Praise for *High St@kes, No Prisoners*

"The *Liar's Poker* of the Internet economy could turn out to be Charles Ferguson's *High Stakes, No Prisoners*. It is a wickedly funny book, in its way just as amusing as *The New New Thing,* but it is also more systematically informative about the technology business. . . . The delightful effect on Ferguson of being rich is to make him an indiscreet writer. Everyone who insulted him in a negotiation or generally got on his wrong side is in for it here."

—James Fallows, *The New York Review of Books*

"Ferguson can write. And as his title suggests, he isn't afraid to demolish people verbally. The result is a minefield of a book that belatedly detonates in the path of venture capitalists, fellow entrepreneurs and Internet titans. . . . Ferguson is a perceptive writer, honest about his own mistakes, and thoughtful about the future. No book I've read has offered a more withering litany of Netscape's mistakes. And few give a better portrait of the financial machinations that govern the life of a start-up."

—Scott Herhold, *San Jose Mercury News*

"Ferguson has a flair for describing the inside angle, and he relishes serving up unflattering descriptions of some of the tech industry's biggest names. . . . This is good old-fashioned dirt, and Ferguson is especially adept at dishing it up."

—Thomas Goetz, *The Industry Standard*

"Industry analysts and consultants usually have little understanding about how difficult it is to run a business. And policy analysts usually don't know how the private sector really works and what government interventions in the market will actually do. Ferguson the entrepreneur has a solid grasp of those issues. Entrepreneurs usually have a hard time articulating their intuitive vision of industry dynamics. Even when successful in business, they can rarely explain what led them to follow their strategies for creating a position in the market. Ferguson can and does. The combination gives the book a wealth of perspective and a streetwise credibility that few books about the Internet economy possess."

—J. Bradford DeLong and A. Michael Froomkin, *Harvard Business Review*

"Ferguson's story about Vermeer over twenty months is strikingly similar to mine at 3Com over thirteen years. A big difference is that Microsoft screwed me while Ferguson 'vermeered' Microsoft. Every would-be Silicon Valley entrepreneur should read this book."

—Bob Metcalf, Ethernet inventor, 3Com founder, and technology pundit

"Once again, Charles Ferguson has managed to condense an unwieldy, complicated, multi-faceted topic into a fast-paced, highly pleasurable read . . . his new book of Silicon Valley intrigue, deception, fierce competition, and colossal egos doesn't disappoint. . . . With refreshing frankness, Ferguson gives the reader a complete picture of the chaotic world of Internet start-ups."

—Gina Fraone, *Electronic Business*

High St@kes, No Prisoners

A Winner's Tale of Greed and Glory in the Internet Wars

CHARLES H. FERGUSON

THREE RIVERS PRESS

NEW YORK

Published by Three Rivers Press, New York, New York.
Member of the Crown Publishing Group.

Random House, Inc. New York, Toronto, London, Sydney, Auckland
www.randomhouse.com

THREE RIVERS PRESS is a registered trademark and the Three Rivers Press colophon is a trademark of Random Houe, Inc.

Originally published in hardcover by Times Books in 1999.

Printed in the United States of America

Design by H. Roberts Design

Library of Congress Cataloging-in-Publication Data

Ferguson, Charles H.
High stakes, no prisoners: a winner's tale of greed and glory in the
Internet wars / by Charles H. Ferguson.
1. Computer industry—California—Santa Clara County.   2. High
technology industries—California—Santa Clara County.   3.
Entrepreneurship—United States case studies.   4. Wealth—
California—Santa Clara County.   I. Title.
HD9696.2.U63C354   1999
338.7'61004'092—dc21   99-34560

ISBN 0-609-80698-X

10 9 8 7 6 5 4 3 2 1

First Paperback Edition

This is for the kind, wise, good-hearted, and supremely tolerant people whose generosity, advice, and examples enabled me to reach this point of extraordinary good fortune; and most especially for Camille and those others who endured me throughout the events recounted here. I hope that my future conduct compensates for at least some of the many mistakes I made, and repays some of the extraordinary gifts you all have given me.

I must study politics and war that my sons may have liberty to study mathematics and philosophy. My sons ought to study mathematics and philosophy, geography, natural history, naval architecture, navigation, commerce, and agriculture, in order to give their children a right to study painting, poetry, music, architecture, statuary, tapestry, and porcelain.

—*John Adams, in a letter to his wife, Abigail Adams*

Never play cards with a man called Doc.

—*Nelson Algren*

CONTENTS

High St@kes,
No Prisoners

INTRODUCTION

A billion here, a billion there, and pretty soon you're talking about
real money.
—*Senator Everett Dirksen*

You are not the kind of guy who would be at a place like this at this time
of the morning. But here you are . . .
—*Jay McInerney, the opening lines of* Bright Lights, Big City

*I*n the late summer of 1993, I got the beginnings of a very cool, very big idea—an idea that could create a huge new industry. After spending the rest of the year timidly thinking of starting a company, I finally decided to try. Randy Forgaard and I shook hands and founded Vermeer Technologies in April of 1994. Barely a month later, we discovered that about two-thirds of my idea was useless—the World Wide Web had gotten there first. However, the Web also seemed to make the remaining portion of my idea even more powerful. We refocused on that and rolled the dice. We secured $4 million in venture capital in February 1995, shipped the first version of the FrontPage product in October 1995, and sold the company to Microsoft in January 1996. It was a wild ride: fascinating, exciting, brutal, tense, unforgettable. Some of it, including my sudden wealth, sometimes feels bizarre. I grew up in a poor family and had finished graduate school thirty thousand dollars in debt only a few years before starting Vermeer.

Yet, by the standards of the Internet industry, we barely made it into the middle class. Jeff Bezos of Amazon and Jerry Yang of Yahoo! are each worth billions; five years ago, nobody had heard of either of them. For better or worse, one of the most striking characteristics of American high technology is that sudden riches like this are almost routine. No other industry, in any nation, makes it so easy to start a business, make a difference, get rich—and do it fast. This is not to say that success is easy, or that there are any guarantees. Our principal competitors were Microsoft, America Online (AOL), and Netscape; many of the other start-ups we either competed or partnered with in 1994 and 1995 got killed or were snapped up at fire-sale prices.

But if you get it right, the results are staggering. As I write this, FrontPage has already become the industry standard for Web site development software. It has nearly three million users and holds about 70 percent of the world market for Web page development software. A rapidly increasing fraction of the world's Web servers are equipped with FrontPage software. As I had predicted, our technology has become strategically critical to Microsoft. FrontPage is being bundled with the new version of Microsoft Office, and from now on, Office will use FrontPage's technology for posting documents to Web servers. Nobody else has that technology.

Since Office has more than 90 percent market share, we can safely assume that within a few years, virtually all Web servers will be FrontPage enabled, and Microsoft will be on its way to securing yet another monopoly. No, this does not make me totally happy, but as you'll see, we had little choice. Netscape under Jim Barksdale was out to lunch, and Microsoft would have killed us if we had tried to go it alone.

And yet even Microsoft's power can't suppress the wave of new start-ups driven by the Internet revolution. Despite its many flaws, the Silicon Valley start-up system unquestionably works. It is the crown jewel of the American economy and a critical driver of American high technology. Silicon Valley itself is an amazing place—electric, addictive, vulgar, full of brilliance, brutally fair and brutally unfair, fiercely competitive, often dishonest, tremendously exciting, and utterly unique. It is no coincidence that the Internet revolution is headquartered there. I'd spent a lot of time in the Valley before starting Vermeer, but I had never really appreciated the sheer intensity of the place until my own future, my own fortune, and the careers of fifty other people who had put their faith in me were on the line.

I've been fortunate enough to observe and participate in the high technology world from several different angles, and at levels ranging from working-level employee to start-up founder to MIT policy analyst to White House consultant. Highest level is not always best; I learned more by starting Vermeer than I did by testifying before Congress. But I think the combination of these experiences has been extremely valuable and has given me an unusual perspective on high technology and the Internet industry, their effects on the world, and the issues they raise. In fact, government policy has been much more important in shaping the Internet industry than most people realize, and it played a major though indirect role in Vermeer's ultimate fate.

Thus, I hope to capture the entire high technology experience in this book: making a start-up really work; raising venture capital; being inside a world-historic revolution; dealing with Microsoft's power, trying to affect White House policy; being forced to deal with the environment that government policy has created. I want to convey the highs and the lows, the electric energy, the brainpower, and the quirky personalities in the Valley, as well as the brutal, ruthless maneuvering that few outsiders ever see. I also want to show how brilliant policymaking by technologists helped create this revolution, and yet how foolish regulatory policies and interest group politics are slowing it down.

Consequently this book tells three interconnected stories. The first is a personal account of what it really takes to do a winning high technology start-up, especially in the Internet industry, where any speed below warp nine doesn't even get you to takeoff. When I started this book, I discovered to my surprise that virtually nobody had written about this experience from the inside. Second, I describe the Internet revolution and analyze the strategic war for control of it, particularly the contest between Microsoft and Netscape and its effect on Vermeer. In doing this I combine my firsthand experience with a broad strategic analysis. And finally, I address the large-scale economic and political issues raised by the Internet and the information era: the question of Microsoft's power, the even worse problem presented by telecommunications monopolies, and the new issues of electronic money, privacy, political censorship, and the effects of information technology on the American and global economies. Forgive me; I still have the MIT political scientist lurking inside.

In fact, I'd primarily been an academic, policy wonk, and consultant before becoming an entrepreneur. After getting a B.A. in mathematics at Berkeley, I focused on international trade and high technology policy for my Ph.D. and postdoctoral research at MIT. In the early 1980s, before writing my thesis, I had also worked in Silicon Valley for two years, first at IBM and then at Oracle. After returning to MIT, I concentrated on Japanese-American high technology competition. I got it about half right, not bad for a graduate student. In the 1980s I was one of the first to warn about the Japanese threat to the U.S. semiconductor industry, which was very real, and I became heavily involved in some extremely useful government efforts to strengthen our industry. But I also made some big mistakes: I overestimated Japan's threat to the U.S. economy, vastly exaggerated the virtues of the Fortune 500, and erroneously disparaged the Silicon Valley start-up system.

By the early 1990s I had learned a lot from those mistakes. I had also gotten to know many people in the White House, testified before Congress, and written a book, but I needed a change from academic life. I became a consultant, which enabled me to make several *new* mistakes, but ones from which I once again learned. I consulted for LSI Logic, Xerox, Texas Instruments, Digital Equipment Corporation (DEC), Intel, Motorola, and, memorably, for the black comedy that was Apple under John Sculley and his successors. Then I had my idea, and there followed Vermeer, FrontPage, and my immersion in the Internet revolution. Since selling Vermeer to Microsoft, I've been investing in start-ups—and that has been quite an education, too.

At Vermeer, we were right in the middle of the battle between Microsoft and Netscape; in fact, we were an important swing vote. They were both out to kill us or to buy us, although Microsoft understood our importance far more clearly than Netscape did. I once thought I'd rather slit my wrists than sell the company to Microsoft, and many of my employees and I initially favored either staying independent or doing a deal with Netscape. But nothing concentrates the mind like watching Microsoft's biggest guns swiveling around to train on *you*.

And when I was forced to think about it, Netscape looked bad. I had seen John Sculley up close as he wrecked Apple. Sculley was a reasonably smart, charming man. But he had an enormous ego, he knew virtually nothing about technology, and he was competing against Bill Gates, who was obviously much smarter, tougher, and more committed. Watching Sculley go up against Gates was rather like watching a rich playboy who was ordering his yacht to attack a carrier battle group. Jim Barksdale, the CEO of Netscape, was Sculley all over again, or worse. Barksdale was moderately smart, charming, handsome, politically adroit, and an excellent manager of large companies. But he was arrogant, ignorant about technology, distracted by politics and glamour, and was running a software company in partnership with a twenty-three-year-old chief technology officer who'd never had a serious job before. Barksdale made a string of disastrous mistakes. It became clear to me that, even playing fair, Microsoft would kill Netscape, and I was sure Microsoft wouldn't play fair. It became equally clear to me that they would also kill Vermeer, although it would take them a few years. So I swallowed my pride, discussed the facts of life with my employees, and sold to Microsoft.

Vermeer taught me other things, too. I had thought I was a pretty tough guy, more than able to take everything in stride; I was wrong. I had never really experienced the industry's rough side, the way you do when there's a billion dollars or so at stake. Starting a company, raising money, and making deals was a constant battle against sharks and suits—some of them ruthless and dishonest, others equally dangerous because they were simply incompetent. Not everyone was like that, by any means; there are many honorable, admirable, highly professional people in the Valley. And playing the start-up game is an incredible high. But it's not a place where the good guys, or the best ideas, always win, and one finds little evidence that the meek shall inherit the earth. A wide array of powerful incumbents, ruthless people, and old-boy networks make life difficult. Some play all hardball all the time, others casually waste other people's money, and they kill far too many good ideas. Your allies become your enemies, and then your allies again, in the blink of an eye. You are constantly at risk of losing your market position, your company, your sanity, and your ethics. In my case, the pressure was intensified by an internal struggle with a self-interested, political, manipulative CEO—whom we had hired on my own mistaken advice. So, yes, I was able to start an Internet company that developed a cool product, and I got rich, but I also didn't sleep through the night for two years. Others tell me they feel less pressure; I don't see how.

Few first-time technology entrepreneurs know much about structuring and financing a start-up and are therefore easy pickings for the suits. Even brilliant technologists and seasoned executives get fleeced. Steve Jobs, for example, is one of the all-time masters of illusion, and he has gotten the best of some very smart people. For example, he used his controlling investment in Pixar (the company that made *Toy Story*) to squeeze out the engineers who had spent a decade creating the technology; one of my employees was among his lesser victims. When Jobs took the company public in 1995, he made $1 billion, but some of the technical founders got almost nothing. Then he sold his own failing company, NeXT, to Apple for more than $400 million, on the grounds that its supposedly revolutionary technology represented Apple's salvation. A year later, when Jobs had become Apple's acting CEO, he announced that upon reflection he had changed his mind, and he flushed NeXT down the toilet—but he didn't give back the $400 million. The Valley is wild, and things like this happen regularly. If you don't stay on your toes, they will happen to you. Although more sophisticated financially than most novices, I was harshly taken to school during my first round of fund-raising and had to learn fast in order to avoid flunking. Then I had to fight the same battles all over again to do our second round, nine months later.

It's difficult to convey how different things were in 1994. The industry is still a rough place, but since the Internet it has been overflowing with money and has become a much more tolerant place for entrepreneurs. Fund-raising for start-ups is enormously easier—maybe too easy. But when I started Vermeer in 1994, things were tough and money was tight. Venture capitalists used their power ruthlessly, lazily, and often stupidly. Few had heard of the Internet, and many didn't care; they didn't have to. It wasn't until I started raising money that I learned what a cozy cartel the venture capital industry actually was. When we talked to one VC, they'd hand us off to their supposed competitors, telling us they wouldn't invest unless their friends did too. We quickly banished any thought of creating bidding contests or playing off one firm against another. Then when business started looking good, some of our first-round VCs worked to keep down our valuation in later rounds so they could own more of us cheaply. We were forced into concealing our fund-raising activities from our own board. I threatened lawsuits and had some of the toughest arguments I've ever been in. But we won.

Venture capital markets and start-up financing are, shall we say, imperfect. Even in lean times, huge amounts of money are sometimes thrown at bad companies. VCs, and even more strikingly large "strategic investors" like AT&T, give money to people with big reputations even if they don't deserve it, often based on hype and dubious grand visions. There is a well-known "second-company" syndrome. Once you've had a successful company, naïve investors throw money at you. But second companies often fail, because rich founders run amok building monuments to their egos. Particularly dangerous are people who really are brilliant technologists, and therefore have credibility when they claim they can produce antigravity next year. John Moussouris, for example, is a brilliant chip designer who co-founded MIPS Computer Systems (now MIPS Technologies), but then wasted more than $150 million pursuing impossible dreams at MicroUnity. Long after it was obvious that MicroUnity was a colossal failure, large corporations were still shoveling money into what had become a bottomless hole. MicroUnity, General Magic, GO, EO, 3DO, HAL, Kendall Square, Encore, Trilogy, Stardent, NeXT, Interval Research—all started by famous people. Between them they blew at least $2 billion of other people's money.

Conversely, Conner Peripherals, which won the record for the fastest ascent into the Fortune 500—zero to $1 billion in revenue in four years—couldn't raise venture capital and got funded by Compaq only because they needed Conner's product. We struggled for five months to raise $4 million. If you've never started a company before, or if you're outside the usual mold, it's a lot harder to open the doors and unlock the purses—or at least it was until all that money came chasing anything with a ".com" in its name.

And, unfortunately, shady deals abound, in part because private companies don't have to abide by the same disclosure and fairness rules that govern the behavior of public companies. Entrepreneurs sometimes deceive their employees and their venture capitalists; the VCs play pretty nasty tricks themselves. When investment bankers suddenly started offering me inside deals, like allocations of hot initial public offerings, I was puzzled for a bit. Then I realized, "Oh! These are *bribes*! They want to manage our IPO." The investment bankers at least had the virtue of subtlety. Some industry analysts came right out and asked us to give them an inside stock deal, or a personal consulting contract, and they'd mention our company favorably. Until we launched our product, I had never known that you literally *purchased* those wonderful analysts' white papers in your launch brochure.

You also need strong nerves; we received unpleasant surprises on a regular basis. One day, for example, a prospective employee who had just learned our entire strategy suddenly backed out, announcing that actually he had been interviewing with Netscape too. I was also slightly shocked when friends at other companies, whom I knew and trusted, said they were interested in partnering with us and requested confidential briefings, only for us to discover that they had already done a deal with a major competitor. Screwing your partners, alas, is an old Silicon Valley tradition. I gradually developed a tit-for-tat policy. I tried to be straight, even generous, with people who were straight with me. But once you screwed me, you were fair game—indeed, it was often a matter of survival.

Altogether, then, you realize how short a window of opportunity any start-up has, how fast you have to move, and how finely tuned your strategic nerve endings have to be, especially in the Internet. We were up against the best—Microsoft, Netscape, and America Online, plus a couple of start-ups who got acquired by Adobe and IBM. We had the first complete product in our category, and by far the best, but that doesn't guarantee victory. Because things are so new, you have to make a lot of guesses, and sometimes you miss. Others watch, avoid your mistakes, and move in—as all of the early browser companies learned the hard way. So you can't announce too early, but you're panicked at the thought of being late. In our case, after some initial self-doubt, we knew that our idea was *so* right, *so* important, and once you thought of it, *so* obvious, that we could not afford to stumble, not once. Once we launched our product, the whole world would know, and if we could do it so could they. It makes you paranoid, and you need to be.

So, if it's that awful, why does the system work so well? For one thing, as Winston Churchill said of democracy, it's the worst possible system, except for all the others. There's also the adage about not watching sausage being made if you ever want to eat it; even when the finished product looks nice, the process is quite messy. And it must be said that the Valley is a place of contradictions and extremes, with virtues as striking as its faults. Despite everything, we *did* assemble a world-class team, we got funded, we were able to develop a highly original product, we made a difference, and we got rich. In fact, doing Vermeer was an incredible experience. The sheer joy of working with some of the smartest people in the world, not to mention competing against the best and winning, is hard to beat.

The opportunity to participate in the Internet revolution was, at the personal level, a remarkable experience. By late 1994 we already suspected that the Internet and the Web would change the world profoundly, in a way perhaps unmatched since the invention of the printing press or movable type centuries before. For a little while, before the world awakened and the suits invaded, a small group of people would be making decisions that could influence history. Thus awe and humility competed with greed, vulgarity, egotism, timidity, accidents, and sheer idiocy. In late 1994, for example, we had one of our countless meetings with prominent venture capitalists. The next day, this venture capitalist had lunch with one of our advisors, Bob Davoli. His opening line to Bob: "So, Bob, what do you think of this Internet shit?"

At the beginning, everything was unformed, and you were invited and even required to consider and reconsider the largest, most fundamental questions almost daily. If you were right half the time, you were doing well. Three quarters of the time and you became extremely rich, like Jerry Yang of Yahoo!, or you immortalize yourself, like Tim Berners-Lee, the inventor of the Web. If you are brilliant but blinded by arrogance, you can go down in history for your mistakes, like the founders and executives of Netscape. If you win through ruthlessness and dishonesty, come to feel above the law, yet also contribute enormously to the industry and establish huge charities in your name, you will have the complicated problem of being Bill Gates.

THE AMERICAN START-UP SYSTEM: AN OVERNIGHT SUCCESS, AFTER FORTY YEARS

The American technology sector has gone through several phases, each of which has widened the role played by venture capital, start-ups, and Silicon Valley. For its first thirty years, the industry was dominated by IBM's mainframes and a handful of second-tier, equally conservative rivals. Then came the personal computer revolution of the 1980s. By then, IBM had degenerated into a politicized bureaucracy that finally imploded in 1992. Nor was it alone in its decline. By the mid-1980s, the whole East Coast computer establishment was looking not much better than the steel industry, GM, or telephone monopolies like SBC and Bell Atlantic—in short, awful. The rest of the computer industry establishment blew the personal computer revolution as badly as IBM did— even worse, in fact. The deterioration of IBM and the East Coast industry allowed Microsoft and Silicon Valley to step in. From the 1980s onward, it was the Valley that drove the PC revolution, as well as everything else that counted in technology—workstations, databases, systems integration, UNIX servers. Lou Gerstner has done an extraordinary job of saving IBM, particularly given that he had to lay off two hundred thousand people in the process, but the company will never again have any power or provide industry leadership.

Thus however imperfect and ruthless the venture capital industry is, it is indisputably a high-octane fuel that drives progress in American high technology. Over the long run it also keeps the big guys honest, or at least punishes their inefficiency and eventually replaces them. Until very recently, venture capital was a uniquely American phenomenon. It had its roots in the commercialization of technology developed during and after Word War II. The first VCs were small partnerships, some of them formed by Harvard and MIT professors in the late 1940s. By the 1960s, the VC industry had split into a conservative East Coast branch, centered in the Boston area, and a West Coast branch with its roots in the high-tech community around Stanford University. DEC was the flagship East Coast venture-funded company, started in 1957 with a $70,000 investment. Others included Prime, Data General, Wang, Apollo, and Computervision. These East Coast companies had two things in common. First, they were all basically in the conservative, vertically integrated, self-contained IBM/DEC mold. And second, they're all basically dead. This is not a coincidence.

The California venture capitalists, and the companies they funded, were less formal, less conservative, less traditional—more willing to back a random kid with a wild idea, even if he didn't wear a tie—although they too missed some big winners out of laziness or miscalculation. At first the Californians focused on semiconductors—hence "Silicon" Valley—and their star performer was Intel, founded in 1968. Then the Valley started to diversify as the VCs funded a steady stream of refugees from IBM, Xerox, and AT&T. Most of the important technologies of the last three decades were developed either through government-funded research projects or by large companies that either didn't know what to do with them or suppressed them for fear of undercutting their cushy franchises. And to their credit, VCs love start-ups that attack lazy, incompetent incumbents. This is a huge factor in American technological leadership over Europe and Japan. And it was exactly what drove the PC industry in the 1980s.

The next phase of American high technology came with the Internet and the rise of start-up investing as a massive, heavily funded industry. For many years the venture capital industry, especially the California branch, was unknown to the public and even to Wall Street. Very quietly, drawing no attention to themselves, a small club of top-tier VCs made a lot of money—*really* a lot, not like those poor guys in New York who slaved away running investment banks. Intel, Apple, Oracle, Compaq, LSI Logic, Sun, PeopleSoft, Lotus, Intuit, Silicon Graphics, Informix, Sybase, 3Com, and Cisco all received VC funding long before the days of the Internet. Those companies alone now have a combined value of half a trillion dollars—yet until quite recently total annual investing by the whole U.S. venture capital industry never exceed $5 billion, and was usually less than $1 billion. Somebody got some pretty good deals there. This is all the more amazing because the VCs turned down some of the largest opportunities in their early stages—they initially refused to fund Oracle, AMD, Seagate, and Conner, which later became some of the Valley's greatest successes. (Sometimes the VCs did come in later, as with Oracle and Intuit.) Despite their mistakes, this small, clubby group produced some of the Valley's first billionaires.

But only in the 1980s did anyone in the media ever start to mention VCs themselves, and only with the Internet revolution did start-up investing employ a significant number of people. Now, venture capital is a huge industry, investing more than $20 billion a year—almost so crowded that nobody goes there anymore.

The industry has always been cyclical and probably will continue to be. The Internet wave brought too much money in, too fast, and at some point there will be a sharp correction. It won't be the first time. The PC revolution of the early 1980s made huge fortunes in the Valley. Then a lot of naïve money— insurance companies, pension funds—began flowing into venture capital just in time for the mid-1980s Japanese assault on the American semiconductor industry, the shakeout in PC hardware and software vendors a couple of years later, and the recession of the early 1990s. Venture capital commitments declined sharply, and VCs pulled out of many areas, focusing on only a few markets they considered safe. When we came along in 1994, it was still hard to get a start-up funded. It was especially hard to fund one with a radically new idea, based on a technology no VC had ever heard of. But I could tell that there was something serious going on, the kind of wave that comes by only once or twice in your life. I was determined not to miss it, so I pushed hard.

The first eight chapters of this book tell the story of Vermeer and the Internet industry from their beginnings through the present day. I discuss the many battles I fought while running Vermeer and our strategy from the moment of my original idea to the final deal with Microsoft. In parallel, I analyze the birth of the Internet industry. The context in which we operated was the war for control of the Internet and Web fought between Microsoft, Netscape, and AOL, as well as others such as Yahoo! and Amazon. Then, in the last three chapters of the book, I revert to my MIT analyst role. Some of the most important strategic, political, and social issues associated with the information era and the Internet revolution remain poorly understood or are rarely discussed, and I take a shot at them.

For example, consider the origins of the new technology that is, after all, the basis of technological revolutions. That technology does not come from the venture capital industry, *and it usually doesn't come from free markets, either.* In fact, we shouldn't be too smug about what the Silicon Valley system can do by itself, for two reasons. First, sometimes the big incumbents—the old IBM, Microsoft, the telephone monopolies—can become too powerful or too lazy, and the start-up system alone cannot always discipline them, at least not quickly. And second, the Silicon Valley system depends for its technology far more heavily on farsighted government policy than your average VC would like to admit, or perhaps even realizes.

It became fashionable in the 1980s to argue that free markets solve all problems. The facts are not so simple, however. As I'll show in this book, the Internet actually provides a beautiful controlled experiment. Virtually all the critical technologies in the Internet and Web revolution were developed between 1967 and 1993 by government research agencies and/or in universities. During the same period, there arose in parallel a private, free market solution—a $10 billion commercial online services industry. The comparison between the two is extremely clear and extremely unflattering to private markets. The commercial industry's technology and structure were inferior to· that of the nonprofit Internet in every conceivable way, which is the primary reason that they were so rapidly destroyed by the commercial Internet revolution. Internet technology was around and available for more than twenty years, continuously evolving under the noses of companies like AT&T, IBM, CompuServe, AOL, and even Microsoft. But somehow these companies managed not to notice. Neither, by the way, did most VCs.

I also discuss the competition between Netscape and Microsoft. Neither company comes off well. Microsoft was inexcusably predatory; Netscape was inexcusably stupid. Chapter 9 offers my analysis of what went happened there. I got a good look at Netscape, including Jim Barksdale, during our deal negotiations, and subsequently interviewed many key insiders at Netscape and Microsoft, once again including Barksdale. Without in any way excusing Microsoft's behavior in the browser wars and elsewhere, I'm afraid that Netscape died primarily by its own hand.

Netscape deserves enormous credit for seeing the Internet opportunity, and it certainly would have survived longer if Microsoft had played fair. But the company was doomed by its own technical and strategic incompetence, by its arrogance, and by the quality of its management. The people running Netscape did not come remotely close to their counterparts at Microsoft in raw brainpower, drive, strategic insight, technical depth, managerial efficiency, or ruthlessness. Jim Barksdale may be great at giving speeches, but he was *way* out of his league, and for a long time he was too full of himself even to realize it. Marc Andreessen is brilliant and should go down in history for his role in creating Mosaic, the first graphical Web browser. But he was in his early twenties, and he didn't know anything about the industry. In a very real sense, Netscape had no leadership and no strategy. It acquired the wrong companies and failed to acquire the right ones, such as us or RealNetworks. Inside, the company was a mess: the kids ran the show, software development was chaotic, strategy and tactics were lurching and confused, and many of their products were second-rate. And by loudly proclaiming themselves Microsoft-killers, they predictably generated a ferocious competitive response.

Just because Netscape was incompetent, however, doesn't mean that Microsoft wasn't out to get them. In chapter 10, I argue that Microsoft's ruthless and predatory use of its power justifies major surgery. Giving due credit for the enormous contributions Microsoft has made to the software industry, and in some areas continues to make, I am convinced that the company's misuse of its enormous power is becoming dangerous to the industry. Although nobody can prove this statement quantitatively, I think the evidence demonstrates that Microsoft's brutality and power already prevent or crush too many alternatives. Moreover, at some point in the future the company will inevitably slow down as all monopolists eventually do, but its power won't decline as fast as its energy. Its excess momentum will then become an enormous dead weight on the industry, delaying innovation at huge cost to the economy. This happened with IBM before 1993, it happened with the old AT&T, it happened in the U.S. steel and automobile industries, it is happening now with the local telephone companies, and it will happen with Microsoft. Neither the present ruthless, effective monopoly nor the future inefficient one is economically beneficial.

There is also an ethical issue. At the moment, Microsoft's leadership really seems to think that anything is permissible. It's not. The industry is rough, and it will stay that way. But dominant firms should not use one monopoly to create others, their CEOs should not make blatantly absurd statements in antitrust depositions, their executives should not show fake software demonstrations in court, and they should not coolly debate the insertion of false error messages in their software to destroy rival firms. And finally, I review the major proposals for curbing Microsoft's power and make several proposals of my own. I argue that there are good reasons for reducing Microsoft's power by dividing it into two successor firms, one each for operating systems and applications.

Dangerous as Microsoft is, however, the continued progress of the Internet is far more endangered from another quarter. I'm currently more worried about the damage being done by the incompetent, and far more politically powerful, monopolists who have a stranglehold on the infrastructure that connects almost everyone to the Internet. I am referring to the local telephone companies, which are among the most retrograde organizations that have ever masqueraded under the name of high technology. (Their friends in the cable industry aren't far behind; I'll discuss them too.) Ask yourself, How does their service compare with, say, FedEx? Can you check the status of your service request on their Web site? Can you even pay your bill online, never mind get high-speed, inexpensive, reliable Internet service? If you don't like them, can you switch to anyone else? Has the price/performance of their services improved 50 percent per year, as every part of the competitive technology sector has? For the most part, the answer is no.

The telephone companies do have certain skills, however. They are extremely good at lobbying, hiring former high-level government officials, filing lawsuits to delay competition, and corrupting prominent economists. Would it surprise you to learn that Daniel Rubinfeld, the UC Berkeley economist until recently in charge of antitrust analysis for the Justice Department, owns over $6 million in stock (representing nearly all his personal wealth) in the largest corporate antitrust consulting firm in the United States? This firm, of which he is a partner, receives a quarter of its revenue from the telephone companies and the rest from just about everybody else Justice is, or should be, investigating. Shocking? Well, he's the third one in the Clinton administration to have a similar problem. The company is the Law and Economics Consulting Group; check them out at www.lecg.com. But there is, unfortunately, even worse behavior than this. In fact, compared to going after the telephone industry, suing Microsoft is easy (although Microsoft hires its share of academics and former government officials, too). In this area, alas, government policy has almost nowhere to go but up. In addition to analyzing the specific case of telecommunications, I will discuss the generally sorry condition of antitrust and regulatory policy in the Federal Trade Commission, the Federal Communications Commission, the Justice Department, the courts, and in Congress, and make a variety of recommendations to improve them.

In the final chapter of the book, I consider these larger issues. I'll outline the inherent tensions between privacy and legitimate information requirements when technology potentially allows unprecedented collection of personal information by companies and governments. I'll examine the problem of the telecommunications industry as a monopoly bottleneck facing the Internet revolution and the technology sector. I will also look briefly at the effect of the Internet revolution on economic productivity, including the dislocations it may cause as it undermines traditional industries. I will not, of course, provide any final answers.

CHAPTER ONE

Starting the Company

The best electric train set any boy ever had!
—*Orson Welles, speaking of the RKO movie studio*

Do you *sincerely* want to be rich?
—*The favorite line of Bernard Cornfeld, a major swindler*

*P*eople start companies for a number of reasons. Obviously there's the money, and frequently there's ego; sometimes there's a passion for improving the world. But in high technology, there's another reason too; it's *fun,* especially when you win. There is an intense euphoria to playing one of the fastest-moving, highest-stakes, flat-out competitive games in the world. Playing the technology game for real is, without question, a serious peak experience. It almost compensates for the tension.

Start-ups are the intellectual equivalent of driving a small, fast convertible with the top down, the stereo playing Keith Jarrett or Bach or J. J. Cale very loud, doing a hundred miles an hour on an empty country road at sunset. You might crash, but the experience is visceral, immediate, and intense. In other words, while competitive energy may not be the noblest of reasons for starting a company, it is an extremely powerful one. Not that I've ever actually exceeded the speed limit myself, of course. . . . Still, others seem to agree that the comparison is apt. Bill Gates used to take his Porsches out at 4:00 A.M. for a spin at

150 miles per hour, and I think that the high produced by competing and winning is a major reason that smart people often enjoy working for Microsoft. And Microsoft is, I think, one of only a few large companies that can deliver that experience. The purest high is found in start-ups. So everyone who spends time in the Valley, and who is smart, ambitious, and competitive, contracts the start-up disease.

I was no exception. I have serious adrenaline addictions, both intellectual and physical. I certainly wanted financial security, along with the ability to speak my mind without worrying about getting fired. But I also had another reason for starting a company, one that for me was extremely powerful: the need to prove myself, to do something *real*. This turned out to be an even more serious matter than I understood at the time. I had gnawing doubts about myself, and I could tell that other people, including many I respected, did too. By the time I was even one tenth of the way into doing Vermeer, I realized that these doubts were well founded. There simply is no substitute for doing something for which you are personally accountable and whose success can be clearly evaluated.

By late 1993, I was making a good living as a consultant, giving strategic advice to the top managements of large high-technology companies. I think that I mostly gave good advice, and by the standards of consultants I was quite courageous in calling things the way I saw them. But I knew that I didn't always go as far as I should have, and I also realized, deep down, that it was a lot easier to give advice than to really be responsible for implementing it. My doubts about consulting were made sharper by the glaringly obvious difference between several politicized, mediocre large clients and the Silicon Valley entrepreneurs who were eating their lunch.

In this regard, high technology is unusual, because it is young and changes so fast. Unlike other industries, which tend to be run by career bureaucrats, the CEOs of the best high-technology companies have generally started and built their companies themselves, and sometimes invented their industry's principal technologies. People like Bill Gates, Andy Grove and before him Bob Noyce at Intel, John Warnock at Adobe, Wilf Corrigan at LSI Logic, Larry Ellison at Oracle, Jerry Sanders of AMD, and Bob Metcalfe of 3Com didn't make their fortunes by climbing up the organization. Bob Metcalfe didn't just start 3Com, which became the dominant provider of Ethernet networking technology. He also invented Ethernet.

Some of these people are pretty arrogant, but they deserve to be. They're very smart, tough, and usually have good academic credentials as well. The founders of Intel all had Ph.D.s in physics; Jim Clark was a professor at Stanford; Bob Metcalfe and John Warnock were researchers at the Xerox Palo Alto Research Center (PARC). But they didn't just get degrees, do good research, and get tenure; they also struck out on their own and submitted themselves to the reality test. Their general view is that this sets them apart, and that only someone who has been there deserves to be taken seriously. So if you're giving advice in Silicon Valley, the unspoken question always hanging in the room is "Well, what have *you* ever done?" Deep in the pit of my stomach I knew that this was a very good question, and that I didn't have an answer.

My personal background fueled both my insecurities and my drive. While I was growing up in San Francisco, my family was extremely poor—we lived on about three thousand dollars a year—primarily because my father was an alcoholic who died when I was in my late teens. Serious alcoholics do not make for fun families, and I fought with my parents continuously from age ten until my mother divorced my father five years later. During most of this time, furthermore, I was crippled by a childhood disease that left me physically dependent upon my parents and almost bankrupted them. I emerged from this experience shy and solitary, but also intensely driven, fiercely independent, judgmental, impatient, permanently on the lookout for threats, and highly competitive. Those aren't the most charming instincts; happily, I mellowed somewhat as I grew older. To my surprise, however, the struggles to launch Vermeer brought everything to the surface again. When I realized what I was in for, I became a tough, impatient, angry, suspicious guy. At times this caused major problems for me, my friends, those who worked with me, and for the company. On the other hand, my toughness and skepticism also served us well. In fact, sometimes I wasn't suspicious *enough*.

I had first noticed computers as an undergraduate at UC Berkeley, where I majored in mathematics but also took some computer science. I discovered that I was a dilettante and also took courses in genetics, economic history, philosophy, art history, literature, political science, and sociology. I started enjoying life a lot and soon realized that I didn't have the personality for technical work. The dominant culture of mathematicians, computer scientists, and superb hackers is solitary and introverted. But with every passing year I grew more attracted to travel, dinner parties, tennis, jazz clubs, political debates, and the company of the opposite sex. In order to postpone adulthood as long as possible, I took leave from Berkeley just before graduating and went to Europe. Because my father had died before I finished college, I qualified for three hundred dollars per month in Social Security benefits if I remained a student. I therefore enrolled in a fifth-rate French university, lived with an extraordinary family in a twelfth-century village in Normandy, and spent a year reading books and jogging on the beach. Lest you regard this as a poor use of federal money, let me say quite seriously that it was not. It saved my sanity and allowed me for once to reflect on my past and future. Every human being deserves, and benefits from, such a period in their youth.

As soon as I returned to Berkeley to finish working for my degree, I read a magazine that changed my life. The September 1977 issue of *Scientific American* was entitled *Microelectronics*. It was a remarkably broad and farsighted survey of semiconductor technology, including microprocessors and early personal computers. It was immediately clear to me that this technology was both fascinating and of great importance. Although I did many things throughout the subsequent decade, I never lost my interest in information technology, and I became ever more intrigued not only by the technology itself but also by its economic, social, and political implications.

So instead of going to graduate school in mathematics or computer science, I entered the Ph.D. program in political science at MIT. It was perfect: I could be a dilettante again. I roamed through MIT and Harvard, taking courses in technical departments as well as in economics, history, philosophy, and—occasionally—political science. I began working with Carl Kaysen, who had just come to MIT. Carl knew everyone, had been everywhere, had done it all: OSS in the Second World War, professor at Harvard, deputy national security advisor in the Kennedy administration, director of the Institute for Advanced Study at Princeton, on the boards of UPS and Polaroid, member of the editorial board of *Foreign Affairs,* et cetera. He's also a wonderful man, incredibly devoted to his students, and has the best collection of wicked one-liners on the planet. In 1981 Carl invited me to join a faculty seminar studying American competitiveness. I noticed that Japan was making inroads against the U.S. not only in steel and automobiles but also in high technology, particularly the semiconductor industry. I wrote several papers arguing that semiconductors were strategically critical to information technology, and that the Americans were about to be hosed by the Japanese, whose superior financial resources, strategic cohesion, and manufacturing discipline gave them an advantage as the industry became more capital intensive. This turned out to be largely right.

Shortly afterward, after finishing my coursework but before my Ph.D. thesis, I dipped my toe into the real world for the first time. In 1982, I took leave from MIT and spent two years working in Silicon Valley—first at IBM's Santa Teresa Laboratory, which developed half of IBM's mainframe software, and then for six wild months at Oracle, which at the time had about seventy employees.

This experience contributed to the first major mistake I made, which was to overestimate large U.S. companies and underestimate the Silicon Valley system. The mistake was not completely weird, given the specifics of my limited experience. Although by 1984 IBM was in decline, it still contained a remarkable number of gifted, ethical, yet tough people. Conversely, life at Oracle in 1984 was quite simply insane.

Larry Ellison, Oracle's founder and CEO, was brilliant, driven, witty, charming, ruthless, wildly egotistical, a superb salesman, a notorious womanizer—and a seriously random number. Anything could happen, and often did. For example, one fine day I was part of a group that had a late-morning meeting with Larry. When we convened at his office, he wasn't there. This was not unusual. Larry had just acquired a new wife—his third—and he apparently liked to go home during the day to make love with her. But our meeting was important, so we piled into a car and took off for his new house in Woodside. My manager, a former classical cellist who was as stunned by Larry's behavior as I was, turned to me in the car and said, "And now, we journey to the land where time has no meaning." When we arrived, Larry came to the door, tousled but in good humor, and invited us into a huge house devoid of furniture, at least on the first floor, where we transacted our business and left. But this was nothing. Larry has since become known, among other things, for buying supersonic combat aircraft for his personal use, securing the felony conviction of a former lover, and winning an Australian yacht race that took place in a storm that killed six people.

I liked Larry, actually. While he was severely warped, he—and the people who routinely saved him from himself—got the important things right. And running start-ups isn't a popularity contest. Larry perceived the importance of relational databases and of SQL (the standard language for dealing with them) earlier than anyone else, including IBM, which had invented them. Oracle grew up to become the third-largest software company in the world. But although Larry was a nice planet to visit, I didn't want to live there. In six months at Oracle I had five different managers, the last of whom was a former CIA agent who was much crazier than Larry was, but nasty and not half as bright. I had a hard time keeping a sense of humor, and eventually I got uppity enough that they canned me. In one of the most hysterically funny conversations I've ever had, Larry called me into his office to give me a sober parting lecture on the importance of maturity, diplomacy, self-discipline, patience, and tact.

I returned to MIT to finish my Ph.D.; with great kindness, my advisor arranged a fellowship for me. I ended up spending the next seven years there, primarily studying the role of technology in economic growth and global competition, first as my dissertation topic and then as a postdoctoral fellow. My thesis focused on the semiconductor industry and correctly forecast the Japanese DRAM (memory chip) cartel that materialized in 1987 and remained in operation until broken by the Koreans in 1991. I became heavily involved in policy efforts to contain the Japanese and help strengthen the U.S. industry, an issue about which I was quite passionate. I testified before Congress; consulted to the White House, the U.S. Trade Representative, and the Defense Department; wrote *New York Times* op-ed pieces and *Harvard Business Review* articles. I became friends with a number of White House officials. I worked on the formation of Sematech—a government-industry semiconductor manufacturing technology consortium—and on the 1986 Semiconductor Trade Agreement that forced open the Japanese market and penalized dumping.

During this time, I argued that in semiconductors the scale, strategic coordination, and massive intellectual property theft of the Japanese posed a major threat to the fragmented U.S. industry. I further argued that U.S. policy should counteract this strategic asymmetry by forcing open the Japanese market, supporting U.S. research and development, and disciplining predatory and cartelistic behavior by the Japanese. This argument was correct, and I think it contributed significantly to national debate. I also argued, however, that U.S. policy should therefore favor a consolidation of U.S. high technology around its largest firms, such as IBM, AT&T, Xerox, Kodak, and DEC, on the grounds that only they had the resources to stand up to Japanese competition. I discounted the value of Silicon Valley start-ups on the grounds that they were too small and fragmented to compete with the Japanese. This was deeply wrong, the product of inexperience and academic disconnection from reality.

Despite this, or perhaps because of it, large technology companies started asking me to consult for them regarding their commercial dealings with the Japanese. Gradually my consulting broadened to include many strategic issues. At this point, my little voice began to nag me. I realized that I wasn't qualified to make some of these decisions, and I learned that often my clients weren't either. Many of the large-company executives for whom I consulted were political and mediocre, while many of the start-ups I talked to were full of brilliant, aggressive people. Moreover, by the late 1980s IBM, DEC, and other large firms were failing to embrace major new technologies, even technologies that they had themselves invented. This problem was particularly serious where new technology threatened the personal empires of executives.

I also noticed enormous differences in governance and personal incentives between the Fortune 500 and start-ups. The boards of directors of my clients were primarily composed of useless decorations, like university presidents or former government officials, with no stake in the company and neither the ability nor the incentive to rock the boat. Start-up boards, on the other hand, were composed of founders and investors who often knew what they were doing and whose wealth depended in an extremely direct way on the company's success. Start-up governance isn't perfect, as you will see in this book, but it is better, on average, than entrenched mediocrity.

By the early 1990s I was forced to admit to myself that the Japanese were not rolling over the American technology sector as I had predicted. In quiet moments, I realized that my mistake derived from my lack of any real, direct experience, which would have forewarned me that the Japanese, and the Fortune 500, each had limits that I might not find described in any academic article. While the Japanese dominated commodity manufacturing businesses such as displays, memories, and consumer electronics, younger American companies were winning in businesses based upon rapidly changing, innovative systems designs. In several major new areas, especially where they had the opportunity to establish a proprietary industry standard, Americans completely dominated the world market. Once Intel's microprocessors and Microsoft's Windows won the market-share battle, they essentially owned the business, and all other vendors, including the Japanese, had to adapt themselves to the so-called Wintel (Windows-Intel) standard. Even in high-volume commodity manufacturing industries such as personal computer systems, the superior designs and flexibility of companies such as Compaq, Dell, and Gateway ensured that Americans dominated the industry.

By 1992, I had figured out what was going on. The key prize in high technology is proprietary control of an industry standard. Windows is again the most obvious example, but there are many others. A number of specific "architectural strategies" can be used to achieve this position, and I cataloged them. While there are many complex variations, they involve two basic goals. The first is acquisition of a sufficiently high market share that your product becomes a de facto industry standard. The other is to create *lock-in,* so that users cannot easily switch to clones or rival systems. The two primary sources of lock-in are user interfaces (UIs), the means by which end-users interact with your product, and application programming interfaces (APIs), which are the standardized technologies used by engineers to create applications based upon your product.

I also noticed that standards and systems architectures played a major role in defining the structure of the industry and the profitability of the various niches within it. There were architectural platform leaders, like Microsoft or Intel; imitators or clones, such as AMD (which copies Intel); architectural losers, such as Apple; commodity manufacturers, such as the PC and component vendors; and point product vendors, such as Intuit in tax software, who create specialized applications for major platforms.

The battle to create and own a proprietary industry standard generates rapid improvements in price and performance, at least until somebody emerges totally dominant. In fact even after a monopolist emerges, there is still considerable pressure to innovate, because unless you can induce your installed base to upgrade frequently, you have a hard time continuing to grow. Again, the most obvious example is the personal computer industry, which has been controlled by Intel and Microsoft since the mid-1980s. There is a risk that a monopolist can misbehave, either through sheer inefficiency (like IBM in the 1980s), or through being excessively predatory, as with Microsoft now. But slow-moving, least-common-denominator, nonproprietary, committee-developed standards are often much worse than any monopoly. Imagine if some international standards committee had created a universal PC standard in the early days. We'd still be using brightly colored, inexpensive, totally obsolete, probably Japanese and Korean PCs today, just as we still use fax machines, VCRs, and television sets that are a generation or more behind where they could be.

Marketplace contests over proprietary, or de facto, industry standards favor the swift and innovative, not the deep pocketed, so American start-ups do well. This helped explain why the Japanese and Koreans dominated cost-sensitive, mass-produced commodity sectors while the Americans dominated more innovative and complex systems. It also helped explain how the apparently fragmented, small-scale Silicon Valley system could organize itself to create large new industries. As soon as the market settled on a standard, large numbers of companies were created quickly through the start-up system, and they could operate quite independently. As long as they adhered to the standard, they had only minimal need to talk to one another directly. This is, in fact, how the personal computer and Internet industries both work. At least in new, rapidly moving industries this enables the Silicon Valley system, collectively, to rival or even exceed the scale and power of much larger firms, whether IBM or the Japanese. And when large firms tie themselves in knots through internal politics, Silicon Valley wins every time.

As I thought about this in 1992, I realized that IBM's day of reckoning was coming soon. I developed these ideas in a *Harvard Business Review* article and a book that I co-authored with Charlie Morris, a fellow consultant. The book (*Computer Wars*) analyzed the rise of Silicon Valley and the decline of IBM and was published within just a few weeks of IBM's crash in December 1992. Charlie and I embarked on a brief crusade, telling the world how badly IBM's management and board of directors had damaged the company. We published several articles, including an open letter to the IBM board, which we FedExed to them. I take great pleasure in the thought that we helped force John Akers out in February 1993; I wish most of the board had been replaced too. Their conduct made hundreds of thousands of layoffs necessary and had probably resulted in several hundred billion dollars' worth of obsolete computers being forced on users over the previous decade. By pointing this out, Charlie and I did the world some good.

But around the same time, I also made my next two mistakes. Both of them provided lessons that helped me later in starting Vermeer. One involved IBM again; the other involved Xerox, for which I consulted intensively in the early 1990s.

IBM's crisis in 1992–93 was enough to wake up anyone. In a few months the company lost over *$30 billion,* and its stock declined by 60 percent. John Akers was forced out, and after a CEO search that to my sheer terror included

John Sculley of Apple—more about that in a minute—Louis Gerstner was hired to run IBM. Gerstner's previous job was running a cigarette company, not the highest calling, but we could overlook that if he saved IBM. Gerstner rapidly laid off more than two hundred thousand people (more than half of IBM's employees), replaced many senior executives, and announced that IBM would build a major systems integration and service business. So far, so good. He also, however, recentralized management of the company; continued to invest heavily in IBM's obsolete mainframe and minicomputer systems; avoided aggressive efforts to develop new products based on leading-edge technologies; and surrounded himself with financial guys rather than real technologists. No strategy was visible. When asked about all this, Gerstner replied, "The last thing IBM needs now is vision."

I thought this was insane and criticized Gerstner both publicly and in some major consulting engagements. I predicted IBM's problems would get even worse because it would be dominated by businesses that were either declining (mainframes and minicomputers) or low-margin commodities (like disk drives and PCs). But Gerstner was right, and I was wrong. IBM was able to restore healthy mainframe and minicomputer sales and profits, even though those systems *are* quite obsolete. Gerstner also saw that IBM's global operations and broad product line were the perfect platform for a conventional, dull, but large and successful systems integration business. Gerstner did save IBM—by turning it into a boring but efficient company, which was exactly the right thing to do. I gained respect for implementation relative to grand strategy.

Then there was Xerox. Xerox asked me to look at Xerox PARC, the famous research center in Palo Alto that fifteen years earlier had invented just about everything in personal computers and networking. I was charmed into suspending my skepticism, despite many warning signs. PARC had become disconnected from reality, even though most of the world's venture capitalists were literally only a mile away, on Sand Hill Road. I fell under the spell of an extremely brilliant, messianic, manipulative, ambitious young researcher there. He asserted that PARC had developed advanced digital technologies that would enable the creation of revolutionary, inexpensive digital systems that would combine image processing, printing, copying, and fax capabilities. In fact, these products would do everything but your laundry.

So I did something extremely stupid: I believed this guy and didn't check his claims carefully. I recommended to Xerox top management the creation of a new division to develop these products. It was a fiasco. In my defense, I wasn't the only one at fault, and some of the work I did for Xerox was extremely good. I would say that on a net basis I helped the place understand digital systems, and Xerox has done just fine. But that new division wasn't my finest hour. I learned the importance of facts and skepticism, which served me well at Vermeer. And once again my little voice told me that if I had some real experience, and if I had known that I would be held accountable for the consequences of my advice, things might have turned out better.

Next came a truly Kafkaesque experience: Apple. Here, I didn't make any big mistakes, but I learned some important lessons nonetheless. Shortly after IBM's crisis began and just after Akers was forced out, in early 1993, I got a telephone call from my colleague Charlie Morris. "We're flying to California tomorrow," he said. "We've just been hired by John Sculley to decide whether he should sell Apple to IBM and whether he should become IBM's new CEO."

We flew out, spent a day briefing Sculley, and then spent a week analyzing the merits of an IBM-Apple merger. In the back of my mind I was already worried about Sculley. Everyone knew that over the previous decade Apple had totally blown its opportunity to usurp Microsoft. Throughout the 1980s the Macintosh operating system had been light-years ahead of Microsoft. But instead of licensing the software to the entire computer industry, Apple had chosen to restrict the Mac OS to its own, second-rate, hardware. As everyone in the industry knew, this was a recipe for a few years of easy profits, to be followed by guaranteed disaster in the long run. Sculley had to bear major responsibility for that, since he had been the CEO the whole time.

We recommended against the IBM merger, and also against his taking the CEO job, which he said was his for the asking. I'll never know whether that was true, but by the time I'd spent a couple of weeks working for him and studying Apple, the thought of John Sculley running IBM scared the hell out of me. Helping to keep him away from IBM during its crisis might be one of my greatest contributions to humanity. Furthermore, it was abundantly clear that Apple was headed over a cliff just like IBM. Sculley seemed to realize that too, but was doing nothing about it.

I nonetheless proposed to Sculley that we change focus, analyze Apple's strategic condition, and make recommendations. He agreed. We were given the run of the place and offices in his building. But the fact that our client was John Sculley posed a dilemma, because John Sculley was a big part of the problem— along with the board that kept him there. We prepared a detailed report, recommending major structural and strategic changes, and scheduled a half-day presentation to Apple's executive committee. At the last minute it was canceled. Suddenly Sculley stopped returning my phone calls, nobody had ever heard of us, our bills weren't getting paid. We asked what was going on and received no answer, although we eventually did get paid. Shortly afterward Sculley was forced out. I tried to contact several board members; none returned my calls. Almost immediately after leaving Apple, Sculley—ever oblivious—took a job as CEO of an obviously fraudulent company, only to quit four months later after the company was besieged by reporters, investigations, and lawsuits. At

Apple, disaster followed disaster as revenues, profits, and market share went through the floor. Sculley was replaced by Michael Spindler, who was as incompetent as Sculley; Spindler was in turn quickly replaced by Gil Amelio, who was incompetent too; and Amelio was quickly replaced in his turn—by Steve Jobs, who had just conned Amelio into buying NeXT, his failing company, for $400 million. Jobs kept Apple afloat, in part by doing a deal with Bill Gates that practically turned Apple into a Microsoft subsidiary. My question: Where's Tom Wolfe when you need him? Or perhaps Hunter S. Thompson would be more appropriate.

In addition to being absurd, the Sculley episode bothered me. Our report was hard-hitting by consulting standards, but it didn't point the finger at Sculley and Apple's board as bluntly as it should have, because that's not the way consultants talk to clients if they want to stay employed. I began to feel as never before that I did not want to spend the rest of my life consulting, and that whatever I did, I wanted complete security to say what I thought.

But it all served a cosmic purpose. After Sculley was forced out, I was asked to analyze Apple's opportunities in electronic publishing, multimedia, and online services. My client was David Nagel, a nice man who rocked no boats, and who was in charge of Apple's software operations. (David is now the chief technology officer of AT&T, which is slightly frightening.) Apple was still a mess, incapable of using my advice no matter what it was. But over the following six months, what I learned from that assignment got me thinking and led me to my cool idea, which in turn led to Vermeer and the Web.

I came to realize that the structure of the online services industry was all wrong. In the months after I completed my assignment, I began to suspect that online services represented a major software opportunity that had been overlooked. All online services used obsolete technology and mutually incompatible systems, which were generally awful, too. America Online at least took advantage of modern graphical user interface (GUI) technology, so its service was easier to use, but otherwise it had the same problems as all the others. There was a problem here, and maybe an opportunity. I came up with the idea of a universal "viewer" or "browser," a single piece of software that would allow you to view and use any of those services. I briefly considered starting a company based upon it, but I came to realize that it was a bad idea. My bad idea, however, was edging toward where my Good Idea was waiting.

I Start to Get It

With the proliferation of personal computers, it became increasingly important for users to get access to information stored in other computers, whether across the hall or halfway around the world. This problem got worse with the advent of powerful, inexpensive "servers," which provided services for workgroups and small companies. By the early 1990s servers costing less than five thousand dollars were being sold in the millions per year by companies such as Compaq and Dell. Organizations were coming to have enormous quantities of electronic information that they wanted to distribute and that people wanted to see—employees, customers, and shareholders, among others.

Thus the incompatibilities between the various commercial online services were just one special case of a far larger problem. Not many people understood this problem well, and only a few products addressed it. Most of them were bad, or at best limited. For example, Adobe was developing a technology, now called Acrobat or PDF, that allowed you to view electronic documents created by other people, even if you didn't have the application software, like Word or Lotus 1-2-3, that originally created the document. But Acrobat had big problems. You needed a small rocket engine to run it, it was a pain to create Acrobat documents, and you couldn't edit them. A few other people, including Apple, developed similar products; they all sank without a trace. The problem, however, was very real: people clearly needed a simple way to publish, distribute, and view electronic documents.

I had learned by now that it was a good sign—for an aspiring entrepreneur—if the incumbent industry was a mess, and it was an especially good sign if the incumbents' business model would lead them to resist innovation and self-cannibalization. CompuServe, Dialog, LEXIS, Prodigy, and the like were all based on expensive, centralized, inflexible, mutually incompatible designs. If a company like Fidelity Investments wanted to distribute its marketing literature through one of these services, it would have to undertake a major effort, pay an absurd amount of money, and even then would not be able to distribute real-time data, like the current market price of its funds. In addition, none of these services would be any help to a company that wanted to deploy a big *internal* information distribution system—like a big insurance company that wanted to make its policy documents and databases available online to all of its agents, for instance.

That was when my lightbulb went on. The solution to this problem, blindingly obvious once you thought of it, was for a software company to develop a single, standardized software product that would allow anyone and everyone to create and operate their own online service. Such a product would logically have a three-part architecture: a viewer, a server, and a visual development tool. Each part would be connected to the others by an open, standardized interface. This would enable any copy of the tool to develop content for any server; for servers to talk to one another; and for any copy of the viewer to look at any service. Moreover, you could use the same system for internal, private services and for public online services.

It was staggeringly clear to me that if a software company could solve that problem—develop an architecture and product for the online distribution and retrieval of electronic information—it would have a golden opportunity to establish a proprietary standard for online services. That was my Good Idea. And I couldn't think of any reason why such a product was beyond the reach of current technology.

It was also instantly clear to me that this opportunity was huge. I could envision a long list of potential users—news media, financial-services firms like Fidelity, catalog retailers like Lands' End, or anyone who wanted to publish information about their company, their financial performance, their job openings. Furthermore, the same software could be used for internal distribution of memos, expense reports, repair manuals, credit information within banks, price changes, legal forms, regulatory updates—the list was endless. The potential market was big enough that the software could be sold fairly cheaply, which would help it proliferate and become an industry standard, which customers and end-users would love because it would solve the problem of incompatibility. If everyone used the same software, users could tap into any service, companies could move information between services, and others could create directories and indexes of services. The software could also interact easily with a company's existing data systems, enabling online access to real-time information. An electronic shopping catalog, for example, could tie into the company's inventory database and accounting systems in a graceful, efficient way and tell you if the widget you wanted was in stock.

At this point you're probably thinking, But that's what the World Wide Web does. Exactly. But at the time, I didn't know that. I had reinvented the wheel. However, it also turned out that my wheel was richer and more complete. At the time, I knew about the Web in a vague way. But I didn't fully realize what it did, or how it worked, and there were only about a thousand Web servers in use, mostly in universities, versus several million now. Likewise I knew about the Internet, but discounted it, too, because it was run by the government, was reserved for research and governmental purposes, and was mainly a convenient way for academics to send one another mail. Bill Gates missed it too, far longer than I did, so at least I had good company.

DIPPING MY TOE IN

Now that I had a truly cool idea, I checked more seriously for competitors. I could see none on the horizon. Microsoft was developing an online service code-named "Marvel" (which became MSN), but it sounded like just an updated version of CompuServe or AOL, which is exactly what it was. The one potentially serious threat was Lotus Notes, a product that allowed big companies to set up and manage internal information services. I have a cousin, Doug Ferguson, who then worked at Lotus, and I asked him for the name of a Notes consultant who could answer detailed questions. I was already getting paranoid about secrecy—a useful emotion, as you'll see, although I should have been more diplomatic about it. So I made my consultant sign a nondisclosure agreement, and even then, I told him absolutely nothing about why I was asking all those questions.

I felt much better afterward, for it was clear that Notes wasn't the answer. For example, it was not designed for large-scale, anonymous public services—every user had to be registered by a system administrator. Furthermore, Notes was complicated and expensive to set up, maintain, and even to use. There were no modern visual tools for creating Notes applications; people did them by hand, the hard way. Notes was also a fairly closed system, with many non-standard ways of performing common tasks.

The glaring deficiencies in Notes were fairly characteristic of Lotus at the time. Much as at IBM and Apple, the Lotus CEO, Jim Manzi, had allowed the company to become politicized and bureaucratized, and it was clearly in decline. The spreadsheet and PC applications business was getting killed by Microsoft, and despite being the first and only "groupware" product, Notes was taking off slowly. It had gotten to the point, in fact, that you didn't have to worry about competition from any Lotus product anymore. Nearly two years later, in the middle of Vermeer's start-up, IBM purchased Lotus for the astonishing price of $3.5 billion. Manzi resigned almost immediately and became CEO of an Internet start-up, which rapidly sank without a trace.

So I decided that Notes posed no major risk, although I also decided that it would be best to focus initially on external, public information services just to keep it simple. But was I ready to take the plunge? I had enjoyed consulting, was good at it, and was earning a good living—in 1993, I made nearly half a million dollars. I was single and, while I lived well, I was financially conservative and had saved several hundred thousand dollars. For me, this was quite a lot of money, but it wasn't enough to give me financial independence if I returned to research or policy work. More important, consulting itself was getting frustrating. I had some great clients, like Motorola, but I couldn't take too many more like Apple. So the idea of starting a company was tempting.

But it was also scary, so I wasted time trying to find some middle ground. I approached some big-company friends, in the hope of working out a deal—an equity stake or royalty if they used the idea. I spoke with Bob Palmer, the CEO of DEC, and some senior people at Intel and Sybase. But it was silly, as well as cowardly. I refused to disclose my idea unless they first agreed to pay me if they decided to use it. But of course they'd have to be morons to promise me money just because I asserted that I had a good idea—maybe one they were already working on. My high-level friends told me, very pleasantly, to go to hell. I gradually resigned myself to the necessity of doing this for real.

I decided to look around for a co-founder, or even two. While I had a good understanding of software, I was by no means the kind of deep technologist I would need to design this system. And while I can do a lot of things well, I knew that I'd want and need management help. I neither enjoyed nor had experience with many aspects of creating and managing an organization, ranging from major functions such as sales to the millions of details—insurance plans, office space, equipment leasing, trade show schedules, accounting—that you must deal with efficiently to make your company work.

So for most of the first quarter of 1994, I concentrated on finding a partner. A good friend at Xerox wasn't interested, but he gave me some names, and of course I had contacts of my own. I had serious discussions, always under nondisclosure, with another half-dozen people. Mitch Allen, a sharp engineering manager at Apple, liked the idea but was surprisingly timid about leaving a large company. Rex Golding, who had just left 3DO (a troubled game company now making a second try) after four tough years as its chief financial officer, seemed burned out and risk averse. Don Emery, who had just sold his small software company to WordPerfect, was still trying to negotiate a severance agreement with his new owner, Novell, and didn't seem very driven or interested. A technical consultant and programmer whom Charlie Morris and I had once hired actually said yes, but backed out a couple of weeks later. Several computer science professors proved surprisingly timid and disconnected from the start-up world. I began to realize that a lot more people talked about doing a start-up than were actually willing to take the plunge.

By this time I was getting nervous. Everybody had signed nondisclosure agreements, and I'd been careful not to give any information to the consultants I'd hired. But I had to disclose my ideas when talking to potential co-founders, and that list was getting longer by the day. Even if they all honored their agreements, I was putting my Good Idea "in play," and the idea was obvious enough, and big enough, that sooner or later someone was going to do something about it. Then one day I called a computer science professor at MIT I knew, John Guttag, and asked him if he knew anybody good. "Well," John said, "actually, yes, I think I might."

It was Randy Forgaard, and Guttag was more right than I could have dreamt. Randy had gotten bachelor's and master's degrees in computer science from MIT and had been a programmer and lead engineer for several small start-ups, so he had good experience. His most recent company had just been sold, so he was available, and while he was not wealthy, he had enough money to take a chance. Although we have very different personalities, we got along well from the start. We checked a half dozen of each other's references. After Randy signed a nondisclosure agreement, I told him the idea. He thought it over and said yes. We made a deal. Neither of us would draw a salary, but I would pay all expenses. We agreed on an initial eighty-twenty ownership split. I said I would give him more if the relationship went well (a couple of months later I gave Randy an additional 6 percent). The whole thing took a week. In April 1994, we started the company.

Getting Started

So we went to work. Randy started designing the product and doing a demo, which showed purchasing a personal computer online. I plunged into getting headhunters, corporate attorneys, patent attorneys, accountants, and marketing consultants and identifying potential users, partners, and competitors. It turned out that I knew very little about how to do this, and it also turned out to take an enormous amount of time. Later on, it also turned out that bad legal advice cost Randy and me millions of dollars.

Even picking a name was harder than it sounds, and even after consulting with lawyers we got into trouble. We came up with a long list of names, like "OnRamp," but when we did trademark searches they were all taken. After wasting a few thousand dollars on searches, I finally had the bright idea of a name that had nothing to do with technology. I proposed Vermeer because by that time we had decided to do a visual development tool, and he's my favorite painter. The trademark search showed that it was ours for the taking, so we became Vermeer Technologies, Inc. A year later, another Vermeer, a company that made agricultural machinery, tried to take away our Internet domain name. In the end they might have won, because they owned a Vermeer trademark and we didn't; according to the rules they would get the domain name.

It was nervous, exciting, and fun, and Randy and I quickly developed one of the smoothest working relationships I have ever experienced. We trusted each other, respected each other, kept each other informed, and rarely had any trouble reaching consensus on critical issues. We had disagreements, and a couple of serious fights, but we always sat down and settled them, and I never once worried for even a microsecond about his honesty or ethics. In this business that counts for a lot. I also came to realize that Randy was not merely smart, as I had immediately deduced; he was *brilliant,* with a rare ability to translate between the technical and business worlds. He was so unassuming about what he knew that it took me a while to get it.

The most pressing task was to put a core technical team in place, and early on, we found a headhunter on each coast. This reflected an initial decision on my part that the company should be bicoastal, which everyone, including Randy, told me was a mistake. It took me several months to realize they were right. But there was a real issue. Randy lived in Massachusetts. I was nervous about Massachusetts start-ups; they had a bad record, and the action was in the Valley. I hired Paul O'Leary, a transplanted Brit, to headhunt for us in California. I picked him, I'm afraid, mostly because he was willing to defer most of his fees until after we got funded. Randy suggested that I should also contact Ed Takacs, in Boston, who had worked with Randy before. Takacs agreed to work entirely for stock. Each of them struck paydirt almost immediately: O'Leary brought us Peter Amstein and Takacs found Andy Schulert, who turned out to be our two team leaders and our most important technical hires. Both were stunningly good, and they had perfectly complementary experience: Peter in graphics and user interfaces, Andy in the internals of server systems. The gods were smiling.

I was inflexible on two issues: I wanted to hire only the best, and I was determined to keep our plans utterly secret. Job candidates had to pass a lot of tests before we told them anything about what we were doing. We wouldn't even talk to someone who was working for a potentially dangerous competitor or even interviewing with one. (At first this didn't exclude too many people, but later it did; a few slipped through anyway, as you'll see.) We screened out people who were unlikely to join a start-up—with seven hungry kids or a huge mortgage—and we insisted that everyone supply references that we checked out *before* the first interview. Then they had to pass both the "Randy test" and the "Charles test," and sign a confidentiality agreement. Only then would we tell them what we were doing.

The "Randy test" was something that Randy had developed in his previous job, and it was amazing. With grace and disarming charm, Randy administered a brutal hour-long series of technical tests on computer science and software engineering. The questions ranged from definitions of abstract ideas such as NP completeness (a measure of how much computing power a problem requires) and public key encryption, to a series of coding exercises that were short but contained tough challenges. Most of our interviewees said that they had never been subjected to such a test before, and a surprisingly large number of highly recommended people flunked. But almost everyone said they were impressed by the thoroughness of Randy's probing, which they took as a sign that we were serious.

The "Charles test" evolved as I learned about hiring; it concentrated on business and strategic analysis, and it was one of the smartest things I did. In a small start-up with a highly original idea, it is invaluable to have engineers who understand markets, users, and competitive strategy. Both Randy and I were stretched very thin, and there's no way that management can ever monitor every decision that the engineers make. They would inevitably make a host of choices without anyone looking over their shoulders, with major long-term consequences for our business position. We couldn't risk being at the mercy of senior developers who weren't sensitive to our market or who didn't have a good grasp of our strategy.

When I interviewed Peter Amstein in San Francisco, for instance, I asked him to analyze the current state of the online services industry. Suppose, I said, I asserted to you that this industry was fundamentally broken. Why would I think a thing like that?

At this point we had told Peter nothing about our plans, and he had never worked in an online business himself. But after less than a minute's thought, he ticked off most of the important problems—the centralized processing model, the inability to accommodate a company's real-time internal data, the incompatibilities between services, and so on. It was very impressive, and I made him an offer shortly thereafter, with an allocation of stock options that was unusually large for a nonfounder. Andy Schulert had already aced the Randy and Charles tests and got a comparable offer in Massachusetts.

The wisdom of this policy proved itself time and again. Whenever a technical or market problem arose, I would discover that the engineers had already thought of it, already designed it in, already coded it. And if I asked for something new, they got it instantly. Sometimes they would argue back, and often they were right. We never had problems with the disconnect between marketing and engineering that plagues so many software companies—our engineers were almost always on the same page with Randy, me, and Ed Cuoco (our marketing director). That's not to say there weren't any fights—there were lots, mostly over resources and time. But everybody understood what we were trying to do.

I was quite struck by how fast Andy and Peter made the decision to come aboard. Each of them told me later that once I laid out the vision, they made up their minds almost instantly. They got the whole picture and knew they wanted to be part of it. They both spent a bit of time thinking and checking our references, but they both came aboard with virtually no bargaining. I told them we expected to be funded in a few months—it actually took longer—and offered them the choice of working at a low salary during the pre-funding period, or taking no salary in return for more stock options. Both of them picked more stock options over current salary.

It's hard for outsiders to appreciate how casually the high technology brains at the technical core of start-ups bounce from one venture to the next. Vermeer was Randy's fourth start-up, Andy Schulert's fourth, and Peter Amstein's second. They enjoyed the intensity of start-ups, the adrenaline of the race, the creative rush from producing something genuinely new, the company of other smart people. They assumed that eventually one of these cool things would make them serious money, but they didn't worry about it a lot. While they cared about stock options, none of them chose jobs solely because they wanted to get rich, and their rewards from Vermeer were far beyond their expectations. They are veterans at business failures—the good guys don't always win—and they knew they were marketable enough to get a job anytime they needed one. After a few weeks off to recharge their batteries, they would put out the word to the headhunters, and offers would start flowing in. People like these never worry about unemployment, although they often don't look after their financial interests very well.

Hiring Peter, who lived in San Francisco, reflected my mistaken belief that we should be a bicoastal company. In addition to my concerns about Boston and the need to stay close to the Valley, there was also a personal angle. As a Californian, I found New England weather inhuman. And until I met Randy I had assumed the company would be located in the Valley. Well, just before meeting Randy, I ran across a modest but lovely house in the Berkeley hills and took the plunge. It was impulsive and dumb. I got a good price on the house and financed most of it, but the down payment was $100,000, which was half my liquid cash, and I now had acquired a mortgage. My house also needed a good deal of work, so it was hard to rent out—in fact, virtually impossible. So when it became clear that the company really had to be located in Cambridge, I realized I had a serious financial problem. I tried selling the house, but the market was depressed and I would have lost money. The combined impact of an 80 percent pay cut, a mortgage, and a few windows falling off the house became one of my many sources of stress over the next eighteen months.

HIRING LAWYERS AND CONSULTANTS; OR, CANNIBALS AND MISSIONARIES

One of the least pleasant parts of my job was organizing our legal team. We needed incorporation documents, employment contracts, nondisclosure agreements, stock option plans, patents—all the legal paraphernalia that makes you a real company. I interviewed at least a half-dozen law firms. I wanted a firm that understood technology and start-ups, that didn't have any obvious conflicts of interest, that would either accrue their fees or take stock instead of cash, that would pay attention to us, and that wasn't run by assholes. That narrowed the field quite a bit. The experience also made me realize that this was yet another way in which I lacked real experience and appropriate contacts, and I paid for it. Picking through the world's supply of lawyers was not, to put it mildly, my favorite activity, and I wanted to be careful about the conflict of interest issue—obviously with regard to Microsoft but also traditional online services as well. Conflict of interest problems abound in the tight universe of high technology services firms. It's fairly common to discover, for example, that your lawyers can't represent you in an intellectual property suit because the firm you're suing also happens to be their client. I even know of cases in which a company's law firm dropped representation in the hope of *acquiring* the opposite party as a client.

Every lawyer, venture capitalist, and consultant I spoke to told me that my secrecy concerns were overblown and that I could rely on their professional ethics to maintain a rigid separation between clients. But venture capitalists, I learned, were surprisingly leaky, and the other professionals weren't much better. One advantage of locating in Massachusetts turned out to be that rumors didn't spread quite as fast as in California. But I was still careful about conflict issues and confidentiality, and I think this was wise.

On the other hand, I wasn't suspicious enough to pick up on the fact that the very impressive senior partners that I met weren't going to be the ones doing the work. I was also naïve enough to think that I could avoid major, straightforward incompetence if I used a highly regarded firm.

The firm I finally chose as our corporate counsel, Brown & Bain, had offices in Palo Alto and were well known in intellectual property law and high technology litigation. They had represented Intel in a huge arbitration case against AMD and were counsel to MicroUnity, John Moussouris's grandiose semiconductor start-up, which has since collapsed. I was on MicroUnity's advisory board, and Moussouris was high on Lois Abraham, one of the B&B partners and a MicroUnity board member. I too was impressed when I met her. She explained that she wouldn't take us on personally because she was a litigator, but she introduced me to an equally senior partner in corporate law. They agreed to work entirely for stock, and I signed them up.

I missed a few things. The senior partner quickly handed me off to junior associates based in Arizona, of all places, so face-to-face meetings were impossible even when I was in California. I never met the lawyers working for us until the closing of our first-round financing. I shouldn't have put up with this, but I did. The young lawyers at B&B, I should say, did a competent job on the routine paperwork, when they didn't really need to know anything serious about the specifics of start-ups. We got incorporation documents, employment agreements, and so forth. They were sincerely helpful and responsive. But the details they missed have cost me, personally, perhaps $10 million, and they probably cost the company something too, although it's hard to know how much. And our lawyers were totally outclassed by the venture capitalists when we finally got down to negotiating funding, which didn't help my bargaining position. Of course my naïveté was part of the problem there, too.

The lawyers made several major mistakes. First, they missed section 1202 of the tax code. If your company meets a set of conditions that are quite clearly spelled out, and that fit Vermeer perfectly, and if you keep your stock for five years, you pay taxes at half the normal (long-term capital gains) rate. Furthermore, as of 1997, if you sell your stock for the purpose of investing the money in another qualified small company, you pay no taxes at all until you sell the stock in your new investment. This is very nice, particularly since I now invest in start-ups. Unfortunately, the lawyers missed one of the qualifying requirements, resulting in what might be called a reverse loophole for me and Randy.

They also missed two other things. One is a mechanism that keeps stock options for employees very inexpensive relative to the price paid by external investors. For arcane tax reasons, this has an enormous effect on how much money employees actually make on their stock. By sheer random dumb luck, I had picked an initial valuation for the company that prevented this from being a major problem, but it was a near miss. And finally, the lawyers should have known—though, to be fair, so should I—that one of the proposed terms of our first-round investment, called a participation preference, was not standard, as our VCs pretended. It could frequently be eliminated, substantially to our advantage. Moreover, our attorneys' behavior confirmed to the VCs that I was an amateur. Although they found that I was tough and learned fast, they realized that they could get away with a few things, and they did.

Our experience with patent lawyers was initially even worse. Early on, I decided to establish strong patent positions. A number of our technical developments would turn out to be patentable, as I expected, and I wanted to get maximum advantage from them. That was an unusual position at the time, especially in the California high-tech sector, and I had to fight everyone about it. Even most of our venture capitalists tended to deride our patenting efforts. We did patent searches on Lotus Notes and the online services companies, and none of them had protected their technology. Nor had Microsoft. The very lack of attention to patenting in the area helped convince me that we had a real opportunity to establish a strong proprietary position over a large technological space.

Just about this time, a major patent infringement judgment against Microsoft was starting to change the casual attitude toward software patents. A company called Stac sold file compression software—it had the effect of roughly doubling usable disk space—for Windows machines. Microsoft, just as the Japanese used to do, engaged Stac in extensive licensing discussions, learned all about their software, broke off the licensing discussions, and, lo and behold, rolled out Stac-like software of its own. But Stac had patented its technical approaches and won a $110 million judgment. Rather than appeal, Microsoft settled, paying cash plus making an equity investment in the company. Enough to get your attention.

I was also aware of another important patent situation, although it was still confidential at the time. To the surprise of the industry, Microsoft had entered into a joint venture with DEC focused on NT, Microsoft's high-end operating system for workstations and servers. The terms were strikingly favorable to DEC. The reason for this was that DEC held patents that could potentially force Microsoft to take NT off the market.

Bob Palmer, DEC's CEO, had told me the story at dinner a year before. NT, as everyone knew, had been designed by Dave Cutler, a former DEC employee, who was also the key designer on an experimental DEC operating system that was never commercialized. When Cutler joined Microsoft, he took his whole team with him, and when they designed NT they relied on their DEC project. But DEC had patented Cutler's work. Not surprisingly, when DEC put NT under a microscope, they found that it included much of the technology Cutler had developed at DEC. Rather than suing Microsoft for infringement, DEC used the patents as leverage to extract a preferential partnering agreement. So I took patents seriously.

Our first patent law firm was a disaster. Blakely, Sokolof, Taylor, and Zafman had one of the best reputations in the Valley. They were referred to us by Brown & Bain, our corporate counsel. Once again the senior partner, Ed Taylor, made an excellent impression. But once again, as soon as we signed on, we were palmed off to junior guys, who were either overworked or incompetent. Weeks went by as they assured me things were going well, but no progress was forthcoming. I finally terminated them, at which point they presented me a bill for $37,000. Randy convinced me that instead of bombing their offices, I should offer them $2,500; they took it and ran. It wasn't until the next year that we found a good patent firm through Tom Blumer, one of our senior engineers, who had extensive patent experience. The firm—Wolf, Greenfield & Sacks in Boston—had several engineering graduates who did an excellent job.

While I have no way of knowing how much our own patents were worth to us, I think they repaid our efforts and could have been even more crucial if we had remained independent. I placed considerable stress on them during our negotiations with Microsoft, and although they argued with me, I could tell that they took the issue seriously. They also pursued our patents fairly aggressively after the acquisition, so they must have given them some weight.

I also got some market research help in the summer of 1994, both to scan for potential competitors and to help us define our product by talking to potential users. I retained Cynthia Pilkington, a marketing consultant I had worked with at Xerox, and Faisal Nanji, who had been head of market research at Charlie Morris's old firm. They both helped us considerably, particularly by tracking down people who were using the Web and conventional online services, learning how these services were developed and what kind of problems developers encountered. Both of them agreed to work for stock rather than cash, and both ended up making quite a lot of money.

But within a month of starting the company with Randy, all of these problems were suddenly made to seem trivial, at least for a short period of intense panic. The problem, of course, was that we discovered the World Wide Web. And it quickly became clear that the Web did a lot of what we proposed to do. For several weeks, it looked quite possible that we would simply have to call it quits and go home.

THE SHADOW OF THE WEB

Almost as soon as we started the company, Randy and I began hearing references to the Internet and the Web more frequently. One of my more fashion-forward friends in the White House, Tom Kalil, had taken to giving me URLs (Web addresses) in answer to some of my questions. One day in a Harvard Square bookstore, I think in early May of 1994, I saw a new book entitled *The Internet Unleashed*. It was a fat paperback, perhaps eight hundred pages. It contained two chapters describing the Web and also Mosaic, the new graphical browser for looking at Web services. For the first time I had the feeling that the Internet and the Web might be serious. I bought the book, read it, and proceeded to become both terrified and excited. It looked very much as if the Web was the embodiment of my idea, at least of some of it.

I called some friends to ask what they thought. One of the people I called was John Markoff, who covered Silicon Valley for *The New York Times*. Without telling him what we were doing, I asked if he knew any experts on the Internet, the Web, and/or online services. He said I should probably talk to Mark Seiden, a contract programmer who had worked for AOL and who was setting people up on the Internet. And then, he went on, there was EIT (Enterprise Integration Technologies—who were they???), and then there were the Mosaic Communications guys (who???). All of them were in the Valley around Palo Alto.

I called Seiden immediately, faxed him a nondisclosure agreement and a consulting contract, and jumped on a plane for California. Seiden was a bright nerd with little business intuition but who was clearly current on the technology scene. He showed me Mosaic and gave me my first tour of the Web. Most Web services were academic, and most were also quite primitive, but they were scarily close to what I had in mind. Worse, one of them was a rudimentary catalog retailing system operated by a publisher of computer books.

Seiden invited me to a weekly meeting at Stanford where by coincidence that week's speaker was EIT's president, Jay Tenenbaum. He was in Seiden's mold: a nice, nerdy, noncommercial fellow, who gave a talk about Internet-based electronic commerce. EIT was funded by DARPA, a Defense Department research agency, which limited EIT's speed and strategic freedom. They had not, apparently, approached any venture capitalists because Tenenbaum wanted to run his playground without commercial interference. I concluded that EIT was probably not a threat, although we warily checked them out for several months just to make sure. But there were more than a hundred people at Tenenbaum's talk, and Mosaic was reportedly already being downloaded at the rate of sixty thousand copies a month, a rate that was doubling monthly. I didn't like this one bit. Sure, commercial use of the Internet was still illegal, but how long could that last? You could already see people bending the rules. Furthermore, the technology could be used commercially if people invested in the creation of private networks. I called up Mosaic Communications, the other company Markoff had mentioned, and got a guy by the name of Marc Andreessen to sign our nondisclosure agreement. Randy and I had a conference call with him, but couldn't get anything out of him. A short time later, Mosaic Communications changed its name to Netscape.

In May, Randy and I gave ourselves a crash course in Web servers and browsers. (Here, a word on nomenclature: the term *server* can mean either the high-performance computers that "serve" networks of personal computer "clients," or the software that implements specific services. This is confusing, even for us. When people say "Web server," or "mail server," depending on context they may be referring either to a computer system on which such server software runs, or to that software itself. Different kinds of software servers are used to store and manage electronic mail, Web pages, directory information, and other data. In this book I will usually be referring to software.)

As we investigated the Web, it immediately became clear that at least in primitive form, two components of my three-part software architecture—the server and the viewer— already existed. And, at least for noncommercial uses, they were already available to anyone, *free*. What should we do? One possibility was to try to develop and sell commercial-grade versions of Web browsers and servers—the strategy Netscape pursued. This made me nervous, because the basic technology was nonproprietary and widely available. Furthermore, if this industry took off, it seemed to me that a collision with Microsoft would be inevitable. It would be one thing to get into a fight with Microsoft if we already had control over a completely proprietary standard. But it would be quite another if we, they, and everyone else had a common, nonproprietary starting point. So I didn't like that idea too much. Another possibility was to concentrate on the one part of my idea that the Web did not yet seem to include. So Randy and I started to think about development tools for Web services. We didn't know whether they existed; even if none did, we didn't know whether any were needed, or if our embryonic ideas were appropriate for the Web.

So we were faced with the unpleasant prospect that the window of opportunity had already closed, or that at best, my three-part idea had now imploded down to just a development tool. We had no idea whether that was a sufficient basis for a new company. But it was quickly clear that whatever we did, we would have to take the Internet and the Web into account. With considerable fear, we forced ourselves to take a hard, careful, honest look at what this meant.

It turned out that there was a very acceptable answer—in fact, a *fabulous* answer. But in order to set the context for the strategy we chose, I should first say something about the birth of the Internet industry.

CHAPTER TWO

The Internet Awakens as the Giants Sleep, 1990–94: The Invention of the Web and Mosaic, Netscape's First Browser, Vermeer Gets a Strategy, and Much, Much More

> The true men of action of our time, those who transform the world, are not the politicians and statesmen, but the scientists. . . . When I find myself in the company of scientists, I feel like a shabby curate who has strayed by mistake into a drawing room full of dukes.
> —*W. H. Auden*

*T*he origins of the Internet reach back into the 1960s. The path leading from its arcane military/academic origins to the fundamental communications architecture for the entire world was extraordinarily long and convoluted. Remarkably few people understood the importance of the Internet, and nearly all of them were in government, nonprofit organizations, and academia, not in private industry. Between 1989 and 1994 they developed critical innovations, both technical and in policy, without which the revolution would not have occurred. During this time they, and the Internet, were ignored by virtually the entire technology sector, including Microsoft, IBM, AT&T, the local telephone companies, the incumbent online services, and nearly all venture capitalists. A few entrepreneurs got it in early 1994 (PSI, the first commercial Internet service provider [ISP], started even earlier, in 1989) but when the government privatized the Internet in September of that year, most of American industry was still asleep. Sometime in 1994, AOL got it, the only established company that did; and, thanks mainly to the start-ups that educated them, the venture capitalists finally began to wake up.

Birth of the Cool: The Early ARPANET and Internet, 1960s–1980s

The Internet began life in the late 1960s as the ARPANET, designed largely by a company called Bolt, Baranek, and Newman (BBN), using contract R&D money supplied by DARPA, the Defense Advanced Research Projects Agency. DARPA was and remains a remarkable place—small, elite, unbureaucratic, generally free from political interference, run by technologists who know how to think big, and with a stunning track record for funding the coolest ideas around. People who maintain that the government can never do anything better than the market have a hard time explaining DARPA.

The ARPANET was created when two very different problems turned out to have a single brilliant solution. First, the Pentagon, which operated the largest computer infrastructure on earth, badly needed a network that would enable its thousands of computers from many different vendors to communicate with one another, just to do daily business. Then, since these were the iciest days of the cold war, defense specialists noticed that the ARPANET architecture was just the thing to use if you were worried about maintaining strategic communications in the wake of a Soviet nuclear attack.

The idea behind the ARPANET was to create a network architecture such that even if large portions of it failed or were destroyed, it would still function. DARPA gave research and development contracts to BBN and a few universities and then subsidized the creation of an experimental, operating network that connected universities and federal government facilities. By current standards it was a toy. In the early 1970s, the ARPANET's fastest backbone operated at about the speed of a current PC modem, fifty-six kilobits per second. Internet backbone speeds are now about twenty thousand times faster, on the order of a gigabit per second.

BBN did great R&D work, but had an unblemished record of snatching commercial disaster from the jaws of technical victory. (In this respect it resembled Xerox PARC, my former consulting client.) After a sad attempt to compete in the real-world Internet industry, a couple of years ago BBN was bought by, God help us, a telephone company—GTE. But its earlier architectural work was brilliant and led straight to the current Internet.

As often occurs, the freedom that DARPA afforded its contractors let BBN and the other ARPANET pioneers do something far better, and more far-reaching, than their contract required. So in addition to designing a decentralized, highly redundant network that would continue to operate after most of it was destroyed, they also designed one that was extremely flexible and extensible. You could add, delete, or replace network devices and addresses extremely easily, without much central control and with no necessity whatever of disrupting network operations. The architecture also was general enough to support lots of applications, including many never dreamed of in the 1960s, and extensible enough so that it could grow by a factor of more than a million without breaking stride.

So the ARPANET started to spread throughout the research world, and people started using it for more and more things, particularly file transfers and electronic mail. When it started getting big, the National Science Foundation took over funding and administration of a new, faster backbone, and the Internet was born. Quietly, unnoticed, for over twenty years the ARPANET/Internet doubled every year. Suddenly, in 1994, there was a global network used by tens of thousands of computers and more than a million people, connecting virtually every university and research center in the world, and everybody wanted in.

INNOVATORS BECOME INCUMBENTS: THE EARLY ONLINE SERVICES INDUSTRY

The commercial online services industry started about the same time the ARPANET did. By the time the Internet went commercial in the early 1990s, online services were a big industry—a dozen large companies, $10 billion in revenues, and growing 15 percent per year. But they had all chosen conventional mainframe-based technology, and they never switched. So the industry's structure and underlying technologies were fundamentally wrong, which is why the Internet and the Web destroyed it so fast. The sudden collapse of the traditional online services industry, however, is less remarkable than its twenty-five-year reign; it is an excellent example of the staying power of second-rate incumbents. Habit, momentum, the high cost of entry, and an implicit ethos of not ruining a good thing made it easy to play along and hard to rock the boat. It was similar to what occurred in the mainframe and minicomputer industry during the same period—a nice little club whose members got lazy and slow.

Most online service companies provided marketing, financial, legal, medical, and technical information to business users. There were a number of specialized scientific services as well. Companies like Lockheed's Dialog and LEXIS-NEXIS offered legal and journalistic research material, economic and financial databases, and repackaged material from the SEC and other public agencies. All of them were mainframe based and completely centralized. In the 1960s and 1970s, you accessed them from a dumb terminal; later, you could use a PC with a modem. These services were expensive, difficult to use, and completely incompatible with one another. The creation of new services, even relatively simple ones, required a $10–$50 million investment in mainframe computers, database software, and much else. People who merely had useful information to distribute—"content providers" or "database vendors"—were at the mercy of the services, which paid them royalty rates of 10 percent or even less.

As personal computers and modems spread to homes, there arose a small number of consumer-oriented services. CompuServe, founded in 1969, was the first significant one. Membership remained small for many years, because few consumers had ready access to computers and the available modems were very slow. Prodigy, a CompuServe competitor offering online news, sports, weather, travel, and some catalog shopping, was founded as a joint venture by IBM and Sears in 1984, but did not complete its full national launch until 1990. At their peak in the early 1990s, just before the Internet obliterated them, CompuServe and Prodigy had a total of about four million users. They were both awful—clumsy, hard to use, slow, and expensive. Developing content for them was a nightmare.

THE PLUMBING GETS INSTALLED: THE RISE OF LANS

At the same time as the ARPANET and the online services industry were growing, the internal operations of organizations were being networked in a way that later had profound consequences for the Internet industry. Starting in the mid-1980s, companies started installing local area networks (LANs), which had been invented by Xerox PARC in the late 1970s. At first, they were mostly used for mundane tasks like sharing files and printers among clusters of PC users. Novell's NetWare operating system rapidly came to dominate this portion—the "low end"—of the LAN server software market. Like much of the industry, it used an architecture copied from PARC's work. Unfortunately for Novell, however, it had designed its own communications protocol, IPX, that was not Internet compatible. Novell was criminally slow to fix this (and many other problems as well), and as a consequence may not be able to survive.

But the "high end" was another story. Through a series of historical accidents, American industry was unwittingly becoming Internet-compatible by adopting servers based on the UNIX operating system for mission-critical applications. UNIX was originally developed at pre-divestiture AT&T, which had licensed it without charge to universities, who in turn used it for their research systems and Internet servers. Then, in the early 1980s, UNIX went commercial. High-end applications such as large databases, enterprise information systems, and custom applications that had traditionally run on IBM mainframes started to shift toward powerful new microprocessor-based UNIX servers sold primarily by Sun and Hewlett-Packard. Their success forced IBM, DEC, Unisys, and others to embrace UNIX too.

We now come to two important decisions—one of them very good for the world, the other rather bad. The good one was the design of "Berkeley UNIX," which became the basis for all commercial UNIX systems (and was another DARPA project, by the way). The primary architect of Berkeley UNIX was Bill Joy, one of the world's software geniuses. He chose the Internet communications protocol, TCP/IP, as the Berkeley UNIX networking standard. In 1982 Joy left Berkeley to become one of the four founders of Sun Microsystems, which used Berkeley UNIX and TCP/IP as the basis for all of its products. Sun's supplier was 3Com, which, in late 1980, had been the first company to ship commercial TCP/IP products for UNIX. Sun rapidly became the largest vendor of UNIX systems, and all other UNIX vendors basically followed them. Lucky for Sun and Hewlett-Packard, lucky for the Internet industry, and lucky for corporate America.

Unfortunately, Sun's founders simultaneously made another choice that in my opinion will ultimately prove a fatal error—they decided to start the wrong kind of company. Although Sun proclaims itself an open-systems company, it is in fact the opposite—a throwback to the obsolete business model used by Apple, DEC, and the old mainframe and minicomputer companies. This is a tragic shame, and it will eventually kill Sun.

In the early 1980s, everyone who was cool knew UNIX was coming and that UC Berkeley's UNIX was the coolest around. I had just joined IBM; I tried to warn IBM senior management about it, and I wasn't alone. Sun was founded in 1982, practically the instant that Berkeley's famous Release 4.2 was finished, and its founders included Joy, who had designed it and knew more about UNIX than anyone else on the planet. At the time, Microsoft was tiny and NT wasn't even a gleam in Gates's eye. Sun therefore had the whole world in its hands.

But like Apple with the Macintosh, Sun was seduced by the immediate profitability of proprietary hardware systems. Apple could have made the Mac operating system the desktop standard for all PCs long before Microsoft developed Windows. Instead, they insisted on bundling it with their limited range of expensive hardware. Sun made essentially the same mistake. Instead of creating a pure software company and becoming the Microsoft of server operating systems, they became a traditional hardware/software computer systems company like DEC or Apple. All of the other UNIX system vendors that followed them—Hewlett-Packard, Silicon Graphics, IBM, DEC—developed their own UNIX variants, because they couldn't risk depending upon a systems competitor for their critical software. And of course they, too, were seduced by the profitability of having a proprietary hardware business, rather than having to fight it out continuously the way PC companies do. As with the conventional proprietary online services industry, UNIX became an expensive club to join.

And also as with online services, the UNIX server industry fragmented, with each vendor's systems incompatible with the others. This left it vulnerable to the assault from Microsoft's NT running on systems developed by Compaq and others. I'll talk more about this in chapter 10; for now, suffice it to say that the rise of the Internet caused an explosion in server demand, and NT is now picking off the UNIX companies one by one. Sun is the last complete holdout. As with IBM and DEC before them, they might take a long time to go down—another five years, maybe even ten. But they're dead; their structure is ultimately wrong, and Microsoft is already starting to tighten the screws.

In the meanwhile, however, Sun had been prewiring corporate America for the Internet revolution.

1990–92: THINGS GET INTERESTING

The Birth of the Web The World Wide Web was invented in 1989 by Tim Berners-Lee, an Englishman with a Ph.D. in physics who was working at CERN, the European particle physics research center in Switzerland. In my brief interactions with him, I found him to be very smart, humorless, angry at the world, and unrealistic—but also principled and committed to what he thought was right. Despite the fact that by late 1994 he was the most marketable guy on the whole planet, he joined a well-intentioned but, I'm afraid, rather useless nonprofit Web standards group based at MIT. There can be few things more futile than trying to develop nonproprietary standards in the middle of a war between Microsoft, Netscape, and AOL.

Nonetheless, if they ever give Nobel Prizes in computer science, and they should, Berners-Lee deserves one of the first. His invention—the Web—was a software architecture that made it easy to post documents on the Internet; to create "hypertext" links, or hyperlinks, from anyplace in a document to other locations within the document or to any other document on the Web; and then allowed anyone to read these documents—from anywhere on the Internet. Berners-Lee intended this system for researchers, not mere mortals with PCs, but his design was brilliant, extensible, and profoundly simple. Via hypertext links, you could instantly navigate at will through dozens, or even hundreds, of papers all over the world using a single Internet connection.

Berners-Lee's architecture included a page-description language for Web documents, called the "HyperText Markup Language," or HTML; a system for identifying the locations that hyperlinks pointed to, called "Uniform Resource Locators," or URLs; and a communications protocol called the "HyperText Transfer Protocol," or HTTP, for requesting and sending Web pages. A piece of software called a Web server managed the documents and "served" pages to users in response to HTTP requests. Users employed a simple, text-only browser to look at pages and request new ones. Any browser could request and display pages from any Web server, anywhere on the Internet, just as any telephone can call any other telephone.

None of the individual ideas in Berners-Lee's design were new. HTML, for instance, was a variant of SGML, a government standard long familiar to federal contractors. But the power of the whole, combined with the Internet, was magical. All Web servers throughout the world were knit together into a vast information repository.

Berners-Lee released the first Web server through CERN in 1991. Like most early Internet software, it was free; Berners-Lee posted it on his Internet site, and anyone who wanted it could just download it. Use of the Web gradually spread through the academic and research community over the next year or so. But for all its magic, Berners-Lee's Web was still hard to use. The main problem, from the viewpoint of end-users, was the crudeness of the browser. URLs had to be typed by hand, for example, and unless you kept careful notes of the URLs you were using, you might not be able to find your way back through the maze of documents and hyperlinks.

Internet Policy, 1990–92: A Brilliant Vision Pursued by a Few In 1990, the year after Berners-Lee invented the Web, the National Science Foundation (NSF) clarified its position on commercial use of the Internet by issuing its "Acceptable Use Policy." The basic answer was no; but there was some wiggle room. The high-speed NSF-funded national backbone was off-limits for commercial purposes. But individual e-mail was deemed private, noncommercial, and therefore exempt. Moreover, commercial establishments were allowed to use the Internet for research purposes—e.g., to communicate with academic colleagues—and there were no objections to commercial use over the regional networks built and maintained by private Internet service providers, so long as traffic wasn't routed through the NSF national backbone.

Nonetheless, the Acceptable Use Policy definitely restricted Internet usage. Consequently, a small group of people, most of them inside the government but a few in the private sector, were working to open the Internet to commercial use and competition.

Mitch Kapor, the founder of Lotus, co-founded the Electronic Frontier Foundation in 1990 and became its first president. Its goal was to educate policymakers about the potential for electronic communication and specifically about the Internet, as well as information policy issues such as electronic privacy and free speech. Kapor also became chairman of the Commercial Internet Exchange, the small trade organization of the regional Internet service providers, and led a lobbying campaign to open the Internet to commercial use.

In March 1992, Kapor made his case in remarkably farsighted testimony before the House Science and Technology Committee. One indicator of growing commercial interest in Internet services was that the small nonprofit regional service providers, such as UUNet, began to convert to for-profit status. Another was that Kapor estimated that 60 percent of registered Internet addresses were already commercial (signified by a ".com" suffix). The following year marked the first venture capital investment in an Internet service provider, when Matrix Capital and Sigma Partners made a first-round investment in PSI, an ISP headquartered in the suburbs of Washington, D.C. It was then a tiny business: PSI's annual revenues were only about $6 million, but it was profitable. Not coincidentally, two years later Matrix and Sigma were the lead investors in Vermeer's first-round financing. They were among a handful of VCs who already knew something about the Internet in 1994. For the same reason, Kapor was also among the earliest Internet investors; in 1994, he invested in Progressive Networks (now RealNetworks) and joined its board.

It was also in 1992 that Ed Krol, who worked at NCSA, published *The Whole Internet User's Guide and Catalog.* It was a difficult, technical book about a collection of difficult, technical services, but it was also the only comprehensive overview of how to use the Internet, and it sold an estimated 250,000 copies. Moreover, the book was discussed in general-circulation publications such as *The New York Times.* Clearly, public interest in the Internet was on the rise.

However, the most important Internet development of 1992 may be the least well known. Robert Aiken, Hans-Werner Braun, and Peter Ford wrote a paper entitled "NSF Implementation Plan for Interim NREN." In it, they described a far-reaching proposal for privatizing the Internet and changing its technical architecture to encourage competition in Internet services while retaining interoperability between competing providers. The paper laid out a comprehensive vision for the development of the Internet and proposed turning over the high-speed government backbone to private industry. It also proposed a revised Internet architecture designed to foster competition and commercial growth, based on the creation of network access points (NAPs), where competing backbones could interconnect with one another and with local providers. It was a brilliant argument that, measured by subsequent practical importance, may rank just below the Monroe Doctrine or George Kennan's 1948 article on Soviet containment. And, for that matter, the government's Internet R&D will surely generate a higher return than any private venture capital investment ever made.

The quiet force behind the ABF paper, as it became known, was Steve Wolff, an obscure NSF official responsible for managing the Internet backbone. They don't give Nobel Prizes for public service either, unfortunately, but

Wolff deserves one. Wolff grasped, as few others did, the importance of the Internet and its potential commercial applications. And he didn't try to block progress because it would mean giving away his empire; on the contrary, he argued for it. Several congressmen helped too. Yet corporate America and the technology sector (IBM, AT&T, Oracle, Apple, Hewlett-Packard, Microsoft) were still years away from figuring it out. Two years later, the NSF announced that NSFNet would be privatized, opened to commercial use, and restructured to provide for competing Internet services—using exactly the architecture recommended in the 1992 ABF paper. On April 30, 1995, the Internet officially opened for business.

It has become fashionable to argue that industrial policy isn't possible in America and is anyway inherently a bad idea. But the record of government-supported Internet development versus the commercial online services industry clearly demonstrates exactly the opposite. The established technology companies, the Silicon Valley geniuses, the online services industry, and the venture capitalists all missed it for twenty years or more. Every brilliant, important, technically farsighted Internet development came either from government agencies or universities. In the meantime, decision making in the competitive marketplace was narrow, shortsighted, self-protective, and technically far inferior to its Internet equivalents.

When you've known both crowds, as I have, it's pretty obvious why. First, the quality of the people in DARPA, the NSF, and the academy was light-years ahead of the bureaucrats running companies like CompuServe, Prodigy, AT&T, and IBM. And second, when you motivate people with money, you shouldn't be surprised if they behave selfishly. If they can get away with something they often will, and in the technology sector they often can, because the vendors are more knowledgeable and better coordinated than the consumers. But if people are doing something for intellectual greatness, for their principles, or for posterity, they think differently. You wouldn't want most computer science professors running your company, but you wouldn't want the average high-technology executive deciding how the world should be wired, either.

This is not to say that the government always gets it right. In highly politicized regulatory arenas such as telecommunications and antitrust policy, the federal government has an abysmal record. (I consider those issues among others in the final chapters of this book.) But when technologists and policy specialists can make critical early decisions out of the political limelight, but subject to open review within the academic and technical community, government policy often outperforms the market.

Meanwhile AOL Grows, and Microsoft Notices America Online went public on March 19, 1992. The company had been founded in 1985 to offer online access to news, soap opera updates, and games. After a money-losing couple of years servicing Apple's private network for Apple II users, the company severed its tie with Apple and built its own subscriber base. At the time of AOL's initial public offering, it had about 150,000 users and a slender profit on revenues of about $20 million. The IPO valued the whole company at about $70 million, versus billions now.

AOL differentiated itself from Prodigy and CompuServe (which at the time were the far larger incumbents) by adopting more modern technology. It was the first to use the Windows graphical user interface and, rather than using mainframes, ran its service on high-end UNIX minicomputers. AOL also started using a clever two-tier marketing strategy that has continued to this day. Publicly, AOL promotes itself as family-oriented, cute, and tame, although in fact a substantial fraction of its subscribers are there for sex, some of it quite adventurous. But it worked. In October 1992 Walt Mossberg, the "Personal Technology" columnist at *The Wall Street Journal,* called AOL "the sophisticated wave of the future" in online services. The other online services remained primarily text-based, were harder to use, and promoted themselves much less aggressively. For years Prodigy, half owned by IBM, was prevented from using Windows interfaces because of the tensions between IBM and Microsoft. CompuServe had a Windows shell fairly early, but it was buried beneath text-based services, and it was awful.

AOL's success attracted unwanted attention. In the late fall of 1992, Paul Allen, co-founder of Microsoft and a Microsoft board member, began acquiring large blocks of AOL stock. Steve Case, AOL's CEO, fought him off by adopting an anti-takeover "poison pill," a provision that forces a company to self-destruct in the event of a hostile acquisition. Case feared that Allen was just a stalking horse for Microsoft, which was apparently not true. But the fact that you're paranoid doesn't mean they're not out to get you: Microsoft *was* interested in AOL. In fact, Bill Gates was upset at Allen because he was getting in the way. Following the advice of Nathan Myhrvold, the physicist who mysteriously continued to act as Microsoft's internal futurist-guru, Gates killed a project aimed at creating an Internet-based consumer service. Gates and Myhrvold became convinced that the future of online services lay with proprietary services such as AOL and decided that Microsoft should enter the business. Gates assigned Russ Siegelman, a bright young Microsoft executive, to come up with a strategy.

1993: Mosaic Jump-Starts the Web

The breakthrough that made the Web accessible to normal people began in December 1992. A group of students at the National Center for Supercomputing

Applications at the University of Illinois, led by Marc Andreessen and Eric Bina, started writing a user-friendly browser for the Web, which they called Mosaic. They did it part-time, on their own, with virtually no support from the center's hierarchy. Despite the fact that some of their later behavior at Netscape was awful, their creation of Mosaic was brilliant, and they deserve a Nobel Prize too. Mosaic left the basic Web architecture untouched, but overlaid it with a GUI, a graphical user interface, that made it easy to navigate. A little hand showed you when you were at a hyperlink, and you could jump from page to page just by clicking on links with a mouse. Mosaic kept a record of the pages you visited, so you could easily retrace your steps. Altogether, it was a very cool piece of software that cleared the ground for the Web's takeoff.

On January 23, 1993, the kids at NCSA posted Mosaic for X Windows, a UNIX GUI used widely in the academic world, on the NCSA Web site. They posted both the program and its source code on the Web, making it possible for anyone to use it, examine how it worked, and even to change it. This was normal in the UNIX/academic world—it was the same way that Berners-Lee distributed his software. This allowed extremely rapid distribution among the cognoscenti, resulting in rapid and intelligent feedback, bug reports, and bug fixes. The phenomenon of "Internet time," the ultrafast development cycle that characterizes the entire Internet industry, is in large part a consequence of using the Web to distribute and receive information and technology about the Web, including software, specifications, documentation, source code, and comments from users.

As soon as their X Windows browser was posted, the NCSA team started working on versions of Mosaic for Windows and the Mac, which were what really opened the Web to the world. Early versions of the software began to be posted on the NCSA Web site in the late spring of 1993. But in the academic-hacker style that would later plague Netscape, each version was written virtually from scratch by separate teams, and none of them was carefully architected. For academic freeware, this is fine. But doing that sort of thing when Microsoft is out to kill you is quite another matter.

In July, Andreessen, Bina, and the rest of the Mosaic team attended an Internet "Wizards' Workshop" in Cambridge, bringing demos of the Windows and Mac browsers, where they met Berners-Lee for the first time. Ironically Berners-Lee had serious misgivings about mass-market browsers and a popularized Web and argued that individual users should create their own browsers, tailored to their own searching priorities. By this time Andreessen had begun to acquire a growing cult-like following, like a rock star about to break into the big time. He easily prevailed.

Andreessen's team posted relatively stable beta versions of Mosaic for Windows and the Mac in October 1993. Downloads jumped astronomically. This was the tipping point for the Web and the Internet, when the growth of Web sites and usage abruptly turned vertical. For the next two years the Web grew 25 percent *per month,* literally faster than any other technology in history. It was also starting in late 1993 that the media finally discovered the Web. John Markoff wrote a long article on Mosaic that appeared in *The New York Times* in December.

The Markoff article, however, added to frictions building inside NCSA. Markoff appeared to give primary credit for Mosaic to Larry Smarr, the NCSA director, and didn't mention the developers. At the same time, Smarr and his managerial team had moved to assert control over Mosaic. The development team got thousands of e-mails a day with fixes, complaints, and questions, which placed them at the very center of ferment. Smarr decided to route the e-mail to a generic response desk and then told the developers that they could not even *see* it, because it interfered with their work. When Andreessen graduated in December, he was offered a $50,000 salary to stay at NCSA—high by university standards—but Smarr would not let him manage Mosaic development. Andreessen quit and headed for California, where he got a job at EIT, which was, however ineffectually, exploring commercial opportunities on the Internet.

THE BIG GUYS KEEP NOT GETTING IT

Outside of the academic Internet community, a lot of the supposedly smart money was betting on ITV, or interactive television. Microsoft spread its money around doing everything with everybody, or claiming to. It joined with Intel and General Instrument to develop set-top boxes for ITV; Microsoft was also part of a group including TCI, Hewlett-Packard, and Cray that invested huge sums in MicroUnity, a failed start-up with grandiose plans for ultrafast memory chips and multimedia microprocessors. Later, Microsoft worked on another deal with TCI and Time Warner for set-top boxes. Oracle jumped into the fray, announcing a video-on-demand system for delivering movies to the home, while Silicon Graphics joined with Time Warner to mount a major ITV experiment in Orlando, Florida. Sybase announced it was developing a similar system. IBM announced a pilot project with Blockbuster Video with the aim of creating a nationwide system for digital distribution of CDs and videos, so every Blockbuster store could produce custom music CDs on demand and would have access to every video in the inventory. Despite much fanfare, all of these initiatives sank without a trace.

In the meantime, Microsoft was simultaneously getting serious about conventional, proprietary online services. On May 11, 1993, Gates, Siegelman, and Greg Maffei (then Microsoft's treasurer, now CFO) met with Steve Case. Siegelman had recommended trying to acquire an existing service before deciding to build one from scratch. He had rejected Prodigy and CompuServe as hopeless, but recommended giving AOL a try. With his characteristic delicacy, Gates said to Steve Case, "I can buy twenty percent of you, or I can buy all of you, or I can go into this business and bury you." Displaying considerable courage, Case replied that AOL was not for sale, so Gates decided to bury him. That same day, Gates authorized Siegelman to proceed with development of the Microsoft Network, or MSN, code-named Marvel.

AOL raised the ante after Gates's visit. In July, AOL started its "carpet-bombing" campaign, blanketing the country with millions—eventually more than 250 million—free start-up diskettes. At first the mailings were limited to subscribers of PC trade magazines, but the response was so favorable that AOL's marketing director, Jan Brandt, began distributing them attached to cereal boxes, on seats at football games, with frozen steaks, to American Airlines passengers. The diskette start-up kit simplified installation and neatly finessed the problem of downloading graphics for the user interface, which in an era of slow modems was a serious problem. CompuServe and Prodigy still installed via much slower and more complicated online downloading and used relatively few graphics. AOL had three hundred thousand subscribers at the start of the carpet-bombing campaign and had been growing quite rapidly, but now it shifted into hypergrowth.

For a while, however, Prodigy and CompuServe were actually ahead of AOL in one area: providing Internet-based e-mail services for their subscribers. AOL caught up to Prodigy and CompuServe by early 1994, offering Internet e-mail and also developing a special, Internet-based version of its client software, which it distributed solely on college campuses—because everybody there used the Internet.

Microsoft continued to be oblivious. In August 1993, for example, Rob Glaser, who had just resigned from Microsoft, visited the Electronic Frontier Foundation, where he was proselytized by Kapor regarding the Internet. Glaser used Mosaic and the Web for the first time and was impressed. A month later, Glaser was hired by Gates as a consultant to advise on Web/Internet issues as they related to MSN. He gave the MSN team a tutorial on the Internet and the Web and strongly recommended that MSN be Web/Internet based. The recommendation was rejected. Gates thought he could control what future online services would look like, in part because MSN would be bundled with Windows 95.

At this point, Microsoft's behavior was still in character, even if it was erroneous. Gates is brilliant, but neither he nor Microsoft has ever been visionary. Microsoft has made all of its money—literally all of it—by entering markets created by others and using technologies copied or purchased from others. In this case, they simply erred in copying a technology that was about to die, and it took them a few years to realize it.

EARLY 1994: THE INCUMBENTS STILL WANDER, BUT SEVERAL ENTREPRENEURS GET IT

Even as late as mid-1994, AOL was the only incumbent, if you can call them that, who had the slightest clue. Apple announced eWorld, a proprietary online service based on Apple's internal network and licensed AOL technology, only to kill it a year later. Characteristically, the effort had no relation to anything else Apple was doing at the time. Ziff-Davis, the largest publisher of computer magazines, announced Interchange—its own proprietary online service aimed at computer users. When Ziff-Davis started to suspect that the Internet would kill Interchange, they had the perfect solution: they sold it to AT&T, reportedly for $75 million.

Without any doubt, in fact, AT&T under Bob Allen (who has since been replaced by Mike Armstrong, the ex-CEO of Hughes) wins the prize for stupidity during this period. Starting in the early 1990s, AT&T spent hundreds of millions of dollars, possibly billions, on a wide array of acquisitions and strategic investments in communications and online services, an effort unparalleled in the perfection of its track record: every single one was a complete, total failure. This was all the more remarkable because of the relationship between UNIX, developed by AT&T's Bell Labs, and the development of the Internet.

AT&T went after everything. One direction was games. In January 1993 AT&T invested in 3DO, a game company that AT&T hoped would stimulate online usage. 3DO's ambitious plans failed; much later it survived by reshaping itself as a conventional game software company. Then AT&T purchased the Imagination Network (a subsidiary of Sierra Online), an online game company that imploded just after AT&T bought it. Then came handheld computers— personal digital assistants, or PDAs. In September 1993, AT&T acquired EO and announced that its PDAs would support Novell's message handling software for e-mail. Nothing came of all this, of course. EO had been carved out of GO, a disastrous investment made by John Doerr of Kleiner Perkins, who was seeking to unload it. Kleiner Perkins actually made money on GO by selling its stock to later investors at a markup—in short, by finding greater fools. When a VC firm offers to sell its own stock, you should think twice.

AT&T, however, was the ideal partner for Kleiner Perkins. They reliably paid high prices for nonworking products and uttered not a word of complaint when their investments turned out to be worthless. GO absorbed $75 million in venture and strategic money before collapsing without having developed a marketable product. Simultaneously, AT&T invested in General Magic. This was truly impressive, first because General Magic was the only company that exceeded GO and EO in its ratio of hype to reality, and second because General Magic's plan was precisely to compete with GO and EO. AT&T said it planned to use General Magic software as the basis for providing wireless online services. Nothing came of that either.

Then in March 1994, AT&T and Lotus announced that AT&T would create and manage a public Lotus Notes network. Notes was the first and most popular "groupware" software product that allowed people within an organization to collaborate by sharing documents and discussions over a corporate network. AT&T and Lotus announced that their network would allow public Notes services and also permit multiple companies to link their Notes applications. Jim Manzi, the Lotus CEO, called the venture "the Business Internet." Recall that at almost exactly the same moment, I was concluding that Notes was not only flawed in general, but was particularly and very seriously unsuited to public online services. Just the thing for AT&T. The network was scheduled to begin operations in early 1995 but never saw the light of day. Microsoft reportedly pushed hard to make its own groupware, Exchange, the basis for the network and was lucky to lose. Then a few weeks later, AT&T reached an agreement with Novell to establish a "virtual LAN," a public network that would provide remote end-user access to all of a company's NetWare-based network services and resources. That plan, also, sank without a trace.

Sharp entrepreneurs, however, were finally catching on. Netscape, Progressive Networks (now RealNetworks), Vermeer, and Yahoo! were all founded during the same period in the first half of 1994 that AT&T, Apple, Lotus, and Novell were throwing away their money.

Jim Clark announced his resignation from Silicon Graphics, the preeminent vendor of high-end graphics-oriented workstations, in late January 1994. Clark was a former Stanford University professor who had founded SGI with six graduate students in 1981. In order to finance it, he gave up control to the venture capitalists and their professional managers, and he was feeling increasingly frustrated and marginalized—to the point where he was willing to walk away from serious money. Clark was already a rich man, worth about $30 million at the time, but he left even more than that on the table. He announced that he was interested in exploring ITV ventures and began a series of conversations with smart young engineers in the Valley.

During Clark's final days at SGI one of his engineers, Bill Foss, introduced him to Mosaic and the Web. Clark was impressed and sent a now-famous e-mail to Marc Andreessen: "You may not know me, but I'm the founder of

Silicon Graphics. I've resigned and intend to form a new company. Would you be interested in getting together for a talk?" They got together.

Clark and Andreessen hit it off, and along with several Silicon Graphics engineers—Tom Paquin, Bill Toy, and Foss—they undertook a series of conversations, often on Clark's sailboat, that stretched over several weeks. Initially they focused on ITV, with some discussion of possible ITV-related applications for Mosaic. Finally Andreessen diffidently suggested the possibility of commercializing Mosaic on personal computers. Accounts conflict as to whether it was Clark or Andreessen who finally decided that the Internet, not ITV, was going to be the big winner. (Both declined to be interviewed for this book.) It required a substantial leap of faith for Clark to embrace the Internet, since his primary interest was high-speed graphics and video. For most users, transmission over the Internet was still limited to modem speeds, and there was therefore no immediate possibility of using it to transmit real-time voice or video. The other engineers at the meetings remember being quite skeptical.

Complicating matters, the University of Illinois had started to license the source code for the Mosaic browser and the NCSA Web server, and the rights to enhance the code and develop commercial products, quite widely. After a dozen licensing deals, the university contracted with a small local software firm, Spyglass, Inc., to act as its master licensee, with Spyglass sublicensing the code to other commercial companies. This was a stroke of luck for Netscape, because Spyglass was and remains quite incompetent. But the clock was ticking, and Clark decided to move fast.

On April 4, 1994—within a few days of Randy and me shaking hands—Clark and Andreessen incorporated, initially calling their firm Mosaic Communications. Clark put up $4 million of his own money; shortly thereafter Kleiner Perkins kicked in an additional $5 million, and John Doerr joined the board. AOL offered to invest, but after extended discussions, Clark wisely vetoed the deal to avoid conflicts of interest.

Clark leased office space in Mountain View, and he and Andreessen promptly flew out to Illinois and hired the entire Mosaic team. They completed their initial business plan, which targeted the business market and included, among other objectives, to "develop, deploy, and widely license a next-generation, commercial-grade Mosaic client, server, and authoring suite." Had I known about that sentence at the time, I would have been terrified—it was very, very close to my own Good Idea.

But Microsoft Still Misses It In January 1994, Microsoft decided to add TCP/IP capability to its next release of Windows, which became known as Windows 95 when its schedule slipped. Although adding the TCP/IP protocol was a crucial step in making Windows 95 Internet capable, Microsoft still had no Internet strategy. It had chosen TCP/IP on its technical merits, and because it wanted to facilitate communications between Windows 95 and corporate UNIX servers, rather than for its role in the Internet.

But there were, within Microsoft, a few people who were becoming increasingly excited, and worried, about the Internet. Their agitation resulted in a series of small, incremental steps. James Allard, the manager of Microsoft's TCP/IP project, wrote a memo to Nathan Myhrvold and other executives entitled "Windows: The Next Killer Application for the Internet," advocating the development of a browser that could be either integrated with Windows or sold separately. The memo was circulated throughout Microsoft, but its recommendations were not heeded.

Then in February 1994, Steve Sinofsky, who at this time was Bill Gates's personal technical assistant (a two-year rotating assignment), went to Cornell on a recruiting trip. His flight home was canceled because of snow, so he returned to the campus, where by accident he ran into a bunch of students using Mosaic to surf the Web and the Internet. Sinofsky got it—immediately. He sent an e-mail to Gates entitled "Cornell Is Wired!" and on his return he gave Gates a demo of the Web. Sinofsky is a very smart guy, with a strong technical background, who I suspect is quite ruthless despite his superficially cheerleading, agreeable demeanor. I spent a lot of time with him when we negotiated the sale of Vermeer to Microsoft. My instinct was to keep my back to the wall. Sinofsky now runs Microsoft Office, which is not a job for pussycats.

On Sinofsky's urging, Gates agreed to hold a Web/Internet retreat in April 1994. The relevant senior people were there, including Siegelman, the MSN manager. Sinofsky gave a Web/Mosaic demonstration. Nonetheless, after considerable discussion, the consensus was that there was no way to make real money on the Internet, and that MSN should not be converted to an Internet-based service. There were a few gestures toward accommodating the Internet. TCP/IP would be incorporated into MSN in order to offer the same Internet-based e-mail services as all the other online services, and a project was authorized to create an add-on to Word that could convert Word documents into HTML, the document language for the Web. But that was about it. During this time, Microsoft's internal networks were deliberately isolated from the Internet for security reasons. In the whole company there were apparently only two PCs, in the library, with Internet access. Gates made no attempt to change this.

Gates's radar had been turned on, but no more. About a month after the April retreat, Gates and Sinofsky saw a demo of Booklink's new Web browser at the Atlanta COMDEX trade show. In late 1994, Gates made a half-hearted attempt to buy Booklink or its technology, but was outbid by AOL. In the summer yet another Microsoft technologist, a developer named Ben Slivka, urged senior executives to start a browser project, and Microsoft finally said yes. But

Slivka was given only five people, signifying that it was a very low priority for the company.

Much later, in the course of antitrust proceedings, Microsoft claimed that as early as the April 1994 retreat Microsoft had decided to integrate Web browsing into Windows. This is ridiculous and directly contradicted by my personal interviews with Russ Siegelman. In fact, a year and a half after the April meeting, in late 1995, when we first began discussing their purchase of Vermeer, Microsoft *still* had not fully embraced Internet or Web standards. They certainly understood by then how important the Internet was, but they thought that Microsoft could enforce its own standards upon it. Chris Peters, who was then in charge of Office, and several of his colleagues suggested to us that Microsoft could replace HTML with the Word document format as the primary document standard for the Web. In the very long run, they might be right, as we shall see later. But the claim that in April 1994 Microsoft had already embraced HTML-based Web browsing as integral to its future systems is absurd.

It is around this time that Microsoft's blindness starts becoming more difficult to understand. Start-up activity was intensifying, and so was public awareness. As I mentioned earlier, *The Internet Unleashed,* a huge trade paperback, was published in March 1994. Unlike Ed Krol's book it was directed at the layperson and was highly readable. There were only two brief chapters on the Web and Mosaic, but they were clear, accurate, and remarkably perceptive about the commercial potential of the Web. It was this book that turned *my* radar on, for real, and got me calling all my friends. Shortly afterward, DEC announced that a Web browser would be bundled with all of its workstations. DEC originally hoped to bundle Netscape's browser, but since it was not ready, they bought a license from Spyglass for the NCSA Mosaic browser. Then Rob Glaser founded Progressive Networks to develop "streaming" audio technology to permit large-scale audio distribution over the Internet. Glaser was a former Microsoft executive who had recently consulted to Gates on precisely these subjects. Mitch Kapor invested in Progressive and joined the board. But Microsoft didn't notice.

April–August 1994: Vermeer Confronts the Web

Randy and I started poking at the Internet and the Web seriously in May and June. As I've said, our original concept was a three-part software suite—a server to store and manage services; a browser for looking at them; and a *visual, end-user* development tool for creating them. Those adjectives turned out to be important; in fact, they probably represent the most valuable contribution I've made to the Internet, and perhaps to anything.

Upon investigating the Web and matching it up against my original idea, we were both frightened and intrigued. We were led to a long list of subtle, difficult questions. The first was, would the Web take off? This was not to be taken for granted. There were only a small number of Web servers in the world, and commercial use of the Internet was still prohibited by the Acceptable Use Policy (AUP). Upon examination, we concluded that the Web probably *would* take off. While the original Web had many limitations, some of which have still not been remedied, it did so many things so well that it was hard to imagine that it wouldn't continue to grow. The Internet and the Web protocol made it possible to skip seamlessly from server to server on a single dial-up connection. Mosaic went a long way toward creating the kind of intuitive, consumer-friendly client software that we needed. We concluded that either the AUP would be changed or private firms would create new, commercial TCP/IP backbone networks. We remained nervous about this for a while and analyzed fallback plans such as converting Web software to operate on non-Internet protocols and networks. Of course this turned out to be unnecessary, to put it mildly.

Next, on the assumption that the Web would take off, we had to consider our own position. The real question was, was there any space left over for Vermeer? It quickly became clear that Web servers and Mosaic embodied major portions of our server and browser ideas. Basic Web servers and browsers were available free, at least for academic purposes. Source code for both could be licensed from Spyglass, and a number of firms were also starting to develop and sell commercial versions, including Netscape. Microsoft's eventual entry, at least in browsers, seemed inevitable. Competing on that terrain didn't look attractive. We might want to bundle server and browser software as part of a complete solution, but it didn't look as if they could supply any real traction.

That left the third part of the architecture—a visual, end-user development tool. Randy investigated how people developed Web sites and found, to our relief, that it was quite difficult, at least if you weren't a programmer. There were no development tools at all. All Web pages had to be written out in HTML, with every detail specified (as in "<CENTER>Vermeer</CENTER>"). Every HyperText link had to be specified in tedious detail, and minor changes such as adding or deleting pages or links generated a great deal of work to ensure that everything still worked properly. Keeping track of links in a site of any complexity, much less a large business catalog, was a nightmare. Adding basic facilities, like a text search facility, or a digitized logo that automatically appears at the top of each page, or a help service, required long hours of programming. Some of the programs were fairly simple, but they still had to be written by programmers. Moreover, they were written in obscure languages not widely used outside of the Web. As a result, there were only a few thousand people in the whole world who had the skills to develop Web sites. As I analyzed the issue, I came to realize that there were also several other fundamental problems with this state of affairs. It was this analysis, I would claim, that represented my principal contribution to the development of the Web.

First, if you believed that this really was a big deal, and that there would be millions of Web services some day, you quickly concluded that there weren't enough programmers in the whole world to develop them. At the time, this was a radical thought, but for me it seemed obvious. Shipments of inexpensive servers—the hardware kind—were growing sharply and would soon exceed ten million units per year. If it was easy enough, every workgroup, every small business, every government agency, would want its own information service. At those volumes, you simply *couldn't* rely on programmers to do everything.

Second, you wouldn't *want* to use programmers, because the content and appearance of online services is best determined by those who understand their purpose, not by people who write computer programs. Just as the first PC spreadsheet programs in the 1980s allowed every accountant and financial analyst to do his own financial modeling for the first time, so too there should be a PC application that allowed people to develop their own online services.

And third, in the absence of appropriate tools, it was, ironically, quite difficult for a Web developer to install and manage Web services over the Internet. You needed either to have direct access to the server hardware on which the service would be running, or to use highly technical procedures. This was absurd. The whole point of the Internet, and the Web, was that it should be easy to get to anything, anywhere. It should be possible to develop services on your PC and then send them across the Internet to wherever they would reside. But you couldn't do that without a fairly complex piece of technology—one that did not yet exist.

So we concluded that, yes, the world needed an easy-to-use end-user visual development tool for the Web, and that if the Web took off the way we thought it might, the market would be enormous.

We reached this conclusion around June. When we interviewed our first technical hires, Andy Schulert and Peter Amstein, we had already worked out the logic of this conclusion, but only in a very general way, and we were still unsure about it. It depended on market and technical conditions that were tremendously uncertain. At the time, Randy and I drew up elaborate fallback plans and decision trees in case the Web didn't take off, or the Internet didn't take off, or they remained off-limits to commercial use, or the proprietary online services started using Web servers over non-Internet systems.

But I became much more confident after a trip to Washington, D.C., that summer. I had dinner with Tom Kalil, a friend of mine on the White House staff who is responsible for coordinating technology policy for the National Economic

Council. Tom is smart, careful with his words, well connected, and utterly reliable. Without telling him what I was doing, I asked him about the status of Internet policy. He told me that the Acceptable Use Policy was soon going to be eliminated via privatization of the Internet backbone, permitting all-out commercial development of the Internet and the Web. Tom was clearly very current on Internet matters and used the Web routinely. He also said that DARPA and other government agencies sensed a great deal of activity in the Internet area. I kept a good poker face and thanked Tom for the update.

We thought we had the field to ourselves. Randy and I had called up Netscape in late April, got Andreessen to sign our nondisclosure agreement, and had had a long conference call with him. He was clearly smart, arrogant, and young. Most of the time was spent fencing, each of us trying to find out what the other was up to without giving anything away. We learned very little, but they hadn't mentioned development tools. It turned out they had already thought about them, but not nearly as carefully as we had, and had decided to focus on browsers and servers instead.

July–September 1994: Netscape in Overdrive

Clark and Doerr decided that they had to move fast, which was undeniably correct, but they overdid it. Netscape started hiring people by the truckload, probably faster than new people could be used effectively—Netscape's first mistake. In July, when we lost a recruit to Netscape, we were astonished to learn that they already had more than seventy people and were still hiring at an extraordinary rate. And some of the hiring choices were odd, at least to me. Mike Homer was hired to run marketing. He came from GO, which had been a dismal failure driven by hype. But Clark was getting recruiting help from Doerr and the Kleiner Perkins network, which is where Homer came from. He also pulled a number of people from Silicon Graphics. The SGI hires included Rosanne Siino, the director of public relations, and Tom Paquin, who became Netscape's first (interim) head of engineering. Siino started a blitz media campaign that quickly produced a very high public profile for the company. This was mistake number two.

The very rapid hiring rate generated a lot of waste and an extraordinarily high burn rate. Far more seriously, by midsummer there were major problems between the kids and the "adults" at Netscape, and there wasn't enough adult supervision. All of the kids came out of the college hacker tradition, and none had any industrial development experience. Andreessen, the chief technology officer, was only twenty-two. Paquin was an old pro, but SGI was a high-end UNIX and graphics company quite disconnected from the world of PC software and Microsoft. No chief architect was ever hired. However, in October Rick Schell, an experienced development manager with a computer science Ph.D., joined as the first permanent VP of engineering. But he apparently deferred to, and/or agreed with, Andreessen and the kids more than was healthy.

Tension between the two cultures was inevitable. Some of these problems were matters of style—like whether or not it's okay to throw food, throw chairs, scream at the top of your lungs, have water balloon fights in the halls, and order pizza at 4:00 A.M. But some of the issues were deadly serious, like whether you thought out a careful architecture before you started writing code, how you cultivated support among software developers, and whether you seriously planned for the inevitable day of reckoning with Microsoft. The kids' philosophy won out: Ready, Fire, Aim. Netscape, and now AOL, are still paying for it.

All my interviews suggest that Clark either chose to side with the kids or simply didn't interfere. Netscape also became infatuated with "Internet time," an obsession of Andreessen's that nobody, apparently, tried to temper. Netscape decided to roll out products at a faster rate than any software company has ever done. This is usually defended—or praised—as the main reason why Netscape won such huge market share so fast. There is some truth in this. But some things shouldn't be rushed. Whether through haste, overconfidence, or ignorance, in 1994 and 1995 Netscape made a series of catastrophic technical and strategic errors that eventually proved their undoing. These included sloppy, indeed almost nonexistent, technical architecture; foolish, immature hype that awakened Microsoft; failure to create proprietary advantage; failure to generate third-party support and lock-in; poor testing and quality control; and excessive attention to minor markets to the neglect of Windows, just for starters. I'll discuss these issues in detail later; suffice it to say that even as Netscape was pulling out in front, it was also helping to dig its own grave.

Netscape's next mistake, in my opinion, was its biggest and most fatal of all: hiring Jim Barksdale as CEO. Given Clark's background and John Doerr's experience, it's a somewhat surprising mistake. Randy and I both hold the view, as do many in the industry, that the CEO of a serious high technology company must have a serious technical background, or at least the ability to understand technology and a deep appreciation of its importance in strategic and organizational decisions. Failing that, it is imperative to have serious technologists with good business judgment nearby at the top of the firm. Barksdale failed this test in every way. He is a smart, smooth, charming, but basically nontechnical manager who started his career as an IBM mainframe salesman. After IBM, Barksdale went on to earn a good reputation as the head of MIS and then chief operating officer for Federal Express, and then became number two at McCaw Cellular. He was offered the Netscape job in August, when McCaw had just been sold to AT&T. Barksdale initially declined the offer. He told me that he did this because he was still involved in the McCaw-AT&T deal, but he agreed to join the Netscape board in September and to think about it some more. He eventually accepted and became Netscape's CEO in January 1995.

In my interactions with him Barksdale seemed to be a nice guy, and many people like him. But he doesn't understand how to design a product, hire a senior technical team, create an industry standard, or compete strategically with Microsoft. He was in over his head from day one, yet at times he displayed extraordinary arrogance.

LATE 1994: THE INTERNET HEATS UP

In September 1994, a month after AOL's subscriber list passed the million mark, Steve Case created an Internet division that reported to him personally. When Microsoft attempted to acquire Booklink and its browser, AOL swooped in and bought Booklink for a much higher price in AOL stock and then embarked on an Internet buying spree that lasted for two years. In November 1994, AOL announced two other deals. The first was the purchase of ANS, one of the early Internet service providers, mainly to government agencies. AOL had decided to piece together its own Internet network, both for technical reasons and to improve its bargaining position with network service providers like Sprint. Case also explored buying a stake in UUNet, but backed off when the company insisted on retaining the right to sell a stake to Microsoft.

The other acquisition was an embryonic competitor of ours, though we only dimly suspected it at the time. AOL purchased a start-up called NaviSoft, reportedly for $4 million in AOL stock. NaviSoft was a few months older than Vermeer and was developing authoring and publishing tools for the Web—almost exactly what Randy and I hoped to do. If I had known their plans in detail, I would have been terrified, because they had a very similar business plan, a head start, and now, a major corporate partner. David Cole, the founder of NaviSoft, had been CEO of Ashton-Tate, developer of the first successful PC database software. Cole became the head of AOL Internet division, with the objective of making AOL the leading Internet and Web solution provider to business. Luckily for us, he and AOL made a lot of mistakes.

All remaining doubts about the commercialization of the Internet vanished in September 1994 when the government announced the end of its Acceptable Use Policy and the privatization of the Internet backbone, effective April 1995. The NSF formally began to implement the privatization plan and technical changes proposed in the 1992 Aiken-Braun-Ford policy paper. It would phase out its funding of the NSF backbone, turn its operation over to private businesses, and implement the network access point architecture to interconnect competing providers.

Around this time, the Internet scene began to explode, and the fog of war started to set in. Within months, a huge number of companies, many of them start-ups, began announcing Internet products. Spry, a small software company in Seattle, released its Internet-in-a-Box, which allowed a moderately sophisticated home user to plug into the Internet and surf the Web. Spry's product included a TCP/IP "stack," the software used to interpret the Internet protocol, a licensed version of the NCSA browser, an e-mail client, a news reader, and assorted other extras. At a list price of $149, it flew off the shelves, selling hundreds of thousands of copies in its first months on the market.

Quarterdeck, another small software company in Southern California, announced a Web server, and IBM announced that its new version of OS/2, "Warp," would include TCP/IP capability and a Web browser based on licensed NCSA code. Interleaf, a second-rate vendor of publishing software, announced Cyberleaf, which converted existing electronic documents to HTML. In the late fall, a Dutch firm, DigiCash, generated a wave of publicity with eCash, an electronic payments system based on purely electronic money, and announced an online experiment using electronic play money called CyberBucks. DigiCash was funded mostly by European Union research grants and was the plaything of David Chaum, an electronic privacy guru and flaky self-promoter. (To the surprise of many, electronic currency over the Internet has yet to take off—people are perfectly happy to simply type in their credit card numbers.) Many of these companies ultimately disappeared. But keeping track of events was starting to get complicated.

One other start-up briefly seemed too close to home in every sense. Open Market Corporation, or OMC, was a start-up created by an MIT professor I knew slightly, Dave Gifford, and an entrepreneur, Shikar Ghosh, who had previously built and sold a cellular telephone software company. Ghosh acted as CEO. They were funded by Greylock, a well-known Boston VC firm. OMC released a high-performance Web server intended for electronic commerce and, more alarmingly, a very crude development tool, called StoreBuilder, for creating Web-based shopping catalogs. Would they be a partner, a competitor, or both? And were they serious? Sometime in the fall I had dinner with Ghosh and was stunned to discover that he didn't know some of the most basic facts about the Web. He didn't know, for example, that Web servers could be used on internal corporate TCP/IP networks (aka Intranets) as well as on the public Internet. I concluded that OMC wouldn't be a major threat even if they tried, but we still decided not to show them what we were doing until our product was almost done, so as not to confuse them.

For us, the good news was that the Web was on the edge of becoming very hot, so our market looked promising. The flip side, for someone as naturally paranoid as I am, was to see so many people walking around on the edges of our product strategy. We were about to embark on VC fund-raising with little more than an idea and a few great technical people. Every week brought more optimism and more panic, more rumors of competitors, more excitement at the opportunity, more issues to struggle with. Was our idea still valid? Had we been beaten to the punch? Had we missed something important? Like soldiers in the fog of war, we had little choice but to fight on. We didn't dare to ask direct questions because they might expose our position, and we probably wouldn't get truthful answers anyway.

OCTOBER 1994–JANUARY 1995: NETSCAPE SKYROCKETS

On October 14, 1994, Netscape posted the beta version of its first commercial browser, which it called "Mosaic Netscape," on its Web site. It ran much faster, had more features, and was easier to use than the NCSA browser or any of its dozen or so early commercial descendants. The response was stupendous. Shortly thereafter, Netscape froze its code in anticipation of final product shipment in December.

Throughout November, Netscape repeatedly changed its pricing policy, trading off its need for revenues against Andreessen's determination to follow the "Microsoft lesson" and make the Netscape browser universal. Netscape had developed three products: the browser, a standard Web server, and a "commerce" server that included encryption capabilities. The original plan was to charge $5,000 for the basic server, $25,000 for the commerce server, and $99 for the browser. Before release, these prices were wisely cut to $1,500 and $5,000 for the two servers and $49 for the browser. But contrary to the myth that later arose in the industry, the Netscape browser was never free. You could download it over the Web for a thirty-day free trial, but then you were supposed to pay. Netscape chased down large business accounts quite aggressively and even developed special software to monitor downloads. It did not follow up aggressively against consumers, partly because it was not cost-effective to do so, and partly because Andreessen did, in fact, want to achieve ubiquitous market penetration. But during its first year of operations, the browser accounted for two-thirds of Netscape's revenues.

Netscape's browser included a number of its own extensions to HTML, which broke with Internet tradition. The company posted them openly on its Web site, in an attempt to avoid criticism from the Internet community. At the time, before the Internet's commercial takeoff, academic and government researchers were still considered influential, although I think Netscape overestimated their importance. But when Netscape initially tried to keep its SSL encryption and security enhancements proprietary, there were both academic and commercial protests. Shortly afterward Netscape backed down, posting the specifications to SSL on its Web site. In the specific case of SSL, this may have made sense. But with its other products, it didn't. Early on, Netscape established a pattern of leaving large portions of the market uncovered by its own products, while at the same time enabling others to clone Netscape's technologies. Netscape's arrogant and careless attitude about proprietary control made it far easier for Microsoft to catch up. Industry standards and proprietary control over them are the core of software strategy. I'll argue later that Netscape's thinking was extremely sloppy and amateurish, leading to major strategic errors.

In November 1994, the University of Illinois and Spyglass threatened to sue Netscape for illegal use of the NCSA code and the brand name "Mosaic." (The company's official name was still "Mosaic Communications.") Clark and Andreessen had never acquired a Mosaic license, insisting that their browser was brand-new code. A forensic software consultant hired by Clark certified that there was "no similarity in form, only in function" between NCSA Mosaic code and the Netscape code. A settlement was reached in December, whereby the company changed its name to Netscape Communications, changed the browser's name to Netscape Navigator, and made a $2.3 million payment to the university. Clark first offered stock, but the university insisted on cash, thereby losing a great deal of money.

By December, however, Netscape was running out of money. Clark had raised more than $8 million, but had already spent most of it. Furthermore, Netscape now had more than 120 people. The Silicon Valley rule of thumb is that a start-up's burn rate is $10,000 per person per month, so Netscape's cash consumption was probably in the range of $1.2 million per month. Clark was forced into layoffs, but when the commercial version of Navigator was posted on Netscape's Web site on December 15, it was a runaway success. Only four months later, Netscape's browser market share exceeded 75 percent and all competing browsers were headed to oblivion. It was the fastest market penetration of any software product in history. Netscape started booking healthy revenues and soon afterward completed a major private financing at a very high valuation.

THE INTERNET BREAKDOWN SCARE

The sudden recognition that the Internet and the Web were headed for hypergrowth prompted scares that the Internet would collapse. Several quite serious technologists, like Bob Metcalfe, warned that the end was near. They said that bandwidth was inadequate; that the Internet's routers (the specialized computers that managed Internet traffic) were not up to the challenge; that the Internet's architecture could not scale to the tens of millions of users now expected; and that the world would run out of Internet addresses.

One of my worst days, in fact, came from one of my last consulting engagements, in late 1994. I had been retained by Bay Networks, a major supplier of Internet and LAN hardware. Toward the end of my engagement, while we were in the midst of first-round fund-raising for Vermeer, I mentioned that I was spending most of my time on an Internet start-up, though I didn't say what we were doing. To my alarm, several engineers warned me to watch out. They said that the Internet would soon collapse or suffer serious performance degradation. One of them told me that the average number of "hops," or connections between routers, needed to deliver an Internet packet was increasing sharply, with the result that Internet performance would inevitably deteriorate.

This was disturbing, since Vermeer was by now totally committed to the Web. But a few weeks later, just after we had gotten funded, I happened to sit next to Mike O'Dell, the vice president of R&D for UUNet, on a flight from Washington, D.C. back to Boston. O'Dell was a serious technologist who was deeply involved with both Internet standardization and also with the Internet industry. I asked him about the Internet's alleged problems, and he told me to forget about it. Some of the factual claims made by the alarmists were accurate, he said, but they were merely a holdover from the Internet's jury-rigged, academic/government roots. Now that commercial players were finally paying serious attention, and spending serious money, those constraints would disappear quickly. O'Dell was absolutely right. Since then, fears about Internet capacity or technology have continued to arise from time to time, but have always turned out to be wrong—just one more example of the almost infinite adaptability of well-designed systems. There are, in fact, some potentially serious problems, but they would arise only in emergencies, not in normal Internet operations.

More Fits and Starts at Microsoft, but Some Forward Movement

As Netscape took off, Microsoft continued developing MSN, despite growing worries within the company. Microsoft was not alone in its confusion. Gates announced in December 1994 that TCI would make a $125 million investment in MSN, giving it a 20 percent share. Apparently the idea was that MSN would be distributed over a future ITV system that TCI would build. Five months later, TCI reversed course, abandoning MSN and ITV and investing instead in @Home, a cable-television-based Internet access start-up associated with Netscape and funded by Kleiner Perkins.

In December of 1994, Microsoft finally started to move; it acquired a Mosaic license from Spyglass. Limited Internet access was planned via MSN, although full Web surfing was not. Then, in January 1995, Microsoft made an equity investment in UUNet in return for a seat on UUNet's board and an agreement that UUNet would develop a dedicated TCP/IP network for MSN users. Microsoft had still made no clear commitment to the Internet and the Web, but the giant was stirring.

Microsoft's Mosaic and UUNet announcements came when Randy and I had finally succeeded in negotiating a $4 million first-round venture capital financing for Vermeer. Getting there, however, was *not* half the fun. In fact, it wasn't fun at all. But it certainly was, as they say, a learning experience.

CHAPTER THREE

First-Round Funding

You can get a lot farther in life with a kind word and a gun then you can with a kind word alone.
—*Rob Aagard, a Linux software engineer at www.stampede.org*

Come closer, boys, it will be easier for you.
—*Erskine Childers, speaking to the firing squad about to execute him*

*A*ndy Marcuvitz is a heavyset guy who wears badly fitting suits. He has no discernible personality, sense of humor, or compassion—ideal traits for a venture capitalist. During eighteen months of extremely intense interaction, we never had a personal conversation, I never heard him make a joke, and he rarely smiled. Indeed, a smile from Marcuvitz is not a good sign. In arguments, and we had many, he's relentless; his voice remains even, he never loses his temper, and he can dig in for hours. If I had known when I started Vermeer that Marcuvitz was going to be one of the most important people in my life, I would have seriously reconsidered. And yet, he was good for me, and in a slightly twisted way, I respect him a great deal.

I first met Marcuvitz in August 1994 when we agreed to have dinner at Harvest, an informally elegant restaurant near Harvard Square in Cambridge. Vermeer was starting to look real. To call us actually *organized* would have been an overstatement, but the core technical team was in place and work was under way on the product architecture, a demo, our business plan, and financial projections. We had hired headhunters, market research consultants, an accountant, and lawyers. We had incorporation documents, employment contracts, a stock option plan, and nondisclosure agreements. Since only one guy was drawing a salary, I could manage our burn rate for a while, but I was feeling a growing sense of urgency.

With every passing week it was clearer that the Web was getting hot, that our opportunity was enormous, but that many other people were starting to notice. As soon as the business plan was done it would be time to start fundraising. In fact, I had just accelerated our schedules, especially for Peter to finish his demo, so that we could begin talking to VCs as soon as the fall season started after Labor Day. (In those days it was pointless to approach VCs during the summer or over Christmas.) So when Andy Schulert called me to say that a former boss of his who had become a big VC wanted to meet me, I agreed, although I grilled him to be sure that he hadn't revealed anything about our plans. I was already paranoid—in some ways overly so, in others not enough.

Marcuvitz and I spent the first part of dinner on introductions—who we were, what we'd done. He was in his forties, the number two guy at Matrix Partners, one of the most prominent East Coast VC firms. Marcuvitz was clearly extremely smart and technically deep. He had a master's in computer science from Harvard and had been one of the original founders, and the first vice president of research and development, of Apollo Computer, which was where Andy Schulert had met him. Apollo had for several years been a stratospherically successful workstation company, later acquired by Hewlett-Packard when it fell on hard times. Of all the VCs I was to meet over the next few months, Marcuvitz was one of the few who understood the Internet. Matrix had already invested in PSI, one of the earliest commercial Internet service providers.

Andy M., as we came to call him, described his background in his typically neutral, unemotional fashion. When it was my turn, I was at my most obnoxious. I listed my glittering credentials—MIT Ph.D. and policy researcher, White House connections, congressional testimony, Fortune 500 consulting clients, powerful friends, important book. I told him Vermeer would be a paradigmshifting company, but he'd have to sign a nondisclosure agreement to hear about our plans, and in any case we wouldn't talk to anyone until we were ready. I told him that I was already lining up private investors as alternatives to VCs, that I planned to drive a hard bargain, and that I would never let the VCs have control of the company.

I suppose I had expected Marcuvitz to act unimpressed, just as a matter of tactics. But it was rather disquieting that, very clearly, he *really was* unimpressed. He smiled coldly and began giving me the Marcuvitz treatment: cool, logical argument, patiently explaining in great detail how you're wrong, and how whatever he wants is not only objectively right, but also in your own best interest.

Kid, he said in effect, if you think you can do it that way, be my guest. But you're already raising warning flags for VCs. In the first place, we don't like nondisclosure agreements, and they're generally a sign of trouble, like husband-and-wife boards of directors. Founders who are obsessed with secrecy tend not to understand what's really important for a company's success, and sometimes they're just crazy. You should be letting us get to know you. You don't seem to have much business experience, and what little you have is not in start-ups. That's okay, but be careful you don't make a big mistake. For example, raising money from random rich people is usually bad; it's dumb money, and it takes too much time to service. If you do manage to fool someone, your valuation will be too high. So then when you try to get serious VC money, you'll either have to explain to your friends why you overcharged them or try to get the VCs to accept a huge set-up for no reason. We don't play that game, so you could ruin your whole deal. And anyway, your fears are misplaced; we don't want to control you, we just want to make money.

Marcuvitz had gotten to me a bit, although I tried not to show it. I replied, What a coincidence you should say all that. Nothing whatsoever to do with your being a VC, I suppose? We fenced the whole evening, exploring each other's opinions—industry trends, people we knew, Microsoft, the decline of Lotus and Novell, and so on. I repeated that we'd be in touch when we were ready, not before, and that he'd have to sign a nondisclosure agreement, period. In retrospect, I'd call it a draw. Despite exposing my naïveté, I think I convinced Marcuvitz that I was smart, understood strategy, knew a lot about the industry, and that I wasn't going to be a pushover. But Marcuvitz was clearly no pushover either. I began to suspect this was going to be harder than I had thought and maybe not too much fun. I was right. Venture capital is a rough game.

Moreover, we were trying to raise money at the worst possible time. The U.S. technology sector was still emerging from the mid-1980s Japanese assault on semiconductors and the early 1990s collapse of IBM and the Route 128 minicomputer industry. Investors were very cautious, and money was hard to come by. In addition, we were dangerously ahead of the Internet curve; nobody knew what the hell the Internet was, and the Internet industry didn't exist. And finally, we had a truly original product that didn't fit into neat, established categories, so VCs perceived us as risky—particularly because a lot of them didn't understand anything we said.

THE VC CLUB

The VC industry in those days was a tight oligopoly, verging on a cartel. While completely informal, it was extremely effective. Superficially, the industry was fragmented. Most VC firms, and certainly the best ones, are small; top firms have perhaps half a dozen partners, managing a few dozen investments at any given time. And there are lots of VC firms. But VCs specialize in specific kinds of companies, stages of investment, and industry segments. And there was a clear hierarchy, with roughly a dozen of the best VCs dominating the highest-quality early-stage deals.

Furthermore, it has long been industry practice to share deals; even when they had more than enough money, no VC would take an entire investment round in a company. So all of the top-tier VCs referred deals to one another, participated in syndicates together, sat on boards together, showed one another business plans, used one another to check founders' references and back-grounds, socialized together, and rarely if ever bid against one another to get a deal. This is not to say that individual VCs never act selfishly; like self-interested participants in all other oligopolies, VCs would sometimes go it alone when they saw an opportunity too good to pass up. (That happened to us in our second round. As you'll see, it isn't necessarily good news for the entrepreneur.) Only in boom periods, such as the Internet-driven cycle that started in mid-1995, is there much real competition. When we were raising money, the club was at its tightest.

Until recently venture capital was a well-kept secret, a boys' club with an invitation-only membership. VCs themselves were a tough, individualistic bunch from diverse backgrounds—many were former technologists, entrepreneurs, and investment bankers. Eugene Kleiner, for example, who co-founded Kleiner Perkins Caufield & Byers (aka KP), was a member of the original Fairchild Semiconductor technical team that also included the founders of Intel. Kleiner Perkins was an early investor in Sun, Intuit, Compaq, Netscape, and Amazon. While KP has become well known, most early VCs shunned pub-licity, in part to keep the gold mine to themselves. They made enormous re-turns, far exceeding hedge funds or New York investment banks. Have you ever heard of Art Rock? No? Well, he funded Intel with a $2 million investment that is now worth billions. Don Lucas? Oracle. Dave Marquardt? Microsoft. Phil Greer? Federal Express. You get the idea. For a *thirty-year period,* from the 1960s through the early 1990s, the top VCs got returns exceeding *40 percent per year.* In their hands, U.S. high technology venture capital investment flows that until recently averaged only a billion dollars a year were turned into companies that now have market value totaling about a trillion dollars. In other words, these people got seriously rich. They also enjoyed playing at the leading edge of tech-nology, knew and helped one another, and didn't need to work too hard. The Silicon Valley boys' club created a somewhat lazy, informally closed industry pattern that persisted until the Internet revolution made the secret impossible to keep any longer. Now, every Harvard MBA wants to become a VC.

Most venture capital deals are shared among two or three firms, and each subsequent round of investment usually adds at least one new investor. The typical cycle for a successful start-up is a first-round investment of $2–$5 million, followed by a second round a year or so later at a higher valuation, when the company has reached some identifiable goal (say, releasing its first product). Then perhaps there is a third and even fourth round, until the company is taken public or acquired several years later. VC funds are typically structured to last ten years; as their investments go public they usually distribute the stock to their "limiteds," or investors. VCs themselves rarely hold any investment for more than six or seven years, although there are exceptions— some people still hold first-round stock in companies like Intel and Oracle. Certain VCs have come to specialize in high-risk early-stage investing, while others, primarily those owned by insurance companies and investment banks, tend to focus on later stages. They all came to use the same fee structure: they charged a 1 to 2 percent annual management fee, and kept 20 percent of capital gains.

The VCs' little club both reflected and reinforced the unequal bargaining power between VCs and founders. Until the Internet revolution and the recent rise of individual "angel" investing, entrepreneurs usually had no alternative to VC terms. Most founders had little or no money themselves, no access to wealthy individual investors, and felt intense pressure to raise money quickly. Many were also naïve about financial negotiations. And of course start-ups really do compete with one another. When was the last time you heard of a dozen competing start-ups sharing information and technology in order to bargain with VCs? Never, is the answer. Conversely, the VCs had time, coordination, and money on their side; they were experienced, well financed, and could afford to bide their time.

This kept valuations low, which is critical for VCs. A rule of thumb in venture investing is that one out of ten investments does spectacularly well, returning fifty dollars or more for each dollar invested. (Including appreciation in Microsoft stock after our acquisition, Vermeer returned over a hundred dollars for every dollar invested by our first-round VCs.) The others range from modest successes to outright failures. To cover the losers, and to pay for the huge inefficiencies of sorting through hundreds of proposals, venture capitalists need to drive hard bargains in order to get high returns. If a fund owns a big percentage of its most successful investment, total returns will be spectacular. The way to own a high percentage is to keep the initial valuations as low as possible; the lower the valuation, the higher percentage of its equity a company must surrender to raise a given amount of money. And, of course, sharing deals is an excellent way to avoid bidding wars. Until recently, the top firms could expect to get referrals on the best deals and share in syndicates if an investment was made. I knew some of this, vaguely, when I started Vermeer; I learned more as I went along, often the hard way.

Recent entrepreneurs may not recognize this picture, because things have changed dramatically since 1994. The basic structure of VC firms and their operations remains the same. But in just a few years the industry has grown enormously larger and more competitive. Since we raised our first round in late 1994, annual U.S. venture capital flows have probably tripled, to over $20 billion. Valuations have probably increased comparably. Dozens of new venture capital firms have been created, and there are many newly wealthy "angels" like myself who are willing to fund young start-ups privately.

As you'd expect, the established VCs lament this state of affairs, and to some extent, they have a point. The fact that bargaining power shifted to favor entrepreneurs didn't make entrepreneurs any more ethical or intelligent. In fact, it probably has had the reverse effect. The Internet is a real revolution, but it also created a financial bubble and brought a wave of greedy nontechnical founders, bad deals, unethical behavior, and hasty judgments. There has been a lot of insane speculation, overvaluation of dubious companies, and many deals in which working-level personnel receive virtually no stock.

This is not to say, however, that VCs are suffering in this new environment, or that the new situation is entirely the result of a speculative binge. Venture capital is now big business. The VC industry is much larger, has many new entrants, and is much more competitive, but this does not mean that VCs are starving. The volume of money pouring into the industry is so immense that even with increased competition, VCs now run much larger funds, charge much higher fees, and take much larger base salaries. Many venture capitalists now have *salaries* in excess of $1 million per year, which come from the annual management fees they charge investors. I think this is a dangerous condition; VCs can now become wealthy even if their investments perform abysmally. Eventually, perhaps their performance will be noticed, but that will be after they've wasted a few billion dollars and then retired. A similar, and I fear also dangerous, situation has arisen in start-ups themselves. It is no longer unusual to encounter venture capital–funded start-ups whose founders have salaries of $150,000 to $250,000 per year, who own two-thirds of the company, and whose stock vests in two years (or is not even subject to vesting at all). I hope, and tend to believe, that some of these excesses will recede when the speculative craze that started in 1996 gives way to longer-term, clearer thinking.

In some regards, I am pleased by the new environment. As one with a long-standing aversion to ties, fluorescent lighting, and working in cubicles ten hours a day, I am extremely happy that I can now go to investment banking meetings wearing jeans, work in Internet cafés, and keep my own hours without having to explain myself. That's nice, and still not to be assumed elsewhere—like North Korea, or Boston. Conversely, I have grown somewhat impatient with the hordes of blond thirty-four-year-olds in the Valley who, while highly intelligent, don't seem to realize that not everyone in the world is Stanford-educated, tanned, utterly self-confident, a superb skier, and worth $20 million.

But in 1994, things weren't like this yet. Our problems were of the opposite kind.

RUDE AWAKENINGS

Any illusions I had of quick, smooth fund-raising soon evaporated. Most of the VC firms we presented to didn't know anything about the Internet, and few of them had even heard of the Web. Worse, most of them didn't care very much. If there wasn't already a buzz in the industry, they weren't interested. A year later, when the Internet and the Web were making headlines, we could have gotten three or four times our initial valuation with no trouble at all. Of course, by that time, we would have been too late, and the investment wouldn't have done nearly as well. One of the ironies of the industry is that some of the earliest and most visionary firms get the lowest valuations because they're ahead of the public tidal wave.

Some of our problems, however, were my fault. Another of my many rude awakenings came as I realized that I didn't have the contacts or experience I thought. I'd been around high technology for a long time and thought I could easily get to the right people. Not true, as it turned out. I had never raised money for a start-up, and my consulting for large firms was irrelevant. I knew who some of the right firms were, but without an introduction, they often don't even return phone calls. Randy and some of the other engineers actually had better VC contacts than I did, from their earlier start-ups. Our headhunter, Ed Takacs, helped a lot by putting us in touch with several VCs and, most especially, with Bob Davoli, whom I'd first heard of, actually, through my girlfriend, Camille. Takacs is a born networker, famous for his seriously wild parties. Davoli is a tough, street-smart Italian American from Boston—the quintessential self-made man. He built a small consulting service, then developed a good database software tool, and then made a fortune when he sold out to Sybase in the late 1980s. A few years later, he took over a troubled company, Epoch, at the request of VCs, quickly turned it around, and then sold it off, making a second fortune. His name was magic among VCs. He came to my apartment in the early fall and was sufficiently interested to let us use him as a reference; from that point most VC doors were open.

Roughly a month after our introductory dinner, I called Marcuvitz and told him we were ready to talk. So our first formal presentation was in mid-September at the offices of Matrix Partners, after Marcuvitz finally signed our nondisclosure agreement. We'd scheduled three hours, but ended up spending all day. Most of the time we presented to Marcuvitz alone. The format was essentially the same one we would use in all subsequent meetings with VCs, though with practice we were able to go much faster. I began with an overview—what was wrong with the current online services industry; the possibilities created by the Web and the Internet; the explosive growth already under way; the huge software opportunity; our product; and a summary of our company status, strategy, and plans.

Then Peter Amstein gave his demo, which was very slick. Peter is a superb engineer who also has excellent market intuition and presentation skills—an unusual combination. He had created a hypothetical Sharper Image catalog shopping site, complete with graphics, order forms, links to inventory databases and FedEx shipment information, and so forth. Then he showed how our product could radically simplify developing such a site, using a state-of-the-art GUI and small drop-in programs that we called "bots," which eliminated the need for conventional programming. Randy presented our architecture. Marcuvitz was attentive and asked some sharp questions. At one point, he raised the Microsoft issue. Wasn't Microsoft a potential competitor, since they were creating many of the same capabilities with Marvel, the online service they were developing? No, I replied, because Marvel is not Internet- or Web-based—it's a conventional, proprietary online service. Oh *really,* said Marcuvitz. I knew then that he really got it.

Marcuvitz listened politely as our consultant presented our financials and then promptly told us that they didn't mean anything. He was partly right, of course. They were beautiful—five years of detailed balance sheets and income statements, Monte Carlo risk simulations, the works. But Marcuvitz said that VCs simply used financials to test whether we'd thought seriously about the size of the opportunity and the cost of bringing a product to market. We don't invest on the basis of numbers, he said, nobody can predict how something like this will turn out. We invest if we like the team and the business idea and we think there's a revenue opportunity of $50 million or more. Then came the first hint of the war to come. He smiled at our proposed valuations, gave us a dry lecture on the impossibility of making accurate forecasts at this stage, and said the only thing he could rely on was VC experience and rules of thumb. Now it's true that our financial projections were wrong, and it is indeed impossible to forecast the path taken by a revolution. For example, our estimated prices were much too high and our unit volumes much too low. But our assumptions were deliberately conservative, and our revenue and valuation projections turned out to be low by about a factor of five. If we had gotten the supposedly ridiculous valuation we asked for—about $25 million—Marcuvitz would only have made measly returns of a few hundred percent per year.

At the end of our presentations, Marcuvitz said he was very interested and would like to go further. He asked whom else we were talking to and was irritated when I wouldn't say. He told us that Matrix rarely invested alone, and he would need at least two other partners. I asked if he had any suggestions; he did. He gave us the names of two VCs to call, Bill Kaiser at Greylock and Geoff Yang at IVP. He was doing us a favor, he said, and he'd be interested in their reaction. I made a dumb smart-aleck remark about the VC herd mentality, which he didn't like. But a more serious alarm bell was ringing in my head. Why was Marcuvitz referring me to his competitors? These guys were supposed to *bid* for the chance to invest in my company.

Marcuvitz continued my education a week later when he asked me to meet with Matrix's founder, Paul Ferri. Ferri was clearly a *very* tough guy—even more laconic and poker-faced than Marcuvitz, and with a long history in the VC business. Coolly, Ferri started questioning me. Did I want to be the CEO? What were my major challenges? How much money did I think the company needed for its first round? Then he came to the main event: valuation. When VCs are interested, they focus on assessing whether the founders will play the game or not, and on what is called "pre-money valuation." This is the value of the company prior to their investment, and it determines the share they get. Marcuvitz said he placed our pre-money valuation at about $1–2 million. This meant that if they invested $4 million, the total value of the company would be at most $6 million, so the VCs would own at least two-thirds of it.

I felt my blood rising. Forget it, I said, you're not going to control this company. Look, forget about control for a moment, Ferri said. Let's just talk about money. Marcuvitz chimed in: When a company works, nobody remembers the first-round valuation. You should focus on getting the best help you can on your board and on making this company as successful as possible. Well, I didn't feel like forgetting about control, but even if I did, I still didn't like what I heard. Their numbers meant not only that we'd surrender control, but that we might not make much money. In fact, this used to happen all the time, and sometimes still does. Randy had been one of the most senior guys at Beyond, his previous company—the fifth employee, and the third engineer. He started out owning 2 percent, but by the time the company was sold for $17 million, he'd been so diluted that he got only about $76,000—not much to show for four years of seventy-hour weeks at a below-market salary.

I told them again that I wanted a pre-money valuation in the $20–$30 million range. Soon afterward I realized that this marked me as naïve and possibly dangerous, because it showed that I didn't know the rules of the game. Marcuvitz and Ferri smiled and began once again patiently explaining VC valuation rules of thumb. We have a lot of experience doing this, they said. We look at a company at your stage of development, take into account what we know about you, your team, the uncertainties of the market, and it's worth about $2 million. I argued back, not quite as patiently, with a long list of reasons why a $2 million valuation was ridiculous. They said, Well, go talk to other VCs. They'll all tell you the same thing. Which, of course, they did.

TORTURE

Anyone who tends toward arrogance, like me, should be sentenced to a term of VC fund-raising during a tight market. The next five months were among the most frustrating and humbling of my life. With the help of Davoli, Takacs, and others, we could at least get appointments with top-tier VCs. From mid-September to early December we presented to more than twenty VC firms, and a few individuals, about half of them in California and the rest in Boston and New York. This meant a lot of travel and large bills, which were paid out of my rapidly dwindling personal bank account.

Worse than the money, the drain on our time was enormous, as were the limitations of working without funding. Everyone was still working out of their homes, which is no way to develop a software product quickly. It was another catch-22: if we did nothing but raise money, we'd miss our window of opportunity, but if we *didn't* raise money, we wouldn't have a chance. But it was partly my fault, too. In retrospect, I should have spent two thousand dollars a month to get us a temporary, minimal, but serviceable office.

By Thanksgiving I had decided that we needed to accelerate our development schedule, bringing our product ship date from February 1996 to the fall of 1995. The Web was taking off, and we just couldn't take the chance of losing the market to a competitor. So we not only needed to raise money fast, we needed to get real work done. Randy took over some of the presentations to let Peter go back to technical work, but he couldn't do them all, so Peter often joined us when we presented. Randy and I tried to shelter the development team from fund-raising demands as much as we could. But whenever a VC presentation went well, the VCs would inevitably send someone to investigate the whole team, often repeatedly. Marcuvitz poked continuously at our technology, sometimes calling engineers at home with detailed questions. But at least his questions were intelligent. Many of the VCs had an infuriating habit of forcing you to meet all their buddies and portfolio companies, many of whom didn't have the slightest clue. This was partly to get their opinions, but partly also to repay favors and stroke egos. All of this blew enormous amounts of time.

VCs run a wide gamut, from brilliant to stupid, from quite decent to stunningly repulsive. When we were raising money they were quite arrogant; money was tight, they were in control, and they let you know it. When you got to a meeting, you usually started by cooling your heels. VCs are prone to schedule a series of back-to-back presentations, but if they get interested, a serious presentation takes two or three hours. If you're scheduled early and they like you, you're fine; but if you come after a couple of presentations that get the full treatment, you can wait a long time. Of course, that meant we couldn't schedule more than two meetings per day, compounding our time wastage. We also got used to disorganized meetings, phone calls, people leaving and then coming back and asking us to repeat everything, and so on.

But the worst problem by far was that most of them didn't know anything. Of the twenty or more VC firms we met with in late 1994, all but about five needed a ground-up education on the Internet, which made their frequent arrogance and occasional stupidity doubly hard to take. Often we had to arrange special meetings to show VCs how to use the Web for the first time, what was available on it, how to get an Internet account, how e-mail worked, how Web sites compared to traditional online services such as CompuServe, and so on. Some were so obnoxious that we simply could not imagine dealing with them. For example, there was our one and only encounter with Ed Anderson, the senior partner at Northbridge in Boston. He was smart, but a sad victim of testosterone poisoning. Every issue triggered a long lecture on his own brilliance and the stupidity of others. After we left I turned to Randy and said, "I'm surprised that man didn't show us his genitalia." (I actually used a different word.)

Then there was the nondisclosure agreement problem. VCs don't like them at all. I got used to VCs objecting pompously—never done in the industry, their word was their bond, the system ran on trust, informality better than legal papers, burned by fraudulent lawsuits, and so on. But only a few actually refused, and when they did we didn't meet with them. In one case this led to an amusing sequel. In 1998 I heard that Mike Moritz of Sequoia, a firm known for its toughness, was backing a company in an area I was considering investing in. I asked him if he could tell me anything about it; I said we might be competitors or partners, depending on the specifics. Moritz asked me if I remembered our last conversation. No, I said. Well, he said, it was when you refused to show me a business plan for Vermeer Technologies because I wouldn't sign a nondisclosure agreement. So I think we'll just meet in the marketplace.

We were wise to insist on the nondisclosure agreements; it let the VCs know we cared. At best, however, this only moderately constrained them. When we were interviewing Tom Blumer, a very good engineer whom we hired soon afterward, he called me one day to talk. He was leaning toward taking the job, he said, in part because the VCs liked us, although they still had some issues with the team. *What!?* I said. How do you know what the VCs think of us? He said he had decided to check us out, so he called a friend who had good VC connections. The friend made a few phone calls, and the VCs basically told him everything—their assessment of our product, our strategy, our team, what they thought of our chances. This did not make my day.

The VC presentations became a ritual, with the tension and anger they provoked in me partially offset by boredom and the predictability of the problems that arose. One was conflicts of interest. We scheduled a meeting with Bill Kaiser of Greylock, one of Marcuvitz's recommendations. Greylock is a tony Boston firm that invests mostly old family money, and they're well regarded. But by this time we checked out *everyone,* and it paid off. Greylock, we discovered, was already a major investor in Spyglass and Open Market, both early Internet companies that we then considered potential competitors. I canceled the meeting. Greylock professed to be shocked, and Marcuvitz was irritated. Greylock protested; Marcuvitz agreed—he couldn't imagine what I was worried about. But while I was naïve, I wasn't insane.

Through my friend John Seely Brown, the director of Xerox PARC, we got a meeting with Warburg Pincus, a huge New York VC firm. The technology group there has eccentric investing habits, in part because it's the personal fiefdom of Bill Janeway, who clearly spends much of his time making sure he's one of the best dressed men on the planet. (After Vermeer was sold, I attended a party celebrating John Seely Brown's marriage to Susan Haviland. A friend of mine pointed to Janeway, who was dressed in a white linen suit, and whispered in my ear: How did Tom Wolfe get into this bash?) But they had money, so we went and presented to half a dozen smart people who clearly didn't understand either the Internet or our product. In the end Janeway explained that they couldn't invest in us because we were really a small and specialized tools company, although we had painstakingly explained exactly why that wasn't true. A few weeks later, Warburg Pincus announced they were investing in EIT, which really *was* a small, specialized tools company, and a mediocre one at that. We were getting used to stuff like that.

Then we talked to Sprout, the venture arm of Donaldson, Lufkin & Jenrette, which sent a junior associate named Virginia Bonker to look us over. She was young, beautiful, and knew it, and cold as ice, probably because she had to tolerate a lot of bullshit. Yet she was also a complete pleasure: extremely smart, with a Harvard computer science degree and a Columbia MBA, and utterly professional, sparing us egotistical lectures and not wasting our time or hers. She heard us out, glanced at the financials, immediately caught a subtle error, skewered our consultant and briefly watched him squirm, then moved on. At the end she said that we were interesting, but didn't fit Sprout's style. Our technology was too novel, the company was too early-stage, and we didn't have the kind of experienced management team they liked. And she got up and left. Ms. Bonker has since founded her own VC firm, Blue Rock Capital.

Back in California, on the other hand, there was Jim Breyer at Accel Partners. Breyer was a former McKinsey consultant and one of the hottest young Internet VCs. When I finally got him on the phone, which took weeks, he oozed arrogance about the great deals he was doing and how little time he had. Well, I replied, then maybe we shouldn't bother, because we're in a rush. Oh no, he said, please do come see us, we can make decisions very fast. So we flew to San Francisco and had the meeting. It seemed to go well, although they got hung up on quite arcane marketing and distribution issues. While it was true that we hadn't thought much about them yet, and they did indeed become a major problem, those decisions were months away, and our whole point was that the Internet revolutionized the marketing and distribution, so we were going to have to play it by ear in any case. Still, we all parted enthusiastically; then, radio silence. When I called Breyer a week later to follow up, he said they were interested and would like to take the next step. Unfortunately, however, he was very busy and they wouldn't be able to meet with us again for at least three months. This was absurd, and I let him know it. I later learned that in fact the partnership had already discussed us and said no, which I should have guessed.

The next step was IVP, another elite Silicon Valley VC firm; Geoff Yang, the other referral Marcuvitz had given me, was there. My problem with IVP was that one of its partners, Ruthann Quindlen, was married to Dave Liddle. Liddle is a world-class smooth talker, a quite nice and charming guy who regularly has big ideas involving large amounts of other people's money. Oddly, while Liddle is extremely smart, he seems to have only indifferent business taste, but without question, he has been very good at staying one step ahead of the bad news. At the time of our fund-raising, he had just started a new company, Interval Research, funded to the tune of $100 million by Paul Allen, the billionaire cofounder of Microsoft, who still sat on Microsoft's board. The idea behind Interval was modest: to do truly revolutionary R&D, of the kind Xerox PARC had done long before, and then make money by being ahead of the world in commercializing the results. Although I'd yet to see anything dangerously valuable come from Interval, I worried about the connection to Allen, and thence to Microsoft. Microsoft was the one large company in the world that I really feared. I did not like the idea of giving them early warning of what we were up to.

I explained my problem to Geoff Yang. He reassured me, of course, and signed our nondisclosure agreement. But Quindlen attended our presentation, which made me nervous and probably more abrasive. I also had noticed the conference room art, which consisted solely of a huge, gold-plated reproduction of a hundred-dollar bill. Subtle. The meeting seemed mostly okay, but Yang laughed outright at our proposed valuation, by this time reduced to ten million dollars. I bristled and snapped, If you think you can get us for a two-million-dollar pre-money valuation, forget it! Yang snapped right back, And you can forget about ten million! They didn't pursue us further.

There were several recurring problems, as I gradually learned. One big one was the stigma of being perceived as a *tools* company. I hadn't realized that this issue existed in the VC mind until it had been raised by Davoli, who was uncharacteristically somewhat confused about it himself in regard to our product. Until we picked up on this, we sometimes contributed to our difficulties by using the T word ourselves. The problem was that many VCs don't like tools because they are perceived to have a poor track record. Tools are usually sold only to professional programmers and therefore have small markets, but programmers love to create them and therefore start too many companies. Some tools companies, like Atria, Business Objects, and Powersoft, have in fact done extremely well, but in the minds of most VCs this is a big problem.

Our problem was made worse, ironically, by the fact that we *weren't* a traditional tools company. We were something better and truly original: software that provided as much functionality as traditional tools, and which handled the complexities of server systems (Web servers in our case), *but which any PC end-user could understand and use.* In fact, this was precisely what set us apart and what now makes FrontPage so valuable. I argued until I was hoarse that, yes, our product could be called a tool, but it was a *mass-market, end-user* tool, and thus far more valuable. The best analogy, I said, was Lotus 1-2-3. Before spreadsheets, you needed programmers to construct financial models, but with them, tens of millions of PC users could create such models themselves. Similarly, Microsoft Word and Publisher were turning into mass-market "tools" for desktop publishing. But if the VCs didn't understand the Web and the Internet, they couldn't see that we were creating a new mass market, and they didn't get our story. Under those circumstances, using the word *tool* was the kiss of death, because that was the only word the VCs understood. It was an unavoidable penalty of being early.

Another major problem that I didn't understand was the VC view of founders versus CEOs. This combined with my excessively confrontational attitude to produce a dangerous mixture in VCs' heads. They were afraid I wanted to be the CEO forever and continuously looked for subtle clues about this. In fairness to them, their frequent experience is that founders profess to be willing to hire a professional CEO, but in fact never relinquish power. VCs are also conservative and conventional in managerial issues generally. And finally, while the VCs were probably agnostic on how competent I was, I'd given many signals that I wouldn't play their game. For me, furthermore, there was a major pitfall here. They wanted to bring in a CEO fast, but they also wanted my stock subject to vesting so I couldn't get it all unless I stayed four or five years. That way they could keep me if they wanted to, but also take my stock back if they decided I was expendable. I didn't trust their taste, either; I wanted to make sure I could be around to see if our strategy was right. We had a few frank and open discussions about that.

But those issues aside, I didn't have the slightest desire to remain CEO. I'd never enjoyed being chained to a desk and wanted to get out of the job as soon as I decently could. But I was afraid to tell the VCs that. I thought that if I showed too much willingness to hire a CEO, the VCs would question my commitment and suspect that I would jump ship too early. So we circled around one another for weeks, in a parody of Dilbert. Finally, I got the joke. I started telling them, hey, guys, it's okay. We can hire a professional CEO as long as I get a role in making the choice. Really.

Not that I wasn't worried about who the CEO would be; I was, and with good reason. I have a generally low opinion of professional CEOs, although some are superb. They frequently have poor technical backgrounds, no concern for anything other than their bank accounts, and skills that are more political than substantive. And their track records aren't great. Of the industry's most successful companies, there's only one—Cisco—that has been run for a long time by a conventional professional CEO. Intel, Microsoft, Oracle, AOL, Compaq, Dell, and Gateway are all run by founders, early employees, and/or former academics who somehow do okay despite not having Harvard MBAs and perfect resumés. When you stack them up against the people responsible for the last twenty years' performance of Apple, IBM, Netscape, Lotus, and many others, you come away thinking that unqualified, socially dysfunctional, impatient, ruthless, egomaniacal founders aren't so bad after all.

I think I did a reasonably good job as CEO of Vermeer, a job I officially held for all but the last four months of the company's existence, and which in many ways (e.g., dealing with Microsoft) I never relinquished. I was far from perfect, and I strained a lot of people's nerve endings, including my own. But I usually did the right thing, with a couple of major exceptions—the biggest one, ironically, being our CEO hiring. Admittedly, however, I never faced the real test: managing marketing, distribution, and sales, the areas where I had no experience, and where both real daring and superb execution would have been required.

PANIC AND COMBAT: LOGICAL NEXT STEPS

By November, I was getting really scared. I was still doing a little consulting, but the graph of my bank account was pointing in a straight line toward zero. I kept kicking myself for buying the house in Berkeley, as I lay staring at the ceiling in the early hours of the morning. A dozen people were working long hours without any cash compensation; that wasn't fair, and I couldn't expect it to last long. The Internet was exploding, and we had to start spending real money soon or risk losing our head start. We continued to hire more people so we could get to market earlier, making the bet that we'd get funded. But we needed to buy computers, reserve trade show space, and most of all, we needed real office space.

Around this time, on a flight from Boston to San Francisco, I used frequent-flier miles to upgrade to first class and found myself two rows away from Andy Marcuvitz. Since the seat next to him was empty, I moved over and sat with him. Our conversation started out reasonably enough, but quickly turned into a full-blown, brutal argument. Marcuvitz never raises his voice, but I sure did, and by the end of the flight, the whole cabin was openly listening or pretending very hard not to. A little piece of my cortex reminded me to be careful, because those flights are full of VCs and high technology types, but I'm sure that "Internet" and "Web" were heard more than once.

I started aggressively and got more so, pushing Marcuvitz about committing to us, and about our valuation. It had been a couple of months since we first presented to him, and he could see the Internet was exploding, just as we had said. Did he have any better bets than us? We sure didn't see anyone else on the horizon. He'd been the first one we talked to and was one of the few who really understood it—was he just going to pass it by? He was completely unruffled.

> We see all kinds of opportunities, Charles, and all kinds of results. Maybe you'll be a great success, like Powersoft or Lotus, but you might be a total failure. Our experience is that so many things can happen that we can't overpay for a young company with inexperienced management.

He started to expand on this:

> For example, Charles, how do we know *you'll* stay with the company? Your strategic insight is obviously crucial to its success. [With anyone else, I would have taken this as sarcasm; but you have to have a sense of humor to be sarcastic.] What if you get into an automobile accident? One of the problems we had at Apollo was that after the first few years our CEO's mind was on other things.

He went on:

> Some founders resist hiring professional CEOs, and others leave even though their stock hasn't fully vested. How do we know you won't give us problems like that? Five-year vesting helps, but it's certainly no guarantee.

I already suspected the vesting issue would arise and realized that it was perfectly reasonable for the VCs to insist on some amount of it. But Marcuvitz had never mentioned it before, and I had serious concerns about how it would be used. So I pushed back hard:

> What do you mean *vesting!*? Randy and I already *own* the company. The idea was mine, we've already worked for six months without pay, and I've seeded the company with my own money. There won't be any vesting requirement for *your* investment, so why should there be for mine?

> Sorry, Charles, he said, but everybody has to vest. It took me five years to earn my stock at Apollo, despite the fact that I was a founder. Why should you be any different? No matter who funds you—*if* anybody ever funds you—they're going to insist that you be subject to vesting, just as your employees are.

I started getting testy:

> Andy, you didn't fund Apollo yourself for six months. Besides, if my stock is subject to full vesting, once you get a CEO, you can increase your share of the company substantially just by firing me. If you get to protect yourself against me, don't I get to protect myself against you? If you tell me to trust you, then I'll tell you to trust me. And I'll stack my ethical track record against any VC I've met. I can give you references a hell of a lot more credible than yours.

> Don't be silly, Marcuvitz said. We want our companies to succeed, and we depend completely on our reputation. We don't go around firing founders just to get their stock.

Then he got tough. He was good at it.

> Charles, he said, vesting is one of many things you clearly don't know much about, and somebody should explain them to you. You don't seem to understand valuations and you don't know how deals work. Do you know that VCs will want to use participating convertible preferred? Do you even know what that is? Do you know your common is already priced too high, so your employees will have to overpay for their options? And who are these consultants you're giving stock to? Do you have any idea how complicated you've made your financing by giving up so much and having so many shareholders so early?

I was reddening. It turned out he was right about some of this, although he exaggerated quite a lot, and we actually hadn't made any fatal mistakes. But I really didn't know much about start-up capital structures and for the moment couldn't respond directly with any assurance. But I fired right back:

> So you know about convertible preferred! I can hire MBAs by the carload to teach me about convertible preferred, and learning will probably take me an hour. I've been teaching *you* about the *Web*. You've picked our brains for weeks. Whether you invest in us or not, we've brought you up to speed on a huge revolution you didn't understand, and that we do. That's worth a lot more than a canned lecture on financing start-ups, but I'll bet you won't give us stock in your next ten Internet investments.

And so it went, hour after hour—about valuations, the industry, my vesting, the VC oligopoly, CEO hiring, control issues, the company's prospects. To my surprise, when we got off the plane, Marcuvitz was truly upset—it's the only time I ever saw him look rattled. Equally surprising, I felt great. I'd worried for months about all I didn't know. But Marcuvitz had just hit me with everything he could think of, one on one for six hours, and while some of it was embarrassing, none of it was fatal, and I'd landed as many punches as he had. As we parted company at the arrival gate I said, Andy, that was fun—let's do it again some time. He looked as if I'd shot him.

But my good mood didn't last. Okay, so Marcuvitz knew he couldn't push me around, and I knew there were no real skeletons in our closet. But the VCs still held the high cards, and they knew it. Another reason it was foolish of me not to get us temporary office space was that it signaled to the VCs that I didn't really have that much money. My cash situation *was* getting dangerous, and we were going to hit the wall without funding, but I should have bluffed better. It was finally dawning on me that time was on their side. The longer they waited, the more I'd be forced to come to terms, and they could tell it wouldn't take that long. Internet time hadn't hit yet, so why hurry?

Throughout this period, I stayed in close touch with Marcuvitz. That may seem odd, because we couldn't spend three minutes together without an argument. But even when we argued, I usually learned something. We disagreed on anything concerning funding, but on substantive issues I valued his opinion. Andy M. is no dummy, and he's *very* skeptical—if you say it's a nice day out, he walks to the window to check. So if he thought I was right about something, I probably *was* right. And he stayed engaged because no matter what he thought of me personally, he acknowledged that I was smart too, that we had spotted a major business opportunity, and that he needed to keep an eye on us.

In the late fall, when it started to look like we might make a deal but before we really had it, we dealt with several important and difficult personnel issues. Marcuvitz was watching, and I made a point of keeping him informed—selectively.

First, we badly needed a VP of engineering. That's a critical position in a software firm, and all VCs wanted it filled. The VP of engineering generally isn't the chief architect, but is responsible for delivering the product—on time, under budget, bug-free, ready for release to manufacturing (RTM, also called *going gold*). This involves crucial judgments on hiring, scheduling, feature priorities, development techniques, workloads, budgeting, and managing the relationships between coding, internal quality assurance, external beta testing, debugging, documentation, the help system, external technology licensing, and even packaging and manufacturing. We interviewed half a dozen candidates; we didn't fall in love with any of them. The only one recommended by Marcuvitz, ironically, was bad—an arrogant ex-researcher, all of whose companies had failed. Shortly afterward he formed another start-up that failed too. Randy finally suggested Frank Germano, who had been the VP of engineering at Randy's previous company, Beyond, and had been at Lotus, DEC, and Apollo before that.

I had trouble with Frank from the start, and Andy Schulert, who had known Frank at Apollo, was anything but enthusiastic. But Randy spoke highly of him, he was a known and acceptable quantity to the VCs, and we needed someone badly, so we made him an offer. Randy's high regard for Frank proves what a nice guy Randy is, because Frank drives many people crazy. Negotiating his contract took months, dozens of phone calls, and much shuttle diplomacy by Randy and even by Andy Marcuvitz. And trust me, if you need Andy Marcuvitz for diplomatic purposes, you're a desperate man.

Frank's demands were outrageous. Part of it was insecurity. Germano was in his late forties, a good deal older than anyone else. He was sensitive about his limited success, and now his previous relationship with Randy was being inverted: *Randy* was the founder recruiting *him*. Often I made things worse through impatience, directness, and occasional arrogance. But once, I was the diplomat: Frank approached me privately and insisted that Randy report to him, rather than vice versa. I said no, politely (rare for me), and then discussed it with Randy. We came up with a face-saving compromise: on paper they would both report to me, so neither would report to the other.

Once he joined, my relationship with Frank was a continuous problem. For example, he liked to hear himself talk; this wasted everyone's time, so naturally I told him so. But it wasn't just me. Technically, Frank was out of date, yet he often issued edicts to technical people whose skills were far superior to his. Fairly quickly, several of our best engineers wanted to strangle him. He insisted on being paid a very high salary—he got $120,000 to my $100,000. This even caused problems (quite properly) with Andy Marcuvitz, who complained to me. I replied: Andy, if you think you can fix this, be my guest. The thought of Andy negotiating with Frank can bring a smile to my face even today.

But we needed Frank, and he knew it. He got almost as much stock as Randy, which in my opinion he didn't deserve. On the other hand, for all his problems, he made a major contribution. There is no denying that without him, we would have shipped our product later than we did. In addition to managing engineering he found us our office space, purchased our computers, negotiated our real estate and equipment leases, and got us our furniture. Not glamorous, but important. His attitude problems cost us time and energy, but he kept our eyes on the prize: getting the product *done*. Most good engineers are overly optimistic about what they can achieve, whereas Germano was a hard-bitten veteran who prided himself on saying no, as often and obnoxiously as possible. I have to say, the product got done on time, under budget, and with fairly high quality. In this business, and given the enormous technical challenge we faced, the novelty of our product, and the unprecedented volatility of the Internet environment, this was quite remarkable. The engineers deserve most of the credit, but Germano deserves some too. And if we had slipped even a couple of months, we probably would have missed our window as an acquisition—but more about that later.

Another personnel decision involved our first problem employee. I hired him, and two months later I was ready to fire him. We'd hired Jim Gettys partly to impress our VCs, which was a mistake. Gettys is a real star—a brilliant computer scientist from MIT and DEC, and one of the two architects of X Windows, a major UNIX GUI standard and a truly important accomplishment. Yet Marcuvitz merely grunted and looked typically unimpressed when I told him we'd landed Gettys. I was getting used to that, but Gettys proved to be a disaster. He talked all the time, tried to order everyone around, generally irritated everybody, and worst of all didn't produce. He had some very good ideas that we used in the product, but he refused to get his hands dirty by actually doing things. At first, I humored him because he was an icon who far outranked me in the technology pecking order. Furthermore, firing him could be dangerous: he might talk to competitors, and I worried about what the VCs would think.

But soon it was clear that he had to go. I held a formal meeting with Randy and Frank as witnesses, handed Gettys a strongly worded thirty-day probation letter, and made him sign a document acknowledging receipt of the warning. The next day, he gave thirty days' notice himself, and eventually went back to MIT. He did okay; the stock he had already vested just in one quarter turned out to be worth a couple of hundred thousand dollars. I worried about telling Marcuvitz, because I had bragged about hiring Gettys only shortly before. But he actually complimented me. Charles, he said, famous academics often don't do well. I was surprised you hired him, but the fact that you fixed it quickly is good. The reaction of the developers also surprised me. Most of them had worked in places where merit lost against politics or appearances. They interpreted the Gettys episode, correctly, as an announcement that bullshit would not be tolerated no matter how famous you were, and they loved it. Scott Drellishak, one of our smartest, most delightful, and most uppity young engineers, said to me one day, "You know, Charles, you might have a zero moron company here."

But I pushed awfully hard and frequently overdid it. A few days after Andy Schulert and his wife had their first baby, I called Andy at home to ask why he wasn't working harder. When Ted Stefanik, a brilliant and extremely hardworking engineer, sprained his arm in a fall while ice skating, I lectured the company that there would be no sympathy for accidents that reduced productivity. Several people were amused, but others were a bit shocked. Long afterward, Rob Mauceri, another gifted engineer and a very nice man, told me that just after my lecture he slipped and fell on an icy street. As he was falling, instead of worrying about hurting himself, he thought, Charles will kill me. By this time I was a pretty tense guy. And I only got worse.

BREAKTHROUGH

The breakthrough that finally got us funded was a call from Wade Woodson at Sigma Partners. Sigma is a small, elite, superb VC firm on Sand Hill Road, the VCs' equivalent of Park Avenue. We had been talking with them for a couple of months. They were one of the firms that Davoli's name had opened up, and they had also been partners with Matrix on their two Internet investments. We had met with them on our first West Coast trip, initially presenting to just one of the partners, Burgess Jamieson. Jamieson is an eminence in the industry and had the courtly manners of a Southern gentleman—unusual for this industry—and while he didn't say much, he seemed to get it. In our first meeting, Jamieson questioned—as others had—the wisdom of being a bicoastal company. When he did so, Peter responded—completely unprompted by me—that if it was critical, he'd move to Boston. Jamieson was impressed, and so was I. Three months later, Peter did indeed move.

A few weeks later, during a trip to Boston, Jamieson came to see us. He brought along Gardner Hendrie, a semiretired East Coast partner who'd been a founder of Stratus Computer, and Wade Woodson. Wade was a Stanford-trained electrical engineer, lawyer, *and* MBA who grew up in the Midwest. He's affable, laid-back, and has a dry wit, not egotistical at all, and razor-sharp. The meeting lasted several hours and seemed to go well. Sigma was the only firm where I actually liked everyone I met. Wade and I had many fights, but he is an ethical guy, and I always liked him. But he could be as tough as Marcuvitz, and like Marcuvitz, he stayed well clear of anything personal when we were doing Vermeer.

Wade became the lead guy at Sigma looking at us. He came back east monthly, and on another of his trips he joined us at Jim Gettys's house to see our prototype. We had decided that both for fund-raising purposes and also for its real value, we should develop a working prototype that implemented most of our architecture. Five weeks later, it was done. It was tremendously impressive, and Wade realized it.

I was in California when Wade called a few weeks later. As I remember, the call came late in the afternoon; he said he wanted to meet me as soon as possible. But I had meetings that night and was flying back to Boston early the next day. I said the only way I could meet him would be at the airport at six o'clock in the morning. He sighed but said okay. I was so tense that I said, Look, I don't want to waste time, so if you're just going to say no, why not save us both some trouble and tell me over the phone? Wade replied dryly, I don't think I would get up at five in the morning for that. If I was just going to say no, I think I'd sleep in. Oh! I thought.

Wade showed up at my airport gate at 6:00 A.M. as promised and handed me a "term sheet"—an informal investment offer—for a $4 million investment at a pre-money valuation of $4 million. It was a far cry from the $10 million pre-money I'd been holding out for, but it wasn't $2 million either. At least we'd keep half the firm. But there were a lot of other terms, too. I decided not to commit us to anything until I had talked it over with Randy. I thanked Wade, told him I regarded it as a reasonable offer that we would consider seriously, that I needed to think about it, but that we'd get back to him soon.

The Sigma proposal was contingent on our finding two other VCs as co-investors. In addition, they insisted on a 20 percent cut in my personal stock holdings. I suspected that this was a control issue, so that I wouldn't have a larger share than any of the VCs. There was a note attached to this point saying that it was absolutely nonnegotiable. Recently, Wade told me that actually they just didn't think it was fair of me to have that much. They also wanted a large stock option pool for future employees, which would come out of our share, not theirs. The net was that I would be left with about 12 percent of the company and Randy with about 4 percent, assuming we vested fully. Issues of vesting, control, CEO selection, and board membership remained unresolved. If the proposal had come two months earlier, I would have been insulted. But after Randy and I talked it through, we decided we had no choice. At least it was twice as good as the deal Marcuvitz had offered—and I liked the people at Sigma.

Wade seemed genuinely pleased when I called back and said we would accept. Then, in his polite way, he gave me a cautionary lecture on life in the VC industry. Now, Charles, he said, we have a deal. You can't use this to go out and shop for a better offer. No reputable firm will give you better terms once they know you've got a handshake deal with us. And we will certainly walk away if we find you're using us as a bargaining lever. If we were to pull out under those circumstances, no one else will be interested in you. I said I understood and would give him my word not to renege, although I was acutely aware how much bargaining power I was giving up. There were still difficult issues of control, board membership, and vesting to be negotiated, and if Sigma wasn't satisfied, they could walk away at any time. If *I* walked away, on the other hand, I risked being blackballed. The truth is that I had no intention of doing an end-run; Sigma, I felt, had dealt with us honestly and straightforwardly, and I suspected we wouldn't do better elsewhere. The Sigma deal was going to be it, and we would just have to try to get the best terms we could.

And we were still not out of the woods: we needed two other investors. I started calling up the handful of firms that had seemed interested. There was Atlas Venture in Boston, which had evinced some interest after what I thought was a mediocre first meeting. They knew little about the Internet or the Web, and the top guy, Chris Spray, had seemed to go out of his way to be unpleasant to Randy. (He actually turned out to be a nice guy when we knew him better.) The rest of the people were nice enough, but didn't seem smart. Then there was Charles River, also in Boston, where we had gotten confusing and contradictory signals after what seemed like a good initial meeting. There were a couple of others, none of whom seemed ready to pull the trigger. Larry Orr at Trinity Ventures, who also seemed like a nice guy, was also interested, and I feel slightly guilty that in the end we couldn't give him the option to invest.

And then, of course, there was Matrix. However much Marcuvitz might detest me, I knew he liked the idea, and I couldn't let Vermeer founder over personalities. It was time for a little humility, so I called him for an appointment. I must have looked pitiful when I showed up at his office—I know I was very nervous—because I actually thought I detected a fleeting note of sympathy. (I was probably hallucinating.) I explained the Sigma deal, told him that we had accepted it, and that we very much wanted Matrix to participate. Marcuvitz was friendly, but cool. The Sigma deal looked reasonable, he said, certainly more so than the terms I had originally asked for. He liked the idea, he thought we were smart, and the business space was promising.

But, Charles, he said, you and I have disagreed a lot, and my partners and I have to think about that.

I swallowed hard.

> I'm new at this, I said, and my diplomatic skills leave a lot to be desired. There's a lot I don't know and that sometimes makes me abrasive. I'm sorry for that.

> Well, thank you, he said, that certainly helps. I'll talk to Paul Ferri and get back to you.

Marcuvitz called back in a few days. Matrix was willing to proceed on the basis of the Sigma term sheet, provided we could find the third investor and resolve all the remaining issues. They wanted a board seat—in fact, Sigma and Matrix eventually agreed to be co-leads, with a board seat each—and they had a long list of other issues. Randy and I would have to submit to a vesting schedule; there would have to be a firm commitment to hire a professional CEO; they wanted a discussion of board structure; they were concerned about stock allocations to consultants; they wanted changes in our employment contracts. I could live with those things, at least in principle. But I needed some minimal security about control issues, and I wanted to get it *done*.

Marcuvitz made it plain he was in no hurry. Then one day he showed me a short article in *The Wall Street Journal,* announcing that America Online had purchased two small Web software companies, Booklink and NaviSoft, for a combined price of $34 million. Tell me, Marcuvitz asked me coldly, Who are they and what are they doing? Nothing in your space, I hope. Nothing important, I replied casually; a browser and a simple HTML page editor, nothing that competed with us. Actually, I was lying. We didn't really know what NaviSoft was doing, and in fact one of our employees had heard a rumor that it *was* something that might compete with us.

Nor was this the only unpleasant fact I was concealing from the VCs. A month earlier, and despite our usual (and serious) precautions, an engineer we were recruiting had suddenly announced he was going to Netscape—after he'd learned everything we were doing, and despite having promised us that he wasn't talking to competitors (Netscape and Microsoft being our main worries). I got a voice mail about it as I came home with a friend of mine, Dale Murphy, for dinner. I called back right then, and in this case I made Marcuvitz and Ferri seem like pussycats. I told him we'd utterly destroy him if he breathed a word about us. I warned him that if he even told Netscape of our existence that he'd be violating our nondisclosure agreement. Furthermore, I said, if Netscape announces similar products, we'll go after you and them for a few billion dollars. Their position will be that they didn't know that you were betraying us, and they'll probably let you twist in the wind. Your depositions and court appearances will take years and your legal bills will bankrupt you. We'll have private detectives going over every phone call you've ever made, every e-mail you've ever sent, every dream you've ever had, every lie you've ever told. Netscape will fire you and you'll never work in this industry again. If you need a demonstration that I can be a complete bastard let me know and I would be happy to provide it. Do you get it? He did; I scared the hell out of him, which was just fine. My poor friend Dale, who had not come over for dinner to hear things like this, was slightly appalled. But for us this was life or death. I thought we'd be okay, at least for a while. And it seems that we were.

But I wasn't in a hurry to describe either that episode or the NaviSoft rumors to the VCs, especially to Marcuvitz. I don't like lying. But with all the bullshit I'd been through with the venture capital industry in general and Marcuvitz in particular, there was no way I was going to give them ammunition at this point in our negotiations.

The third investor problem briefly seemed to solve itself when Charles River Ventures called and asked for another presentation. This was a major positive surprise. After our first presentation a couple of months before, they had assigned a new hire, Steve Coit, who had previously been at Hewlett-Packard, to do a more detailed review. They would make reassuring noises, Coit would continue to miss his deadlines for getting back to us, and we finally wrote them off as a waste of time. Now, suddenly, they were back.

For the new meeting they wanted the entire technical team, a good sign. I couldn't go because I was in California, but Randy reported that the meeting went perfectly. Our guys performed well, and Charles River finally seemed to get it. But a few days later, one of the senior partners, Rick Burnes, called to say that they were not interested. I was shocked and demanded that he explain. He said that our market would probably be small and fiercely competitive, with lots of cheap products fighting it out. I pointed out that our software was not simple, that at the moment we were the only ones addressing this market, and that it was a very big and rapidly growing problem. Burnes arrogantly retorted that the number of Web sites was exploding and people seemed to be able to create them somehow without our tool.

I blew up, because by this point we understood approximately ten thousand times more about this issue than he did. Of course, I said, Web growth is going through the roof—that's the *whole point*. It's hard to develop sites now, but people are doing it anyway, because the Web opens up so many possibilities. We know *exactly* how people are developing sites now, and the Web can't keep growing that way without consuming every programmer in the universe within a year or two. Burnes retreated into VC hauteur. I don't want to get into that, he replied; we have a lot of experience at this, and our decision is final. I was truly astounded. After weeks of inactivity, they took half a day of our whole technical team and then turned us down for the stupidest of reasons. Having now made a few investment mistakes myself, I understand how things that are obvious to those involved can be opaque to outsiders, but this was pretty bad.

So we still needed a third investor. Then at the last minute, Atlas resurfaced. They wanted in, perhaps prompted by Matrix, but I wasn't overjoyed. Chris Spray, the lead guy, is extremely smart and quite the urbane Brit. But we had been assigned to his partner Barry Fidelman, a former salesman who didn't strike us as the sharpest tool in the shed, nor the cleanest. Barry at first insisted on being a co-lead and having a board seat, which was absurd. There Sigma and Matrix did my work for me: *they* flatly refused and told Atlas what the terms would be if Atlas wanted to invest. After a brief, tough negotiation, Atlas capitulated. They agreed to take a nonvoting observer seat on the board and to invest only half as much as the other two. The $4 million investment was therefore split up as $1.6 million each from Sigma and Matrix and $800,000 from Atlas. Davoli, my original introduction to Sigma and Atlas, was allowed to put $50,000 into the first round on the same terms, and Davoli would also be an observer on the board. Davoli's $50,000 came entirely out of *Sigma's* share, which I should have noticed. In fact, Davoli was negotiating to join Sigma, which nobody mentioned until nine months later.

LITTLE DETAILS LIKE CONTROL

There was still a long way to go: control, vesting, board makeup, CEO selection. By now my paranoia needle was permanently in the red zone. They could walk away any time, and we would just die. I became difficult to deal with—sarcastic, openly mistrustful of the VCs and their motives, angry that they kept whittling away at our positions. At the same time, I felt increasing concern about our lawyers, Brown & Bain. After the initial meetings in Palo Alto, they had turned me over primarily to kids, very nice and smart kids, who however were in *Arizona* and who were totally outclassed by the VCs when it came to deal terms.

The Christmas season was awful: five-way conference calls day and night—me, Randy, the VCs, and the lawyers fighting over the control issues. I would go to parties, my cell phone would ring, I would disappear for hours and then come out furious and exhausted—not the ideal guest. One conference call in particular sticks in my mind. Our lawyers were part of the call, mostly listening. Marcuvitz asked me why they were on the line. I said, Because I fucking *want* them on the line, Andy! I know *that,* he said, in his most maddening, studiously even tone. My question was, *Why?* As far as I can see, they're just running their clocks, taking away my stock and yours. Of course, Andy said this in part *because* the lawyers were listening.

Throughout it all, even when I was at my worst, Randy was wonderfully supportive and willingly gave ground on many of his own issues. At one point in December, I almost blew everything by asking for the right to do some consulting even after we were funded. My $100,000 CEO salary would be a fifth of what I had made as a consultant, I was temporarily supporting my girlfriend, Camille, I had a mortgage, and my liquid savings were getting low. Nonetheless, it was stupid. That I would even dream of asking suggests how tense I had already become. I raised the issue to Wade on a call from my car phone in Cambridge while he was in California. He responded, very calmly, that this was a deal breaker—if I insisted, they would walk, period. It didn't sound like a bluff—and later, he told me it wasn't. I pulled my car to the side of the road, thought for ten minutes, and called him back. Of course I'll be full-time, I said, I realize it would be best for the company and for me. Thanks very much, he replied, that means a lot to us. By this time, I was coming to like and respect Woodson a great deal. He was cool and tough and we had some harsh arguments, but he was smart and efficient, had a dry humor that eased tensions, and he was as aboveboard as our frequently conflicting interests permitted him to be.

Of course, we did the deal, or I wouldn't be writing this. The final documents covered an enormous conference room table in a layer of paper a foot thick. Their details shed light on the many pitfalls of early-stage financings. For example, one argument over vesting arose from differences between East Coast and West Coast venture capitalists. West Coast firms are used to the intensely competitive, freewheeling style of Silicon Valley: companies are born, make money, and die quickly; everyone moves on to the next hot business. Four-year vesting schedules are the norm, and I had used that formula for our first employees. East Coast VCs are stodgier; they think the California style encourages a wandering eye, and they prefer five-year schedules, with a one-year "cliff"— you don't get anything until you've stayed for a year. Marcuvitz wanted us to switch retroactively to East Coast rules. I refused—I'd already given my word to the employees. After a long argument, we compromised: current employees got treated like Californians, but all new hires vested like easterners.

Even though I offered to fight the issue for him, Randy volunteered to accept the same vesting schedule as the other employees. But I wasn't willing to accept it for myself. Randy was a key system architect, a brilliant technical presenter, and the one person who kept everyone together—the highest-level technologist, but also the critical mediator between me and the developers, Germano and the developers, and me and Germano. So the VCs needed Randy, arguably more than they thought they needed me—indeed, replacing me with a professional CEO was a key part of the deal. Furthermore, Randy was an incredibly sweet guy; safeguarding our interests was my department, not

Randy's. As my friend Charlie Morris once said in another context, my relationship with Randy was that I kept him from going broke and he kept me from getting killed. I clearly had no compunction about getting into fights. The VCs would surely be able to control the company more easily through Randy or a new CEO than through me.

I was worried both for myself and for the company. I thought I had the clearest strategic view and needed to be there at least until I was satisfied that others with equal vision were in place. But once the VCs owned it, and certainly once a professional CEO had been hired, they might decide I was more trouble than I was worth. And I was much more expensive than Randy. If my stock was subject to normal vesting, especially if there was also a cliff, the VCs could take back 12 percent of the company simply by firing me. And even if they didn't fire me, my bargaining leverage would be severely constrained by the knowledge that they could. So I did not like this picture.

It took a while, but we hammered out a deal. I vested, but with one huge exception. Upon the hiring of a CEO, half of my stock vested immediately, so the VCs' incentive to fire me was greatly reduced, while conversely I was strongly motivated to cooperate in hiring a CEO. With regard to corporate control, we agreed that the VCs would own 50.1 percent of the company. But the shareholder's agreement would specify that the board would comprise two directors from their side, initially Woodson and Marcuvitz, and two from ours, initially Randy and me. Randy would resign from the board in favor of the professional CEO once we had hired one. Critical issues, like choosing the CEO or independent directors, required three votes, so at least one of us (Randy or me) had to vote in favor. If we were acquired, everyone's vesting would accelerate one year. Finally, I demanded, and they conceded after a fight, that I would be chairman for two years. The job was purely symbolic, but I thought it would give them a larger public relations problem if they wanted to fire me.

The VCs and their lawyers took me to school on the capital structure of start-ups. In general, I give them high marks on this score. For the most part, they explained things clearly and honestly—in fact, I learned much more from them than from our own lawyers—and they treated us fairly. One of the points that Marcuvitz had rubbed my nose in on our plane ride was that it was important to have at least two classes of stock, usually a convertible preferred layer for investors and a common layer for employees. (The preferred is later converted to common at the investors' option or upon some "liquidity event" like an initial public offering or an acquisition.)

While you're still privately held, the two-layer structure allows you to raise the price of the preferred far above the price of the common. This is because preferred stock has attributes, such as liquidation preferences, which give preferred shareholders the first call on the company's assets. That way, as you keep hiring employees, you can give them low prices on their stock options, so they can make a lot more money if you're successful. It also makes it cheaper for employees to exercise their options and purchase their stock early, so they can qualify for long-term capital gains treatment sooner and also avoid arcane but serious problems associated with the alternative minimum tax. A further nuance is that you can own unvested stock in the form of "restricted" stock, which you can't sell but can still vote. Randy and I held such stock, which was an important safeguard for us, albeit only in an extreme situation. Since we could vote all of our stock, if necessary we could vote a professional CEO off the board and put Randy back. The VCs had a potential countermove in that event: they could convert their preferred stock to common and outvote us as common shareholders. But that would be legally questionable, they would all have to do it together to outvote us, and they would lose some money due to them as holders of preferred stock. It didn't come to such extremities, although as we'll see, a couple of times I thought it might.

The VCs did pull one fast one, although in the end it didn't matter. Their preferred carried a "participating preference" equal to their invested capital, which was triggered by either acquisition or initial public offering. I heard them say it repeatedly, and it was written on the first page of the term sheet, so there was no concealment, but they presented it as normal and unquestioned, which turned out to be false. My expensive lawyers didn't tell me that this provision was far from standard and often is negotiated away. The effect is as follows. Assume the VCs had invested $10 million in convertible preferred and owned half the equity. If we then sold the company for $30 million, they would get their $10 million back first, and then would *still* get half of what was left, for a total of $20 million, or two-thirds of the deal. In our case, the buyout price was so large that the advantage didn't amount to much, and our second round eliminated the provision, because we'd figured out the game by then.

Finishing the deal saddled me with one final, very unpleasant task. On our plane ride, Marcuvitz had beaten me up for giving away too much stock for professional services. As usual, he was at least partly right. Because I was anxious to conserve cash, I had paid most lawyers and consultants in stock, which seemed innocuous enough, but some of them had built up big positions. For Marcuvitz and the VCs, the answer was easy—Charles, either it comes out of your hide, or you call them up and take it back! Marcuvitz took a particularly hard line with Ed Takacs. He made Ed take an especially big haircut, pressured me intensely about it, and eventually went through a convoluted charade in order to pretend that Ed had invested in us rather than receiving stock for his services. This puzzled me at first because Takacs had not built up an outrageous position and had been very helpful to us. However, I gradually realized what was going on. Takacs was in a subtle but serious way a VC competitor, and Marcuvitz was both punishing him and trying to avoid setting a dangerous precedent. By helping us build a team without cash, and by introducing us to people like Davoli, Takacs was indirectly acting as a VC substitute. We'd be further advanced when the VCs finally came into the deal, wouldn't need as much money, would be in touch with more potential investors, and could command a higher valuation. I fought the issue, but eventually made a half dozen very difficult phone calls and clawed back about 15 percent of what I had given out. Quite understandably, Takacs was absolutely furious. But he, and most of the consultants, still made very large sums of money.

When we finally got a deal, we had a company party at my apartment. Randy brought Dom Pérignon. Peter Amstein and Tom Blumer surprised us with T-shirts. Under a reproduction of one of Jan Vermeer's paintings taken off the Web (probably illegally), there was written:

VERMEER TECHNOLOGIES, INC.
We can't tell you what we do, but we do it better than anyone else!

THE PROTECTION—AND SCREWING—OF EMPLOYEES

Many start-up employees are naïve about legal and financial matters and insufficiently aggressive in protecting their interests. In my experience, engineers, women, and people just out of school are particularly vulnerable. As a result they are often fleeced by management. At one point, for example, our lawyers explained to me that companies often retained the right to repurchase employee stock options at their original strike price. That sounded unfair to me, so we didn't do it, but I later learned that it does occur. It is one of many tricks used against the innocent and unwary.

Most people have heard of Pixar, the company that did the animation for the movie *Toy Story* and that made its principal owner, Steve Jobs, a billion dollars when it went public in 1995. Pixar was founded by Alvy Ray Smith and Ed Catmull, who are legends in the world of digital animation. Smith is a veteran of Xerox PARC from the 1970s, where, far ahead of his time, he created some of the earliest technologies for manipulating images. In 1979, Smith and Catmull were recruited by George Lucas's Industrial Light and Magic—Smith was its first director of computer animation.

At Lucasfilm, Smith created a stir with a spectacular 3-D sixty-second sequence in Paramount's *Star Trek II: The Wrath of Khan,* which would have been impossible with conventional technology. But Lucas got into financial trouble, and in 1986 Smith and his team were spun off as Pixar and sold to Jobs, who'd been kicked out of Apple and was looking for something to do. Jobs made himself CEO and kept about 60 percent of the stock for himself, while the rest was widely distributed among employees. Jobs was his usual impossible self, and Smith finally left in despair in 1992. He's a good man, and I'm pleased to say has done well since. He founded a software company that was eventually purchased by Microsoft, where he seems to have found a home as their top graphics guru.

Jobs put a lot of money into Pixar—Smith guesses $50 million over ten years. But the company's future, including the *Toy Story* contract and a long-term relationship with Disney, had been constructed before Smith left, the result of fifteen years' work. At this point, however, Jobs reorganized the company, selling off a money-losing hardware business to focus on software. Then Jobs pulled a neat trick. "Old" Pixar was shut down and all of its shares sold to "New" Pixar, which Jobs created solely for this purpose. The paperwork was easy. The controlling shareholder of Old Pixar and the controlling shareholder of New Pixar, both of whom happened to be Steve Jobs, simply voted the deal through.

As part of the reorganization, Jobs exercised a clause in the employee stock option agreements that allowed him to buy back their options at the original strike price, which was a pittance. Peter Amstein had worked at Pixar, and all he knew was that one day he had stock options, and the next day he didn't. During the public offering, the underwriters forced Jobs to distribute about 15 percent of the stock among key employees, because nobody would have invested otherwise. Smith was allowed to buy a small allocation of stock at Catmull's insistence, but many employees were shut out entirely, including some who had spent many years creating the technology. If you look at Pixar's Web site now, you'd never guess that the company existed before Jobs got there.

As I said, the industry can be pretty nasty. So I told our lawyers that, no, we did not want the right to buy back people's stock options.

The sad fact is that many of the people who supply the brainpower for America's leadership in high technology are highly exploitable and are regularly exploited. I was determined to prevent this in our case. When our deal was about to close, I held a meeting of all the employees to explain the capital structure of the deal, including what they personally would end up with, and was surprised to learn that none of them had ever been in such a meeting. For smart guys, most of them didn't look after their interests very well.

The government should do something about this, and it would be easy. The Securities and Exchange Commission provides extensive protection for investors, particularly in public companies, by requiring disclosure of critical financial information. But none of these protections are provided for start-up employees, who, in proportion to their wealth, are usually making much bigger and riskier investments. I think this should be fixed. Every firm using stock-based compensation should be required, annually, to provide all full-time employees and holders of stock or options with a one- or two-page description of the company's capital structure and the critical terms governing the stock option plan.

Even though I was comparatively sophisticated and was paying a battery of lawyers and accountants, one oversight cost me about $10 million. As I mentioned earlier, shareholders in small companies are eligible for privileged tax treatment under certain conditions—one of them allows you to get taxed at half the normal capital gains rate if you hold your stock for five years. But I had originally organized Vermeer as a Subchapter S corporation (so I could deduct my losses on my own taxes). We then converted to normal corporate status before the financing. But the attorneys didn't realize that if I *exchanged* my Subchapter S stock for common stock in the new company, that this disqualified me from favorable treatment. It would have been trivial to fix if the lawyers had known about it . . . but, easy come, easy go. I made an enormous amount of money and, all things considered, am very fortunate.

On January 31, 1995, Randy and I, Andy Marcuvitz, Bob Davoli, and a small army of lawyers assembled for the closing of our first round in a conference room at the VCs' law firm's offices.

There had been one more big explosion before getting there. Andy Marcuvitz had repeatedly assured us over the previous months that Matrix was ready to proceed as soon as we could reach agreement. This was a question we routinely asked of all VCs, because we didn't want to get caught waiting for them to raise money. But when our deal went through, Matrix was winding up one venture fund and opening another. They decided that they wanted us to be the first investment for their new fund, which they hadn't closed yet, but they didn't tell us. At the very last minute, in early January, Andy Marcuvitz told me that Matrix had therefore decided to delay *our* closing by three weeks. I was furious, and had every right to be. Three weeks may not sound like much, but for us it was a very serious matter—about 8 percent of the time remaining to our product shipment date, which was already impossibly ambitious. The Net and the Web were getting hotter by the minute. We were ready to move right away into new office space and start full-scale development. Now we had to wait three weeks so Marcuvitz's fund numbers would look better. I screamed; Marcuvitz, as usual, refused to budge; the other VCs, as usual, supported him; so I gritted my teeth and endured it. What was I going to do? Go to the competition?

It seemed like forever, but the time passed, and finally there we all were, actually closing the deal on a gray, rainy Boston winter day. Marcuvitz and I managed to be pleasant to each other. Randy counted that he signed his name 123 times. I signed mine even more times than that, but didn't count. Bob Davoli realized that he hadn't brought his $50,000, and his checking account didn't have enough money in it; he had to call Goldman Sachs for a funds transfer. Then the VCs handed Randy and me a half dozen checks totaling $4 million made out to Vermeer Technologies, Inc.

I remember that we all milled around for a few minutes. I felt distinctly strange, almost embarrassed, about holding $4 million. Then it was time for Randy and me to go. I put the checks securely into the inside pocket of my jacket, and the meeting broke up. Randy and I walked for a few minutes, and I said:

Randy, do you realize that we have $4 million?

I do, he said. And we have check signing authority.

Yes, I answered, but only up to fifty thousand dollars. Over that we need board approval.

But the bank doesn't know that, Randy said. They just have our signature cards.

So we could just leave for Brazil? I said.

Yep, he said.

We decided not to go to Brazil. Instead, I took the checks home and then, a couple of days later, to the bank.

For a short while, I almost developed warm feelings toward Marcuvitz; it must have been the Stockholm syndrome. About a week after the closing, Marcuvitz called and suggested holding a celebration—a pizza party for the VCs and the whole company. The party was pleasant enough, and Marcuvitz wore a plaid shirt instead of his usual bad suit. My goodness, I mused, maybe he has a human side, after all. But just before dinner ended, Marcuvitz stood up, shook hands, and departed. He had stuck me with the bill. I thought, That's more like it.

CHAPTER FOUR

Vermeer, Fall 1994–Summer 1995: Making a Beautiful Machine and Preparing It for War

Then it was just a blur of eighty-hour weeks.
—Andy Schulert

If you're not having a bad week, you're not in a good start-up.
followed by: Vermeer—A Great Start-up!
—The third Vermeer T-shirt, by Tom Blumer, Peter Amstein, and Ted Stefanik

God is on the side not of the heavy battalions, but of the best shots.
—Voltaire

*R*eluctant as I was to turn away from the tranquility of first-round fundraising, we had a product to develop. Even before we got funded, with the engineers working out of their homes as I bounced around the country groveling to VCs, we did some amazingly good and very important work. We were *thinking.* As a result, when we finally moved into our offices, we hit the ground running, and we were running in the right direction. We had already designed, developed, and refined a demo, a strategy, an architecture, a prototype, a functional specification, and a development schedule.

Not that this was all neat and clean. In principle, and in the textbooks, software development is done via an elegant "waterfall" sequence. You proceed genteelly from product requirements to architecture to specification to design to scheduling to writing code. Unfortunately, the real world doesn't cooperate. Each activity actually depends on the others, and in our case they all kept changing, so we drove around the circuit several times, iterating everything. The Web's rate of change meant that we had to do this fast, taking the corners on two wheels, and soon we also had to just start coding it, ready or not. All of our analysis was informal—no bureaucracy, three-hundred-page documents, elaborate charts, or fancy software design tools. But the fact that we took the time to think carefully, deeply, and ruthlessly about the problem was vital to our success.

In fact, this process of analysis and design is a major determinant of success in high technology generally, not to mention of the quality of the products we must all use. Yet it's not widely discussed, even within the industry. This is a curious situation. The analysis of software engineering found in Frederick Brooks's 1975 classic, *The Mythical Man-Month,* has in many regards not been improved upon, in part because it is a work of genius. But although Brooks revised his book in 1995, it isn't current. More seriously, Brooks's book and the many lesser works devoted to the subject confine themselves to technical and managerial issues. There is little discussion of how strategy affects software design and development. Yet these issues are at the heart of Netscape's mistakes, Microsoft's success, and the behavior of the industry. You have to design your strategy alongside your product; in fact, you have to design and build your strategy *into* your product. A devious mind is a major advantage; in this domain nice guys definitely finish last. On the other hand, the best strategy in the world is worthless if you don't get your product done, so you need great implementation too.

Our development process, which ran from late 1994 through September of 1995, was an unusually clean example of how a start-up designs and develops a new software product, whose success depends upon combining market analysis, demanding technical design, and complex strategic and business considerations. It's quite an art form, grand strategy of a high order; when you do it right, you're in rarefied air. Nobody gets it completely right . . . but we came damn close, and Microsoft's conduct shows that they fully understood and appreciated what we did. In describing how we designed and built FrontPage, I would therefore like to convey how complicated, difficult, and fascinating this process is, how big the payoff is to being clear-headed and tough-minded, and how completely you slit your own throat if you blow it.

In our case, we did well in part because we educated one another. Randy, Andy, Peter, and many of our engineers proved not only brilliant in technical matters, but astoundingly quick studies in strategy and business. To be sure, there were certainly tensions. I clashed with some of the engineers over the importance of strategy and patents, and there were also disagreements among the engineers about the relative importance of technology versus appearances. At first Andy Schulert's attitude was technology-dominated, UNIX-y, and academic; he felt anything except creating the best product in purely technical terms was vulgar, unfair, and/or a waste of time. Patents were evil, broad patents intended to block competition were especially evil, and demos of user interfaces were smoke-and-mirror tricks. But while we sometimes argued, the engineers always got it; I never had to say anything twice. On the contrary, they often had to repeat themselves to *me,* because they picked up strategy faster than I learned technology. This proved yet again that in an ambitious start-up, it is tremendously valuable to hire adults and to hold out for the very best. One of the many now-famous aphorisms in Fred Brooks's book is that the best professional programmers are ten times as productive as poor ones. I would say that if anything he underestimates. Another of Brooks's aphorisms, taken from a French restaurant in New Orleans: "Good cooking takes time. If you are made to wait, it is to serve you better, and to please you."

Of course, we were in a serious hurry. But we were also extremely ambitious, which meant that we couldn't afford the quick cheap shot. We wanted to build a large, highly profitable company. This translated into a simple goal that is very difficult to achieve: becoming the proprietary industry standard in our market. In designing and building FrontPage, we therefore wanted: (1) to create the best possible product, reaching the broadest possible mass market, with the best and most flexible architecture to accommodate future requirements; (2) to create "lock-in" to our product and architecture so that neither users nor the industry could easily switch to a competitor; (3) to maximize our proprietary control and value relative to other firms and segments of the industry; (4) to make it difficult for anyone to clone us, which would allow them to undercut our price and potentially wrest control of the standard from us (as Microsoft is doing to Netscape and RealNetworks); and (5) to do this cost-effectively, within a schedule considered impossible by normal standards.

Notice that designing the best possible product was only one goal among five. These five objectives translated into a complex list of strategic, business, and technical issues, goals, decisions, and trade-offs. For example, we needed to decide how we related to the other segments of the industry. While we were primarily concerned about Netscape and Microsoft, there were many others: AOL, the Internet service providers, the emerging Web hosting industry, second-tier vendors of Web servers and browsers, various minor tools competitors, and freeware such as the Linux operating system and the Apache Web server.

In our case, developing the best possible product and covering the broadest possible market happily coincided, for the most part, with our strategic and financial objectives. It doesn't always work that way; I would argue that for Microsoft, the two goals are sometimes antithetical. Even for us, there were some trade-offs, mostly financial but sometimes strategic. I'll begin by describing the "pure" work we did to understand the market, what the product should do, and the kind of architecture and technology this implied. Then I'll circle back to our strategy and how it affected our product and architecture.

MAKING A NEW MACHINE I: IMAGINING THE MACHINE

What functions should our product perform, and how should these functions appear to users? Once we decided that we were in business, these were among the first questions we had to answer. They were hard questions, and the obvious ways to find the answers to them would have been wrong. You might think, for example, that we could find a bunch of Web developers and ask them. Or we could collect a bunch of PC users into a focus group and ask *them*. Both of those things would have been fruitless at best. The only Web site developers in existence, and there weren't many, were academic UNIX nerds, i.e., exactly the opposite of the normal person who was our target market. This was a great danger for another reason: software products are designed and written by *programmers,* who often impose their own highly technical preferences and mind-set on the products they develop for mere mortals. One reason for administering the Charles test to our engineering candidates was to minimize this problem. As for gathering a focus group of normal people, no way. In 1994, normal people had never heard of the Web, much less used it, and the services we envisioned didn't exist. Remember, commercial Web services were still against the law.

So we guessed. Some engineers have great intuition about user interfaces and end-user preferences; we tried to find them. Peter Amstein is fabulous, as was Rob Mauceri, who arrived a few months later; Randy turned out to be quite good too. We all looked at the available models, none of which fit perfectly. We borrowed ideas from word processors, Windows, the Mac, desktop publishing products, database development tools, and even software development tools. Then we thought, discussed, and thought some more. And then Peter did a demo. The initial impetus for Peter's superb demo, actually, was to help the VCs understand our product. But we quickly realized that it also helped *us* understand our product. Then we had to match our ideas against what was technically feasible. The architecture of the Web didn't allow us to do just anything we pleased.

Randy and Andy started working on technical requirements and feasibility, while Peter concentrated on the user interface. Andy also worked on the server-side architecture. Throughout the summer and early fall, the four of us designed the product. I was the least technical of the four, but the business vision was mine, so I participated in defining market requirements, user interfaces, and functionality. I would conceive of new services—yellow pages advertising services, bulletin boards where users could post and respond to messages, electronic newspapers, customer support services, etc.—and then I would ask what it would take to develop these services, and what kind of tools would help. I also thought of new functions, such as automatically generating an e-mail based on a browser request, or copying a Web service onto your PC, and asked the same questions.

It was all too easy for me to have ideas, since I didn't have to write any code, and I drove everyone slightly nuts. But when I look back at the material from that period, I am amazed at how complete our vision became. There are very few Web services that we didn't think of, including many that are only now being developed. We also conceived of many features that are only now being put into FrontPage. Our biggest misjudgment was to underestimate the length of time it takes to implement such a rich set of ideas.

Peter played a more visible role than Andy in the early days, in part because his work *was* visible; you could look at his demo screens. He's quick, funny, and likes an audience; he was the star demonstrator of his own demo. Peter is also a superb developer and manager in his preferred domain—personal computers (i.e., not servers), Windows applications, graphics, user interfaces. He has excellent business sense, and while his software was always well designed and well written, he was willing to compromise when commercially necessary. He had no problem at all with patents, proprietary control, or ruthless thinking about how to compete, win, and make money.

Peter wrote the demo using a Microsoft tool called Visual Basic, which lets you build slick user interfaces quickly. The original version was only about five hundred lines of code—basically just a sequence of screens—and it took Peter only three weeks. Over time, as we received feedback and refined our product ideas, the demo evolved quite a bit, in ways that helped our design effort considerably. In fact, the demo was an important development milestone. It brought the product down from the realm of pure ideas to that of real software. It put a stake in the ground and made us ask: Well, does *this* look right? It also became a terrific recruiting device. Instead of talking about our plans in the abstract, we'd show the demo to candidates and watch their reactions. Most good people got it immediately. We used it for more than six months, well into the spring of 1995, when we started discussions with potential partners.

Andy understood that we needed a demo to get funded, but he regarded the exercise with distaste. He thought that mock-ups of cool screens done with Visual Basic were useless toys, a rather irritating distraction to real work. He was wrong about that, as I think he now realizes. But he also thought that I didn't sufficiently appreciate the importance of what he, Andy, was doing, and for a while he was *right* about that.

Our first-generation product design was done by mid-September 1994, when Peter's first demo was ready and we gave our first VC presentation to Andy Marcuvitz. At that time, we planned to release the product in February 1996. But we were still confused about one thing. While we were very clear on developing a product for end-users, we also wanted an upper tier of the product to provide database connectivity, custom scripting, and support for electronic payments systems; realistically, however, only "power users" and professional programmers would be able to use these functions. This distracted everyone, made the product more complex, lengthened our development schedule, raised our costs and price, and called into question our ability to use mass market distribution channels.

By Thanksgiving, when we had gone around the design cycle again, we had fixed those problems. We brought in our delivery date from February 1996 to September 1995, so we could make the fall product release and trade show cycles. In order to achieve this we eliminated the high-end functions, deferring them to some later release of a "professional" product; we thereby gave ourselves much more flexibility on costs, price, and distribution channels and allowed ourselves to focus completely on end-users. This helped greatly. In fact, we even *added* end-user features, such as the ability to create discussion groups, when we were already writing code. We were able to do this only because we had developed a superb underlying *architecture,* which is a subject in itself.

MAKING A NEW MACHINE II: ARCHITECTURE FOR THE SHORT TERM AND THE LONG HAUL

The popular image of the software industry is dominated by stories of how people like Steve Wozniak, Jerry Yang, Paul Allen, and Bill Gates got their start, and sometimes got wildly rich, as solitary kids hacking software in garages and college dorms. There is some truth to this image, but early academic or prototype software is typically quite simple; a single brilliant hacker can do it just by pulling a few all-nighters. The resulting code is as quirky as it is brilliant and is unusable for commercial mass production. If you try to do a real product that way, you get a mess that is impossible to disentangle—hence its pejorative name, "spaghetti."

Thus, writing a clever piece of code that works is one thing; designing something that can support a long-lasting business is quite another. Commercial software design and production is, or should be, a rigorous, capital-intensive activity. Software products should be based on a broad, deep structure that can support much more than whatever the product contains at any given time. In addition to code that works, you need documentation, help functions, error handling, multi-platform support, and multiple languages. You also need an underlying *architecture* that allows you to add and change features, purchase and integrate external software components, and allows other software vendors to make their products talk to yours, add customized widgets to it, or embed your product inside something larger of their own. A good architecture, one that will carry you for a decade's worth of unpredictable technology and market changes, takes months to develop. But if you skip this step, as Netscape did, you have made a truly Faustian bargain.

So if you want to be around for a decade, you need to understand that by the fifth or sixth release of your product, it will probably be twenty times bigger than the first release. And the first commercial release has to be ten times larger than a prototype. Another of Fred Brooks's aphorisms is that a software *product* takes three to nine times as much effort as a program written for private use. He's right. For example, the first freeware Web browsers, those written by Tim Berners-Lee at CERN and the kids at NCSA, were a few thousand lines of source code each. This means they each took a few person-months to write. This, in turn, means that they required no real management, no coordination, no serious testing. But they weren't commercial grade, in the senses I listed above. Netscape's first commercial browser was one hundred thousand lines of code. For various reasons that number probably overstates its real complexity; still, it was surely at least five times the real size and difficulty of NCSA Mosaic. Of course Netscape was in a rush; they were starting from scratch, playing catch-up with all the Mosaic licensees. In such a situation it's tempting to build just what you need right then, instead of making your code bulletproof and planning ahead.

The problem with this is that these systems start getting ferociously complicated. It comes time to fix a mistake, add a feature, replace something, and you discover that everything is connected to everything else in ways you can't even begin to understand. Because you're doing something more ambitious than the initial academic prototype, it's big enough that you need to partition it across a team. The members of the team need to have a clear idea of how their work relates to everyone else's, and they need to be able to communicate to the testers whose job it is to find errors. Otherwise, you give the patient a kidney transplant and his heart suddenly fails; then you give him a heart drug, but that makes his lungs collapse. You don't know why, and you're screwed.

And then the future comes, and you're *really* screwed. Later releases of the product inevitably are more complex, because they must continue to support previous versions while adding new capabilities. (As stated above, Netscape's first browser was one hundred thousand lines of code; four years later, their

Communicator product was *three million* lines.) You discover that the original developers have quit or been promoted or have forgotten what they did, and it's time to keep up with the competition by adding new features, supporting more platforms, translating into Japanese, and so forth. The engineering team has to quadruple in size. You start discovering things like three different groups need to change the same piece of code, and each set of changes causes problems for the others, and nobody else can test their work until that piece of code is stable, so a hundred people twiddle their thumbs for a week. Or you want to use an existing function for some new purpose, but you can't isolate it from everything else, so you have to write it all over again. This not only means that you have the extra time and cost of writing and maintaining twice as much code, but you probably have to ensure that the two versions work exactly alike, which they almost certainly won't. (This happened to Netscape when they tried to compete with us.)

With each successive release, these problems get worse. By the time you're on your fifth release, the decision to do your first product the quick and dirty way has probably cost you ten times what it originally saved. (The first chapter of *The Mythical Man-Month* is entitled simply "The Tar Pit.") A program like Microsoft's Windows 98 is tens of millions of lines of code. The company employs more than thirty thousand people, and probably more than a thousand of them wrote some piece of Windows 98. Probably another several thousand people who worked on previous versions no longer even work there anymore. Nobody can keep that much complexity in their head or hope to manage it effectively. So you need an architecture that says to everyone, Here's how this thing works, and to do your part, you need to understand only these five things, and don't you dare touch anything else.

So we did an architecture. By current standards, the first release of Front Page was a moderately complex software product: it had about two hundred thousand lines of source code, written in C++, the standard "high-level" language for PC software development. This source code "compiled," or expanded out, into a million lines of machine instructions, or "object code." The real complexity of the product was greater, because its functionality was novel and unusually rich; this wasn't the twentieth word processor, spreadsheet, or browser. FrontPage was by no stretch of the imagination something that a couple of kids could cobble together in a garage. By the time we shipped product, our engineering team had grown to about twenty people, most of whom ranked among the best programmers anywhere; our documentation, testing, and customer support people were extremely good too.

Andy Schulert started our architecture, in part because he was the first person we hired and for a couple of months there was nobody else. Later, he was in charge of the server side of our product, which is all technology and no showy demos or screens. He is a quiet, serious, tightly wound guy who stays in superb physical shape; he was in his late thirties in 1994, a few years older than Peter. He had been burned by suits, and he didn't like them or anything they stood for. His idealism coexisted with a cynical humor that is common in the industry and that often showed up in terse, wry comments.

But Andy is also brilliant, rigorous, completely honest, and ridiculously disciplined. I gradually learned that Andy underpromised and overdelivered and that there was usually about a hundred times more going on inside his head than came out of his mouth. If he thought the rest of us were wrong, he might say so, but quietly and just once, and sometimes he didn't bother, which could be a problem. He'd been through more start-ups than I had, for instance, and he later told me that he thought my initial valuation demand was ridiculously high, which was true. Why didn't you tell me? I asked. Well, it was your company, he said, and you were the suit, I didn't think the price was my business. Thus at first, because Andy was not very communicative, and because I was insensitive, I found Andy opaque, even difficult. I began to fear that he wasn't doing much. Boy, was I wrong. Luckily I eventually figured that out.

What Andy was doing in his first couple of months, when I wondered whether he was doing anything, was laying the groundwork for our future. Andy later admitted that he felt out of the loop through that first summer. For a while Andy didn't really have colleagues to talk to, because he was the only server technologist. He was working at home alone, was tight for money, and even thought about quitting. I fault myself for not paying more attention to this, another problem that was compounded by my decision not to spend money for a temporary office. Andy wouldn't have been so isolated, the team could have begun bonding earlier, and I could have watched everyone's body language. Instead, I started getting on Andy's case.

Andy's laconic style didn't help. He was doing brilliant work, but was disinclined to waste time explaining it. We had meetings, of course, but a typical exchange would be:—What did you do this week, Andy?—Well, I'm pretty sure we can use HTTP for remote Web development.—Oh? Anything else?— No, that's pretty much it. *Those are very close to exact quotes.* What I didn't know at the time was that this was a little like:—What did you do today, Albert?— Well, I'm pretty sure $E = mc^2$.—Oh, anything else?—No, I don't think so . . .

WHAT ANDY, PETER, AND RANDY DID THAT SUMMER AND FALL

The architecture that emerged was a collaborative effort by Andy, Peter, and Randy. Other key engineers, including Rob Mauceri, Ted Stefanik, and Tad Coburn, started contributing as they joined. My involvement was essentially nonexistent, with the exception of describing strategic requirements that the engineers folded into the technology. But I want to explain what they did, because it gave us major competitive advantages.

One goal of good architecture is to enable systems to be partitioned so that people can work effectively in parallel, their progress can be measured periodically, and everyone can finish at the same time. FrontPage was therefore divided into the client, or tool, side—the PC application—and the server side, which was the back-end engine that talked to Web servers and implemented the tool's orders. Early on, these were separated by a clean interface so that the client and server teams could design, and then develop, their systems independently. In turn, the client side was divided into three major parts: the HTML editor, the Web site manager (called the FrontPage Explorer), and the to-do list, which provided administration functions. Similar subdivisions were made on the server side, so that our engineering team of over a dozen people could work on the same product at the same time. Even smaller subdivisions were made so that their work could be measured weekly against our plan and schedule. This also paid off in dividing up the later work of testing and bug fixing. Finally, the architecture helped us to use other people's software components, so that we wouldn't have to reinvent things that already existed.

But architecture is not ideology or religion, either. We made some impure, politically incorrect, but extremely wise decisions. For years, many graphical PC software products were developed first on the Mac. But that era had clearly ended. Microsoft had won the war, and also had better software development tools. So we did Windows first. The Mac would come in time, and we never even planned a version for UNIX clients. But from day one, the FrontPage client ran on Windows 3.1, Windows 95, and Windows NT. By targeting Microsoft operating systems first, we saved months relative to Netscape's early practice of developing simultaneously for Windows, the Mac, and UNIX. Sometimes, architecture is just saying no.

At other times, good architecture means saying yes even when you would prefer not to. Our tool had to enable development of good Web sites without any programming. For example, our vision was that if a FrontPage developer wanted a site to include a text-search capability, they would just bring up a dialog box and mouse-click through a series of options. That's all: just click on some choices, and the Web site would be indexed automatically and would become searchable. We could easily get a decent text-search engine, and it wouldn't be hard to write a layer of code that would interpret mouse clicks and order the engine to behave as the user requested. So far, so good.

But now we come to what this implied. I've already mentioned that Front-Page has two parts, a PC "client" side and a "server" side. This was necessary, but not nice. Our lives would have been far simpler if we could have written just a shrink-wrapped PC application like Word. The problem was that, no matter what Andy and Randy tried, Web technology dictated that many of the functions we wanted to provide, like text-search engines, had to run alongside the Web server. In part, this is just the way servers work. In part, it was the result of our extremely ambitious goals. In part, it reflected the fact that Berners-Lee had not designed the Web architecture with mere mortals or PC applications in mind. Furthermore, his architecture was incomplete, with the result that every Web server was subtly different in those areas where he had not specified a standard. Thus to make our product work, Andy and Randy quickly realized, we needed a "client-server" architecture, with a substantial piece of our product running on the server side. Andy and Jim Gettys concluded that it would be okay for the client and server components to communicate using the Internet protocol, TCP/IP, and the Web protocol, HTTP, so at least we didn't have to reinvent those. *But there had to be a server side.*

Not to mince words, this was a bitch. First, it threatened our ease-of-use goal. The linchpin of our strategy was to democratize the development of on-line services, which made it important that the development tool be a normal PC application residing on the *client,* so anyone who could use PCs could use our software. Conversely, most servers are complex systems that PC users don't understand and in most large organizations are not even permitted to touch. Next, there were platform and Web server compatibility problems. There existed a half dozen different Web servers, each with unique access controls, image map formats, and so forth, and Web servers were commonly found on computers running on a dozen operating systems: several varieties of UNIX (including Linux, the freeware version), NT, the Mac OS, and occasionally Windows. One solution would be to integrate the necessary FrontPage server software into every Web server, but we couldn't imagine that Web server vendors would let us do that. Microsoft certainly wouldn't, and we didn't think Netscape would either; it would lessen their proprietary control. Furthermore, by the time we could ship our product, there would already be a large number of Web servers in operation; we wanted access to them too, as part of our market.

That was the mess we gave Andy. He couldn't make the problem go away. But he developed an architecture of extraordinary elegance that would let FrontPage software colonize the world of existing Web servers and effectively turn them into FrontPage servers, without any cooperation from the Web server vendors. Furthermore, in the best tradition of judo, he turned many of the difficulties of the situation into advantages. Once you conceded that you *needed* a server side, you could make it do some extremely cool things.

Andy took advantage of a feature that the NCSA had added to the Web architecture—the "common gateway interface," or CGI, which lets Web servers connect to external software programs. It is the same on all Web servers and is something that server vendors don't dare to change. Andy worked out a method by which our server software, which we called "server extensions," could talk to any Web server through CGI. Once our server software was installed, whenever that Web server got a signal from a FrontPage client, it would automatically activate the FrontPage server functions. We didn't need the cooperation of server vendors. Any "Webmaster" could install our server extensions on any Web server without affecting other server functions.

Even better, Andy's architecture gave FrontPage features that no other tool could match. FrontPage became the only development tool to allow remote development across the Internet. A corporate Web site, for example, may include data from many parts of the company, like press releases updated by the PR department, product announcements maintained by marketing, graphics done by an advertising agency, or repair manuals maintained by customers service. FrontPage makes it possible for people scattered throughout the company, or even outside the company (if they have permission), to contribute to any Web site anywhere. Access controls keep out unauthorized developers. You can develop remotely over the Internet, any private TCP/IP network, or both. You can even come in over the public Internet, pass through the "firewall" server that maintains corporate security, access the internal network, and update an *internal* corporate Web server. We applied for broad patents on these and other features, several of which have already been awarded.

Andy's architecture was not only elegant, but also robust. You could push it hard and it would still work beautifully. We added things, changed things, and forced every limit; Andy's technology never broke. For example, we realized one day that we could put a Web server on the same PC as the client application. In fact, we could include a personal copy of the whole server infrastructure—a Web server plus our server extensions—as a standard part of the PC product. This "personal Web server" would bring huge benefits. You could use your PC to develop Web sites even when you weren't connected to the Internet—using your laptop on an airplane, for example. You could operate a Web site from your own desktop PC. Or you could set up another PC, install FrontPage on it, and run a Web service from it without having to touch the centralized corporate server system at all.

Furthermore, the server extensions allowed us to save people enormous amounts of work. The Web makes it possible to use portions of images as hyperlinks, for example, but you had to write out the image map design by hand. Furthermore, different Web servers store image maps in different formats. Peter had the terrific idea of a software widget in our client application that lets you simply draw on a picture with your mouse; FrontPage automatically translates those instructions into a Web image map with an appropriate hyperlink. Andy's server software handles the rest and hides the differences between various Web servers, so the user of the PC application never even knows it's an issue. In fact, Andy's architecture allowed us to hide most major differences between Web servers (access control, for example, is another un-standardized area). This meant that services developed from FrontPage could be easily transported across different Web servers and operating systems, while traditionally developed services can't. That story was repeated over and over. Furthermore, as I've said, the architecture wasn't just technically excellent; it also supported some extremely important strategic and business goals.

My early experience with Andy illustrates a risk peculiar to high technology. I'm not a true technologist, but I know much more about software than most nontechnical executives, and I understand the importance of good architecture. Yet I still underestimated the value of what Andy was doing for a while. Most marketing MBAs don't have a clue, and that can be very dangerous if they become CEO of a company. It is astonishing how often executives underesti-mate the importance of technology in general, and of good architecture and code in particular. Four prominent examples were IBM under Akers, Apple under Sculley, Netscape under Barksdale, and Lotus under Jim Manzi.

Doing the Prototype: Trust, but Verify

No matter how well you understand something intellectually, you always learn much more by getting your hands dirty and doing it. In mid-October 1994, therefore, we decided to create a prototype of FrontPage. Andy thought this was a very good idea: a prototype is not a product, but it is real working software, not a smoke-and-mirrors demo. Basically, the engineering team stripped away gnarly details and set themselves the task of writing just enough code to prove that our basic concept was feasible, and to learn what we needed to change. The objective was to build FrontPage server extensions sitting on top of a Web server and then to write client software that would let someone use a PC to create Web pages that could be uploaded to the server. We wanted the client to have a WYSIWYG editor ("what you see is what you get")—some-thing that would feel like a word processor and would create HTML pages that would look exactly as they would appear on the Web. We then had to show that we could transfer the new pages to the server over the Web and access them from another client equipped with a standard Web browser. And every-thing had to work over the current Web and Internet. The goal was to do it in five weeks.

The team plunged in with amazing energy and enthusiasm. Peter hadn't moved east yet, and he and Scott Drellishak did the client side from California. We had originally thought we would just buy a WYSIWYG HTML editor, but to our surprise, no one had produced one yet. There were lots of editors, but they were all primitive and bad. Scott, who is wonderful, got the editor assignment. He was still in his mid-twenties at the time, ponytailed, the classic California software engineer—a total stranger to physical exercise and clothing stores, with a stratospheric IQ and an encyclopedic knowledge of *Star Trek,* alien cultures, and all technical gadgets. At the same time, his tastes and education are quite broad, and his wit is quick, dry, and biting; I felt its sting more than once, always deservedly. In less than a month, he produced, single-handedly, a real WYSIWYG editor; it was primitive, but it worked. By this time, I had come to take it for granted that I could make utterly unreasonable demands on the engineers, and that whenever they said they would do something, what they actually did was five times better.

Andy wrote the server software with some conceptual help from Jim Gettys. Gettys was technically superb and contributed some important ideas, but this was the project that confirmed that he couldn't do real work. In the last week or so of the project, Andy shanghaied Tom Blumer to help him out but otherwise did it all himself. Tom had joined the server team in early November, but I had drafted him to work on patents. Tom was quiet, very smart, a former graduate student in mathematics who had also written extensively, was the principal inventor on three patents, and had run his own software company. One day Andy called him and said that he needed Tom to write a fairly complex piece of code in Tcl, a Web scripting language, and in a hurry. Tom went home with a five-hundred-page book on Tcl and told his wife that he had to learn it that night. Tom later reminisced, not at all fondly, that during his first months at Vermeer, he came home at least a half dozen times with another thick textbook—on HTTP, HTML, C++, CGI scripting, all things that he hadn't worked with before—and told his increasingly skeptical wife that he had to learn it overnight. Tom is great, or we would never have hired him, but for some years he had managed programmers instead of doing coding himself. Furthermore, he was pulled between the demands of patent work for me and real work for Andy. The first few months were hard on him, but he adjusted well and always with dry good humor.

No one claimed that the prototype was beautiful software. We hadn't even finished the detailed product design yet, and Andy was still working out his ideas for the Web server extensions. And we didn't care if it was modularized, componentized, or followed any of the other rules of well-architected software. We just wanted to see if we could make the basic idea work. At a certain point, the team said it would. So, just to add some excitement to life (but with the team's agreement), I scheduled a prototype demonstration for the venture capitalists. Wade Woodson, the VC from Sigma, was going to be in Boston right after Thanksgiving; this was still at the most critical stage of fund-raising, before

Sigma made their offer. The prototype was supposed to be done that week, so naturally, I suggested that he come and see it. That was a bit reckless, because the prototype wasn't finished yet. Wade said he'd be delighted to come.

A few days before the scheduled meeting with Wade, Peter and Scott flew out from California with the client code and stayed at my apartment. We allowed a couple of days to integrate and test the client and server software working together—not much room for error there. We used Jim Gettys's house for the demonstration because he had the computers we needed. Peter remembers that they actually cheated a little, although I didn't even know it at the time. After struggling with Web protocols for a few hours, the team dialed up the server we were using through a Netscape browser and "sniffed" the precise command sequence that was used. Then they hard-coded precisely that command sequence into Scott's editor. From that point, the Web server "happily and obliviously," in Peter's words, did whatever we told it to do. Working through those protocols for our real product took work. Peter also remembers that Andy was characteristically bored and impatient much of the day. *His* stuff worked fine, of course; it was the client guys who were having all the problems. By the end of the first day, the prototype wasn't quite running, but the guys were confident enough that they didn't work through the night. The meeting with Wade Woodson was the next day at two o'clock in the afternoon. The team reassembled at Jim's house that morning, and had everything working within a couple of hours. The challenge for the rest of the morning was just to keep their hands off.

Randy and I showed up in the afternoon. We had not verified that things were working before Wade showed up; we were trusting that all would be well. Wade had already met most of the team, so we ran through the introductions quickly and got on with the show. We stood and watched Scott use a PC to create some Web pages. His HTML editor obviously wasn't very sophisticated, but it was clearly a genuine WYSIWYG editor—he could center text, change its size, edit sentences. Wade suggested a couple of lines of text to verify that the Web page was real. When Scott finished, he published to a remote Web server running on another machine right next to him; the two were connected to each other over the Internet. This was no smoke-and-mirrors trick; you could see the modem dial up an Internet access number and then watch Scott locate the server. Then Scott closed down the client and opened a Netscape browser, went onto the Internet, surfed to our server, and opened those same Web pages. Then he did it a second time from a different PC using a different Internet service provider. Then he showed that the browser let us navigate around our new site just like any other Web site.

Seeing the prototype produced a rare moment of affection between myself and Frank Germano. I was quite properly awed. Frank saw my reaction, read my mind, and grinned. "No, Charles," he said, "we can't sell it."

Wade was impressed too. He later told me that the prototype did indeed help clinch Sigma's decision to fund us. But he said it wasn't the prototype itself that was decisive, impressive as that was. It was the obvious quality, collectively and singly, of the team we had put together. My own reaction was similar to Wade's. I was amazed at what they'd done, but I was even more amazed at how good they were. It was clear that there was a very unusual collection of energy, brainpower, and excitement in that room. I think the prototype effort was what turned us into a real company. The engineers had worked together intensely for six weeks, had produced something extraordinary—and they made it work the first time. Andy later told me that the experience convinced him to stay. After working so closely, intensely, and successfully with Peter and Randy, he decided that, yes, these guys were good, the product was going to happen, and it would be a big success.

A couple of days later, at a meeting at Matrix, Andy Marcuvitz gave Randy and me another of his humorless lectures. He said that he was glad we had done the prototype, but he certainly hoped we hadn't written throwaway code. His experience was that you lost a lot of time if you threw away a prototype, so he hoped we had done something good enough to use as a starting point for full product development. Andy Marcuvitz is a very bright guy, but it had been ten years since he'd written code, and both we and the Web were moving much too fast for us to freeze the design at that point. Furthermore, by now I realized that we had absolutely world-class people who were better engineers than Andy M. had ever been, so he had no business lecturing them. But instead of kicking him in the balls, we said yes absolutely, and then the engineers threw all the code away and started over, which was completely the correct thing to do.

MAKING A NEW MACHINE III: ARCHITECTURE AND SOFTWARE ENGINEERING FOR *PROFIT*

In parallel with analyzing what the product should look like, what it should do, and what its architecture should be, we were also considering our strategy and how that strategy should be integrated into the architecture. This was vital, in part because we anticipated an impending collision with Netscape and Microsoft, and in part because we were aiming so high—we wanted to dominate the entire tools market by becoming and controlling the industry standard.

Some of the engineers, especially Andy Schulert, were somewhat shocked, even offended, at how cold-blooded my thinking was. But the difference between first and second prize in these contests is usually at least a factor of ten, and we were up against a rough crowd. In the end, the Netscape people turned out to be amateurs. But Microsoft is another matter. They set the gold standard in strategy, and even though the quality of their purely technical work is uneven, they usually win because they're so clever, ruthless, and powerful.

You can't become the industry standard unless your product covers every major portion of the market. (Amazingly, Netscape didn't find this obvious.) This had many consequences for us, some of them quite complicated. Consider once again our need for server-side code. If we had just wanted to make a little money, we could have gotten ourselves a Web server and added just enough code to make our client software work against only that server. We could then have sold a two-part package, the client application plus a Web server; this would have been easier to design, and some people would have bought it. But then we couldn't have become the industry standard, for two reasons. First, with Netscape, good freeware products, and prospectively Microsoft all in the Web server market, there was no way we were going to dominate the whole Web server market, no matter how good our tool was. And second, the fact of selling our own Web server would undermine our status as an honest broker—for example, we'd be tempted not to support Netscape's features because they were a server competitor, or so people would reasonably suspect. Netscape and NaviSoft/AOL both made precisely this mistake, among others.

Thus, we needed an architecture that would allow our PC client to work with all of the major Web servers in the market. This would require more work, but once done would serve us well, both technically and strategically. The same issue came up in a number of other areas: security and encryption systems; text-search engines; scripting languages; database connectivity; electronic payment systems; and, of course, the operating systems that Web servers used. So at the cost of considerable time and effort, we designed an architecture that allowed us to support just about whatever platform turned out to win. In some areas, such as text-search engines, this turned out to be overkill; the market simply didn't care, and anything we supplied was fine. But in the case of Web servers and operating systems, this turned out to be critically important. The Web server market is fragmented, and Web servers run on a wide array of operating systems. The Apache freeware product, Microsoft's IIS, and Netscape's products each have substantial market share, and there are also many lesser contenders. We could cover them all. This also helped in our negotiations with strategic partners and software component suppliers, who realized that we had the technical ability to support them or not, and use their technology or not, as we chose.

Our goal of becoming the standard led to many other, more devious, strategic choices. I wanted FrontPage to be addictive, both to its users and to the industry infrastructure, so that once you started using our product, it would become very difficult to stop or to switch to a competitor. In the language of the industry, I wanted *lock-in*. Lock-in may not seem nice, but it is very, very important. Microsoft has lots of it. The techniques used to achieve it are subtle and vary according to the community you want locked in.

With end-users, we could generally do well by doing good. If we provided easy-to-use features that performed highly complex functions, end-users would have access to those functions only through our product—unless someone cloned us, a problem I'll discuss later. A harder problem, however, was to achieve lock-in with various parts of the industry: professional programmers who wrote additional functions on top of our product, Web hosters who based their businesses on it, large corporate customers. And we wanted to do this in ways that seemed innocuous and helpful.

So, for example, we made it easy to design a site that contained advanced functions that normally required programming. We did this by developing "bots," or little programs that we wrapped up neatly so that users could add them, delete them, change what they did, or move them around quite simply (just by clicking the mouse). We developed bots for date-stamping a page, for adding text-search functions, for creating navigation bars, and a number of other functions. But we also developed an architecture for bots and an API that allowed third parties—other programmers, large corporate customers—to use this architecture to create new, customized functions.

All this was cool for users, and it was also cool for us. As a FrontPage user, or as the operator of a Web site, once you started depending on bots in your Web site, you were hooked on FrontPage, because only FrontPage understands how to deal with bots. Furthermore, we designed the API and architecture so that you could easily post your new custom bots on a Web server, allowing users to download them to the client, so they could then design Web sites with them. Every large company could customize their Web sites in all kinds of cool ways. Programmers could sell packages of bots, the way people sell word-processing templates for legal documents. This would be cool for the industry, and again it would also be cool for us, for two reasons. First, it would allow our product to be customized for niche markets we couldn't reach directly, and second, it would once again get everyone, including programmers developing bots, hooked on FrontPage. We created analogous programming interfaces—APIs and software development kits, or SDKs—for creating FrontPage "wizards," software widgets that walk a user through a simple set of dialog boxes to create an entire Web site. It turned out that programmers and large customers were slow to use these APIs to create their own bots and wizards, so we didn't get much traction from them early on.

But we got lots of traction from remote development and the whole server side of our product, which also locked people into FrontPage. Once it became clear that it was absolutely necessary for us to have a big piece of technology on the server side, we used judo, or stealth if you prefer. We deliberately kept the interface between the client and the server extensions closed, so that you need our client to get access to those functions. We also patented that area heavily. If a Web hoster or corporate Webmaster wanted to offer remote development capability they needed to use both our client and the server extensions. Once used, they stuck; bots wouldn't operate otherwise. But for us, it was even better. We freed our customers from the lock-in that their Web server supplier would otherwise have acquired. Our server extensions hid the differences between Web servers and made services developed with our tools transportable across different Web servers for the first time. So we could argue that by adopting our technology, users actually gained freedom from lock-in; of course, what we were really doing was commoditizing Web servers and transferring proprietary lock-in from the Web server vendors to us.

We also wanted, at the same time, to subvert corporate controls on the use of Web servers and tools. We did this in two ways. First, we gave the server extensions away, a decision I'll discuss later, and second, as I mentioned earlier, we included a personal Web server and server extensions package inside the PC product itself. In this way, individuals could begin using our tool to design and operate small Web sites from PCs, either their own PC or another one set up just to provide the Web service. But this could occur without the approval or even the knowledge of corporate administrators. By the time they found out, we hoped, our technology would be so entrenched that they wouldn't be able to remove it. This hypothesis proved to be correct.

Finally, we designed our architecture so that we could not only use software components developed by others, but could switch them easily. We wanted to use, and did in fact use, a considerable number of other people's components rather than develop them ourselves. We wanted a dictionary and spelling checker for our HTML editor; file format converters, so that users could import word processor documents into the editor; a Web server to include inside the PC product; graphics format converters, so users could import images and place them on their Web sites; and so forth. These were generic objects; we could save a lot of time by using other people's work rather than recreating it. Our long-term plans, e.g., for database connectivity and scripting, required the use of even more complicated components.

But this posed several problems. First, we had to make sure that we didn't become locked in to anyone else. Second, things change and suppliers can go bankrupt; we needed to be able to switch if necessary. And third, we didn't want to pay royalties on anything. So we designed our architecture so that we could swap components and vendors easily. We also tried to purchase source code rights for a flat fee, or, even better, to use nonproprietary freeware code whenever possible. We generally succeeded. To his credit, Frank Germano was very tough on this.

These decisions would have been vital to our future had we needed to compete with Microsoft, or even Netscape, for a significant period of time. To see this, let us briefly consider what might have occurred if we had remained independent and Microsoft had either acquired someone else or developed its own product a year later.

Upon acquiring us, Microsoft promptly reduced the price of FrontPage by about 75 percent, even though the product faced no significant competition at the time. They could have done more than that. You see, as with airplanes, so with start-ups: takeoff is the most dangerous part of the trip. Suppose you are a start-up undergoing rapid growth via the success of your wonderful new product, which threatens the position of a larger rival. You might think this is a wonderful position to be in. Yes, if the big guy is incompetent, but otherwise, not necessarily. You have only one or two products; the incumbent has many. You are young and growing fast, which means you are consuming a lot of cash to fund your growth. In these circumstances, the incumbent can suddenly and dramatically reduce its prices—but only on those products that compete with yours. In these circumstances, paying royalties to someone on every copy of your product is very dangerous. The incumbent forces you to respond, which cuts off your cash supply, which forces you into layoffs, et cetera. In our genteel industry, an incumbent who employs this strategy is said to "perform a cashectomy" on you. Microsoft has performed at least two: one on Borland, in the early 1990s, and on Netscape more recently. So even though we initially set too high a price for FrontPage, I was quite aware that we needed maximum flexibility in the event that sudden reductions were required.

MOVING IN AND STARTING TO WRITE CODE

Although we reached an agreement with the VCs in the first week of January 1995, it was at least six weeks later that we actually moved into our new offices, the engineers starting writing code full-time, and we began to behave like a real company. First, as I said, we had to wait three weeks because Matrix had screwed us by putting us into their new fund, which hadn't closed yet. Then we had to wait until the offices were ready and we had a decent work environment. This was a combination of computer hardware, furniture, networking, telephones, leases, and other random details. When your industry is growing 25 percent per month you get very, very impatient with delivery services, personal computer retailers, NYNEX telephone installers, locksmiths, landlords, insurance salesmen, and electricians.

Moving into a real office made a huge difference, both for morale and productivity. Frank had found three possible sites; I chose the best and most expensive, which while by no means palatial was at least civilized. This was wise, even though it seemed slightly extravagant at the time (the lease was $100,000 a year), because we would be spending *a lot* of time there. Our office occupied the entire top floor of a six-story building directly across from Fresh Pond reservoir in Cambridge. We had taken it over from a bankrupt software company; we joked about holding an exorcism. We had about eight thousand square feet divided into enough offices to accommodate thirty to forty people comfortably. There was lots of light, a conference room, a small kitchen, and even a patio for which we purchased deck furniture and a barbecue.

I persuaded the Gardner Museum to make us a huge print of Vermeer's *The Concert,* which was and remains one of my favorite paintings in the entire world. It had been stolen several years before, and at this writing is still missing, but the Gardner had excellent archival negatives. The curators were extremely kind and patient; I still feel guilty that we never had a party to which we could invite them (the few parties we had were confidential). I had the print framed and hung it in our reception area facing the front door; it now hangs in the entry hall of the FrontPage business unit at Microsoft. We covered the office walls with whiteboards, which added a feeling of lightness. The bathrooms had showers, so people could take a break during the day and jog around Fresh Pond, which was nice, and a shopping mall right up the street supplied all the food, both junk and real, that we needed to keep going.

When we initially moved in, there were only sixteen of us and there was more than enough space. In addition to Randy, myself, Andy, Peter, and Frank, there were our two marketing and business development people, Ed Cuoco and Philip Werner; the other engineers we had already hired (Scott Drellishak, Tom Blumer, Ted Stefanik, Rob Mauceri, Stu Kolodner, and Tad Coburn); and our astoundingly efficient then-office-manager Manda Schossberger (who later moved into marketing) and her basset hound, Beethoven. But the engineering teams weren't complete, and as development proceeded we also needed to hire people for documentation, testing, and customer service. By the time we entered beta testing in late summer, many people were sharing offices. But until the product got done, the space crunch was low on the priority list. By March, the engineers were pushing themselves—and one another—very hard.

During February and March, I started to relax a little, comparatively speaking. I had to adjust to life without a consulting income while still paying my mortgage in California, but the atmosphere at work was comparatively calm. We were in our new space, we were bringing on more developers of very high quality, and it was now in the engineers' hands. They had a lot of code to crank out before we had a real product, but between Randy, Andy, Peter, and Frank, I had little doubt that we would get it done. Moreover, there wasn't anything *I* could do about it, so for a few weeks I could take it easy.

The first two post-funding board meetings with the VCs went smoothly enough. We developed a budget that made our $4 million last through the following November. The VCs, to their credit, told me that they thought I was planning to spend too much money. They were about half right; our initial budget was too heavy on overhead, but the VCs also forced us to cut back on long lead-time marketing expenses, such as PR, advertising, and reserving space at major trade shows. This would have proven a mistake if we had not been purchased. We also started our CEO search, which went through the summer and into the early fall, and which I'll discuss further below. But for a couple of months my life was quiet and fairly regular as the engineers dug into their work.

Then the shit hit the fan. For about a week, life looked ugly.

THE NAVISOFT SHOCK

Engineers often have the best grapevine. Sometime in late March, I got a call at home from Tom Blumer, who told me that a friend of his was a consultant to AOL and that they had a business unit called NaviSoft that was about to announce a product that sounded just like ours. NaviSoft was the company that Marcuvitz had asked about during our fund-raising, and which I had dismissed as unthreatening. I actually didn't have any real information about NaviSoft at the time, but I *had* heard a vague rumor that they might be too close for comfort. I hadn't worried about them since, because (a) they never made a sound, and (b) I thought it unlikely that a subsidiary of AOL could be a credible competitor. This turned out to be correct, but for a couple of days it didn't look that way.

I called Tom's friend, Rich Levandov. At first Levandov said everything was ultrasecret and he couldn't discuss it; then, once I got him started, I couldn't shut him up. He freely described what AOL was up to, and he flat-out scared the hell out of me. Later, I realized that Levandov tends to exaggerate quite a lot, but at first I didn't know this, and his analysis and description of NaviSoft were terrifyingly credible. NaviSoft had been founded by David Cole, who had been CEO of Ashton-Tate, which had developed dBase II, the first serious PC database software product. Cole had also spent some time as a VC. According to Levandov, NaviSoft had developed Web authoring tools and a strategy that, point for point, was almost exactly like ours, and they were coming to market *now*.

Levandov said that AOL realized that it had to cannibalize itself and intended to become the dominant Web-based supplier of both software and online services. AOL would turn the Web into "Microsoft's Vietnam." AOL was prepared to sell its new Web software completely independently of its online services, which would all be migrated to the Web, even though this would cannibalize AOL's proprietary business. AOL would win by making its browsers, tools, and Web servers ubiquitous. Since AOL's existing business was dominated by evening peaks and home users, it could easily offer inexpensive daytime business services. Levandov insisted that AOL would not make the mistake of limiting its software sales to AOL users, although AOL expected to obtain strategic advantage from its ability to offer both software and services using the same architectures and technology. AOL was fully committed to the strategy, Levandov said. The software would be very inexpensive (the tool might even be given away free), it was ready now, and it would be heavily promoted.

I tried not to panic, but only half succeeded. This looked bad. For about two days, I forgot the careful thinking I had already done about why AOL couldn't be a serious competitor. I wondered how they could do something so good, so complete, as fast as Levandov's description implied. I had never deluded myself that no one else could conceive of our business idea, but an important premise of our plan was that no one already had. Once we had gotten our funding and our engineers started cranking code, I thought we had six months' head start, maybe a year. If we didn't make any mistakes, this would be (barely) enough to establish a dominant position before Microsoft and/or Netscape offered real competition.

I talked with Randy and Ed Cuoco about what to do, and they panicked a bit too. We decided to beat NaviSoft to the punch by *announcing* first, and we wasted some time and money on a PR firm, putting out press releases and arranging press interviews. This was stupid of me. We didn't even have any real code, and I was (properly) still concerned about secrecy, so I wouldn't give away any details. The trade press hears sentences like "We've got something even better, but it's still a secret" about five times a day. Virtually nobody paid any attention to us, and for that reason, in the end, our failed announcement turned out not to do us any real damage.

But the real question about NaviSoft remained. What did they have, and how serious were they about selling it? The official NaviSoft launch was scheduled for the Seybold conference in Boston. We bought a couple of passes and showed up the instant it opened. We took turns visiting NaviSoft's booth repeatedly, watching their demos and then pulling their people aside to ask sharp, pointed questions in private, while concealing who we were. I felt awful doing this. This is the inevitable downside of the start-up adrenaline addiction:

when you compete, sometimes your job is to defeat another company whose engineers are just as nice, just as ethical, just as hardworking as yours. Often there's a large enough pie so that everyone can do well, but not always. I felt myself sympathizing with the very nice kids who ran the NaviSoft booth. They were just like us, working hard to bring out a product, worrying about their stock options, and now being grilled by a succession of extremely smart, vaguely hostile aliens who sure didn't act like enthusiastic potential customers.

I assuaged my conscience by thinking that at least they'd already been bought out in AOL stock. In fact, I think they may have gotten a bad deal, although I don't know. NaviSoft was sold to AOL for only $4 million in late 1994. Cole, NaviSoft's founder and CEO, became an AOL executive through the acquisition, probably with lots of AOL stock options, and he was wealthy anyway. But I doubt that NaviSoft's engineers got rich, although since they got AOL stock they probably did reasonably well. I didn't enjoy picking their brains, and despite its importance to us, I derived little pleasure from discovering the seriousness of their mistakes. Nonetheless, it was my job. We spent the morning cycling through the NaviSoft booth and began to debrief each other. As we analyzed what we had learned, we began to realize that, below the surface of their demo, NaviSoft had made some very serious mistakes indeed. But this took time; that first day I was still very tense.

The inevitable phone call from Marcuvitz came as soon as I got back to the office.

He was even colder than usual. —Hello, Charles, he said, I've just been to the NaviSoft booth at Seybold. Have you seen it? I said yes. —Well, what do you think? It looks exactly like your business plan. I replied that we were still analyzing it, and that while it looked serious we sensed that it was less dangerous than it initially appeared. —Well, we have a board meeting in a couple of days, and we'll certainly want to discuss it then. —Sure, I said. We hung up. It had not been a warm, caring conversation. Uncharacteristically, though, Andy M. had at least been sufficiently gracious (or diplomatic) not to remind me that he had asked me about NaviSoft once before; I'm certain he remembered.

But upon reflection, most of my original analysis still held; NaviSoft was unlikely to become a major threat. First, AOL faced serious, inherent problems even if Levandov was describing their strategy accurately and they had completely committed themselves to the Web. AOL could not portray itself as an honest broker. Its natural customers for Web tools and Web servers were primarily either competing Web hosters and Internet service providers, on the one hand, or potential corporate content providers on the other. These people simply would not trust AOL with their business, nor should they. Second, there was evidence that AOL was *not* completely committed to cannibalizing its business. There were many things AOL could have done to accelerate this process, and it wasn't doing them. Rather, it appeared that AOL wanted to add Internet service on top of its proprietary online service, in which case it would not, in fact, engage in scorched-earth cannibalization.

Third, their behavior at the Seybold conference suggested an astonishing lack of understanding about how to market software. The kids at the booth rarely gave the same answers twice to standard questions, such as what their product cost and how you could buy it. Even worse, they let you try out the product by using a live Internet connection *to their own corporate Web site*. They would play with their corporate Web site, destroying it before your eyes, which was truly crazy. During their period of greatest publicity, when they could expect the maximum traffic to their site, their own demos were constantly screwing it up.

Fourth and finally, there was a reason that NaviSoft was able to market a product so fast; it was bad, both technologically and strategically, and they had taken many of the shortcuts that we had decided against. Instead of targeting Windows with their tool, they had used a layer of cross-platform software that made their product easily portable to the Macintosh, but which prevented them from using many important features of either Windows or the Mac. Also, like us, they had realized that some important software had to reside on the server side. We had solved this problem for real, with Andy's server extensions, which could work with any Web server from any vendor. But NaviSoft had hard-wired their server code into their own Web server, which was a huge beast they planned to bundle with their tools. Their tools would therefore work fully only for Web sites running on their own Web servers.

But this shortcut doomed them. There was zero chance that AOL would dominate the Web server market or even have more than a small share of it. First, they had their "honest broker" problem. In addition, Netscape and Microsoft simply wouldn't let them dominate the market, and there were also excellent freeware Web servers that held considerable market share (and still do). Moreover, they had alienated the entire database software industry— Oracle, Informix, Sybase, and even Microsoft—by making a bizarre decision to bundle a new, untested, nonstandard database software product with their Web server. And finally, they hadn't gotten rid of programming. They proposed to "solve" the Web server programming problem through a national seminar tour in which they would teach Web server programming to the world, using one of the more arcane scripting languages. That was silly.

So although I was still pretty wobbly for a week or so, we rapidly concluded that on the available evidence, NaviSoft was a paper tiger. We had our story together by the board meeting and even managed to sound reasonably confident. But it was not a pleasant experience. Marcuvitz was skeptical and unpleasant; Barry Fidelman, the observer from Atlas, acted like he simply didn't understand, which may not have been an act. Wade seemed more relaxed, but I found that scant consolation at the time.

By the fall, NaviSoft had practically disappeared. But now some of our ideas were in play, and the experience confirmed that we had to get to market, *fast*.

THE PARTNER SEARCH AND UNDERGROUND EVANGELISM

By May, less than two months after the NaviSoft scare, we had our first working code—very fragile, not even beta-test quality, not even *alpha* quality for internal use, but enough to demonstrate what the real product would do. I decided it was time to start looking for, and educating, some potential partners and large customers. This turned out to be a remarkably frustrating exercise with no direct payoff, but it also turned out, indirectly, to be quite valuable. In addition to obtaining actual partnerships, I wanted to begin sensitizing the world, selectively, to our existence and to all the problems we solved. On the one hand, we didn't want to hand Netscape or Microsoft a copy of our product; on the other hand, I wanted to start serving notice that anybody interested in Web site development software should consult with us before doing anything rash.

I drew on all the contacts I'd built up in my years as a consultant, academic, and speaker and set up dozens of meetings. I targeted big companies in information-intensive businesses like financial services, Internet service providers, large content providers, proprietary online services that had announced they were moving toward the Internet, and influential firms with good contacts, such as investment banks and consulting firms. We presented to technology executives at Citicorp, Alliance Capital, Fidelity, S. G. Warburg, UPS, the New York Times, Time Warner, the Chicago Tribune and Tribune Media Services, U.S. Trust, the White House, Xerox, J. P. Morgan, Prodigy, the Chicago Board Options Exchanges, Bank of America, Refco, CompuServe, Dow Jones, Merrill Lynch, and probably two dozen other organizations I've forgotten.

Gradually, as time passed and our product stabilized, we started widening the circle. We started going after slightly more dangerous people, who were in closer contact with potential competitors: industry analysts, the organizations that ran the major industry conferences, computer systems vendors, and the like. On that crusade, we talked to Forrester, Meta, the Gartner Group, Esther Dyson, Dick Shaffer's Technologic Partners, Sun Microsystems, Intel, UUNet, John Young (who had just retired as CEO of Hewlett-Packard), Tim Berners-Lee and the MIT World Wide Web Consortium, and many others. We made nearly everyone sign NDAs, and we never left either code or documentation behind except with a few major potential partners, in order to minimize the rate and quality of information leakage. I'm sure there was some, but I think we did a pretty good job of maximizing impact while minimizing risk.

I usually went to these presentations with Randy, who did all of the technical presentations and demos, and sometimes with Ed Cuoco. Once in a while I brought Peter instead of Randy, although we were careful to minimize outside demands on Peter—delivering the code was his top priority. For the most part, the experience was an extraordinary lesson in the backwardness of big-company information-systems organizations and the executives who ran them. This was precisely why it was dangerous for Netscape to put all of its eggs in this basket: it would take most of these people *years* to get it. The movie clip that runs in my head is us sitting in a conference room at a huge, highly polished, expensive table, presenting to a group of overweight guys in their mid-fifties who'd spent thirty years working with COBOL and IBM mainframes and who hadn't learned anything since. There were exceptions: the White House had a smart woman who was in charge of a bunch of young interns, running what my friend Tom Kalil described as "an HTML summer camp." The Intel people were smart, although they screwed us. The people at J. P. Morgan and Merrill Lynch got it, too.

But most companies didn't. The Prodigy executives laughed indulgently when we said that the Web threatened their basic business model. They clapped us on the back, said we were spunky kids to say things like that straight to their faces, and told us, hey, good luck guys, stay in touch. Less than two years later they were virtually bankrupt. Then there was the UPS guy in charge of MIS who knew nothing about the Web and told us that his company had no Web sites. When he left the room, one of his assistants said to us that actually there were dozens of Web servers running inside UPS. "But you can probably see why we don't tell Frank very much," he added. Then there was the Citibank meeting. This was a surprise, because I knew some smart people there, and Citicorp was considered a technology leader in banking. But here they had blown it. There was exactly one serious, and disturbing question. "Why use you? Why don't we just wait until Microsoft does it for us?" asked one guy. But they knew nothing about the Web and showed no interest even when I told them that Wells Fargo was already way ahead. Later, my contact told me that nobody at Citibank was interested in anything unless John Reed, the CEO, was interested first; and that Reed was preoccupied with globalization and finding his own successor.

IBM called, and two guys came to our office for a demo. They liked it and asked if they could come back with more people. I said no, don't come back until you have a coherent story about what you're doing, and bring your checkbook. Ed Cuoco was appalled, but I said, Look, IBM just made a huge investment in Notes, which is non-Internet, and is half-owner of Prodigy, which is non-Internet and brain-dead. In the last two years IBM has laid off two hundred thousand people and it's still pushing OS/2, which everyone knows is dead. IBM could have bought the whole Internet industry with what it paid for Notes. So we'll deal with IBM if and when they can prove they're serious. We never heard from them again.

With Intel we had a different problem. I called a friend there, Les Vadasz, one of the original Hungarians from Fairchild, wealthy and powerful, who was in charge of external strategic relationships, including all of Intel's quite extensive venture investing. He said, yes, we're working on a lot of Internet stuff and we'd love to talk to you. As a matter of policy, however, he said, we don't sign other people's NDAs; we'll give you our NDA, you'll have to trust us. I said sure. Randy and I presented to a group in California including Vadasz, and then flew up to Intel Architecture Laboratories in Oregon, where their Internet development was based.

Randy and I presented to a crowd of smart, knowledgeable people, including Steve McGeady, who later testified in the Microsoft antitrust case. They said they were building a system that would have everything a small company needed to set up a Web site: an Intel-based computer, the NT operating system, a Web server, and—of course—authoring tools. Great, I thought. We presented for two hours, showing them our entire product. Then, at the very end, one of the technologists asked me, Could you get your server extensions working for the NaviSoft Web server? Sure, I said, but why would we want to do that? They're a competitor, they have their own proprietary tools, and in any case they don't have enough market share to justify the work. Well, he said, we've decided to bundle NaviSoft with our stuff, but we thought that maybe we could bundle you too. I was shocked, and the meeting ended quickly. I actually made another try later, to see whether they might be for real, but they weren't. Later, it dawned on me that the NaviSoft Web server came with that quirky new database product, Illustra. Intel was an investor in Illustra, and NaviSoft was one of Illustra's largest customers. So Intel had an indirect financial interest in NaviSoft, which my friend Les Vadasz had never mentioned—along with not mentioning that they had already chosen NaviSoft for their product. He hadn't quite lied; he just hadn't told me the important things. At the time, I was rather angry. But you live and learn. Intel is rough, the industry is rough, and this was business.

Nothing substantive came of our meetings with CompuServe either. They were a huge waste of time, but they also improved our morale. CompuServe was naturally one of the partnering tickets we had to punch, and I tried to contact them at least a dozen times with no luck. Then I got a call from a young CompuServe business development guy who had heard about us. He said they were moving into the Web in a major way and were looking for authoring tools. Randy and I flew out to their headquarters in Columbus, Ohio, and presented to a roomful of executives, including the ones who had never returned our calls. They loved our stuff and sent a team to Cambridge, who met the development team, learned more about FrontPage, and got even more excited. We flew out to Columbus again for another big meeting that ended with their telling us that we should do something together—something big.

But there were also some disquieting signs. Besides some weird technical decisions, they had just made this very foolish purchase of Spry. Dave Pool, the former CEO of Spry, was arrogant, greasy, egotistical, and had a big say in CompuServe's Internet strategy. If we joined CompuServe, we'd blow his cover and expose how dumb the Spry acquisition had been. CompuServe also raised some legitimate questions as to whether we could scale to their volumes. That was a fair issue, but our architecture was robust enough that some investment would have gotten us there, and we were by far the best show in town. I began to suspect that one of the technical guys dealing with us, who now works at Microsoft, was a little greasy too.

But talks proceeded, and they assigned a marketing executive, Dave Bezaire, to do a deal. We mapped out an arrangement that would let them use our server extensions and a CompuServe version of FrontPage, while assuring that their servers would still work with versions of FrontPage sold through normal channels. At the huge volumes they were projecting, our royalties would have been tens of millions of dollars. Bezaire asked if they could make an equity investment and get a board seat. I said no. We'd be willing to give them an exclusive license for a limited time, but we didn't want to be chained to any online service—especially not them. Well then, he said, could we buy you for $50 million or so? I replied that he could buy us, but we'd need more money than that. Bezaire indicated that they might be willing to do it.

Initially to my surprise, Randy was strongly opposed. He wanted more money for himself, but equally important he wanted the working-level engineers to get more. Randy sensitized me to this in a very important way. I had thought it would be hard to turn down a quick profit like that, but Randy and the engineers had a different view. They had each been through several start-ups and knew that only a few worked. So once they had a real winner, they weren't willing to sell cheaply. They were more than willing to put in the additional several years' work required to take us through an IPO in return for enough money to secure their families' future and their kids' educations. They were also properly skeptical of the value of CompuServe stock, a view I completely shared. But I realized how different my position was: I had much more stock than the other employees did, and even more important, I didn't have a family. From then on I became much more careful about how any potential deal would work out for *them*.

When Randy and I explained the potential CompuServe offer to the board, they were intrigued, a bit impressed, but skeptical. Fine, they said, but let's wait until there's a firm offer, and it's awfully early to cash in. But to their credit, Wade and Andy M. also indicated that the decision was primarily ours, because we knew the company and the market better than they did. As it turned out, the issue was moot. CompuServe began to implode; within days both its CEO and the CEO of its parent company, H&R Block, resigned. Bezaire finally called to say they'd decided not to proceed. Still, it was a sign that some big guys were beginning to take us seriously, and it got us a bit of respect from our investors.

THE ANALYSTS

Any remaining illusions I harbored about the workings of my industry were dispelled by our meetings with analysts, market research firms, and industry newsletters. Some, like Esther Dyson and the people at Technologic Partners, Jupiter, and Simba, were absolutely wonderful: fair, honest, responsive, straightforward. Others, however . . .

Most of the market research firms push you to buy their services in return for mentioning you in their reports. Individual analysts also cut private deals, a practice that seemed so widespread that the companies must know about it. For example, one of our first meetings was at Forrester Research. We gave the guy a demo, and he said it was cool, but of course a lot of other people are doing the same thing. The first time you hear that, you go, Oh God, how can we find out who he means. But I was learning by now. The guy was probably lying; it was a trick to get *us* to tell *him* if we had any competitors. Then came: Well, I'd like to write you up, but I think you need to clarify your message, so how about if I do a few days' consulting for you first? I stayed diplomatic and said that it was still a little premature for us to think about marketing. He responded, Well, would you consider me for your CEO, or maybe marketing VP? A few days of consulting in advance would be a good way for us to get to know each other. This guy was *really* greasy. Sure, I said, we'll give you a call when we're ready for that. Outside, Randy asked me in a worried tone if I was for real. I burst out laughing. No, Randy, I said, I don't want to have to bathe that often, that guy's truly filthy. At Gartner, the VP we met with gave us a long lecture demonstrating how little he knew and then suggested he might be able to slot us into their conference, but their services started at $15,000 per year.

We had to reengage with these clowns when it was time for our product launch in October. You always see gushing analyst white papers as part of the press package when a new product comes out. We needed one too. Well, it turns out that you *buy* them. We negotiated with several firms. Aberdeen wanted $16,000, preferably in stock, but Seybold would do it for $15,000 in cash. So we used Seybold, who sent us a nice man who wrote exactly what we told him to. I didn't like it, but everyone made it very clear that this was standard practice, that it was necessary for us, and that I should keep my mouth shut and stay out of the way. So I did.

Almost There

The developers got the alpha product out in June—they met every schedule we set, which is extremely unusual in software. Andy Schulert later told me that he didn't think we had a chance in hell of finishing by October. The developers were under terrific pressure, particularly because we were still making some major decisions as late as May. Fairly late, we added "wizards," which use a series of dialog boxes to walk a user through the entire process of creating a complete Web site, or major functions within a site. We also added the ability to create threaded discussion groups for a site, with questions, comments, replies to comments, replies to replies, etc. Ted Stefanik decided that our discussion group feature needed "Next" and "Previous" buttons, which was correct, but Frank banned them as an unacceptable extravagance. Ted put them in anyway, but made a mistake, which gave Frank an excuse to yell at him. "Naughty boy," I told Ted, laughing. "Very naughty. Very very naughty. Now go do it some more." By this time many of the engineers were giving Frank "the mushroom treatment," as we say in the industry. Mushrooms, you see, are kept in the dark, fed manure, and eventually canned.

Another problem, though, was becoming more urgent. As I mentioned earlier, we had concluded that it would be extremely cool to include a personal copy of the server extensions, and a personal Web server, inside the product, available on everyone's PC. As with HTML editors, we assumed it would be easy to find one. As with HTML editors, this proved not to be true. To our astonishment, we could not find a decent Web server that ran on all the operating systems we needed: Windows 3.1, Windows 95, and Windows NT.

Including a personal server was clearly the right decision, but I couldn't ask Andy to meet our schedule *and* simultaneously write a new Web server. We looked hard—very hard. We found and rejected at least half a dozen products, which had various technical, legal, or financial problems. (Remember: no royalties, and no lock-in.) Time passed. We began to get nervous.

Then Ed Cuoco finally tracked down a fellow named Bob Denny, a smart, eccentric, and cantankerous developer who had at least part of what we needed. He had a Web server that ran on Windows 3.1 only. The problem was that he had just sold his software company. He was spending some time promoting his product on behalf of the company he had sold out to, which was a potential competitor of ours, but he mainly seemed to want a vacation. In fact, he was on vacation most of that spring and wasn't particularly interested in talking to us or anybody else. But Ed is good at nagging, *gently*. Ed finally wore him down, and sometime in May, when I was getting pretty tense, Ed convinced Denny to sell us unrestricted rights to his Web server for $25,000. Denny thought he was raping us. But we didn't need a *good* personal server— we emphatically intended to stay out of the high-end server business, in order to keep the goodwill of commercial server vendors and preserve our "honest broker" status. We just needed something minimal, so that a stand-alone PC user could try out the full system. We hired a sharp contract programmer who ported Denny's code to Windows 95 and NT, and we finally had all the essential platforms covered. Our last problem was security: we wanted to provide encryption for communications between our client and the Web server. We couldn't license anything cheaply. But Randy knew a lot about encryption—so he did it himself.

In general, our development process went incredibly smoothly, given the intense pressures to which we submitted the engineering team. Aside from Jim Gettys, we lost only two developers. One was just lazy. Andy Schulert told him dryly, You're allowed to be the slowest developer, because somebody has to be. And you're allowed to be the first one to leave at night, because somebody has to be. *But you're not allowed to be both*. We started getting ready to fire him, but he quit first—the day after his first stock vested, only three months after he'd joined, but he ended up with a fair amount of money. I began to see why VCs wanted a one-year cliff for vesting; although I think a year is too long, I didn't like giving this guy stock for three months of unsatisfactory work. The second case was just very sad. We'd hired a young woman from mainland China despite some doubts about her skill level. She could not cut it as a development engineer, unfortunately, but we offered to try her as a tester. Peter, and especially Frank Germano, had been quite tough on her, and I think she felt humiliated. She decided to resign, because her mother was coming from China; she hadn't seen her mother in five years. She had absolutely no idea how large a mistake she was making. She was breaking an unwritten rule—you don't resign just before a product is released. She was also giving up her stock. If she stayed only a few months longer, she would have made hundreds of thousands of dollars. I gave her six weeks' severance pay, which she considered very generous, and which Frank, rather nastily, tried to block.

Marketing, however, started to pose problems. As our launch date approached, it became necessary to start getting real. But I had deferred hiring a marketing VP until we found a permanent CEO. Ed Cuoco and Phil Werner were working as joint number twos, which made them both tense and insecure. It got worse when I hired a sharp, tough marketing consultant, Shelley Harrison. I like Shelley a lot, but like me, she isn't shy. And while I don't think she totally understood our large-scale strategic issues, she was absolutely, utterly infallible on tactics and implementation. She knew every consultant, vendor, PR firm, trade show, telemarketing firm, shipping company, and distribution channel. When she took a position in those areas against Ed or Philip, she was almost always right, which threatened them. They tried to freeze her out. Philip and I clashed frequently, and he finally resigned after I had reamed him out quite hard over a weekend. He joined another Internet company, FTP, with which we were negotiating, which bothered me a bit. But it cost him a lot more money than it cost us.

Frank Germano remained a problem, too, and not just with the engineers. When the product was nearly done, our critical path became preparations for manufacturing and launch—documentation, customer support, diskette production and shipping, packaging, telesales, credit card processing. Frank knew more about this than I did, and he wanted to own it. This caused friction not only with Ed but, of course, with Shelley. Frank's instinct was always to take the cheapest route, which Shelley thought was usually wrong. Ed would uncharacteristically agree with Frank if it meant disagreeing with Shelley. To prevent a complete explosion, I sometimes sided with Frank and Ed even when I shouldn't have.

But for all our tensions and difficulties, by late summer a shippable product was coming together with remarkable speed and smoothness. Soon it would be time to engage seriously with the outside world. Of course, the world hadn't been sitting still either.

CHAPTER FIVE

The Industry, January–August 1995: Netscape Lights Its Roman Candle, Bill Gates Wakes Up, and AOL Rolls with the Punch

It is a very humbling experience to make a multimillion-dollar mistake, but it is also very memorable.
—*Frederick P. Brooks, Jr.,* The Mythical Man-Month: Essays on Software Engineering

We will bury you.
—*Nikita Khrushchev, speaking to Western diplomats, 1956*

*M*uch of the future structure of the Internet was decided by the fall of 1995, although this fact was temporarily camouflaged by an explosion of excitement, surprises, mistakes, and lies. Netscape and the new Internet industry's challenge to Microsoft superficially reached their height. Yet much of this challenge was built on quicksand, while Microsoft was preparing to wage war for real. It was also in 1995 that the Web, through new firms such as Yahoo! and the Internet service providers, began to sweep aside older systems and the incumbents backing them. Among those incumbents, only AOL moved aggressively to embrace the Internet, becoming one of its leaders. IBM, Oracle, AT&T, Prodigy, CompuServe, Novell, and many others either failed or did not even try. The Department of Justice allowed Microsoft's bundling of MSN with Windows 95, which was released in August, shortly after Netscape's spectacular initial public offering. And finally, 1995 saw the first stirrings of the electronic commerce revolution that we were all expecting.

During most of this time we deliberately stayed out of the fray. Vermeer's engineering team had its collective head down, working insanely hard to develop the product, which was far more complex than the browsers and Web servers dominating the news—especially if we were going to do it right. Randy and I were watching, talking to people, trying to figure out what the hell was going on. It wasn't easy.

NETSCAPE: THE FIRST HALF OF 1995

In the industry, a "Roman candle" is a company that has a spectacular take-off, but that quickly burns out and falls back to earth—at which point, in the Valley's terminology, you "crater." This often happens to companies built upon a single clever idea, but which due to managerial and strategic error fail to create a sustainable position. Their hallmarks are excessively rapid, chaotic growth and overreaching born of arrogance. In 1995 Netscape showed signs of being one of the biggest Roman candles in the Valley's history. Conversely Microsoft was strangely quiet—too quiet, as the movies say. Over the summer, however, word spread that Gates had written a major Internet strategy document, referred to as The Memo.

With Barksdale starting as CEO in January, Netscape now had most of its top management; only a few other people would be added, after the acquisition of Collabra in September 1995. On the surface, their credentials were glittering. But all that glitters . . .

In fact, some disquieting signs were visible. We monitored Netscape intensely but from afar. After our initial conversation with them in May 1994, we were running silent; we didn't want them to learn about us until we had an unassailable lead. Until quite late, it was unclear what their tools plans were and what our relationship with them would be. I was thus deeply ambivalent about the emerging picture of Netscape's strengths and defects. On the one hand they were our most immediately dangerous potential competitor. On the other, they were also a potential partner and a vital counterweight to Microsoft if we were to survive as an independent company.

Shortly after Barksdale's hiring was announced, I was discussing our own prospective CEO search with Paul Ferri, Andy Marcuvitz's senior partner at Matrix. Ferri is even more impassive and poker-faced than Andy M., and he rarely volunteers opinions. So I was quite surprised to hear Ferri say he knew Barksdale and that Barksdale was "absolutely the wrong kind of guy for that company." Barksdale, Ferri said, was a "big-company guy" who didn't understand start-ups or technology—"exactly what Netscape doesn't need." I took

Ferri's opinion very seriously, and my wheels began to turn, because I was worried about some of Netscape's *other* top management.

I don't believe in coincidences. I had never met Mike Homer, Netscape's VP of marketing, but his background bothered me. He had been at Apple under Sculley for a long time. Knowing Apple and Sculley as I did, I considered this a bad sign. From there, Homer had become an executive at GO and then EO. This was a *very* bad sign, because GO and EO were among the worst smoke-and-mirrors tricks in the Valley's history. This resumé suggested to me that Homer might be good at PR, especially when it involved promoting Mike Homer, but that he also might not have the brains, depth, and judgment required for war with Microsoft. Then there was the technical side. I didn't know Rick Schell, so I couldn't judge him either, but the overall picture wasn't good. There were lots of kids and UNIX people, but few seasoned technologists with PC software experience. Andreessen's job as chief technology officer was supposedly deciding what Netscape's future products should be. But he had no experience, and *there was no chief architect;* so for architectural strategy, who was minding the store? Moreover, of the entire top management team, only one person—Schell—had *any* experience with a successful PC software company. The chief financial officer, Peter Currie, and the general counsel, Roberta Katz, were Barksdale's friends from McCaw: again, big-company people. And there was nobody, period, who had either been at Microsoft or who had competed successfully against it.

But in 1995, especially in Silicon Valley, it was heresy to question Netscape's management or future prospects, and its immediate results were unquestionably spectacular. The Valley has a tendency to embrace uncritically anyone and anything perceived to be challenging Microsoft. This was clearly a factor in the length of time that Sculley and Apple were immune to criticism. It is charming, in a way, that the Valley falls prey to this very human need to believe in a savior. But it can cloud your mind.

The stunningly successful launch of Navigator effectively ended the first round of the browser wars. There existed many other browsers, mostly based on NCSA Mosaic code, but none of them was as feature-rich or as fast as Navigator. Virtually overnight, Netscape obliterated them and took a commanding lead; by summer, its market share was something like 80 percent. Its browser revenues were nearly doubling every quarter, and the company was on the verge of both profitability and a wildly successful initial public offering. The only credible threat was Microsoft, which showed no *public* evidence of getting serious.

Furthermore, in March 1995 Netscape announced a blizzard of server products: new releases of its two basic Web servers, plus an Internet news server, a proxy server (also known as a firewall, a server that provides security and translates between public Internet and corporate private addresses), and several specialized applications products (based on customized Web servers) for publishing, electronic retailing, and other markets. These latter products in particular were described as having powerful features such as integrated relational database support. We wondered at the time how a start-up could possibly do all this; the answer was they couldn't. Some of these announcements were real, but others were essentially vaporware, and not all the products were good. This was far too much for such a young company to bite off at once, but few people said so at the time.

Thus by the spring of 1995, only a few months after its cash crisis and layoffs, Netscape was famous and very bankable. A $17 million private placement closed in April. The investors included Adobe, the Hearst Corporation, Knight-Ridder, TCI, and the Times Mirror Company. Their $17 million bought a 12 percent stake in the company, for an implied valuation of about $140 million—not bad for a year-old company. Investment bankers were already sizing up Netscape as a superb IPO candidate, an extraordinarily early stage in a company's history for this step.

Netscape didn't stop there. On May 23, Netscape and Sun Microsystems jointly announced that Netscape would become the first licensee of Java, the language and software environment that allowed Web sites to download programs over the Internet that would then run inside browsers. This announcement was the first official statement by Netscape that threatened Microsoft, because the Java environment was an application programming interface (API) that Microsoft did not control. Then a so-called point release of the first browser, Navigator 1.1/1.2, was released in June. Like the first release six months earlier, the point release was available almost simultaneously on a wide array of platforms, including the Macintosh and obscure variants of UNIX as well as Windows 3.1. A browser for Windows 95 was under development, but was not yet commercially available because Windows 95 hadn't been released yet.

And this brings us to Netscape's dealings with Microsoft in mid-1995. Sometime in April, Gates and other senior executives including Paul Maritz and Brad Chase started getting serious. Microsoft clearly became aware of Netscape's ambitious plans to become a platform rival by creating browser APIs that would allow applications to be written directly for browsers without much need for a PC operating system. If successful, this would deeply threaten Microsoft's power. This threat turned out to be less real than Netscape asserted and than Microsoft feared, but both sides took it very seriously for the next three years. In April and May 1995, senior Microsoft executives discussed how to approach Netscape, with the risk of platform competition in mind. They realized that they had to retain control of critical platform standards—for the operating system of course, but also for new Internet technologies including TCP/IP, Web browsers, and Internet security software. E-mail messages made public in the antitrust trial make it clear that they understood, even before Netscape's May 23 Java announcement, that Netscape's browser was a potentially serious platform threat.

In May and June 1995, senior Microsoft personnel repeatedly attempted to dissuade Netscape from becoming a platform competitor, and to persuade Netscape to use Microsoft APIs for browsers and security functions. Apparently Netscape executives, including Barksdale, Clark, and John Doerr, told Microsoft, dishonestly, that they had no plans to threaten Microsoft's APIs and wanted to cooperate, but it was too late. Netscape had already said and done too much in public, and Microsoft wasn't fooled. Barksdale and Andreessen allege that, in June, Microsoft proposed dividing the browser market between them, giving Netscape control of the Windows 3.1 market if Netscape would agree not to compete on Windows 95. Barksdale also alleges in his antitrust trial testimony that Microsoft began to withhold technical information necessary to Netscape, and that Microsoft executives linked provision of this information to Netscape's agreement not to compete in the Windows 95 market.

Microsoft executives deny all this, but given Microsoft's history, it's quite plausible. Microsoft had induced IBM to accept an almost identical deal in their operating systems "divorce settlement" three years earlier. IBM got rights to Windows 3.1 but not to future releases, which doomed IBM completely as an operating system competitor. Later, Microsoft also made a somewhat similar deal with RealNetworks, and Microsoft is now in the process of strangling RealNetworks using strategies virtually identical to those used against Netscape.

But whatever Microsoft did or did not propose, by July 1995 it was evident to senior Microsoft executives that Netscape would not play along. So Microsoft started preparing for war. Instead of reacting with extreme concern, Netscape began openly taunting Microsoft and became if anything more arrogant toward the software community, whose support would be critical in any platform war with Microsoft.

In July, Netscape started work on Navigator 2.0. This would be the first version of the browser to incorporate Java capability, and it would also for the first time provide an API, called the Plug-In interface, that permitted other third-party programs to run inside browsers. The Plug-In interface, for example, was used by Progressive (now Real) Networks to allow browsers to play Real-Audio files on demand. Other plug-ins allowed video clips, animation, music, and Adobe PDF files to be played and/or displayed within a browser.

However, the ratio of noise to reality in Netscape's announcements was extremely high. Netscape did not actually offer a browser with any APIs and/or platform characteristics until the beta release of Navigator 2.0 was posted on the

Web in September 1995, and the final product wasn't commercially released until February 1996. But by the spring of 1995 Netscape had endorsed Java and made it known that it would create browser APIs, thus becoming a platform rival to Microsoft. Worse, Netscape executives, particularly Andreessen but others as well, began to brag that they would eviscerate Microsoft. So there was a six- to nine-month period between Netscape *announcing* that it was a threat to Microsoft and its actually *becoming* one.

Furthermore, both Java and Netscape's APIs were initially of mediocre technical quality and limited functionality, and Netscape's arrogance alienated much of the software development community that would be using it. Consequently Netscape received considerably less technical and marketing assistance than it could have received and badly needed. One of Netscape's worst mistakes concerned Java. Almost as soon as it had licensed Java from Sun, Netscape initiated efforts to *compete* with Sun by developing and selling its own Java technologies. This not only threatened to splinter the Java standard, but alienated Sun and many Java developers. Sun's own behavior was far from blameless, but Netscape clearly made things worse. Every developer we spoke to complained of Netscape's arrogance, outrageous demands, and lack of responsiveness.

In mid-1995 Netscape also decided to focus its future efforts on enterprise software, particularly Internet-based groupware for large companies. This decision was not an entirely unreasonable strategy, nor, moreover, was it free of problems. The first difficulty was simply that this very young company was spreading itself way too thin, particularly given an impending browser war with Microsoft. The second is that large corporations are slow to adopt new technologies and products, so it takes a lot of time and money to build that kind of business. This meant that Netscape would have to depend upon browser revenues for a significant period, until the corporate herd was finally moving toward the Internet. And third, in this market Netscape would be competing with several preexisting, non-Internet-based products—primarily Lotus Notes, Microsoft Exchange, and Novell GroupWise.

This was not an insuperable problem—the Internet was clearly the coming thing, and Internet-based groupware potentially offered major advantages relative to traditional proprietary systems. As I've already indicated, for example, Lotus Notes had a lot of problems. But to realize the potential of Internet-based groupware, you would have to design a new and different product, one that explicitly leveraged the Internet and the Web. And you couldn't just throw something together; you had to think about the problem carefully. And once again, to the skeptical and discerning observer, even Netscape's publicly visible behavior soon suggested that something was wrong.

In September, Netscape announced that it would acquire Collabra for $100 million in Netscape stock. Collabra was a moderately successful Silicon Valley groupware start-up that was starting to run into trouble precisely because its products were not Internet-compatible. Then why did Netscape buy them? Excellent question. We wondered that ourselves, particularly because one of our engineers had good friends at Collabra and knew what the deal was. We were truly confused; if Netscape was so wildly successful, could this be as dumb as it seemed? However, in 1995 Netscape could do no wrong, and press coverage of the acquisition was almost entirely favorable.

Finally, in mid-1995, Netscape also decided that it would compete with *us* by entering the tools market. They telephoned me in the summer, offering to talk; I said thanks, but no thanks. In September we announced FrontPage and demonstrated it at two major industry conferences; at one of them Randy and I spoke just after Mike Homer. By a striking coincidence, one week later, on September 18, 1995, Netscape announced three tools products. I will discuss this later. For now, let's just say that here, *we* were skeptical and discerning. While we respected and even feared Netscape, we weren't impressed with what we saw, even if it was real. Furthermore, we didn't think it *was* real—and we were right. It largely wasn't.

Thus by mid-1995, Netscape was already blowing it, and if you looked carefully you could tell—even if you were restricted to the public evidence. And if you could have looked *inside* both Netscape and Microsoft, you would have run away screaming into the night. Netscape's position and decisions in 1995, and to some extent during the following two years as well, represent one of the great missed opportunities in recent business history.

In fact, Netscape had a much longer free ride than most people, including me, predicted that it would. It was clear to us that the Internet was a huge new market of precisely the kind Microsoft goes after, and it was also a profound threat to Microsoft, because it offered opportunities to supersede and marginalize Microsoft's strategic position. Furthermore Netscape, a major new competitor, had publicly announced by mid-1995 that it would attack the core of that position.

The ultimate source of Microsoft's power is its monopoly control of the software platform used by PC applications—Windows. This is not because there's anything particularly wonderful about Windows as a product—but, like driving on the right side of the street, it has become the standard that we all assume, and without which using PCs would be impossible. Microsoft has brilliantly leveraged this control into another monopoly, the MS Office application suite, and is now using both Windows and Office to secure further monopolies in server operating systems and applications, via NT and BackOffice. Even now, if Microsoft were deprived of its monopoly over the underlying platform for creating PC applications, Microsoft would be left with only a fraction of its current power. Windows directly accounts for one-third of Microsoft's revenue and profits, and in the absence of PC platform control, Microsoft's positions in other markets would inevitably—and significantly—deteriorate.

So when Netscape announced that it would turn its browser into a platform for writing applications, and one that would render Windows unimportant, it was announcing nothing less than its intent to destroy Microsoft. Furthermore, as I argue in chapter 9, if Netscape had mounted its attack *competently,* there would have been some reality to this threat—less than Netscape claimed, but a great deal, nonetheless. When Netscape said its browser would supersede Windows, it was doing something akin to Saddam Hussein announcing that he would conquer all of OPEC. Netscape, however cool, was a start-up with fewer than a thousand employees and no proprietary leverage. Microsoft was a $20 billion company with more than $10 billion in cash. Moreover, the software industry is littered with the decaying bodies of companies whose resources were greater and whose threat to Microsoft was far less serious. Thus Netscape should have expected even faster and more brutal retaliation than it received. When I recently asked a Microsoft executive about the company's response, he smiled. "War is hell," he said dryly. Then he shook his head and added: "They threatened the platform." That was all he needed to say.

Bill Gates Finally Gets It: The Memo; or, How to Turn an Aircraft Carrier

On January 13, 1995, Gates had announced that MSN would at some point offer Internet access, eventually including access to the Web. But there was no indication that MSN's essentially proprietary structure would change, or that Microsoft felt that the Internet was a major discontinuity. Randy and I were stunned as most of 1995 passed before there was the slightest evidence that Microsoft was waking up. But then the evidence started to appear. Netscape should have understood this much sooner than we did, as a result of Barksdale's meetings with Microsoft executives in April, May, and June. When Barksdale and Netscape declined to play nice, Microsoft went to Plan B. We now know that by late May, Gates had concluded that Netscape was a serious threat.

But to the outside world Microsoft still seemed brain-dead, and in fact parts of it still were. Even after Gates told the company that the Internet was its highest priority, there were several further months of stumbling around. Most of the company remained paralyzed until the fourth quarter of 1995, a month after the release of Windows 95 in late August. The company's public pronouncements, and to some extent its actions as well, were confusing, mutually contradictory, and ineffective. A number of people, including Paul Maritz, one of the company's most senior and technically deep executives, became increasingly alarmed about this.

Russ Siegelman, the MSN manager at the time, told me that it wasn't until relatively late in 1995 that Microsoft finally realized that it could not replace HTML with Word formats and MSN standards. I saw direct evidence of this myself in late 1995 when I was dealing with the senior people at Microsoft. Some people in Microsoft even thought that MSN still had a chance, and they continued working on MSN and its proprietary development tool, code-named Blackbird.

Microsoft's public attitude toward the Internet was visible in the Blackbird announcements starting in March. Blackbird would allow MSN developers "to implement on-line publications, consumer-oriented applications, business-to-business services, interactive advertising, electronic-commerce applications, and even interactive games." For a while the MSN people believed, or at least pretended to believe, that MSN and Blackbird could get away with only minor concessions to Internet standards. One announcement said that Blackbird would support "key publishing standards," the list of which did *not* include HTML. But, the announcement went on, Blackbird would "also read standard HTML documents so those documents can be easily converted to more sophisticated" Blackbird standards. Blackbird, in short, would come to the rescue of developers who were forced to deal with primitive technologies like the Web and Internet. Later the spin changed: Microsoft spread rumors that Blackbird was becoming a Web development tool. I'll return to that later.

But in mid-1995 Microsoft still had not begun work even on an HTML editor, much less advanced Web servers or other Internet servers such as mail servers or "firewalls," the servers that shield corporate TCP/IP networks from unauthorized users. Work also continued on Microsoft Exchange, a non-Internet groupware product that was released in 1996. The browser project based on licensed Spyglass code was still a low priority; Microsoft decided not to integrate it into Windows 95, and it was far behind Netscape's browser in features and speed. Microsoft made no immediate attempt to provide any browser at all for Windows 3.1 or the Mac, and in fact the contract with Spyglass *prohibited* Microsoft from using that code on Windows 3.1.

Bill Gates finally "got it," however, and served notice that Microsoft would change. On May 26, 1995, he authored a memo to his senior staff called "The Internet Tidal Wave." The document rapidly acquired iconic status within Microsoft and was soon referred to simply as "The Memo." It started to leak shortly afterward, and several months later it was apparently deliberately leaked to the press to demonstrate that Microsoft understood the Internet. This is somewhat curious, because The Memo provides a rather unflattering portrait of its author, and of Microsoft culture.

I learned of The Memo in the late summer of 1995, roughly two months before we announced in September. I received a visit in Cambridge from a friend of mine who had retired from Microsoft at age thirty-five with $10 million or so. At Microsoft this is nothing special; the place has already produced over ten thousand millionaires. My friend, who retained good contacts at Microsoft and occasionally still consulted for them, described The Memo in terms that made it clear that, even if no movement was visible from outside, the Softies were coming in force. In early September, I talked with Doug Colbeth, the CEO of Spyglass, who confirmed that Microsoft was mobilizing for all-out war. The problem that had delayed them, Colbeth said, was their entrenched routine for periodic releases of Windows and Office, which made rapid redeployments difficult. But they were working on it.

Gates's memo is noteworthy in several respects, some but not all of them good. It is eight pages long and single-spaced, addressed to "Executive Staff and direct reports." Not many Fortune 500 CEOs sit down and write such detailed technology and strategy assessments. And Gates clearly wrote it himself; it's full of sentences like "[The Internet] is an incredible opportunity as well as incredible challenge. I am looking forward to your input on how we can improve our strategy to continue our track record of incredible success." But while Gates's next career may not be literary, the document is perceptive and proves beyond any doubt that he finally got it.

It opens with Gates noting how his own attitude has changed: "I have gone through several stages of increasing my views of [the Internet's] importance. Now I assign the Internet the highest level of importance. In this memo I want to make clear that our focus on the Internet is critical to every part of our business. The Internet is the most important single development to come along since the IBM PC was introduced in 1981." That statement seems to belie Microsoft's subsequent claim while defending antitrust suits that it assigned top priority to the Internet a full year earlier, in the spring of 1994. More generally, it is a bit strange that Gates had to write this in mid-1995. Jim Clark, Marc Andreessen, John Doerr, Randy, myself, Jerry Yang, Rob Glaser, Mitch Kapor, and a number of other people could have written that memo a year earlier, as our actions attested.

Gates provides a technical primer on the Internet, obviously assuming that his employees don't know much about it. He describes the advantages of Internet and Web protocols and standards—TCP/IP, HTTP, and HTML. He talks about interesting sites, like Yahoo!, explains what they do, and gives instructions for connecting to them. Another sentence in this section suggests that Gates, too, still thought that Microsoft could replace nonproprietary Web standards with its own: "The strength of the Office and Windows businesses today gives us a chance to superset the Web."

He goes on to explain packet switching, problems with real-time transmission, and lists the start-up companies trying to solve these problems. He discusses telecommunications technologies and the potential of cable modems. Then he notes: "Amazingly, it is easier to find information on the Web than it is to find information on the Microsoft Corporate Network. This inversion where a public network solves a problem better than a private network is quite stunning." The technology section ends with: "The On-line services business and the Internet have merged. What I mean by this is that every On-line service has to simply be a place on the Internet with extra value-added . . . [W]e will have to explain to content publishers and users why they should use MSN instead of just setting up their own Web server. We don't have a clear enough answer to this question today."

The next section reviews the competitive scene and notes the "default [Internet] server is still a UNIX box and not Windows NT . . . Many Web sites, including [Microsoft co-founder] Paul Allen's ESPNET, put a SUN logo and link at the bottom of their home pages in return for low-cost hardware." He goes on. "Browsing the Web, you find almost no Microsoft file formats. After 10 hours of browsing, I had not seen a single Word.doc . . . or other Microsoft file format," although he noted a large number of Apple and Adobe formats. The reference to ten hours of browsing is interesting. By May 1995, Randy and I *each* had probably spent a couple of hundred hours browsing.

Finally, Gates says: "A new competitor 'born' on the Internet is Netscape. Their browser is dominant, with a 70% usage share." And Gates is clearly aware of the first stirrings of the "thin client" and "network computer" hype that became ubiquitous later in the year: "[Netscape is] pursuing a multi-platform strategy where they [use the browser] to commoditize the underlying operating system. . . . One scary possibility being discussed by Internet fans is whether they should get together and create something far less expensive than a PC which is powerful enough for Web browsing." Note Mr. Gates's touching concern for the welfare of users, regardless of Microsoft's profits. In the antitrust case, Microsoft has maintained that it bundled its browser to benefit consumers. But describing an inexpensive thin client as a "scary possibility" does not suggest that consumer welfare is uppermost in Mr. Gates's mind.

But Microsoft didn't turn on a dime. MSN development continued, and it was released, bundled with Windows 95, as a proprietary service with virtually no Internet capabilities. The first browser barely made it into the Windows 95 Plus Pak, never mind the operating system, and it was bad. Blackbird continued along in the same non-Internet path for months. But Microsoft began wholesaling FUD about how Internet-friendly Blackbird would be. FUD, for those fortunate enough never to have encountered it, stands for "fear, uncertainty, and doubt." It's a time-honored but underhanded tactic available only to prominent firms. When confronted with potential competition, you deter users from using or allying with your competitor by spreading rumors—or even making formal announcements—implying that, any day now, your new products will obliterate them. Even when this is pure horse manure, it often works. The rumor that Blackbird was becoming a Web development tool created some alarm at Vermeer, as you can imagine. It also caused us problems with several potential investors and partners; Mitch Kapor cited it as a major reason he didn't invest in us. Later, we resorted to skullduggery ourselves. We obtained a bootleg copy of the Blackbird beta release in September and discovered that it had *nothing whatsoever* to do with the Web or the Internet. So while Gates had mostly gotten it, and Microsoft's public rhetoric and FUD became more Internet-centric, action didn't follow until after the Windows 95 launch.

I recently pressed Russ Siegelman, the MSN manager at the time, on why it took so long for Microsoft to react. He's a sharp guy, but I didn't find his explanation convincing. His principal response was that switching MSN strategy to the Internet and Web would have raised horrendous practical problems. Windows 95 was originally scheduled for release in the summer of 1994, incorporating MSN. Then Windows 95 was repeatedly delayed, but each time ostensibly only for a few months. So there was never enough time, Siegelman argues, for a fundamental redirection of MSN.

But that doesn't explain why the first release of Windows 95 did not include a browser. In that instance, Siegelman said, the company was completely consumed by the Windows 95 release. Windows 95 had been delayed so many times that it was becoming a laughingstock. Only Gates could put another feature "in the box," which might delay it again, and he chose not to.

I think that in fact there were a number of reasons for Microsoft's slow reaction in 1995. First, and most important, was that for whatever reasons, it took Bill Gates quite a while to get it. Microsoft doesn't go anywhere Gates doesn't want it to. Second, along with many others, Microsoft did not expect the Internet to move as fast as it did. Thus, even some of those concerned about the Internet and the Web thought that Microsoft could afford to take its time. Third, there seems to have been a strong belief within Microsoft that it would have the power to impose its own standards on the Internet and make the world adapt to them, rather than the other way around. Fourth, the rise of the Internet caused some internal political problems that delayed analysis of, and reaction to, the Web. There was MSN, threatened by the Web; there was Blackbird, threatened by the Web and by us; there was MS Exchange, a non-Internet groupware product potentially threatened by Web-based groupware; there was the corporate e-mail software, threatened by Internet e-mail; and there was Word, which had a bad add-on for HTML generation that would be threatened by a real HTML editor. There were also powerful individuals, such as Nathan Myhrvold, who had been slow to appreciate the Internet and whose judgment would be called into question by its ascent.

And there was the platform-cycling problem. Microsoft makes a lot of money by periodically forcing people to upgrade their operating systems and applications. Microsoft was just about to launch Windows 95, the largest operating system upgrade in years. The goal of killing Netscape, which implied distributing a browser and other Internet technologies for the installed base of Windows 3.1, thus conflicted with the goal of promoting Windows 95. In the end, Gates would decide that killing Netscape was paramount and shot anything that interfered. But that decision took a while—until Pearl Harbor Day. And finally I think that Microsoft, including possibly Gates, had just gotten somewhat lazy and complacent. Nobody had given them a run for their money in quite a while, and they began to think that nobody could.

But they hadn't lost their touch. When they got the wake-up call, they not only got serious, they probably had a lot of fun in the process, and they certainly proved that they were still capable of playing rough. So although they had gotten dangerously close to becoming the kind of incumbent they had previously delighted in gutting, they were pulled back from the brink just in time—by Netscape's blatant challenge.

Gates also had another matter to attend to during the summer. Intel tried an end-run, but Gates caught it. He successfully coerced Intel into dropping plans to enhance its microprocessors' ability to handle audio, music, graphics, and video, and to provide an Intel software API for these functions. Gates, according to Intel memoranda, was also "livid" about Intel's Internet investments and "wanted them stopped." Gates made it clear that while it was okay for Intel to cooperate with Netscape as it would with any one else, he expected the closest relation to be with Microsoft. He was particularly upset that Intel was supporting non-Microsoft versions of Java. Andy Grove, one of the toughest men in the industry, conceded that he "caved" before some of Gates's demands because Microsoft held the high cards.

JAVA: SUN CONTRACTS THE HYPE DISEASE

The first public mention of Java came on March 23, 1995. It was a front page story in the *San Jose Mercury News,* the local newspaper that doubles as a Silicon Valley trade journal. Prominently featured in a sidebar was a quote from Marc Andreessen that Java was "undeniably, absolutely new. It's great stuff." Andreessen was also the keynote speaker at the May Sunworld conference, where the new language was officially unveiled, and he announced that Netscape would incorporate Java into its next browser release, due in the fall. The Java hype machine was off and running full-tilt.

Java is a terrific language and a real intellectual accomplishment. But its many virtues have been obscured by exaggeration not seen since the days of cold fusion. When I talked to Jim Gosling, the veteran Sun developer who headed the Java team, he stressed that none of the hype came from him or the other developers. When I pointed out that his boss Scott McNealy, the CEO of Sun, had been among the most outrageous offenders, he replied, "Yeah, well, Scooter's quite a character." Aside from McNealy, the major hype producers were Oracle's Larry Ellison, Netscape's Andreessen, and later in the summer George Gilder, who perhaps holds the record.

The project that turned into Java got its start in 1990, when Gosling thought of developing software to simplify the operation of household devices like microwaves, VCRs, stereos, and alarm systems. Sun gave him a small budget and allowed him to assemble a team and go to work on his idea.

Gosling initially assumed that his software would be written in C++, the dominant language in desktop software, but he quickly found that it wasn't suitable. The low-performance chips in home devices could handle only small amounts of code, and C++ wasn't compact enough for them. Even worse, it was a compiled language, meaning that instructions in C++ had to be translated into machine-level instructions that each different processor could understand. There were lots of different processors, and you didn't necessarily know which variety was in the stereo or heating control you were trying to talk to. So Gosling and his team developed a new language, which they called "Oak," named for the tree outside Gosling's office window. It was rechristened "Java" by the Sun marketing team just before its official release.

Gosling and the Oak team simply designed a language that incorporated state-of-the-art software principles. For example, Java is object-oriented, forcing a developer to work in small, tightly self-contained, reusable chunks of code. The Oak team solved the problem of enabling programs to run on different processors by creating a "VM," or virtual machine—effectively, a software emulation of a generic processor that could run Java programs on almost any chip. The VM would have to be ported to each type of processor just once; from then on, all Java code would be interpreted by the VM, so any Java program could in principle run on any processor without knowing in advance which kind it would be. Finally, since Java was designed for sending programs across networks, the team built in tight security. For example, a Java application, or "applet," transmitted over the Web will not take up residence on your hard disk and generally cannot get access to the data residing on it.

Then came the Web. One of the obstacles to generating early excitement about the Web was that Web pages were static, like "televised pamphlets." But with Java applets, you could bring the medium to life with little cartoons, rotating pictures, rolling stock quotes. Java was *designed* to run over networks, so its compactness minimized the communications burden over modems, and its built-in security meant that users didn't have to worry that applets would destroy their machine or steal their secrets. In addition, Java is a good language, better and more modern even than C++. Developers love it. But there are two problems, big ones. First, the use of an interpreter as opposed to a compiler imposes a substantial performance penalty; Java programs run slowly. And second, the security features prevent Java from using many PC software features, including the graphical user interfaces provided by Windows. So although Java might evolve into something very valuable, it wasn't going to take over the world instantly. But that's not what Netscape and Sun wanted to hear, or to say to the world.

In the spring of 1995, Kim Polese, who was then the Java marketing manager, e-mailed Andreessen, who downloaded a copy of the Java software and got it immediately. But he got it excessively, and between him and Sun, the Java-Netscape-Web-network-computer illusion was born. Shortly afterward Polese left Sun to become the founder and CEO of Marimba, which supplies Java-based Web content distribution systems. Marimba doesn't seem to be an enormous success. But Polese has become quite the media star. She is extremely smart, self-assured, articulate, and likable; she's also gorgeous, aware of that fact, and slightly outrageous. When I interviewed her—in her office at Marimba—she was wearing tight black pants and a leopard-print blouse, which even in Silicon Valley is not standard CEO attire.

The truly off-the-wall Java hype may first have surfaced publicly with an August article in *Forbes ASAP* by George Gilder. Gilder, who I've known for a long time, is an odd combination of very smart guy and wacko self-promoter. (One example among many: his first major book was an antifeminist tract entitled *Sexual Suicide.*) Gilder announced that Netscape and Java would obliterate Microsoft and supersede Windows. The argument was as follows: If a Java virtual machine were ported to all the major personal computer systems, then applications would need to be written only once, in Java, and could run on any machine. And if most machines were connected to the Web, the applications could be stored on Web sites and downloaded whenever needed. In principle you could dispense with Windows and Windows-based applications by using Java-based applications that required only a browser and a Java virtual machine, which could therefore run on an inexpensive "thin client" or "network computer."

All theoretically true, but not in the next five years. Java applications run slowly because they are interpreted; they don't yet have access to a complete user interface or other important facilities comparable to Windows; and—little detail—*virtually no applications had been written* when Gilder made this comment. They still haven't been. To duplicate the infrastructure, tools, and applications of the Windows environment is not something that happens overnight, if it will ever happen at all. Furthermore, to download large Java applications and their data files would require faster Internet connections than most people possess, certainly faster than current PC modems.

So Gilder was largely selling magazines, and himself. Some have suggested that McNealy was just selling UNIX boxes: Java was a fabulous PR tool to convince the world that somehow Sun was the coolest vendor of Internet server hardware. And Andreessen was only a kid. But Barksdale and Netscape management should have known better. McNealy and Andreessen were soon telling the world that Java plus the Web spelled the end of Microsoft. Shortly after Gilder's article appeared, Andreessen was quoted in the trade press as saying that Windows would be reduced to a "poorly debugged set of device drivers," with Java-enabled browsers taking over most PC software functions. This was surely one of the stupidest, most arrogant statements in the industry's history, and that's saying a lot. Soon afterward, pictures of Andreessen appeared in the halls of the Internet group at Microsoft—as the bull's-eye of targets.

Siegelman commented to me: "They mooned Microsoft way too aggressively. Netscape had one of the best Trojan horse strategies in the history of personal computer software. Their browser got distributed electronically just so quickly, in such vast numbers. And if they had just said, 'Oh, this is just a little piece of software, nothing to do with the operating system. We love Windows. We're going to use all Windows formats.' Marc's a smart guy. I like him. But pissing in front of Microsoft's face on stuff like that. What did he think was going to happen?" I'm doubtful, actually, that if Netscape had developed major APIs for its browsers, that Microsoft would have failed to catch on for *too* much longer—even if Netscape had been cleverly dishonest and worked hard to remain low-key and seemingly innocuous. In part I say this because it was already nothing short of astonishing that Microsoft gave Netscape as much of a headstart as they did. But even an extra six months would have been extremely valuable for Netscape, so Siegelman is still right. And Andreessen used the same attitude in dealing with people who should have been Netscape's friends. Furthermore, Andy Grove was completely correct in the title of his book: *Only the Paranoid Survive.* In this industry, the penalty for blind arrogance is, sooner or later, very severe.

AND IN THE REST OF THE WORLD . . .

The other companies that could have done something about the Internet (and in some cases needed to in order to survive) were AOL, the other proprietary online services, Oracle, IBM, Hewlett-Packard, Novell, and the telecommunications companies. AOL got it. IBM was an intermediate case, while the others missed their window. For HP, Oracle, and the telecommunications companies this was a missed opportunity, but not a mortal blow. HP was growing its UNIX server business rapidly, but unaccountably failed to move into the Internet server arena, leaving most of it for Sun. Oracle would have been a logical vendor of Internet server software, particularly Web servers, but failed to notice until it was too late. The telecommunications companies were either local monopolies who didn't care because they didn't have to, or large long-distance carriers. They could survive, at least in the short term; in the long term, Internet telephony may do them major damage. But for Novell, the proprietary consumer online services, and AOL, this was life or death. Most of them chose death.

Novell Novell's failure to adapt to the Internet was an extraordinary lapse for a company that was still the leader in server operating systems by a huge margin in 1995. During that year, in fact, Vermeer held extensive discussions with American Internet, a start-up that planned to Internet-enable Novell's flagship product, NetWare, and sell Web servers that ran on NetWare. But Novell dropped the ball, continuously. Ray Noorda, Novell's founder and longtime CEO, was elderly and no longer functioning effectively when he was finally forced out in 1994. Novell's culture required a Mormon or at least someone from Utah, which limited the CEO search. Noorda was replaced by Bob Frankenberg, who had been general manager of HP's PC and networking hardware operations. He was completely ineffective, and he totally missed the Internet. None of us understood why this man was just letting his company die.

Interestingly, in his May 1995 "Tidal Wave" memo, Gates was equally puzzled. "Novell is surprisingly absent [in Internet competition]," he wrote, "given the importance of networking to their position," but he expected Frankenberg to change that. It never happened, and Novell proceeded to implode. Frankenberg resigned after two and a half years and was replaced by Eric Schmidt, the former chief technology officer of Sun. Schmidt certainly does understand the Internet, and he has completely remade the company. Novell still has a technical lead over NT in some areas, but it may be too late.

IBM/Lotus Earlier I remarked that Gerstner was right to focus on improving IBM's efficiency rather than on grand visions and new frontiers. The rise of the

Internet illustrates both the virtues and limits of that decision. In principle, IBM was in a position to use the Internet to challenge Microsoft and to establish a proprietary position in a huge new industry. But IBM failed to do so, whether deliberately or otherwise, in part because its top executives did not have the technical background necessary to make accurate strategic judgments in a dangerous, rapidly changing industry. And when IBM did make a daring move, it sometimes chose poorly. It invested heavily in Java and network computers, for example, and got burned badly. Gerstner was probably wise to concentrate on making IBM an efficient implementer of other people's visions.

IBM's acquisition of Lotus was this kind of middle-of-the-road decision. It was certainly a daring move in some ways—any time you spend $3.5 billion you're going at least a little bit out on a limb. But it was also conservative. It gave IBM a predictable and profitable position in corporate groupware, but simultaneously doomed it to second-tier status. It also had elements of low comedy: Jim Manzi resisted the acquisition, perhaps because he knew he would never get another important position in the world. He forced the price up a bit, conceded, and then left shortly afterward with his $78 million. He then became CEO of an Internet commerce start-up that sank without a trace.

Notes was the first major groupware product and suffered from the problems of many pioneering products: it contained lots of mistaken guesses. It was designed for internal, highly secure corporate networks with extensive MIS and administrative support. It was expensive, hard to use, lacked development tools, and suffered from poor performance. It was and remains unsuited to public online services. To Lotus's credit, Notes had improved substantially since its first release and in limited ways had been adapted to the Internet. For example, Lotus added features that made it possible to place a Notes database onto a Web server, for use either on a corporate Intranet or the public Internet. But Notes was, is, and will always remain a limited, pre-Internet product.

Thus by purchasing Lotus and committing to Notes, IBM both guaranteed itself a substantial corporate groupware position and forever denied itself anything better, including any possibility of establishing industrywide standards for *Internet-based* groupware. IBM also set itself up for some nasty internal political fights, because some of its business units needed to promote Internet-based systems while others promoted Notes. This meant that potential partners were exceptionally (and wisely) skeptical about dealings with IBM. This was one reason, for example, that I was so rough and skeptical with the mid-level IBM executives who wanted to start negotiations with us. I asked them to explain the positioning of Notes versus IBM's Internet plans and Netscape's Internet-based groupware. They couldn't. IBM did make money from Lotus: it ported Notes to all of its hardware and has been able to raise Notes's user base to 35 million, which is impressive. But again, IBM could have purchased literally the entire Internet industry in early 1995: Netscape, the major Internet service providers, Vermeer, *everyone*. Web usage has now grown to 250 million people. And at some point, somebody is going to develop good Internet-based groupware. But Gerstner was working with the material he had. He probably made the right choice not to do anything daring, given that he couldn't evaluate the issues himself and he couldn't trust his people to do it right. And in fact IBM later made a big bet on Java, which proved disastrous, so Gerstner's instincts weren't foolish.

AOL and Others All three of the big online service providers continued to reconfigure their operations to become more Web compatible. Prodigy and CompuServe did so in a halting and confused way, while AOL understood that it needed to act aggressively, and did. All of them faced two structurally similar, potentially fatal problems: the Web potentially allowed all of their content providers to establish their own Web sites, and the Internet was replacing traditional communications networks. AOL survived, and then flourished, by becoming a value-added Internet service provider, by giving content providers a better deal, by selling advertising, and by exploiting certain respects in which the Web's user interface remained behind AOL's.

During 1995, AOL was not only converting its internal operations to become Internet-based but was also pursuing an aggressive, and generally intelligent, Internet acquisition strategy. It purchased Medior, an interactive multimedia company, and WAIS, an Internet text search company, in May; in June, it bought the Web Crawler, a Web search tool, and one of the first commercial Web publishers, Global Network Navigator, which published the "Whole Internet Catalog." In total AOL purchased several dozen small Internet software companies over the following three years. And, of course, one of AOL's failures, NaviSoft, gave us a few heart attacks, when they announced authoring tools that competed with us.

CompuServe and Prodigy sank fast. CompuServe had purchased Spry in late 1994 for $100 million, which was one of the dumbest deals in history—almost an AT&T-class mistake. Spry was the company that sold the Internet-in-a-box product, which was just a TCP/IP stack, an NCSA browser, and a few other widgets like a primitive e-mail client and news reader. But by the spring of 1995, Netscape totally dominated the browser market and was working on adding e-mail to its browser, the Eudora e-mail client was gaining fast, and Microsoft had announced that TCP/IP would be built into Windows 95. In other words, the product was predictably about six months away from being completely worthless. But David Pool, Spry's CEO, was a slick operator, and he found someone at CompuServe to swallow his story. CompuServe's management either didn't understand anything, panicked, or both. They also approached us in the spring, then rejected us for silly reasons. Later in the summer they announced various Web and Internet services, but it was too late. They were later purchased by AOL and chopped up a couple of years later. Prodigy sank just as fast, was sold, and later reinvented itself as a small Internet service provider.

The Internet start-up scene exploded during this period. Rob Glaser's Progressive Networks launched RealAudio, enabling streaming audio transmission over the Internet, in April. VeriSign, a start-up supported by a number of strategic investors including Intel, announced that it was developing Internet authentication and certification systems. CheckPoint and others announced firewall servers to screen access to corporate networks from the public Internet. VocalTec, an Israeli start-up, unveiled two-way Internet telephony. The sound was poor and transmission was slow, but it was far cheaper than metered long-distance rates. Given the technology's high rate of performance improvements, it became increasingly clear that Internet architectures and technologies would eventually absorb the telecommunications industry. Another competitor of ours, a small start-up called Ceneca, released a Web authoring tool in August called PageMill. It provided only very simple functions, perhaps a quarter of ours or even less, but its truly *fatal* problem was that it was designed only for the Mac, which excluded about 90 percent of the market. We thanked God for the blindness and religious zeal of Macintosh bigots. Adobe acquired them shortly thereafter.

People started going public. Wall Street now understood at least one thing about the Web—there was money in it. Spyglass's IPO was in June. At about the same time, PSI, a Matrix-Sigma investment, and UUNet both had successful IPOs. And then there was a tidal wave of pure hype, coming from all quarters. A consortium of the largest newspaper chains and publishers, including the New York Times, Cox, and Knight-Ridder, announced that they had formed the New Century Network to develop Web-based publishing and advertising systems that they would all use. It sounded like the ideal Vermeer prospect and potentially very important. After dozens of e-mails and phone calls, we finally tracked down the consortium's interim CEO and met with him in Atlanta. He didn't have a clue about what was going on. NCN was quietly disbanded in 1998. Oracle announced in July that it had licensed a browser from Spyglass and would market a browser with an integrated, *free* relational database engine. I don't believe the product ever saw the light of day—just one more of Larry's many amusing statements.

I found it interesting, however, that the Oracle announcement engendered an almost immediate and identical counter announcement from Netscape. Netscape announced that it had entered into a relationship with Informix, one of Oracle's main rivals, and that it too would shortly offer a free, integrated database engine in its browser. As far as I can determine, this was simply vapor.

It was also around the same time—the second half of 1995—that Netscape also announced products that competed with ours and began its extraordinary barrage of hype about Java, obliterating Microsoft, thin clients, network computers, and ultrafast Internet access via @Home, a start-up of which Barksdale was a director. I think this period was another fateful transition in Netscape's history. Microsoft has been justly criticized, even sued, for FUD and vaporware announcements, but Netscape quickly proved that it could play the FUD game with the best of them. One reason for the hype, clearly, was arrogance. But another factor may have been the desire to boost Netscape's IPO price, and then to maintain that high price afterward. In his defense, Barksdale quite reasonably wanted money and a publicly traded currency for stock-based acquisitions. Cisco and AOL had demonstrated the effectiveness of purchasing R&D, products, and engineering teams by acquiring young companies with public stock.

The problem with this strategy, however, is that once you're on the stock price merry-go-round, it's hard to get off. As long as your stock does well, you don't need to spend a nickel of real money. But Cisco not only showed better taste in what it bought, its stock kept going up because its business kept doing phenomenally well. To retain employees with options, and to make stock-based acquisitions, you must keep your stock price up and convince people that it will stay there. Our (quite justified) skepticism about Netscape's stock price, and Barksdale's absurd statements to me about it, was one factor contributing to my concern about our being acquired by Netscape.

Microsoft and Netscape: August 1995

After many delays, Microsoft finally announced a release date of August 24, 1995, for Windows 95. The launch reportedly cost $250 million, more than the total proceeds of Netscape's IPO. The launch included licensing a Rolling Stones song, a televised midnight gala on Microsoft's Redmond campus hosted by Jay Leno, and the illumination of the Empire State Building in Microsoft colors. But you still could not yet access the Net and the Web from MSN, although you could buy a lame browser. On the night of the launch, AOL rented a huge blimp and floated it over the Microsoft campus with a big "Welcome" sign.

For months prior to the launch, however, AOL had been complaining to the Justice Department about Microsoft's plan to bundle MSN with Windows 95. The Antitrust Division investigated the issue but decided not to do anything. Shortly before the Windows 95 launch, Justice announced that it would not attempt to block either the launch or the bundling of MSN. This was, I think, a mistake, for reasons I'll discuss later, when I consider the entire Microsoft antitrust problem.

Netscape scheduled its IPO for two weeks before the Windows 95 launch. By conventional standards, that was ridiculous timing, even if Microsoft had not been hogging the media with the Windows 95 blitz. Netscape was a very young company for an IPO—total revenues through June were only $16 million—and investment bankers are accustomed to spending August in the Hamptons. Clark and Barksdale, however, pushed hard for an early date, and the underwriters (Morgan Stanley and Hambrecht & Quist) were acutely aware of the building Internet buzz. Part of the impetus for an early IPO, it seems, was the pleasure of tweaking Microsoft. What better way to announce your entry into the big leagues than to steal some of the thunder from the Windows 95 launch?

Netscape's failure to exploit its early opportunities was unquestionably a disaster. But one must also give the company credit for some major achievements. Between April 1994 and August 1995, Netscape took control of the browser market and pioneered a new method for commercial software distribution that enabled it to move with unprecedented speed and flexibility. Netscape had also created valuable partnerships with Internet service providers, online vendors, and software companies to ensure that its logo would be ubiquitous. Its revenues grew very fast, and by late 1995 the company was profitable. Had Netscape's opponent been anyone but Microsoft, its overall performance would have been adequate, even stellar.

The IPO, of course, was a smash hit—too much of one. Clark, Barksdale, and Andreessen went on a worldwide road show, playing to packed audiences everywhere they went. The toughest question they got was "How can I get an allocation?" When the offering was first discussed, price expectations were in the range of $5 a share, but as the investment bankers watched, they began raising their goal and finally filed an expected top price range of $14 with the Securities and Exchange Commission. Netscape was selling five million shares. At $14 a share, that would have meant gross proceeds of $70 million; fully diluted, the newly issued stock would have represented a bit more than a 12 percent stake, placing a value of about $550 million on the whole company.

Early SEC filings are not binding, and in the days before the offering, Morgan Stanley kept raising their recommended price, to $18, then to $21, and the day before the offering, to $31. Barksdale made the call to come out at $28, valuing the company at $1.1 billion. He didn't want to risk a price drop after the opening, and Netscape would still be the first stock in history to double its asking price over the top range in its filing. In the event, the price was far too low: on the first day, it took an hour and a half for trading to open, because so many traders had posted buy orders at any price. They finally opened at $71, and the stock shot up from there, until finally settling down to close out the day in the mid-fifties. In just sixteen months, according to investors, Clark, Andreessen, Doerr, and Barksdale had created more than $2.2 billion in value.

In short, the Internet craze was on. The 280,000 shares that Clark had given Andreessen for $28,000 in April of 1994 were now worth about $15 million, and he held options worth a lot more than that. Clark himself still controlled more than a fourth of the stock and was a very rich man indeed. Within a few months, he would be a billionaire. But outside of the public craze, Microsoft was getting ready for Pearl Harbor Day, and we were getting ready to enter the big time ourselves.

CHAPTER SIX

Wins and Losses;
or, No More Mr. Nice Guy

Whatsoever therefore is consequent to a time of war, where every man is enemy to every man; the same is consequent to the time, wherein men live without other security, than what their own strength, and their own invention shall furnish them . . . and the life of man, solitary, poor, nasty, brutish, and short.
—*Thomas Hobbes,* Leviathan

However many ways there may be of being alive, it is certain that there are vastly more ways of being dead.
—*Richard Dawkins*

*I*n a ten-week period beginning in early September of 1995, Vermeer Technologies went from being an unknown development-phase company to being the hottest, coolest start-up in the United States. In part due to this change, but also for other reasons, my life simultaneously went from being demanding but manageable to being completely, totally insane. September through Christmas 1995 would prove to be the most exciting yet punishing months of my professional life.

One year earlier, we'd had to fight for months to raise $4 million. Even in March, when we had tried to counter NaviSoft's product launch, nobody had paid us the slightest attention. But by the end of September, we had the opposite problem, and it was a very serious problem indeed. Everyone either wanted a piece of our hide or they wanted us dead because we threatened them. And my problems were by no means confined to the outside world. To the contrary, I needed to defend both Vermeer and myself against our investors and our newly hired CEO just as much as against external threats. Events were moving at the speed of light, everything was connected to everything else, and there was essentially nobody I could talk to about it. So these developments brought astonishing highs and great personal fulfillment, but also brutal fights, extreme stress, and painful lessons.

Even through August, we had been quite secretive. While we had been speaking to potential partners, large customers, and analysts, we did so very selectively, under nondisclosure, and usually without revealing sensitive technology or strategic plans. But by September our product was nearly done, and it was time to announce ourselves to the world. Our timing was perfect; as we had planned, we could launch in the peak of the fall season. We wanted business, and there was no further point in concealing what either we or our product did. Furthermore, it was also time to raise more money. So it was time to show our stuff. When we did the response was, as they say, overwhelming.

So when Peter Amstein and I arrived at the room we'd been assigned for our presentation at Dick Shaffer's Digital Media Outlook conference on September 11, 1995, we found the place packed and the atmosphere electric. Every seat and every square inch was occupied. Venture capitalists, investment bankers, technology executives, and industry gurus were lined up along the walls, with more straining to hear from the doorway and the corridor outside. Everyone had already heard of us, but none of them had ever seen our presentations or software before. They liked what they saw. Afterward we were surrounded by people shoving cards at us, wanting meetings, asking if we were raising money, inviting us to conferences, offering partnerships.

Several factors contributed to our sudden fame. In the period between the NaviSoft fiasco and our unveiling in September, everybody in the world—meaning VCs, investment bankers, the Fortune 500, and the media—had finally figured out that the Internet was a big deal, even though most of them still didn't understand why. It also turned out that our campaign of underground evangelism had yielded powerful though indirect dividends. Word had spread that we had something cool, were well connected, and were looking good. And finally, our product was almost done, it worked, and it was seriously good.

Unfortunately, at the same time that these great things were happening, the organic matter was hitting the fan again—from three directions at once. On September 18, Netscape announced three products that competed with ours and that sounded great—until you looked carefully. As we strongly suspected, their announcement turned out to be mostly hot air, but at the time, it was still a bit scary. Second, I was going to war again with our venture capitalists—especially my favorite guy in the whole world, Andy Marcuvitz. The issue was second-round funding—we needed to raise more money, a lot of it, but I didn't want to give away the rest of the company to get it. For this fight, it turned out to be *very* convenient that we made a big splash at the Shaffer conference and started to attract a tidal wave of investor attention.

Third and most serious, I saw growing evidence of big trouble from another quarter: our newly hired CEO. Almost as soon as he was on board, serious personal tension erupted between us. I discovered that I just couldn't trust him.

At the same time, there were many decisions to be made, and everyone had real work to do. I was determined to protect the company, the employees, and myself from the machinations of our CEO and the VCs, and to prevent these tensions from interfering with everyone's work. I believe I largely succeeded. But I failed to protect myself, Randy, and my girlfriend, Camille, at least emotionally. Beginning in September, for the first time in my life I could no longer sleep through the night, a condition that endured for two years. I became angry and tense even with Randy, my closest friends, and Camille. Then Camille's stepfather had a series of heart attacks. Although I am very happy to say he recovered, his condition worried Camille greatly and necessitated a series of late-night three-hour drives to his hospital in New Hampshire. When a young cousin of mine died, my mother decided not to tell me until I was done with Vermeer. In short, this was not a relaxing time. In fact, it was often a nightmare.

THE CEO PROBLEM

My agreement to hire a professional CEO was a condition of our funding, a rare area in which the VCs and I agreed. I had no management experience, and the VCs regarded me as dangerous, so they wanted a pro who would play the game. But I had been worried that they could dump me once they had a CEO, while they clearly were equally worried that I'd never really consent to hiring one. I found this concern of theirs amusing, not only because I had no desire for organizational power but also because I assumed that we could easily find and attract a good CEO. This was to prove an extremely stupid assumption. However, during our first-round negotiations we had reached an agreement whereby half my stock options would vest upon hiring a CEO, which both protected me and gave the VCs comfort that I would make it happen.

So I had been all for hiring a CEO. In retrospect, I think that I was in fact too eager to do so. It was a hard call, but I probably should have prepared myself and the company for me to remain CEO for another several months. I certainly needed help at some point; I had never managed a high-growth organization and didn't particularly enjoy it. Furthermore, we urgently needed to build a serious marketing, distribution, and sales organization, as well as a PR effort to launch the product and, in fact, the company. I didn't know *anything* about those things, and despite Ed Cuoco's great ability and intelligence, neither he nor anybody else in the company really had the requisite skills and experience. So I was nervous about reaching product launch without a CEO, as were the VCs. This was particularly worrying because, in another decision that in retrospect was probably mistaken, we had deferred all further marketing and sales hiring so the future CEO could pick his own people. Thus, aside from Ed, our marketing and sales functions were essentially nonexistent.

Given these circumstances, getting a CEO as early as possible clearly made sense. On the other hand, we paid dearly for trying to do it before product launch. First, this meant that we were in a rush, and we grew increasingly panicked as our launch date approached. And second, because we were still quite secretive, we had a difficult time attracting people. We were trying to hire someone into a company that nobody had heard of, founded by people with no entrepreneurial track record, in a completely new industry that nobody understood. Finding a superlative person and persuading him or her to join such a company was quite difficult. If we had waited a few months longer—when the Internet was suddenly everywhere, and we were suddenly famous—we could have had our pick of almost anyone in the industry. We probably could have gotten a better person, I could have done more comparison shopping, and we (and I) certainly would have had *much* more leverage over the terms of his or her hiring. Given my generally dim view of professional CEOs, this would have been extremely useful. But the VCs wanted someone fast, and for better or worse I agreed with them. So we started looking for a CEO shortly after we closed the first round.

The problem of attracting a good CEO to an unknown company was worsened by our location—Boston versus Silicon Valley. In early 1995 the Boston area ("Route 128") high technology sector was still conservative and full of dead wood, in part because it was still dominated by the dying minicomputer companies (DEC, Prime, Wang, and Data General). There was relatively little start-up activity, and most of it was in networking hardware. The only major PC software company was Lotus, which was almost as bad as DEC—highly politicized, too cushy for too long, going downhill fast. The last thing I wanted was some guy who had been at Lotus or DEC for ten years because he was too comfortable and timid to move, or even worse had been successful there because he was a master politician. Ironically, the handwriting was on the wall at all these places (in boldface, in fact), and hanging on at these supposedly secure companies turned out to be a recipe for infighting, layoffs, and unemployment. Taking the "risky" path of start-up life was actually, in the long run, the safer thing to do for any competent person. And for this reason, the Boston area has changed for the better as the traditional companies fell apart and Internet start-ups have arisen. There are many more start-ups and potential CEOs now. But that didn't help us with our problem in 1995.

So we had trouble finding good candidates, which in turn made us too eager to hire whoever was interested, and left us at the mercy of the few qualified people we found. Hence, despite growing misgivings about the individual we chose, I nonetheless agreed that we should hire him. The route to this mistake was highly instructive.

Soon after the first round closed and the board was organized, we formed a CEO search committee. The members were Andy Marcuvitz, Wade Woodson, and myself. But as a practical matter, since Wade was in California, most of the work fell to Andy and me. (I should have forced Andy to keep Wade more involved; mistake number one.) My first shock was discovering that the East Coast VCs weren't as well connected as I assumed, and that the pool of potential East Coast CEOs was very thin. I had thought that Matrix and Atlas would have half a dozen good suggestions; they only had a couple. One was a woman who had been at Apollo, with a fabulous reputation, but I already knew of her myself (through Camille), and then it turned out that she wasn't available. The few others Andy M. suggested didn't impress me—they struck me as bureaucrats and politicians. I was also surprised that Andy seemed inexperienced and uneasy with the whole process. Gradually I realized that while Andy was assuming a senior role at Matrix, he was new at CEO searches, which previously had been handled primarily by Paul Ferri, the senior guy.

Then we tried to find someone through people we knew ourselves, before resorting to a headhunter. We came up with about ten names between me, Randy, Andy Schulert, Bob Davoli, Tom Blumer, and Frank Germano. We talked to a couple of guys from Lotus, but one of them seemed too political—under Jim Manzi, Lotus politics were Byzantine—and the other one, although seemingly decent and smart, kept talking about spending more time with his kids. A friend of Frank Germano's recommended several good people, including a sales VP at a software tools company that had recently gone public. He seemed unusually straightforward and smart for a sales guy, but he had too much money locked up in unvested stock options to change jobs. Then Bob Davoli recommended two guys from Sybase. One of them was John Mandile. Mandile had spent almost a decade at Davoli's database software company, rising to a senior job, and had stayed on after Bob sold the company to Sybase. He had done well at Sybase, too, and was running the Sybase database administration tools business; in just a few years, he had grown their sales dramatically to more than $50 million. The business was based near Boston, so we agreed to meet for dinner.

After that dinner, I vetoed him right away. He didn't feel like a CEO—he seemed nice enough, quite kind and even timid, only moderately smart, and was clearly uncomfortable and nervous when challenged. As we shall see shortly, I can say with confidence that I have never formed a first impression that proved more disastrously incorrect.

The other Sybase executive recommended by Davoli was Richard Yanowich, who was then Sybase's vice president of corporate marketing. I liked him a lot. Although some people I've encountered since have faulted him for being erratic and disorganized, I found Richard to be smart, honest, direct, and well informed about the industry. So did Randy and Ed, although a couple of the technical people worried that he didn't really seem to understand the product when they demonstrated it for him, and indeed Richard had no technical background at all. But his marketing credentials seemed impeccable, and Davoli strongly endorsed him. We conferred with Andy and Wade, who agreed that we should make him an offer. But Richard had just started a relationship with a woman in California and told us he couldn't move. He suggested that he run the company from San Francisco, which was ridiculous, and for the first time made me question his judgment. With some regret, we said no and parted ways. Richard went on to become VP of marketing at VeriSign, a start-up specializing in Internet security systems, which has since gone public.

By March, we were out of leads. So, despite my reservations about headhunters, I agreed it was time to get one. The first one we met, David Beirne from Ramsey Beirne Associates reinforced all my prejudices. Though young, he was already the hottest executive headhunter in the country. We called him on Ferri's recommendation, even though he had just placed Jim Barksdale at Netscape, which Ferri had quite presciently told me would turn out badly. But Ferri endorsed Beirne anyway, and we called him.

Beirne was tall, handsome, and knew it; well dressed, every hair perfectly combed, full of arrogance. He was amusingly gung-ho, "as if he was storming the beach at Iwo Jima" in Marcuvitz's words—and for Andy to say something like that takes quite a provocation. He also seemed utterly uninterested in the substance of the assignment, the content of the job he was filling, or whether the people he found were appropriate. Instead, he bragged about manipulating the process—keeping the board, the VCs, and the founders on track until they converged on a candidate. I think we would have offered him the assignment anyway, because the alternatives were poor. But he must have sensed that I disliked him, and he called a few days later to say that he was too busy to handle our search right now. Beirne has since changed professions; he has become a venture capitalist.

On the other hand, not all executive headhunters are bad. Like VCs, they run a wide gamut. Many of the prominent ones have gigantic egos and can be quite unpleasant. Like PR executives, they frequently have good looks, elegance, and superficial charm, behind which is utter ruthlessness. But a considerable number of them are efficient, professional, and even ethical.

Unfortunately, we got one who was about to retire. We interviewed a half dozen headhunters—most of them in Boston, possibly a mistake. The large ones who specialized in the Fortune 500 were hopeless. We finally settled on a small firm specializing in technology companies, Fenwick Partners, but the partner who handled our search, Jim Masciarelli, told us that we might be his last search, which turned out to be literally true. He didn't seem to work very hard, and his results were not impressive. He was hard to get hold of even after repeated phone calls, rarely met a deadline, and at first he did little except produce long lists of candidates, obviously from some database, with minimal screening. The typical interviewee was a sales or marketing VP at a mediocre software firm—good haircut, firm handshake, about one-third of a brain, clueless about the Internet, trying to connect with me by talking about the stock market, cars, the weather, stereo equipment, and sports. I thought I would die. Sometimes our engineers had worked at their previous companies and had uniformly negative assessments. As the process dragged on, I started getting testy. Masciarelli turned up only one truly interesting candidate, a guy who had a senior engineering management position under Larry Ellison at Oracle. I liked him, and he was clearly smart, but I didn't pull the trigger; at some deep level, I suspected that anyone who had survived that long with Larry was crazy, dangerously political, or both.

HIRING JOHN MANDILE; OR, WATCH OUT, YOU MIGHT GET WHAT YOU'RE AFTER

At a low point in the search process, about mid-May, Davoli urged us to take another look at John Mandile. This time I brought Randy with me. We had dinner at the Harvest in Cambridge, and it went stunningly well. Mandile came across as genuine, smart, thoughtful, relaxed, sincere, ethical, an all-around nice guy. He agreed fervently when I described my hatred for politicized companies, and how good businesses were destroyed by dishonest company cultures. We talked about roles—how my strength was in strategy, partnering choices, and future product directions, while Randy had the key role in charting the company's technical strategy. I said I had no particular desire to manage, no experience or ambitions in marketing or sales, and that we both knew we needed someone to run the show. Mandile was completely enthusiastic.

The job fit his skill set well, although not perfectly. He came from a technical background, which I liked, but had strong general management experience. His marketing background was in expensive business software, which was a different world from ours, but if he was smart and open-minded he could make the shift. The combination of the three of us—me as the strategist, Randy as the technologist, and John running the store—looked fabulous. I distinctly remember a *very* small voice telling me that this was too good to be true, that the contrast with our first dinner was too great. I also wondered just a bit how it could be that Mandile agreed with us about everything we said. Any smart, independent person talking with two others will usually disagree about *something*—that is, if they're being honest. My little voice was right, but it was timid and faint, and I didn't listen to it. The next day, Randy and I told the other board members that we thought we had found our CEO.

I've subsequently thought a lot about how I could have misread Mandile so badly. First, I think he's just a very, very good actor, and he is extremely smart. He's not imaginative, but he calculates quickly and well, is often good at telling people what they want to hear, and almost never reacts emotionally. He always thinks before speaking. He has trained himself to submerge his emotions and to subordinate them to his long-term self-interest; he never gives offense unless he thinks his self-interest requires it. Second, I let my guard down because of his background. He seemed like a smart guy with a technical background from the wrong side of the tracks—just like me. Technical people are usually more direct and less political. I have since learned, however, that there is a huge difference between engineers and executives who used to be engineers, and I have become less naïve about the latter. I was also lulled by the fact that, like me, he came from a poor family. In a subtle way, Mandile played this card well. I'm trying to be less naïve about that, too; poverty isn't always ennobling. Then there was Mandile's shy, slightly awkward, unpretentious, utterly unthreatening, yet relaxed manner when Randy and I had dinner with him, in contrast to his nervousness the first time. Randy's presence may have been a factor there; he has a calming effect on everybody that undoubtedly helped Mandile perform to best advantage. Mandile, I found later, tends to come apart in front of groups, or when facing people who are stronger, quicker, or better educated than he is—I've seen him literally shake with nervousness. At some level I also let my anxiety about needing to find a CEO override my skepticism about human nature. And by the time my doubts about Mandile became truly serious, it would have taken a big fight to dislodge him—at a time when I already had plenty of fights on my hands.

Finally, I didn't realize until later the degree to which Mandile had apparently become a surrogate son to Davoli, and I may also have been naïve about Davoli himself. Mandile, the son of a police officer, had needed to push hard in order to go to college. Both Mandile and Davoli came from blue-collar Italian families, had struggled, gotten second-tier educations in class-conscious Boston, and had done extremely well financially. They were both tough and, in different ways, a bit on edge about their backgrounds and credentials. Once again this lulled me into complacency; I too have a low tolerance for the spoiled preppies and WASP idiots you still see around Boston. But I think there is one fundamental difference between Mandile and Davoli. Although he conceals it extremely well, I gradually came to the conclusion that Mandile is a deeply angry, cynical, frustrated, envious man. It is therefore both natural and in his self-interest to assume the same of others, which allows him to rationalize his behavior toward them.

The point of all this is that I suspect (though I must emphasize that I can't prove) that Davoli helped Mandile during our negotiations with him, including coaching on how to please me. Davoli was no sweet innocent young thing either; I later learned that he had a reputation as a ruthless negotiator, and of course he had concealed from me the fact that he'd been negotiating with Sigma to become a VC ever since I'd met him.

In any event, while Mandile's early conduct did raise a few questions, for the first several weeks my emotions were primarily quite enthusiastic. But the whispering in the back of my head got louder when this salt-of-the-earth, aw-shucks, nice, quiet, common-man fellow turned into an excruciatingly tough, relentless, and very clever negotiator. The VCs occasionally complained that I had gotten an unusually good deal, even though the company was my idea, I had funded it out of my own pocket for eight months and had run it for over a year. Yet despite the fact that Mandile didn't start working full-time until only one month before the product shipped (and only four months before the company was sold), he ended up with a deal that wasn't just good—it was *ridiculous*.

How did this happen? The short answer is that we were desperate, I was naïve, and Mandile outmaneuvered us. By late May or early June, when we concluded that we would try to make Mandile an offer, we were getting fairly desperate for a CEO. The engineers were cranking out superb code at a frightening rate; ready or not, we were going to have a real product by October. So we had a huge amount of work immediately ahead of us—a PR campaign, the major trade shows, building a marketing team and sales force, negotiating distribution channels and partnerships, pricing, customer support, planning the next generation of products. I had no serious experience in any of these areas, and nobody else in the company really did either. In deference to the incoming CEO, we'd also held up hiring, since we thought the CEO should pick his own team. So I was getting worried that we were headed for a train wreck, and the VCs agreed.

Consequently, after Mandile had met everyone, we had agreed fairly quickly that we'd try to get him. Then the fun started. Suddenly everything started to get very complicated and to take an extraordinarily long time, even though we were ready to proceed quickly. Randy and I were positive; Marcuvitz had met Mandile and liked him; and Davoli was enthusiastic. I kept Davoli informed of all of our discussions, including on compensation, which was undoubtedly a mistake, since he was almost certainly on Mandile's side as much as the company's. Mandile became very hard to pin down on anything, although he always insisted he wanted to proceed as rapidly as possible. He also started to make requests, ask questions, and encounter little problems that, taken together, caused major delays. This also started to open my eyes. For example, he wanted to meet the senior people in the company and some of the engineers, but without revealing his name or that he was a CEO candidate. I was impressed but a little disturbed by how quickly he suggested a plausible lie so that we could bring him to a staff meeting using a cover story. His insistence on absolute secrecy bothered me too, especially as the process stretched out for week after week.

Secrecy naturally complicated the question of references. Mandile was very reluctant to give us names and said it was very important that we not ask *anyone* about him without his permission. We agreed, and moreover kept our word, which was stupid. I later found several people who shared the opinion of Mandile that I later came to hold; they described him as political, dishonest, and ruthless. But we spoke only to the two references he gave us, so we didn't hear any of the negatives. One of these references, however, set off an alarm signal anyway. He was a guy named Mark Pine, who, I later found out, was also in the process of leaving Sybase, and he and John had agreed to be mutual references. Neat trick. At one point in the conversation, I asked him about John's weaknesses, and he embarked on a disquisition about how John's distaste for politics had put him at a disadvantage at Sybase—all very reassuring, until I realized with a shock that he was using the *identical words* that Mandile had used at our dinner. I was listening to a prepared script. I was upset and told Marcuvitz. He was disappointed, but reacted unemotionally—I wish it didn't happen, Charles, but many people do it. Besides that, John seems like a good guy, and we need a CEO.

I was also slow to realize that these delays, nearly all caused by Mandile, were working in his favor. The product train was thundering down the tracks, so the need to shore up management got more urgent by the day. But as the CEO search came to focus on Mandile, we'd stopped looking for alternatives. In the meantime, he could watch the product take shape and see how the customers were responding to the trial releases. So his risk was going down while his bargaining position kept improving. The cynical side of me had to admire the performance.

The next mistake I made was to cede control of the negotiations to Marcuvitz. We agreed on a set of fairly reasonable terms at a board meeting, with Davoli present, of course, which I shouldn't have allowed. Andy M. reported back that Mandile accepted in principle, but wanted to discuss some of the financial details. At least a week went by, and I called Mandile. He said that he was very enthusiastic, but had to make it work financially. Nothing outrageous, he insisted, but he thought he deserved a fair amount of stock to make up for options he'd be losing at Sybase, and for taking a big salary cut when his wife was about to have their second child. I just need enough to pay my mortgage, he said, I'm sure you can understand. Sure, I said.

Then it dragged on—and on. Every few days I'd hear from Marcuvitz that there was some new thing. Mandile needed to own some stock right away to lock him in. Then how much he needed to own. Then vesting. Then salary again. Starting bonus. A mix of common and preferred stock to keep his buy-in price down. A loan to finance the stock purchase, because he didn't have any money. A higher salary. Greatly accelerated vesting in the event we were acquired. Whenever I talked to Mandile, he'd apologize for the delay and emphasize his enthusiasm—was not trying to be difficult, was really excited about joining, we just needed to understand that he had a family and a mortgage and he had to protect himself.

As the deal got richer and richer, I started to get upset. If we were acquired Mandile's options would vest much faster than anyone else's, including mine. And if we were acquired quickly Mandile would get a huge payoff for very little work. In fact, if we were acquired the day after Mandile started, he would get about *70 percent* of his stock. Marcuvitz pooh-poohed that. If we get bought out that fast, we'll all be happy, he said, but the chances of that are small. To make any money, he said, we probably have to take the company public and fight and win over the long term. Besides, he said, we want John's interests aligned with yours. We don't want him to have a dramatically different incentive structure than you do for acquisition relative to IPO. This was horse manure, of course, because the effect of John's package was precisely to give him an extremely disproportionate incentive to sell the company.

I called Davoli and said that I was getting disturbed. Furthermore, I was somewhat puzzled. Davoli had told me that Mandile had gotten a substantial amount of stock before the sale of his company to Sybase. So I asked him for the details, and he told me that Mandile had gotten about a million dollars, plus some options from Sybase. I was surprised. A million dollars is a *lot* more money that I had when I started this company, I said, so why do we have to lend him money to buy stock? Well, Davoli said, I think he put a lot of it into his house, so he wouldn't have a mortgage. Oh really, I thought.

I called Mandile. John, I said, I'm getting concerned about the compensation issue, and how much time and energy it's taking. For example, since you got a million dollars from the Sybase acquisition, why do you need a loan to buy your stock? —Well, he said, you were poor too, Charles, so I'm sure you understand. I didn't want to have any debt so I paid off my house. We're planning more children and I just didn't want to live with the thought that it could ever be taken away. —But, John, I said, I thought you needed a good salary so you could pay your mortgage. You've said that maybe three or four times in those exact words. But, John, you don't *have* a mortgage.

Silence. With no exaggeration, one of the loudest, most eloquent silences I've ever heard. I could practically hear Mandile's brain moving at top speed as he screamed to himself, OH SHIT I blew it. After maybe fifteen or twenty seconds, Mandile said, That was just a figure of speech, I just meant that I have expenses, my wife doesn't work, we have some help, and I have two children. I said something like, okay, John, but I think it's time to decide. We've made you a generous offer, we really like you, but we have to get going, and this has taken a long time already. Yes, I understand, he said, but you've dealt with Andy Marcuvitz, and you how difficult he is.

I told Davoli that I had just caught Mandile not telling the truth, and that I thought he was stringing us along. Davoli dismissed my concerns. He said, I've known this guy ten years, he's one of the most honest people I know, you simply don't have to worry about that at all. But Davoli said he agreed this had gone on too long and said he'd talk to Mandile and tell him it was time to make up his mind. I was confused and disturbed; Davoli *did* know this guy well, yet I was becoming very, very worried.I called Randy and told him about the mortgage incident. Oh really, Randy said; he took it quite seriously. He was concerned about the lying, but we agreed that we'd reached a point of no return and should still proceed. My little voice was now clamoring that this was a big mistake, but I didn't let even Randy know how worried I was.

By this point, backing out would have been painful. We were about six weeks from product launch, Ed Cuoco was our entire marketing and sales staff, and we had *completely* stopped searching for other CEO candidates. Not to mention the fact that I was starting a world-class fight with the VCs over second-round funding, and another battle with Andy Marcuvitz was just what I didn't need. Furthermore, canceling on Mandile would undoubtedly have led to serious tension with Davoli, who until now had been an extremely helpful guy. All that said, let me be clear: I screwed up. I should have had three marketing and sales managers in my back pocket and I should have had the nerve to say no. I should have had the courage of my convictions and bet that in another two months, once we had started announcing ourselves to the world, we could get anybody we wanted.

Marcuvitz and Mandile finally settled on terms. Mandile became president and CEO, replacing Randy on the board, with a $99,000 salary, $1,000 lower than mine. I found this bizarre when I discovered it and supposed that either Marcuvitz or Mandile had thought that it would soothe my ego. We lent him $106,000 to buy shares equal to about 1.6 percent of the company, and on top of that gave him options representing another 6 percent of the company. His basic vesting terms were the same as everybody else's: the options vested over five years with a one-year "cliff" (he had to stay for a year to get anything) and a year's acceleration if we were acquired. But there was one exception that nobody else had. *In the sole event of acquisition, John's vesting would be accelerated by an additional twenty months* beyond the one-year acceleration of vesting upon acquisition that was the standard provision for all of us.

I thought this was outrageous, and it was. To start with, the stock purchase loan bothered me a lot. In effect, he walked in the door, and could turn around and walk out again the next day, owning an amount of stock nearly as large as what Andy and Peter would earn through full vesting of their options. John received this stock without doing any work or putting up a nickel of his own money. I didn't mind the large block of options we gave him—if we had a five-year fight for market share against Microsoft and Netscape and he ran the company well, he would deserve every penny. But the special acceleration provision bothered me *a lot*. If we were acquired on the day Mandile started work, he would own about 5.6 percent of the company, more than any of the other employees except me. I objected strenuously, but finally gave in not because Marcuvitz persuaded me on the merits but because I was simply too tired and worried that we had no other serious CEO options. So the offer was made and Mandile *said* he accepted.

But had he? Still more time went by—many weeks, in fact. There were more arguments on little details, and John wanted his lawyers to review everything before signing his employment agreement. He also dragged out the process of resigning from Sybase. First he didn't want to tell anyone at Sybase; he wanted to wait until he could find "the right occasion." I had to start applying pressure; then John said he had told Sybase, but we had no independent evidence that this was even true. Then he said Sybase couldn't announce his resignation, even internally, until a replacement was found. More time passed. All this time, John demanded secrecy, so we couldn't even tell important potential investors that we had a CEO. Then he insisted on a month's vacation before he joined us, despite all the urgency we felt about bringing him on board. The whole process, from start to finish, took four months, from May to September. Mandile's first day as Vermeer's CEO was September 11, 1995—the same day that Peter and I made our presentation at the Shaffer conference in San Francisco.

Puzzlingly, when Mandile finally permitted us to introduce him to the employees sometime in late August, he was so nervous that his hands shook, he stumbled over his words, and he spoke so softly that many people in the room couldn't hear him. That's the side of him I had seen at our first dinner, and it had initially convinced me he wasn't tough enough to be a CEO. But although Mandile was extremely insecure and timid in certain situations, his management of us had been masterful. As I was to learn over the coming months, we had just hired one of the most perfect self-interest-maximizing machines I have ever encountered. From now on, I would be fighting a two-front war. And the other front had opened about a month before Mandile officially started work. We needed to raise some serious money, which meant it was time for another conversation with my favorite people, the VCs.

ROUND TWO WITH THE VCS: THE FIGHT OVER SECOND-ROUND FUNDING

I didn't know much about organizational infighting when I started Vermeer, and it's a domain in which I am neither naturally gifted nor eager to improve my skills. But by necessity I was gradually learning. One essential strategy was to suspect the worst and plan accordingly, well in advance. The negotiations over first-round funding had been a good lesson in this regard. Then, just as I went to war with my VCs again over second-round funding, the CEO hiring experience opened my eyes to the power of delaying tactics. By saying yes but then stringing out the process until we were desperate, Mandile had stopped our search for other candidates and enormously strengthened his bargaining position. Hmmmm. What about my second-round funding? I wasn't afraid that the VCs would let the company fail, but I suspected, correctly, that they would love to buy more of it, and as cheaply as possible. One way to do this would be to employ exactly the same strategy, i.e., to wait until we were out of time.

This suspicious thought had first crossed my mind in the late spring. Mitch Kapor, whom Andy Schulert knew well and I knew slightly, came in to talk with us. We showed him the demo, at which point Mitch pulled me aside and said he wanted to consider making an investment. We discussed a pre-money valuation of $12 million, a 50 percent premium over the first round that had closed only a month previously. But when I raised the issue to the VCs, Andy Marcuvitz objected. He argued that most celebrity investors don't add much value and that Mitch's investment would dilute us if we could get more than a 50 percent markup in our second round. In the end, the issue was mooted; Mitch decided not to invest, in part because he believed Microsoft's FUD about Blackbird. But

Andy Marcuvitz's response to the possibility was most revealing. I noted with interest but not surprise his rapid production of a spreadsheet demonstrating the diluting effects of a wide array of investment scenarios. This was in response to a possible $500,000 investment by one of the most famous and successful entrepreneurs in high technology. If this is how he behaves now, I thought to myself, what's going to happen when it's time to raise $10 million or so?

Our projections, based on very conservative spending plans, indicated that we had enough money in the bank to last until about the end of the year. If we spent heavily on our launch, we would burn out even faster. Since it could easily take at least three months to raise money, waiting until the fall would be cutting it very close. Furthermore, the Internet was heating up so fast that I increasingly suspected that we *should* spend more money than we had planned, particularly for marketing and sales. I started testing the waters for second-round money at a board meeting in June. The VCs shot me down. They said it was ridiculously early; we needed to get the product finished first; there were too many other important things going on. Their objections made sense at the time, but as I watched Mandile's hiring process drag on, and the Internet heat up, I was determined not to let the VCs catch me in a squeeze.

The board meeting in early August was supposed to be a happy, pat-ourselves-on-the-back, hey-great-job-guys experience. It was the first one that Mandile attended; although he wouldn't start for another month, he had just signed his contract, so we decided to invite him. This meant that half my options had vested. The VCs may have assumed that this would put me in a good mood, but if anything it gave me the security to be tougher. At the board meeting, we demonstrated the first functionally complete version of our product, which was about to enter beta testing. We were very close to the schedule I had set the previous winter, the code looked good, and the VCs were pleased. Suddenly, though, I found myself making a speech that I had not planned. I distinctly remember that I surprised myself at the determination and barely suppressed anger in my voice. The rest of the room was stunned and uncomfortably silent.

We have now completed the first visual end-user development tool for the World Wide Web, I said. The Internet is now white hot. Furthermore, we have done an amazing job. Our product is on time and under budget, and you know perfectly well that it will be a very important and very successful product. But to grow and to compete with Netscape and Microsoft, we need to raise a large amount of money. This company is now extremely valuable, and I do not intend to sell it cheaply. I would like to hear how you intend to help us raise a second round at the highest possible valuation, and I am determined to *get* a fair valuation with or without your help. I intend to start fund-raising in September.

My tone was tense and confrontational. A shocked silence followed until Marcuvitz, tough and cool as always, replied evenly, Charles, we all want this company to succeed as much as you do. The product looks good, but there's a lot more to do before this company is successful. He paused, and then went on: But you're right to worry about the time it takes to raise money. Perhaps we should think about doing an inside round, just with the people here. You already know us, and we know the company. I think we'd be happy giving you a very attractive step up in valuation, and it would save you time when you need to be running the company. We could probably close a deal in a couple of weeks.

I suspected a trap, and I was right. I replied that we could certainly discuss it, but it would depend on getting a fair valuation. The meeting broke up shortly after that, rather tensely.

I proceeded, over the next several months, to become a serious hard-ass—not just in substance, but also in style. Even with Wade, whom I liked and trusted more than our other VCs, I was hostile and challenging. To this day, Marcuvitz tells me that it was all wasted energy. Once a VC has committed and invested in a company, the VC's interests, this line goes, are aligned with those of the employees—everyone just wants to make the company as valuable as it can be. If the employees get rich, the VCs get rich. So you can trust the VCs to do the right thing. To this day Andy Marcuvitz insists, with a straight face, that the VCs had no interest in pushing for a lower valuation.

To put it bluntly, this is complete bullshit.

Allow me to elaborate. If you're starting a company, you might want to read this rather carefully—it could save you a lot of money. It's a bit complicated, but let me tell you, it's worth the effort. You won't hear this from your average VC.

Andy, and most VCs, try to keep the argument vague—after all, we're all shareholders, and we all want the same things, right? *Wrong,* as you'll see. Then, when pinned to the wall and forced to make a rigorous case, Andy based his claim on VCs' "pro-rata" investment rights. As is typical, our first-round investment agreement contained a provision that guaranteed the VCs the right to invest exactly enough money in later rounds to maintain their original ownership share. In other words, since the first-round VCs got a 50.1 percent share of the company, they had the right to maintain their 50.1 percent position by making the indicated fraction of any later investment. There is indeed a reason that most VC investment contracts specify the right to invest exactly this much. The reason is that the financial arithmetic turns out such that, in this situation, the first-round investors are *exactly indifferent* to the valuation of later rounds.

However, it also turns out that this is an extremely special case. In fact, pro-rata investment is the *only* case where the VCs are financially indifferent to valuation. So, yes, it is true that if early investors maintain exactly the same share of the company through later rounds, they are indifferent to the valuations of these rounds, because they dilute themselves just enough to offset changes in valuation. The higher the second-round valuation, the more they have to pay, but the less they dilute their earlier holdings, and at pro rata these two effects exactly cancel each other out. However, even this condition can be unhealthy. A company's investors and board shouldn't be *indifferent*. They should have incentives to do the best thing for the company, its employees, and *all* of its shareholders—i.e., increasing the value of the company. Otherwise, inappropriate factors can tip the balance. Like whether the VCs will look good to their limited partners, or whether they can let a pal into the deal at a low price, or whether they're just too lazy to do the work required to get the best achievable deal.

But first-round investors have the correct incentives only if their share of the company *declines* over time, either because they don't invest in later rounds at all or, preferably, because they do invest, but less than their pro-rata share. In this case, the VCs do indeed have the same goal as employees, i.e., to get the highest valuation possible.

But in the real world, and in our case, the indifference produced by pro-rata investing isn't the worst problem. The worst problem is that in reality, when a company starts looking really good, the first-round VCs often try to invest *more* than their pro-rata share. This is what Andy Marcuvitz proposed at our board meeting, and both Andy and Barry Fidelman later continued to propose privately. And if the VCs' share of the company increases over time, e.g., because they are the principal or sole investors in the second round, then their incentive is to minimize the valuation of the round so they can own more of the company for a given amount of money. In other words, *their interests are exactly opposed to those of the employees*. The lower the valuation, the larger the VCs' share, and the more profit they earn at exit. The employees, on the other hand, are *always* better off with a higher valuation. In our case, the outside deal we eventually obtained was even better for the employees, for interesting reasons I'll get to later.

If we had done the friendly, simple inside deal that Marcuvitz and Fidelman wanted, the VCs would have owned two-thirds of the company, not the 53 percent they actually owned when Microsoft acquired us. For the employees, the difference was far more dramatic: we owned nearly half the company instead of a third. This meant that we collectively made almost $19 million more *on the day the deal closed*. This effect was greatly multiplied by the stratospheric increase in Microsoft's stock—a factor of ten since the acquisition. Since almost everybody expected Microsoft stock to rise, we held on to most of it. By 1999, on conservative assumptions, and even allowing for substantial sales, the difference between the two deals was therefore worth more than $150 million to the employees. So, yes, I admit it: for a mere $150 million in additional wealth for Vermeer's employees, I acted like an asshole for three months and ruined my loving, close, tender relationships with our VCs. Later, our position was further improved by special provisions that permitted us to take only part of the round. This was an urgent last-minute change, made for reasons I'll explain later.

We wanted to raise about $6–$8 million in our second round. The higher the pre-money valuation, the smaller the share the new investors would get for their money. So the big question was, what pre-money valuation could we get for our second round?

There is no science to VC valuations; it's mostly rules of thumb, chance, and market conditions, which fluctuate wildly over industry cycles. Ironically, the more important and novel and powerful your idea, the worse you're likely to do at first, because it won't yet be conventional wisdom, and you'll be forced to educate your VCs. When we were raising our first round, few VCs had heard of the Web, and their ignorance and skepticism contributed to keeping our valuation low. I knew that the world had changed a lot since then; the VC herd mentality ought now to work in our favor. We knew that Netscape's second-round financing in April had been done at a valuation of about $150 million, or more than ten times higher than their first round the year before. And we expected their public offering, coming up shortly, to be at a much higher valuation than that, as indeed it was. At that time, the only real products Netscape had delivered were early browsers and Web servers, which were a lot less complicated than FrontPage, not nearly as well engineered, and easier for Microsoft to clone. I was quite aware, as the VCs constantly reminded me, that I wasn't a famous and experienced founder like Jim Clark, and that we didn't have a name-brand management team, so I didn't expect the tenfold increase in valuation that Netscape had obtained. But I thought a multiple of three to six should be feasible, and I wasn't in a mood to settle for less.

A few days after the August board meeting at which I threw down the gauntlet, I called Wade. To his credit, Wade suggested looking for an outside investor. He also suggested that we ask for roughly a 50 percent markup. That is to say, our second-round pre-money valuation would be $12 million, 50 percent up from the $8 million *post*-money valuation as of the first-round closing. Wade said that a step-up of two times would be generous, and that I shouldn't even think about a step-up of three times. I rejected this instantly. We argued a bit over the validity of a comparison with Netscape, and he suggested that I talk to Marcuvitz again.

Marcuvitz and I thereupon had a series of conversations, after several of which he proposed an inside round at a $16 million pre-money valuation, a two-times markup. I summarily turned it down, whereupon things began to get edgy. He said, Charles, you should think about this. It is a very attractive offer by industry standards, and we could all agree on it quickly and easily. No thanks, I replied. We deserve better, and I think we can get it.

Then I said, Andy, we're going to proceed, and I will expect you not to interfere with us. Directors of companies are supposed to serve the interest of the company, not their own interest, and it would be unethical and possibly illegal of you to block any action that was in the best interest of the company. In fact, it's probably unethical for you to propose an inside round without helping us try to do better. Marcuvitz came back coolly and quickly: Charles, the interests of the company are decided by the collective judgment of the *entire* board, not just me and not just *you* either. I have a perfect right to make a reasonable proposal, which by industry standards is quite generous. I replied, Andy, the interests of our company are clear: to get the most money while giving up the smallest possible share of our equity. No, Andy said, there is also value to having known investors and avoiding the disruption of fund-raising during a critical period. The conversation ended with me saying something pleasant like, Andy, this is bullshit and you know it. To myself, I thought, Uh-oh, here we go again.

So I started the process of raising money, almost as if it were the first round again. The VCs asked me to keep them informed. I told them to go to hell. I also told them that I would require potential investors to speak to me before having any contact with the board. I began writing a second-round business plan that I could circulate to outside investors. I spent at least half my time on it for two weeks in late August and early September, and, if I say so myself, by the time we started sending it out in late September, it was very good. Meanwhile, I had several more conversations with Wade, which at first were more amicable than those with Marcuvitz. To his credit, Wade didn't try to persuade me to do an inside round, although he still asserted that my ambitions were off the wall, and I didn't exactly see him pounding the pavement on our behalf. I was aware that I had complicated our first-round funding by asking for an excessively high valuation, and the VCs took every opportunity to remind me. But I made it clear to Wade that I wouldn't give in this time, at which point things got rough.

In one telephone call Wade told me, If it will make you feel better, go out and shop around. I asked him what he thought our asking price should be. He said, Make your asking number high, but not crazy. It should start with a two. We were speaking about pre-money valuations, so that was more than Marcuvitz proposed, but Wade stressed that this was an asking price, and that I'd probably have to settle for a Marcuvitz-like number. I asked him, What about opening with a number that starts with a three or a four? Not a chance, he said. And if you go around asking for excessively high valuations, you'll discredit yourself just as you did before. And by the way, if you did get something that high, we'd probably pass on the round, so you'd have to raise the whole round outside. I didn't like that at all; I don't know whether Wade meant it as a threat, but it sure sounded like one. We then argued through the Netscape comparison again, as well as comparisons with other Internet companies and various tools companies. By this time, of course, the Internet IPO wave— UUNet, Spyglass, PSI, and, above all, Netscape—had overturned all previous benchmarks, and I started getting angry. My relations with Wade got quite rough during this period, although I always trusted him more than Andy or Barry.

After a few weeks they realized I wouldn't listen to reason. What happened then would have been highly entertaining, if it hadn't been happening to *me*. My determination to go it alone, and my refusal to let the VCs control the process, set off a series of complex interactions, negotiations, and alliances as everyone jockeyed for position. It was like palace intrigue in fifteenth-century Florence, or perhaps present-day Iraq. You just assume that anyone might try to kill you at any time, that everyone has a hidden dagger, and that the dagger is probably poisoned. Your food taster becomes your best friend, especially if he has a food taster too, and even more so if they have to taste your food *after* you've eaten it as well as before.

Barry Fidelman, our second-tier investor and board observer from Atlas, approached me with a proposal to beat out Matrix and Sigma for the second-round lead. He proposed a $20 million valuation if we gave Atlas the lead. I thought, Hell, let's see how far Barry will go. I told him that I'd let him have the lead position, as long as he brought in at least one outside investor and agreed to a valuation of over $30 million. He replied that he'd consider it seriously. But nothing happened, as I should have realized. I don't think Barry had the guts to piss off Wade, Davoli, and Andy Marcuvitz that much, not to mention Paul Ferri, who could eat Barry for breakfast without even swallowing hard. Wade played tough at first on valuation, but proved to be a moderating (and civilizing) force on the inside-round issue, which was his natural role. Marcuvitz, of course, dug in until he realized it was hopeless.

Things got *really* Byzantine when Bob Davoli approached me and said *he* wanted to break in as an angel investor, pretending that he was helping me against the VCs, when in reality he was in the process of becoming a VC himself. The morning before a board meeting, in early September, I believe, Davoli came to see me privately. Note: *me*, alone, not Mandile, who was about to become our CEO and was Davoli's old friend. Davoli offered to lead the new round at a $17 million pre-money valuation, $1 million more than Marcuvitz had offered, with a personal investment of $500,000 to $1 million. He also asked for a seat on the board. I'm a former entrepreneur, he said, and I'm always inclined to favor the entrepreneur over the VCs. The VCs will try to screw you, as I'm sure you realize. Then, in the board meeting, Davoli repeated his offer. I turned him down flat. The valuation wasn't high enough, and furthermore I sensed there was something weird about it.

There was. I've never figured out exactly what was going on, and who knew what when. But a short time later, Wade called to tell me that Davoli was joining Sigma, and that they'd been negotiating this for almost a year, in fact even before the first round had closed. If Davoli had in fact led the round and joined the board, Sigma would have acquired two votes on the board, which neither Andy Marcuvitz nor I would have liked at all. To say that I wouldn't have been amused is the understatement of the decade—perhaps the only time that Andy M. and I have agreed on a question of corporate governance. Soon afterward Marcuvitz and Wade clearly had, as the diplomatic press releases say, a frank and open exchange of views. I had not, of course, been invited to participate. However, at the next board meeting Wade said he had a brief statement to make. He announced that everyone had cordially agreed that Bob Davoli was joining Sigma Partners, that Davoli would remain a *nonvoting* observer on the Vermeer board, and that any further personal investments by Davoli would come out of Sigma's share—whatever that share turned out to be. At this point, I really began to think that life as a triple agent would be simple by comparison.

And then there was John Mandile, our new CEO, who finally started on the job in September. Midway through the process, he started trying to marginalize me. I fought this, quite successfully, but it didn't make matters any easier to pretend in public that Mandile and I were the best of friends when in reality I could never turn my back on him. In private, Mandile told me that he agreed that the VCs were trying to screw us, and said we could beat them together. At the same time, he took care to let me do most of the fighting; he was happy for me to be the bad cop while he was the good one. I strongly suspect that John was already thinking about life after Vermeer, and at a minimum, he wanted to avoid giving offense to people who he realized could be valuable to him in the future—and, in fact, who were. Andy Marcuvitz, one of the toughest negotiators I know, had just given him an amazingly favorable compensation package. And Davoli, his mentor, had already been negotiating with Sigma for a year. Mandile has in fact followed Davoli to Sigma, where he now works. Mandile also received an offer from Matrix after Vermeer was acquired.

As soon as Mandile started to work as our CEO, two incidents strikingly confirmed to me how manipulative he was. The first was when I told Mandile about Davoli's private conversation with me, in which he had requested a board seat. Mandile professed not to have known about this. I asked him what he thought was going on, and what he thought we should do. Don't worry,

Mandile said, it's not hard to manage Bob. The key is making him look good to the world. Then we'll be fine. I've been doing it for years. Believe me, it's a very manageable problem.

This truly shocked me, although I tried not to show it. True, Davoli was a tough guy; but Mandile owed a *huge* debt to him. Davoli had extremely kind and paternal feelings for Mandile, had made him rich, had made him the god-father of his children, had introduced Mandile to Vermeer, and had been critical to getting him the job as Vermeer's CEO. No matter what Mandile did and how I discussed my growing concerns, Davoli loyally defended John and had never spoken of him except in the most glowing terms. Yet Mandile was now telling me, casually and without the slightest emotion, that Davoli was an easy guy to manipulate because of his ego, and that Mandile had been playing him like a violin for years. That conversation really made me shudder.

Shortly afterward, we were discussing potential competitors and how to acquire information about them. Oh, it's pretty simple, Mandile said, I had this problem at Sybase all the time. You just take a couple of your best engineers, make sure that you have them locked in with lots of stock options, and then have them call headhunters and ask for interviews with your competitors. A full set of interviews for a senior engineer or a development manager will tell you all you need to know, and nobody can ever prove anything. Engineers will tell other engineers everything, you know that. Trying to control myself, I replied that perhaps we didn't need to do that.

What I still don't understand is what effect John thought these statements would have on me. Bizarrely, it seemed that somehow he thought that these kinds of revelations would help me trust him and make me feel in his debt for receiving valuable life lessons. Rather, I found myself trying hard not to show how completely appalled I was. One consequence of John's cynicism, I think, is that it blinded him to the possibility that others might not be like him. Perhaps he assumed that as long as I made money, I wouldn't care about anything else.

But at the same time that getting to know John Mandile was scaring the hell out of me, many other things were going spectacularly well. I was finishing the second-round business plan, as well as an article for *Upside* magazine. *Upside* is not well known outside of Silicon Valley, but it is one of the few magazines aimed primarily at technology executives and investors, so it attracts an extremely influential audience. They agreed to publish my article in the November issue, which was actually distributed fairly early in October—i.e., when we launched our product. I circulated several hundred copies privately even earlier, prior to the Shaffer conference in September. It wasn't the first article to describe the future of the Web, but it was early, and the message was clear. It not only described what was attractive about the Web, but mercilessly listed what was wrong with traditional online services, including Notes and MSN.

I also got in a couple of advertisements for Vermeer, although I was fairly genteel about it. I mentioned Vermeer's tools only in a line or two, along with a list of other available products, including NaviSoft's. I did say, however, that unfortunately NaviSoft's tool "requires NaviSoft's proprietary Webserver, database system, or Web hosting services. My company, Vermeer Technologies, has created an end-user, client-server visual development environment that provides server- and vendor-independence." In my defense, this self-serving comment was true, and it was in part because of their closed, proprietary nature that NaviSoft's products sank without a trace. In fact, one could argue that I was taking a risk by giving NaviSoft a wake-up call. But they slept right through it. Interestingly, it turned out that Microsoft *didn't* sleep through it, even though my comments about them were comparatively brief.

Far more important than the *Upside* article, however, was the fact that we had been invited to Dick Shaffer's Digital Media Outlook conference (now called Internet Outlook). It was there that we were catapulted into the public eye, instantly became one of the hottest properties in technology, and got ourselves within reach of my insanely high valuation goals.

THE SHAFFER CONFERENCE

Dick Shaffer is a class act. He clearly enjoys the part, with his elegant clothes, gray hair, bow tie, and courtly manner. And although he's sometimes quite the showman and also probably a tough businessman, he is also, in my experience, one of the industry's few gentlemen. He is an electronic media guru who specializes in publishing high-end (and expensive) newsletters and running annual executive conferences (also expensive) on the major sectors in high technology. So he was naturally one of the people I called when we started our selective evangelism campaign in early summer. Randy and I visited his ultra cool Manhattan offices (the former headquarters of the Perry Ellis fashion business, complete with runway) and made a presentation to his staff, who seemed to like what they saw. A month later, Dick called to say that if we had something to show, he'd like us to be among the companies making presentations at his September conference. This invitation was a big deal, and it got even bigger when he called back later inviting me to participate in a panel discussion on the Web, in front of the whole conference, which was several hundred of the most important people in the industry, including lots of VCs. I accepted instantly.

A Vermeer buzz was just becoming audible when Randy, Peter, and I flew out to California for the conference, which like all of them was held at a huge, ugly hotel just south of the San Francisco airport. My panel discussion came early and was composed of a half-dozen industry executives and analysts. This was just a month after the Netscape IPO, so everyone suddenly knew that the Web was Something Really Big, but, to my surprise, many people in the industry still didn't know much more than that. When we were raising our first round, very few people in the financial community had even heard of the Web. A year later, it seemed, the level of real technical knowledge hadn't changed much, except now they all knew that Kleiner Perkins had made a ton of money on Netscape, so they wanted to learn how to do it too.

Randy and Peter were watching the panel discussion. I provided an overview of the Web's inherent benefits and argued that it would supersede all proprietary systems trying to do similar things, roughly the argument in my *Upside* article. Online services like MSN and AOL, document exchange systems like Adobe's Acrobat, corporate groupware like Notes, and much else, would all be replaced by the Web/Internet architecture.

Chuck Geschke, the co-founder of Adobe, was the next speaker. He's nice, smart, and technically deep, so I was stunned to hear him discuss the Web by making wildly inaccurate claims about its technical limitations. I was sure that he was wrong, but I had enough respect for Geschke that I wanted confirmation. I looked into the audience at Peter, who had positioned himself so that I could see him. He shook his head wildly, signaling that Geschke was indeed full of it. I don't know whether it was an attempt to save Adobe's huge investments in Acrobat, or just ignorance. I tried for statesmanlike regret when I said that Mr. Geschke was, unfortunately, misinformed.

My presentation apparently had some effect; afterward I was surrounded by people with lots of money. Our company presentations came soon after. At Shaffer's conferences these are very tightly scheduled, exactly twenty minutes each, and they run in parallel, so you're competing for the audience. Some are virtually empty. But when Peter and I found our way to our assigned room, we could barely get in. The crowded room, the pushing to be able to see, the people straining to hear from the doorway and the corridor beyond all created an atmosphere that was simply electric. Then came one of those trivial problems that can kill you. Our projector failed; without it, Peter couldn't give his demo. One of Shaffer's people told me they'd get us one from another company, after they'd finished their presentation. With a regret I could not afford to show, I said that in five minutes, the time we had allotted for my introductory talk, my personality would undergo a dramatic change if a projector didn't appear, fast. I gave a crisp overview, and the projector appeared the instant we needed it.

Then Peter gave one of his most dazzling presentations. I hadn't even seen it before; it was a clever re-creation of how FrontPage could be used to develop, and improve upon, Shaffer's own Web site. Afterward we were practically assaulted by bankers and VCs wanting deals. We did it all over again two hours later, the room equally packed with yet more VCs, investment bankers, and Fortune 500 executives. We had their complete, undivided attention. Vermeer was on the map, and I knew now for sure that we were a hot property. Several VCs, including Hummer Winblad, approached us on the spot and offered to invest. When we told them it would be expensive, they didn't blink. I liked that. Hambrecht & Quist invited us to an enormous Internet conference they were doing in New York several weeks later, at which Randy and I spoke shortly after Mike Homer of Netscape. That conference, attended by several hundred VCs and investment bankers as well as all the major Internet companies, also helped significantly.

But the Shaffer conference was the catalyst. From that moment on, we were deluged with calls from venture capitalists, investment bankers, and potential strategic partners. At least two dozen would-be investors and partners approached me within the couple days of the conference, including most of the blue-ribbon firms—Morgan Stanley Venture Capital, Hambrecht & Quist, AT&T Ventures, Hummer Winblad, Montgomery Securities, and many others. In addition, at the conference itself we got our first strategic overture from AT&T. An executive named Kathleen Early gave me a survey of the "platforms" she operated—i.e., the many obsolete proprietary services AT&T had purchased and would shortly write off as failures, plus the Web, which was, hey, another great platform. I couldn't tell whether she really believed it or not; I tried to keep a straight face, which was hard, and agreed that we should talk. During the weeks that followed, we got so many calls and meeting requests from AT&T and its venture capital organization that they became a serious time problem.

But we weren't out of the woods yet. As soon as Netscape saw our stuff, they retaliated by announcing products of their own. If you believed them, if you didn't read carefully, and if you didn't know the technology intimately, you could be pardoned for thinking that they really had something serious. And we had the makings of a similar problem with Microsoft, even though we had just learned that they didn't have anything at all. In both cases, however, sufficiently convincing FUD could impede our fund-raising and partnership efforts, which is doubtless just what they wanted.

We Dissect a Blackbird, and Netscape Announces It's Competing with Us

Microsoft was beginning to worry us. My friend had already told me about The Memo, and at the Shaffer conference Spyglass CEO Doug Colbeth had told me to "fear the worst," although he also said it would take them some time.

Furthermore, Microsoft had started referring to Blackbird as "Internet Studio." Rumors gave the product wonderful features, yet specifics were lacking. We had decided during the summer that we needed to get a look at it, but for quite a while we couldn't. We suspected that "Internet Studio" was pure FUD. Blackbird had initially been designed as a development tool for MSN, which had been launched along with Windows 95 in August. By exercising MSN, and watching how it behaved, we could infer a lot about its design, and it looked very, very unlike the Web. Consequently we were extremely skeptical that any product already under development could be retargeted from one platform to the other. Architecture again: we concluded that you'd essentially have to start from scratch.

But for a long time we didn't *know,* and it bothered me. Then, sometime in early September, one of our senior employees came into my office to tell me that he had a friend who could get him a copy of the current Blackbird beta test product. I didn't ask who the friend was, didn't want to know, and never learned. But I decided that this was one case where some underhandedness was justified. Remember my tit-for-tat policy: I was virtually certain that "Internet Studio" was FUD, but we needed to know for sure. We soon had it up and running and learned how to use it.

We had been right. Blackbird had nothing to do with the Web, *nothing whatsoever,* and the software was designed in such a way that they would have to tear it all apart and start over to shift to the Web. It wasn't even a good authoring tool for MSN, but worked more like a high-end desktop publishing program, the kind that professional graphics houses bought. In fact, the Blackbird team were mostly high-end desktop publishing types, from a start-up called Daily Planet that Microsoft had acquired. We later learned that just about this time, Microsoft trashed the Blackbird code and told the team to start over, so they were quite demoralized. I couldn't publicly say that we'd inspected Blackbird, but I became expert at telling VCs, potential investors, and strategic partners that we were *quite* certain we had nothing to fear from Blackbird, and that we knew exactly what it did.

Netscape's FUD attack came in mid-September, and we knew why. We had given the first public demonstration of our software at a minor conference, called Windows Solutions, in San Francisco on August 31. We thought it was close enough to the Shaffer conference, and to our public launch, that we could afford it.

Well, perhaps we should have waited. I got an urgent call in Cambridge from Peter, who was telephoning from our booth. Peter had been approached by a fellow named David Pann, who said he was a senior product development executive at Netscape and insisted on a demo. Pann was very pushy and threatened to make lots of trouble right then and there. I told Peter to go ahead. Pann specifically told Peter that Netscape didn't have any competitive products under development, which was a lie. Mr. Pann eventually became something of an office joke. He applied to be a beta tester, but we refused. Then he applied under false pretenses, but we sniffed him out from electronic trails that led to him and/or Netscape. That was fun. But now they had seen our stuff, and what happened next wasn't quite so enjoyable.

One week after Peter had given Mr. Pann his demo, a couple of days before the Shaffer conference, I got a "This is serious" e-mail from Ed Cuoco, saying that Netscape would soon announce competing tools products, with availability in the fourth quarter. On September 18, Netscape did indeed announce three tools products: Navigator Gold, LiveWire, and LiveWire Pro. According to the announcement, Navigator Gold was a low-priced WYSIWYG editor that could be integrated with Netscape's browser. It would let you create HTML pages and would allegedly work with any Web server. LiveWire would be a full visual environment for creating and managing sophisticated Web services—building and managing links, handling forms, and dropping in live objects, or other multimedia data. It included a list of development wizards that sounded a lot like ours, and once again it would work with any Web server. LiveWire Pro added an integrated Informix database, but supposedly worked with any relational database a customer might prefer on the server side. LiveWire Pro was almost one thousand dollars, but the others were inexpensive—under one hundred dollars. All three would supposedly be available in the fourth quarter—in at most four months.

If you believed this, it was catastrophic. By now, however, we were getting hardened to FUD. I won't pretend that we weren't a bit rattled, but the notion that Netscape was that close to a major tools release was inconsistent with everything we knew, and the substance of the announcement didn't hang together either. First, about a month before Pann showed up at Peter's booth, I had gotten a call from a different Netscape executive, Len Feldman, who described himself as the product marketing manager for their future tools. He said they were early in their development process and might be interested in licensing FrontPage instead of building their own. I said no—the last thing I wanted to do was show Netscape all of our thinking. But Feldman seemed fairly straightforward, and I was inclined to believe him when he said that they had just started. So while we knew Pann was lying when he said there was no development under way, we also suspected that there was no way in hell they could have such a complete product line by the end of the year. Tellingly, this was one of the few times that Netscape had announced a major product without also announcing the availability of beta software.

Furthermore, Netscape's announcement didn't make technical sense—and we were confident that we now knew as much as anyone in the world about Web authoring tools. Netscape strongly implied that the tools would enable remote development over the Web and would work with any server. Well, there's no way to do that without building server extensions the way Andy did for FrontPage, and their news releases made no mention of server extensions. We also doubted that Netscape would support competitors' Web servers. Even if they tried, the "honest broker" problem would once again interfere.

The claim of a high-end tool with an integrated Informix database was similarly suspicious. We knew what a complicated development challenge it is to integrate database software with a Web authoring tool. We had estimated it would take several additional months, and we had awfully good engineers; once again, it seemed vanishingly unlikely that Netscape would really field such a product in the fourth quarter of 1995. And if this was a fabrication, as we suspected, it was also dumb. Oracle had recently announced a browser with an integrated database management system, and Netscape was probably doing FUD to two companies at once. But it was foolish to antagonize the database vendors unnecessarily—Oracle, but also Sybase and even Microsoft.

Of the three products, only Gold, the low-end page editor, was actually released anywhere close to Netscape's publicly announced schedule—it went into beta testing in January 1996 and shipped in March. It was a decent editor, with maybe a fifth of the functionality of FrontPage, but it was not a serious authoring tool and it did *not* support either true remote development or other vendors' servers. Netscape bundled it with its browser, and it therefore came to have quite a large presence. The two higher-end LiveWire products didn't come out until late in the spring; neither was successful, and they were later withdrawn.

I TRY TO REFORM THE GOVERNMENT

I had long anticipated that we would be a target for both Microsoft and Netscape, because both of them needed our authoring tools. Our preference was still to stay independent, but our best chance of thriving on our own would come with a competitive standoff between Microsoft and Netscape. Failing that, we could let one of them acquire us. And by September, as I've already mentioned, I saw increasing evidence that Microsoft had finally got it.

This led me to be concerned about the structure of the industry, and about antitrust policy. First, I didn't want Microsoft to be able to crush Netscape. And second, I wanted to understand what the Justice Department's posture would be toward acquisitions by Microsoft and/or Netscape. So in late August, I decided to find out what the Justice Department was up to. They had blocked Microsoft's acquisition of Intuit that summer, which was a hopeful sign. But they had also allowed Microsoft to bundle MSN with Windows 95, and they had caved when investigating Microsoft's Windows licensing practices. I was even worried that they might make things worse; other than blocking Microsoft's acquisition of Intuit, their track record was awful. In 1992, for example, Borland acquired Ashton-Tate, which was the vendor of dBase, the leading PC database software package. Insanely, Justice blocked the deal because the combination of dBase with Borland's Paradox would control about 70 percent of the PC database market. The fact that everyone in the industry knew Microsoft was out to kill Borland and everyone else seemed not to penetrate, or to count. As a condition of Justice's allowing the deal to proceed, Borland was forced to license dBase's intellectual property to a major vendor of dBASE clone software, FoxPro. One month later, Microsoft purchased FoxPro and proceeded to effectively obliterate Borland. Thus, antitrust policy had actually helped Microsoft eliminate its strongest rival. This, unfortunately, was not out of character. The high technology expertise of the Justice Department leaves much to be desired.

Thus I was particularly concerned about a Vermeer acquisition because Netscape's position in 1995 resembled Borland's in 1992. Microsoft's position in the Web and Internet was vanishingly small compared to Netscape's, just as it had been in database software compared to Borland. Unless Justice understood that whenever Microsoft entered a market, it was *always* the dominant threat, I feared that it might actually be more difficult to get approval for an acquisition by Netscape than by Microsoft. So in my current situation, I wasn't going to take anything for granted.

I had several colleagues who knew Anne Bingaman, who was then in charge of the Department of Justice Antitrust Division. Joe Farrell, an economics professor at Berkeley who had consulted for Justice, and Lois Abraham, a senior partner at Brown & Bain, our attorneys, also knew her. I'd also once spent a few hours with Senator Jeff Bingaman, her husband, who had seemed like a very intelligent and well-intentioned man. I sent Bingaman a letter, enclosing a draft of my *Upside* article on the Web, and asked if we could talk. She replied promptly and quite courteously that she would be pleased to meet with me, and in fact, gave me two hours in mid-September.

I'm afraid I behaved badly at the meeting, and I'm still embarrassed about it. Things started going wrong immediately. I walked in for what I hoped and assumed would be a fairly private discussion and found a dozen people in the room, mostly lawyers with no technical or industrial experience. And I started out much too confrontationally, asking Bingaman why she didn't do something serious about Microsoft. Bingaman, to her credit, kept her cool and said, Well you're not being very polite, but I've made time for you, so I will ask you what you think we should do.

I launched into an explanation of how Microsoft was taking over the entire industry, and especially targeting the Internet. I admitted that Justice probably couldn't chop up the company yet, but said that they should tilt the playing field every chance they had. They should keep withering scrutiny over Microsoft's bundling of software and services with its operating system, its acquisitions, its predatory pricing, and its OEM contracts. I said it was inexcusable that the Antitrust Division had no one who understood the industry or technology, which was true, but not the most diplomatic thing to say in front of a dozen of its employees. Bingaman replied, Well, we understood enough to prevent them from buying Intuit. I said something like, Thank God for small favors. But now here's the Internet, this huge new thing, and Gates is going to kill it and you're not doing anything about it. She shot back, Bill Gates didn't see the Internet coming, and you know it, and right now Netscape dominates it completely. I said, That won't last long, just watch. Bingaman said, We'll cross that bridge when we come to it. And you should be more polite, because you requested this meeting, and there are a lot of industries, and a lot of people who want my time. If you have any constructive suggestions, make them. I did make some—including telling her to get tough on Microsoft's acquisitions.

When it was over, I felt bad for two quite different reasons. First, I was ashamed of my manners. From what I saw and knew, I liked and respected her, and she had a very difficult job. Bingaman wasn't responsible for Justice's bureaucratic condition, and she had taken a lot of heat for blocking the Intuit acquisition. That eminent high technology policy genius, Bob Dole, had directly attacked her for suing Microsoft, and Republicans were accusing her of hurting national competitiveness by going after a successful company. So I should have been much more respectful of her problems, which were large.

On the other hand, she had confirmed some of my fears. First of all, she didn't seem to understand that Gates almost always waited until another company invented a market before taking it over, and that Microsoft's structural position would let him do this with the Internet unless Microsoft's natural conduct was sharply curtailed. So I couldn't count on much help from Justice when Microsoft set out to obliterate Netscape and all the rest of us. Her comments about Netscape bothered me too; she thought *Netscape* dominated the Internet. This made me seriously concerned that Justice might block an acquisition by Netscape. I knew that I owed Anne Bingaman an apology, but I was too angry and upset to make one. I flew home thoughtful and depressed, because once again, it was all too clear that we were on our own.

Back to Fund-Raising; or, How to Herd Cats

After the Shaffer conference there was no shortage of outside investors who wanted to get in. But I wanted to make sure that they didn't cut a deal with our first-round VCs. This was a real risk, in my view, since Matrix and Sigma were heavy hitters that every VC would have to live with in future deals. And I respected Paul Ferri; I was certain that he ate large iron bars for breakfast. So I insisted that potential new investors were to talk only to me, and not call the VCs without my permission. This made some of them very confused. I also told my board that if I caught them screwing around with our negotiations, they would see my very worst behavior.

In many ways the VC industry is a cartel, but a cartel is not the same kind of animal as a monopoly. Cartels can be broken. They are always at the mercy of market conditions and the self-interest of their members. Now that the Internet was exploding and we had been anointed a white-hot property, the VCs—both our existing investors and prospective second-round investors—began to see the handwriting on the wall. So many VCs and investment banks wanted in that we could now play them off against one another, documenting enough offers that Andy M. and Barry Fidelman would have to think long and hard before trying to block an outside deal. Indeed, another of my motivations in bringing in new investors was to dilute their control. In addition to the risk of their scalping us on valuation, an inside round would give them virtually complete control of the company, a prospect I did not regard with joy.

I also wanted to be sure that the new VCs wouldn't form any coalitions, either. So in addition to conventional VCs, I made a point of soliciting bids from the venture arms of investment banks and corporations. The investment banks, like Morgan Stanley and H&Q, used their venture funds partly to generate IPO deal flow, so their interests diverged somewhat from the traditional VC partnerships. For exactly the same reason, we didn't really want them as major investors, and we certainly didn't want them to have a board seat— they would push us to use them for our IPO. But I wasn't above using them to discipline other venture capitalists. The same was true with the corporate venture organizations. AT&T's venture arm was very interested in us, partly because their Internet unit wanted to negotiate a marketing partnership. But I wasn't very interested in them—their strategic investments in online services had demonstrated an almost comical degree of incompetence—but they were a big player, with barrels of money, and they helped keep the others in line.

Hence I was determined to control the process myself. Here, my confrontational instincts served me well. We'd had two very rough board meetings before the Shaffer conference, plus many private conversations, in which I essentially accused the VCs of trying to control the second round in order to keep our valuation down. Their response had been, in effect, okay, wise guy, go see whether you can do any better without us. Great, I said, glad to oblige. I not only took up the challenge, but refused even to tell them who we were talking to, although I let enough information out so they knew we were getting serious interest. Did I mention that this period was tense? Yes, it was tense.

In late September, Mandile and I developed a list of potential investors and sent them my new business plan, along with a cover letter written by me but signed jointly by both of us. Mandile and I were still superficially working well together, but I already distrusted him and was beginning to act accordingly. I wanted to see anything that was sent to outside investors, and I wanted to make sure that my name got equal billing with his. The cover letter was tough, arrogant, and clear. It basically said, We're opening our second round; minimum opening bid is $30 million pre-money; investors will not get a board seat; we'll give you a couple of weeks for due diligence, but don't even think of bothering our engineers, and don't respond unless you can meet our conditions.

In addition, I included a requirement that potential investors were not to communicate with the board or any of the first-round VC firms without my permission. I didn't want Marcuvitz trying to filter the market or reduce competitive bidding. Nobody liked this. Here is a plaintive e-mail from Bill Kaiser, a partner at Greylock, one of the oldest Boston venture capital firms:

> Monday, October 2, 1995, 4:35 P.M.
>
> Your message asked me not to talk to the existing investors except through you. Before I got your message, I had already had a brief conversation with Andy Marcuvitz. I have also received a call from Bob Davoli, which I have not returned.
>
> Charles, your request puts me in a somewhat awkward position to say the least. It is also a unique request in my experience. These are people that I know and it's quite unnatural for me not to talk to them. I would like to understand why you have made such a request. Please call me tomorrow if you can . . . In any event, I look forward to moving ahead to the next step. My enthusiasm remains intact.
>
> Regards,
> Bill Kaiser

Yes indeed, I thought, I was going to make sure that this was a "quite unnatural" process. I reconfirmed the rules to Kaiser, who somehow managed to swallow them. A few weeks later, we presented to the entire Greylock partnership.

We had innumerable meetings with potential investors throughout September and October. Generally they went easily. Everybody was finally starting to get up to speed on the Net, and the smart VCs could see the value of what we were doing. Furthermore, many people didn't care; VC herd behavior was finally working in our favor. Because we were in the middle of product launch, I worked hard to limit their access to the engineering team. VC presentations were usually attended by Randy, John, and me. Usually I gave the overview presentation, and either Randy or John would do the demo. Once again, I was surprised at how nervous and inexperienced Mandile was in public presentations. He stumbled and made obvious mistakes such as not bringing an external mouse for his laptop, so that he blocked the view of the audience and slowed down the demo.

The first *written* offer came from Barry Schiffman at Weiss, Peck & Greer. We'd presented to him on the first round, and I liked him. He'd been one of the few people back then who appreciated what we were doing, but his management had been reluctant to invest in such a risky company. He didn't want to miss out again, and in mid-September he produced a term sheet for a $30 million pre-money valuation. It wasn't one I was disposed to accept, since it was conditioned upon due diligence. But it was a serious offer at a valuation almost double the proposal that Marcuvitz was still pushing. I put it in my pocket until the October board meeting.

The board meeting opened with the usual housekeeping, but quickly moved to a contentious discussion about funding and valuation. After a bit, I interrupted, enjoying every second, and said, I have a piece of paper I'd like to show you. I distributed copies of Schiffman's offer to everyone. Davoli was the only one to maintain his good humor. Oh, it's a *term sheet,* he said, smiling. But nobody else was smiling. Wade was actually shaking; I've never seen him so upset. I think he was utterly furious, at everyone and the whole situation: at me, for playing so rough, and equally at Andy M. and Barry Fidelman for provoking the confrontation.

They read the term sheet in silence for a few minutes, then, his voice quavering as he struggled for composure, Wade said, Well, this is a conditional term sheet, I don't think it's in our interest to proceed except with an unconditional offer. Fair enough, I replied, but I'm confident that this is a serious offer seriously made, and it shows that we really can demand and receive a high valuation.

Wade and I had some brutal exchanges after the October board meeting; I was still angry that he had tried to push me into a low valuation. I'm not proud of the way I behaved toward him, and although he hasn't directly mentioned it, I suspect he's not totally happy with his own behavior either. Here's some e-mail on the subject, from an exchange that took place over several days ending on October 11, 1995:

Wade to me: If you think I've tried to subvert your efforts to get the best deal, that's bullshit. Of *ALL* of the people in the board group (both VC and management), I have been the only one who from the start said to you *and* the other investors that the right thing to do was to price the deal outside. Following that course is once again proving that the free market sets the best price.

Me to Wade: I will change my mind, instantly, the next time you make a mistake that doubles my net worth at your expense. Please inform me as soon as this happens . . . Until then—no free lunches. I am very much a consequentialist.

Wade to me: If your beef is that I was wrong about where the market price would end up, you have a fair point. I congratulate you on the likely close at a valuation well above what I thought was possible. Whether you remember that "forever with acidity" is your business but I resent any implication that I wasn't trying to promote the best interests of the company. My vote is that we've spent enough time on the issue.

Me to Wade: I think you're right. And I assure you that I hold you, and Andy, in high regard, as to competence and ethics. But Wade: we (me, you, Andy M., us collectively) have tangled about several things. Do not try to persuade me or to pretend—as Andy has REPEATEDLY tried to do—that your interests and ours are perfectly aligned, and that we can do no better than to entrust ourselves to you.

However, the fact that I was rough on Wade should not lead you to think that I neglected Andy Marcuvitz. Andy was tough, and I was concerned until quite late that he would try to block outside offers. I started planning to lay a strong paper trail in the event that I decided to sue him later, and I told him so in order to shake him up. I had a private telephone conversation with him in which I said, Andy, you might be able to screw us in this round, but I'm documenting everything. I can't sue you right now without wrecking the company, but I would have one hell of a lawsuit if we got acquired or did an IPO. And if it turned out that other companies have had similar experiences, this could get expensive for you. Don't be ridiculous, Charles, he said, nobody's trying to screw you. I have a perfect right to make a reasonable offer for a trouble-free inside round. Nobody is going to get in the way of whatever makes sense for the company. Great, I said, I'm so glad to hear that. Your offer is flatly refused, so stop wasting time by bringing it up.

Shortly afterward, the dam broke. In addition to the Weiss, Peck & Greer offer, we started getting both verbal and written offers from an increasing number of VCs. Greylock came up with a competitive bid, $32 million pre-money. But they still had the same problem they'd had before: conflicts of interest. They were investors in several companies that were potential partners and/or competitors—particularly Open Market and Spyglass. Spyglass, in fact, had already tried to acquire us. Bill Kaiser assured us that we had nothing whatsoever to worry about, but frankly, I didn't believe him then and I still don't now. I have since heard several entrepreneurs complain about exactly this kind of problem.

But we could afford to be picky. By mid-October, we had received firm $32 million pre-money offers not only from Greylock but also Weiss, Peck & Greer, AT&T, Menlo, Hambrecht & Quist, and Hummer Winblad. Many others were clearly interested too. For a variety of reasons, the choice for the outside lead came down to Menlo and Hummer Winblad, both of which are among the most reputable, high-powered West Coast firms. I was essentially indifferent. For some reason Mandile had a preference for Menlo, so that's what we did. At my request we let Barry Schiffman and Weiss, Peck & Greer in for a small investment, as a reward for his having been the first to break the logjam with a high-valuation term sheet. Hambrecht & Quist also got a small piece, partially because they had been helpful in slotting us for important conferences. But it was also partially a favor to them motivated by fear. Their venture capital fund was actually the personal money of the partners, and if they wanted in for a small amount, it didn't pay to refuse them. If we got them angry, it might hurt us later, either when it came time to do an IPO or in some other situation. For example Dan Case, the president of Hambrecht & Quist, is the brother of Steve Case, the CEO of AOL.

Shortly afterward, speaking of H&Q, I did something stupid and mildly improper at their behest. A banker at H&Q called me and said something like, Charles, we're giving you the right to buy five hundred shares of the Arbor Software IPO. You'll get a call. Thanks, I said. And, sure enough, I got a call, from a charming woman whose job was to be charming, and with zero effort I made several thousand dollars. Then a month or two later, it happened again, and then a third time. I realized that this was leaving the realm of innocent favors, and I became uncomfortable. I told them to stop, though I kept the $25,000 or so that I'd made, which was probably wrong. Although nobody said a word, my guess is that they wanted our IPO business. In 1997 *The Wall Street Journal* ran two long articles focusing on H&Q and several CEOs who had each received millions of dollars in return for steering them IPOs.

In any event, we finished negotiating our round. I asked the employees if they had any friends who were qualified investors and said that if possible we would get them the right to make small investments. We let in a couple of my friends for small amounts, as well as an uncle of Randy's. Sure enough, despite earlier threats to the contrary, all of the first-round VCs exercised their rights to purchase their pro-rata share. The nonmonetary terms were pretty much the same as in the first round, except that there were no new board seats, and the new investors didn't have the "participation" provision that gave special liquidation privileges to the first-round investors. Furthermore, the first-round participation provision was canceled if we achieved either an acquisition or IPO valued at more than $75 million. The total new money was $7.2 million, bringing Vermeer's post-money valuation to $39.2 million, or a fivefold step-up in just nine months over our first-round post-money. Not quite Netscape, but not bad.

A truly mature, wise, and generous person—say Mother Teresa—would have resisted rubbing the VCs' noses in this and would have been magnanimous and conciliatory in victory.

However, I have never claimed to be Mother Teresa. I reminded the VCs frequently that a foolish, reckless amateur had been accurate while they, with their rules of thumb and decades of experience, not to mention their altruism and concern for employee welfare, had blown it badly. But at least now, I thought, we're finally done. *Wrong again.* Shortly before we were scheduled to close the deal, we got the first calls from Netscape and Microsoft. This changed everything. In fact, closing our second round could have been disastrous for us in the context of an acquisition, for reasons I'll discuss shortly.

CHAPTER SEVEN

Wins and Losses, Continued:
or, Things Get *Really* Complicated

Why, I remember when you were just a country boy with a Ph.D.
—*An acquaintance of mine at IBM, reacting to a colleague's devious plans*

The odds are five to six that the light at the end of the tunnel is the headlight of an oncoming train.
—*Paul Dickson, paraphrasing the poet Robert Lowell*

*I*n October and November, the engineers could finally relax a bit, but everything else at Vermeer took on a truly insane velocity. We faced the requirement to transform ourselves from merely a development organization into a real company, at the same time as the world decided to ask us some serious questions. The tasks before us included our product and corporate launch; choosing and implementing marketing, distribution, pricing, and sales strategies; partnership negotiations with AT&T, FTP Software, Sybase, Spyglass, BBN, American Internet, Novell, Open Market, and others; planning for our next products; and dealing with strategic overtures from Netscape and Microsoft. The complexity of *my* life was further increased by the fact that this period forced me into a definitive but bleak assessment of our new CEO. I concluded that John was highly intelligent and an excellent manager, tactician, diplomat, and negotiator, but that he had little strategic ability, was extraordinarily political and selfish, and wanted to marginalize me as rapidly and completely as possible.

More than ever, these developments interacted, making every decision dizzyingly complicated. Pressure to generate major news for our launch affected partnership negotiations with brain-dead but prominent companies such as AT&T, which affected in turn our pricing and marketing decisions. My assessment of John implied that in the long run it would be necessary either to force him out—which would be extremely difficult—or to sell the company, rather than to go public and remain independent. I simply couldn't endure years of political combat with John, and in my absence I didn't trust him to run the company either well or ethically. In the short term, I had to prevent him from cutting me out of the information and decision loop for critical issues. At the same time, the overtures from Netscape and Microsoft had many additional implications. They forced us to renegotiate our second round at the last minute, and also forced me to assess not only *our* prospects in competition against them, but also *their* prospects if one of them acquired us, since we would be paid in their stock. In addition, either an IPO or an acquisition had major financial implications for employees and executives, not all of them automatically good. This led to two particularly nasty incidents with John, one of which nearly derailed our acquisition negotiations with Microsoft. In short, life got very complicated.

LAUNCH

Launching, i.e., proclaiming your arrival to the world, is extremely important, particularly to a start-up. Your goal is to draw as much favorable attention to yourself and your product as possible, not just from potential users but from the industry, investors, the press, potential employees, and potential strategic partners. Doing launches has become an industry in itself, populated with an enormous array of consultants, public relations firms, trade shows, conferences, product reviewers, Web sites, traditional press, newsletters, and advertising agencies. Launching a product is complicated and *hard,* even for large and powerful firms such as Microsoft, and even when it's a new version of something that everyone already uses. Launching a completely new product while simultaneously launching a new *company,* as we were trying to do, is much harder. We not only had to release our finished product, but we had to build our launch infrastructure at the same time, make a large number of decisions quickly, and attract enough attention to rise above the general noise level. As a start-up, we had to convince the world not only that our product was good, but also that we would be a reliable vendor—i.e., that we wouldn't go bankrupt or sell ourselves to someone's competitor.

We got it done, in some ways quite successfully, but we also made some serious mistakes. The PR, product review, trade show, and press coverage side of things generally went very well. But launch also forces you to choose, announce, and implement your initial pricing, marketing, distribution, and sales strategies, and there we did very badly. None of our mistakes would have been fatal if we had fixed them promptly, but they indicated an extreme amateurishness and timidity in these functions that would not have been sustainable in real competition with Microsoft and Netscape. We never faced a final report card because of our acquisition, but our midterm grade was at best a D. I'll say more about this shortly.

We settled on an official launch date in mid-October. The conventional wisdom in the industry, which is probably true, is that it's vital to hit the world with everything at once—the availability of the product, an updated Web site, trade shows, press coverage, advertising, product reviews, conference appearances. Timing is important in other ways, too. You want to be in the middle of the fall season, but you don't want to be obliterated by a much larger concurrent launch (such as Windows 95). You also have to be careful that competitors don't steal your thunder by announcing something, either real or fake, just ahead of you. We had used that tactic incompetently against NaviSoft in March, and Netscape used it semi-competently against us in September.

Another reason that launches are tricky is that many components of them must be decided long in advance. You have to bet that everything will converge on the same date. This is extremely difficult, in part because many of these processes are interdependent. For example, in order to write product reviews, reviewers for monthly magazines and quarterly newsletters need your product, long in advance—i.e., before it's done. If the beta copy you send them has too many bugs, your reviews will tear you to shreds. Alternatively, you might not finish your final product in time, because you need not only code but also documentation, collateral materials, the CD, the box, etc. In that case you spend a fortune on launch, hordes of people surround your offices wanting to buy, and you have to tell them to go away for a while. And you often don't get a second chance if you're an unknown start-up. If you solve all of these problems by choosing a conservative launch date, you risk having rogue press coverage that destroys your leverage with the media, as well as damage caused by competitors sowing FUD.

We had the additional problem that we were generally in a psychotic rush because that's the way the Web was. Nonetheless, we couldn't afford a disaster. We had made some launch preparations before John arrived, but not many. Ed Cuoco had reserved space for some trade shows, and Shelley Harrison found us an excellent PR firm, Davé-Bairey. When I saw what most of the PR industry is like, I realized that Peter Davé was a rare find, and I remain extremely grateful to him, and to Shelley for finding him. But there were a million other things to do, and we had essentially no experience doing them.

In the mechanics and logistics of launch, John's arrival was extremely helpful; it was precisely in areas such as this that his managerial and tactical skills served us well. In early September, for example, I argued for accelerating our launch to counter Netscape's upcoming September 18 announcement of competitive tools. John decided that we should wait, and he was absolutely right. He wanted us to be ready and organized: to have stable code to send to reviewers, customer support, public relations, press tours, the logistics of telesales, fulfillment, a professional presence at the correct trade shows, and the thousand other details that make the difference between a bad image and a good one. The September 18 Netscape announcements turned out not to damage us much, and we wouldn't have looked nearly as organized a month earlier.

Furthermore, nearly a year earlier Ed Cuoco had reserved us prime space at Fall Internet World. Fall Internet World would be held in Boston at the end of October, and it was becoming a major trade show. In 1995, about thirty-two thousand people attended, versus ten thousand the year before. So we settled on a mid-October launch, and Peter Davé decided that we would embargo press coverage and avoid public demonstrations of our software until then. We did, however, start cultivating the press through interviews and meetings. We also made a few exceptions to the embargo on software demonstration in order to appear at smaller, elite industry-only conferences such as Dick Shaffer's and the Hambrecht & Quist Internet conference in New York.

This still left us with many problems. First, we needed a sufficiently stable beta version to send to product reviewers, many of whom, despite their occupation, are far from expert in the use of PC software. Then, of course, we needed to be able to ship the final product. Here, Frank earned his keep. He knew how to drive products to completion and he did a good job as keeper of the schedule.

Frank made some mistakes, though. As I mentioned earlier, he was cheap, and when buying outside services, he always chose the low-end option. He insisted on using the least expensive telesales and order fulfillment house, for instance, which was predictably awful. Shelley Harrison had warned us about this, and in fact it would have hurt us badly if our sales had been any higher. (Ah yes, our sales. We'll get to that.) And despite Frank's effectiveness in getting the product done, his behavior hadn't improved. I was gradually coming to the conclusion that we should look for a new VP of engineering once the product was done and try to find Frank a job that wouldn't let him do much damage. Randy had a milder, more favorable view of Frank, but agreed that there was a problem, particularly because Frank infuriated some of our best engineers. Neither of us looked forward to that conversation, to put it mildly. But with all his faults, without Frank we probably wouldn't have shipped our product until months later. And the fact that we had a real product made an enormous difference in our acquisition negotiations.

Even in engineering, where we had the greatest confidence, we had unpleasant surprises that risked derailing our launch and our strategic negotiations. In late August, for example, we started getting reports from Fidelity and some other key customers that our software didn't always install. Since I talked frequently with George Bukow and Kelley Hardwick, the superb customer support people just across the hall from me, I knew about these as they occurred. I noted with increasing alarm that these reports continued for weeks. I started getting upset, and becoming progressively more so when I thought that neither Frank nor the engineers were taking the problem seriously enough. It took quite a while to hunt the bug down. The engineers finally tracked it to some code in Windows that affected the operation of TCP/IP stacks, including the one built into Windows 95. There were a great variety of stacks out there, most of them buggy, and many of them subtly different from one another. So it wasn't our bug, it was Microsoft's, but users blamed us anyway when they couldn't install our product. And I would argue that they were partially right, in the sense that it's our job to give them something they can use, even if it means cleaning up after other people's messes.

This was potentially a quite serious problem. It risked undermining our early credibility with reference accounts, reviewers, and potential partners and would surely cut down on sales through word-of-mouth recommendations. Even worse, it surfaced in our early negotiations with Microsoft. In early November the senior Microsoft executive we were dealing with, Chris Peters, called me to say that two of the four people he had assigned to exercise our product had been unable to install it. And these were not end-users; they were Windows software engineers. I explained that the technical problem was on his end, not ours, but that's *not* a great position to be in. It took some sharp e-mails to get the engineers to treat the issue as seriously as I felt they needed to.

We developed a workaround, of sorts, which included diagnostic and customer support procedures, and if necessary we directed customers to a good freeware TCP/IP stack available on the Web. But the problem didn't go away completely until Microsoft finally fixed its own stack and then, as Windows 95 took over the world, proceeded to obliterate all others. The appearance of such a problem just at launch—a problem that prevented people from even being able to use the software at all—didn't make my day.

Producing final product code, however, was just one of many preconditions for shipping the full commercial product, which in turn was just one of many preconditions for launch. You need documentation, manufacturing, telephone support, and a Web site with order taking, bug reporting, software downloading, and support functions. You need reference accounts, name-brand users who are willing to talk to the press and potential customers. You need marketing litera-ture, a telesales organization, and a fulfillment house that actually ships the product and handles credit card payments. And then you have launch itself: weeks of press and analyst tours (two separate ones, a "long-lead-time" and "short-lead-time" tour, both national, a month apart), trade shows, confer-ences, support for product reviewers, and so forth. And you need to educate the strategic partners and sales channels who will be selling your product, and who generally start out knowing nothing about it.

All this gave me my first close-up look at the Silicon Valley PR industry. Be-fore Shelley Harrison found us Davé-Bairey, I had talked to a half-dozen others, and in the course of launch and making partnership announcements another dozen or more afterward. PR is the only part of the technology sector that is dominated by women, and it has a hard-edged Hollywood glitz. The top exec-utives are about half men and half women. The men generally reminded me of my reaction to Clinton advisors like Dick Morris or David Gergen—greasy, overweight, amoral, somehow pathetic even when extremely successful. The women are smart, hard as nails, ruthless, and often stunningly gorgeous. The rank and file is *completely* dominated by attractive young women, various com-binations of dragon lady and bimbette, whose job is social lubrication—open-ing doors, getting interviews, pushing you through a crowd toward someone they're just dying to have you meet. This basic model was pioneered by Regis McKenna, who built one of the first Silicon Valley PR firms in the early 1980s using his army of "Regettes." A lot of the front-line PR women marry their clients; the stereotypical marriage is the forty-year-old wealthy entrepreneur and his twenty-five-year-old PR blonde.

I was courted by a couple of PR executives. They were good at it, and I found myself getting invited to industry parties full of people I wanted to meet, et cetera. A couple of them tried to invest. Peter Davé, who also had the UUNet account, was in every way atypical, and did quite a good job, especially consid-ering our budget.

FLIRTING WITH DISASTER: PRICING, MARKETING, DISTRIBUTION, AND SALES (OR MORE PRECISELY, THE ABSENCE THEREOF)

In pricing, marketing, distribution, and sales, we did almost everything wrong. Most of our errors ultimately derived from our timidity and inexperi-ence with high-volume software markets, which in turn derived from our choice of CEO, which was ultimately my fault.

On the surface, our marketing and sales disaster was a collective effort. John blew it by treating our product as if it were an expensive database tool product, rather than mass-market PC software. The VCs were overly nervous about spending money in general, and on marketing and sales in particular. Frank was always pushing for the cheapest solution, and none of the rest of us knew much about advertising, marketing, distribution, or retail sales channels, *especially* for mass-market software. I sometimes expressed discomfort with the approach we took, but I didn't have the courage of my convictions, and initially I even contributed to the problem in some areas. As time passed, I began to wake up and in fact was becoming quite alarmed, but by then the prospect of acquisition superseded these concerns and dominated all other issues. Furthermore, I had agreed to step back from running the company once we had a CEO; in my ostensible new role as strategic guru, initially I didn't think it appropriate to provoke a fight with John in an area where I knew so little.

Ultimately, however, there is one person to blame for our mistakes: *me*. My mistake, quite simply, was hiring John Mandile, after having summarily rejected others who might well have served us better. Not only was John ruthlessly and dangerously selfish, he was also not entirely qualified. In retrospect, it was a mistake for me to reject a couple of the Lotus people as abruptly as I did. One in particular probably would have been pretty good, or in any event better, at least for some initial period. He understood PC software markets, was an experienced manager, and was probably much less dangerous than John. I had met him early in our CEO search and rejected him after several interactions. He had openly stated he wanted to spend more time with his family, not a major qualification for Internet start-up CEOs, and he had seemed timid. (Ironically, he later founded an Internet software start-up, not very successfully.) I suspected that he had survived at Lotus by saying yes far too often and taking no chances. Probably so, but he was smart, he could have quickly found us a pretty good VP of marketing, and my guess is that our relationship would have been reasonably free of political maneuvering. It was foolish of me to reject him summarily and break off our discussions. My doing so derived from an arrogance with regard to my judgment of people, and with regard to our ability to attract anyone we wanted, neither of which was borne out by subsequent events.

Immediate responsibility for our marketing and sales disaster rested primarily with Mandile. Aside from the fact that since he was now CEO, and therefore in principle running the show, his value-added was supposed to be in general management and marketing. But his previous experience was confined to expensive database software, for which direct sales and large corporate partnerships are the principal channels of distribution. For high-volume PC software, however, other channels, especially the retail distribution channels and increasingly, the Internet, are far more important. But Mandile was naturally conservative, averse to admitting ignorance or weakness, and *extremely* averse to sharing power. (I do not think that I have ever heard Mandile admit to making a serious mistake.) My supposition is that he chose a strategy that he understood, even though it was wrong, for these reasons. He overruled Ed when Ed suggested, correctly, that we should reduce our prices and go for volume. He also overruled me when I objected, also correctly, to dangerous entanglements with large but dumb partners such as AT&T and FTP. Wade got worried about those deals as well and raised his concerns in a couple of board meetings. Frank was also worried about the AT&T deal because of its potential burden on engineering. Between us we were able to slow down the FTP deal enough to prevent it from closing, but the AT&T deal went through.

In fairness to Mandile and all of us, it was a difficult problem. In 1995, and even to a considerable extent today, PC software start-ups—and indeed almost the entire PC software industry, with the exception of Microsoft—were forced to obtain most of their revenues by selling through the retail distribution channel. Even in Microsoft's hands, at least until the bundling the product with Office, most of FrontPage's revenues came from this channel. The "Channel," as it's known, is a grotesquely inefficient two-tier industry with a handful of large distributors, who distribute product to retailers, both the large chains and independent stores. Collectively, the Channel takes a huge bite out of your revenues; Vermeer probably would have given up 40 to 70 percent of retail price to the Channel.

Problem number one for a start-up, however, is *getting into the Channel at all*. The distributors serve so many retail outlets that they need to take several tens of thousands of copies of a product to place just one or two with each of their customers, so they take heavy inventory risks. Furthermore, shelf space is a scarce commodity for the retailer, so unknown products without heavy advertising are not looked upon with great favor. For the Internet software industry, the Channel is a kind of cosmic joke, although by now direct Internet retailing is starting to improve things. But in 1995 it was ghastly.

These conditions predispose the Channel to focus on products with proven high-volume sales records and huge advertising budgets. Assuming a conventional 1995-style launch, to crack the Channel we would have had needed either to demonstrate extremely rapid sales growth, or to commit to enormous marketing expenditures, and then also to give the Channel most of our profits. It was six months after the commercial release of its browser, which had already been distributed by the millions, before Netscape introduced a retail browser product through the Channel.

How did start-up companies sell without access to the Channel? By telesales and indirect use of the Channel and other distribution mechanisms via partnerships with large firms. But all of these methods had extremely serious problems. Web sales were still novel in 1995, PC modems were slow, and our product was large. So for users who had only a modem, it literally took hours to download even the first release of our product. But partners like FTP and AT&T would have taken an even bigger bite out of revenues than the Channel—especially when they use the Channel themselves, so you're hit with their margins *and* the Channel's. Mandile's letter of intent with FTP Software called for selling FrontPage through the retail channel under the FTP brand and logo, paying us a royalty of only about 5 percent of the retail price. Wade and I objected to that, and as I said, we managed to slow that down enough that a final contract was never signed.

Conversely, we didn't even try to enter the retail channel. In fairness to John, none of us argued that we should, but it was John's job to handle that issue, or to get someone who could, and he didn't. During the history of Vermeer as an independent company, it was never possible to purchase FrontPage in a store. This was an understandable mistake, but it was an extremely serious one.

As a result of our timidity and John's misjudgments, our actual sales performance was a complete, unmitigated disaster. By the time Microsoft acquired us in January 1996, three months after launch, we had sold a grand total of 289 copies of FrontPage—that's right, count them, *289 copies.* Furthermore, the AT&T contract that Mandile negotiated was awful. It placed huge support burdens on us, yet contained no guaranteed revenue or sales levels. AT&T told us that it would sell twenty thousand copies of FrontPage in the first year of the contract. AT&T's actual sales of FrontPage in that year, even after Microsoft took over the product, were less than five hundred copies. Despite this appalling performance, or perhaps because of it, AT&T absurdly continued to insist that Microsoft maintain expensive custom programs such as round-the-clock support personnel accessible by pager only by AT&T.

During Microsoft's due diligence prior to our acquisition, Chris Peters, who was selling a million copies of Microsoft Office each month, joked to me that he would call each of our customers to thank them personally. If Microsoft had not bought Vermeer when they did, Peters was going to develop a Microsoft FrontPage equivalent; in fact, he was already starting the planning for it. Peters estimated that it would have taken about a year, which strikes me as realistic, especially since they had our product to look at. If we had sold only a few thousand copies of FrontPage by the time Microsoft rolled out its own product, the Microsoft marketing machine would have quite simply obliterated us.

What should we have done differently? Everything. First, our price was much too high—$695, with trade show promotional pricing of a mere $495. Given John's background, $695 felt cheap to him, and Frank pushed for prices even higher than that. Ed Cuoco and I wanted lower prices, but even we never mentioned a price lower than $299, and at first Ed was more sensitive to this issue than I was; I focused on it only after our sales disaster became apparent. When Microsoft took over FrontPage and relaunched it, they listed it at $149, and offered rebates that brought the effective price down to $109, so the "street" price at large retailers was even lower.

I had known that, led by Microsoft, PC software prices had been declining dramatically, but the degree to which this affected us didn't register with me. The pricing comparisons we used for FrontPage were primarily products like PageMaker, Illustrator, and QuarkXpress—desktop publishing and graphics programs that sold in the $500–$800 range. But Microsoft was already attacking those franchises with low-end, inexpensive programs like Microsoft Publisher; more important, if we believed our own arguments, FrontPage would be a very high volume product, more analogous to Word and Excel than to desktop publishing programs.

And those products had become quite inexpensive. By bundling multiple applications into the Office suite, Microsoft had driven down the implied prices of products like Word and Excel to the $100 range, from $400–$500 just a couple of years before. Netscape's browser pricing—$39 at retail, $10 or so for high-volume corporate licenses, and essentially free for individuals—continued this trend. Significantly, Microsoft still hasn't added most of the professional developer functions we cut from the product. Instead, Microsoft kept prices low and the product's functionality accessible to end-users, with the result that it sold millions of copies. Brilliantly, Microsoft then made use of the FrontPage server extensions in creating a *separate* product, Visual InterDev, for professional developers.

But our pricing misjudgment was just one special case of a far more general, and dangerous, unwillingness to take risks. The truth is that we had plenty of money—we'd just raised $7.2 million, remember—and if we thought about it realistically, we had only a year or two to build our market position before Microsoft, and perhaps also Netscape, lowered the boom. If we were successful, we could raise as much money as needed; if we failed, everyone would lose heavily anyway. There was no logic to conserving our cash; the superficially "safe" route was actually the riskier course by far.

Thus we should have been more aggressive. We should have blanketed every trade show, spent heavily on real advertising, lowered the price of the product, and committed serious money for co-marketing agreements in order to penetrate the retail channel. We should have paid for better documentation, packaging, and telesales. We also should have spent heavily to cover all the major market spaces quickly: rapid translations into the half dozen or so largest foreign languages, especially Japanese, and porting FrontPage quickly to the Mac. (We were doing a Mac port, but slowly, because we had only assigned one guy to it.) We should also have aggressively promoted the free downloading of the software for a trial period—perhaps even before we officially shipped the product. Although PC modems were slow, many corporate users had access to fast Internet connections, and I'm quite certain that if we had advertised heavily, we would have increased downloads by at least tenfold. When Microsoft posted the beta version of release 1.1 on its Web site in April 1996, four hundred thousand people downloaded it.

We should also have much more aggressively exploited our free Web server. We had bought the Denny Web server code and ported it to all the major PC operating systems, so we could package up a low-end "personal server" with FrontPage on Windows 3.1, Windows 95, and Windows NT. Then it dawned on us that we had the only Web server that would run on all PC operating systems, free of royalties. We had packaged our server extensions with this server and posted both the bare server and the server with extensions on our Web site, available for free downloading. But since we didn't advertise, we had few takers. If we had advertised this heavily, and perhaps also ported the server (with our server extensions) to other operating systems such as NetWare, the Macintosh, and Linux, we could have had a *very* interesting opportunity, both for publicity and for populating the world with our server extensions.

If we had done all these things, would it have worked? I don't know, and I certainly didn't fight for this strategy when we made our initial decisions in September and October. But it certainly would have been a lot better than what we did; it's damned hard to sell *fewer* than 289 copies in three months. And as time passed, I began to panic.

My initiation in marketing, distribution, and sales issues, including the difficulty of cracking the Channel, drove home the massive distribution advantage that Microsoft has, which is one of the company's largest competitive advantages. In the first place, for a very large proportion of its sales, Microsoft doesn't even use the Channel. Most operating-system sales occur via original equipment manufacturer preloading by PC companies like Dell, IBM, and Compaq, as do a high fraction of Office sales. On these sales, Microsoft cuts out the Channel completely, can charge lower prices, and keeps most of the profit itself. Besides making more money for Microsoft, preloading also greatly simplifies life for consumers, a major competitive advantage. A high fraction of Microsoft's remaining sales also avoid the retail Channel by using volume or "master" licensing agreements with large companies. Large users purchase corporate or site licenses; Microsoft sends them one master CD, and the MIS organization is responsible for installing it, tracking users, etc. And finally, when Microsoft *does* use the Channel, it gets better pricing and business terms than other companies because its volumes are far larger and it has so much power. Microsoft also has a major organization with custom software tools for internationalization, enabling it to market products globally soon after the U.S. version is completed.

Microsoft's software preloading advantage is another reason that it has fought so ferociously against PC manufacturers' preloading of other vendors' software, such as Netscape's. It wants to force other vendors to use the Channel, with its inherently higher costs, inconvenience, and slower distribution. Thus, when you add up all of Microsoft's marketing advantages, you find that they equate to six months to a year of extra lead time and nearly a factor of two in costs. For example, translations into major foreign languages and establishment of foreign distribution arrangements would have taken us six months to a year even if we had moved aggressively. For Microsoft, these would have come at least six months faster.

Consider what happened when the Microsoft marketing machine took over FrontPage. Randy remembers being simply blown away by the sheer competence and efficiency of the release. On April 8, with a great burst of fanfare, "Microsoft FrontPage" was announced at the new $149 price, with a $40 rebate coupon essentially for anybody who had ever bought Microsoft software. By early May there were massive FrontPage displays at all the major retailers. The following year, "FrontPage 97" was released in six languages simultaneously (all on the same CD; only the boxes were different), and the Japanese version was actually in stores before the English version.

In the first four months after Microsoft FrontPage hit the shelves, it sold 150,000 copies. By early 1999 Microsoft had sold more than 3 million copies of FrontPage and completely dominated the Web authoring market. With the integration of FrontPage into Office 2000, FrontPage's installed base will probably exceed 10 million by the turn of the century. So if we had wanted to stay around as an independent firm, we would have had to wake up and get very serious, very fast, about marketing and sales strategy. However, I don't think even then that we could have survived as an independent firm over the long run, for strategic reasons I describe below. For now, suffice it to say that our marketing and sales efforts were pretty hopeless. But the issue turned out to be moot. In late October, we started down the road to acquisition.

FIRST PROBES: OUR IDYLLIC EXISTENCE COMES TO AN END

A couple of weeks before Internet World, sometime in mid-October, Manda Schossberger, who was then still our office manager, took a call from Marc Andreessen's secretary, who said that Andreessen wanted to speak to the president of Vermeer. Manda put the call through to John, who had a brief conversation with Andreessen. John then came to me to say that Andreessen wanted a meeting; John had already told him we'd be happy to meet, but that he would get back to him on place and time. We told Randy and the three of us discussed how to handle it. We decided that he could come to the office, but we would keep it low profile, with just the three of us in attendance. We would give him a demo and answer questions about external features of the product and any nonsensitive questions about the company, but would discuss nothing sensitive until we had assessed his intentions. Andreessen was planning to be in Boston for a Forrester conference toward the end of October, so John called him back and set up a meeting at our office; I think it was for the twenty-sixth, a Thursday. None of us had ever met Marc, although Randy and I had talked to him on the phone a few weeks after we started Vermeer in the spring of 1994, when he had oozed arrogance.

On the day Andreessen was scheduled to visit, in the morning before he had arrived, I got a telephone call myself. A man introduced himself as Chris Peters and said he was the Microsoft vice president in charge of Office.

I had never heard of him. But since Office accounted for more than half of Microsoft's total revenues at the time, it was safe to assume that Peters was not a file clerk. Conversely, his assumption that I wouldn't know his name was typical of his understated but confident style. In the following months, despite many tensions, I came both to like and respect Chris Peters a great deal. It quickly became evident that he was *seriously* intelligent, as nearly all the top people at Microsoft are, but he was also refreshingly free of the crude, overbearing arrogance that the company's culture fosters. He was also excellent at dealing with me, even when I was extremely angry, tense, and aggressive, which was often. He kept our interactions calm and substantive, which I liked, and I tried to respond in kind. But I had a lot on my mind, as you will shortly see, and it was valuable to all of us that Chris stayed remarkably cool.

Peters said that he and a number of people at Microsoft had looked at our product. We already knew they were interested. We had been carefully tracking trial product downloads, looking at our server logs and the electronic forms we asked users to fill out. We knew that we'd gotten a very large number of Web page hits and product downloads from Microsoft, although only a handful from Netscape. Peters told me that he thought our product was very cool, that he would be asking Steve Sinofsky to give Bill Gates a personal demo the following Monday, and that Gates would be taking the software with him on his PC during his annual "Think Week." Every year, Gates isolates himself for a week of thinking about the industry and the world in general. And now, he would be thinking about us. How comforting.

Chris also mentioned that he had read my *Upside* article, which had just appeared. He said that he thought it was quite good, and mostly right, but he didn't quite agree with all of it. What didn't you like? I asked him. Well, he said,

I don't think that we're so crippled by our established businesses that we can't shoot something in the head if it makes sense. (As they indeed demonstrated shortly thereafter by downgrading MSN—the Microsoft Network—to an "interesting place on the Web.") Peters didn't mention that in the article I had also called Microsoft the most predatory, ruthless, and dangerous company in the industry. I decided not to bring it up either, but I think that it was actually useful that Peters had seen that opinion. It saved us a lot of bullshit; otherwise they would have wasted time trying various tricks that work on the naïve, and we would have gotten irritated.

Peters continued: One reason we like your product is that we've been thinking along similar lines ourselves. Since you've already got a product, we might be able to cooperate somehow. I replied that in principle, we'd be open to that. What do you have in mind? Well, he said, there's various things we could do. We might like to bundle your product with Office, either as a separate product or as part of the suite. Would you be interested in talking about that? I noted how carefully he kept this from sounding like a Voice-of-God announcement that the Goths were coming. Sure, I said, we'd be happy to talk. Peters asked if there was any chance we could get to Redmond, because it would let us do it sooner. Sure, I said. Randy, in fact, was scheduled to go to Redmond the next week, just after Internet World, for a Microsoft Internet developers' conference. I suggested we might be able to coordinate with Randy's trip, and we agreed to talk soon.

Much later, I learned how we had come to Peters's attention. Mike Mathieu, a program manager in the Word group, had downloaded an evaluation copy of FrontPage from our Web site, liked it, and brought it to the attention of Steve Sinofsky. Sinofsky was one of Peters's direct reports, who later succeeded Peters as head of Office. Sinofsky had just finished a two-year rotation as Gates's personal assistant for technical issues and had been one of the first at Microsoft to understand the importance of the Web. He had written the famous 1994 "Cornell Is Wired!" memo to Gates when he was snowbound on a recruiting trip there and saw students surfing the Web in their dorms. Sinofsky immediately recognized the value of FrontPage and showed it to Peters.

Peters himself, it turned out, was deeply technical, had done graduate work in electrical engineering, and had been one of Microsoft's best developers. He had been at Microsoft since the early 1980s, knew Gates very well, and was intensely loyal to Microsoft. He lamented the fact that he could no longer code new features in Office himself, even though he was running a $5 billion organization. When he realized the Web would be important, his response was to create his own Web site by hand, which had taught him how difficult it was. So when Sinofsky showed FrontPage to Peters, he got it immediately. And although our first telephone conversation was fairly general, I could sense that Chris Peters was, in a quiet way, a very serious guy, not someone to underestimate if you wanted to stay alive.

When I hung up the telephone, I told John and Randy about the conversation. We decided to propose a meeting in conjunction with Randy's trip to Redmond. Privately, I told John that I would be the one to go, and that I expected to be present and involved at every meeting with Microsoft. I already distrusted him, and events would prove that if anything I wasn't being careful enough.

A few hours later on that same day, Marc Andreessen showed up, by himself. We whisked him into a meeting room without anyone seeing him except Manda. Outwardly Andreessen was just a big, bland-looking twenty-four-year-old. But he was clearly *very* smart, and after a year as software's newest and biggest rock star, he exuded self-assured cool. Randy, John, and I introduced ourselves. Then Andreessen said that he'd heard great things about what we were doing, he would love to see our stuff and explore whether there might be some way that we could work together.

We started with a Randy demo. Andreessen watched it all the way through, saying virtually nothing. When Randy finished, Andreessen said something like, Cool product. We asked him about Navigator Gold and LiveWire, the competing tools that Netscape had just announced. He answered smoothly, They're broadly similar, same general idea, but you're a few months ahead of us, and you've got a few things we don't. (This turned out to be complete bullshit, as we already suspected, but he carried it off extremely well.) He went on, We'd be interested in working with you, even potentially acquiring you, if you were interested. Okay, we said, we'll think about it and get in touch if we think there's something we can do. Aside from the offhand remark about acquisition, neither Andreessen nor we suggested anything specific about potential relationships, either commercially or technologically.

Andreessen asked if anyone could give him a ride to Harvard Square, and I volunteered. On the way out of the office we ran into Tom Blumer, so I introduced him. Then I took Andreessen to the Square in my convertible. During the ride, we discussed the industry in general, and it became clear that Andreessen had a wide-ranging intelligence and curiosity. He asked me about George Gilder, who had made Andreessen the star of his absurdly irresponsible piece of hype published by *Forbes ASAP* a couple of months previously. Andreessen brought it up in a carefully neutral way that made it impossible to decipher his motive. He may have been promoting Gilder and himself, or he may have been worried that the hype about Netscape-as-Microsoft-killer was getting out of hand. If he wasn't worried about that, he certainly should have been. Most of the hype came from him, Barksdale, and Gilder, although Scott

McNealy and Larry Ellison had contributed their share. But Gilder's article pushed it to a new level. Eric Schmidt, now the CEO of Novell but then the CTO of Sun, and thus deeply involved in the Java negotiations with Netscape and Microsoft, told me that Gilder's article had especially infuriated Gates and made Netscape into number one on Microsoft's target list.

In his typically lurid prose, Gilder made the "ursine" Andreessen "the Archimedean man who sharply shifts the center of the sphere, alters the axes of technology and the economy and . . . [inherits] the imperial throne in the microcosm and telecosm currently held by the Redmond Rockefeller." The Net, a place of "callipygian naked-lady bitmaps and voluminous digital ululations of the Grateful Dead" was making "all forms of desktop software—operating systems, applications, and utilities—. . . similarly peripheral. The ever-growing gigapedal resources of the Internet will always dwarf any powers and functions that can be distilled on a desktop or mobilized on the backplane of a supercomputer." The combination of the Net and Java "emancipates software from computer architecture. It offers a software paradigm radically different from the Microsoft model . . . The computer hollows out, and you no longer are concerned with its idiosyncrasies, its operating system, its instruction set, even its resident applications." By the way, I am informed that "callipygian" is a word derived from ancient Greek that means having a good-looking rear end; Gilder has quite a way with language. Unfortunately, he doesn't seem to care about its consequences. The main effect of these particular words, aside from promoting George Gilder, was to ensure that pictures of Marc Andreessen, placed inside a bull's-eye, began appearing on the walls of Microsoft's Internet group. I told Andreessen to watch out for Gilder, but it was already too late, even if he took my advice.

I dropped Andreessen in the Square and returned to Vermeer. Now it was time for some hard thinking.

IMPLICATIONS AND DILEMMAS I: FOOD FOR STRATEGIC THOUGHT

We had known, of course, that we would eventually confront the issue of strategic relationships with Netscape and Microsoft, ranging from warfare to nonexclusive relationships to exclusive relationships to acquisition. But I had decided to wait a while before trying to *initiate* any relationships and had deferred careful strategic analysis until the issue became real. Now, it was real. The top levels of both companies had approached us, in both cases in ways that made it clear that we had a narrow window of time in which to decide whether we would be their friends or their enemies. As a result, I was forced to undertake a serious analysis of our alternatives, and fast. Furthermore, the prospect of such relationships, and particularly acquisition, raised some major *internal* issues as well.

Strategically, the principal alternatives were as follows: We could go it alone and compete with both of them, being the honest broker and providing a vendor-independent industrywide standard. We could try to form a sufficiently close relationship with one of them to prevent them from competing with us, which might compromise our honest broker status. We could try to form relationships with *both* of them, although I doubted that they would swallow that unless market conditions forced them to. Or we could get acquired by one of them. With both Netscape and Microsoft, there were potentially enormous benefits to cooperation, such as bundling our server extensions with their Web servers. Both companies, for different reasons, were also potentially lethal competitors. In both cases, however, much would depend on how smart and tough they actually proved to be.

In competing against us, Netscape could potentially bundle their browser with their tool, and if and when they woke up to the requirement for server extensions, they could bundle those with their own Web servers. However, those measures wouldn't be enough to kill us: Microsoft was entering browsers and Web servers, and there were a number of other Web servers, including freeware servers, that held substantial market share. In order to really kill us in the tools market, Netscape would have to develop open-architecture server extensions like ours and make them available for competing Web servers, including Microsoft's products and freeware. I doubted that Netscape would do that, because those measures would undercut Netscape's position in Web servers. Furthermore, Netscape had announced three products that seemed fairly brain-dead, even if they really existed. If those products had powerful internal political support within Netscape, as I suspected they did, then Netscape wouldn't be much of a threat for quite some time.

Unfortunately, the same logic implied that Netscape might not be very excited about cooperating with us. If they didn't want to support other Web servers, they would appreciate only part of the value of our server extensions (remote development, but not vendor independence). And if their competing tools had powerful internal political support, those people would oppose a deal that would strengthen us relative to them. Some but probably not all of these problems could be addressed by acquisition. In that event, Netscape could decide to discontinue our server extensions for competing Web servers, and they would have our patents to prevent Microsoft or others from providing equivalent functionality. They could also provide superior support for their own browser and Web server features in our tool if they chose. I didn't like the idea of closing our architecture, and I even thought that in some areas it would be contrary to Netscape's own interests. But I recognized that Netscape might think along these lines, and that in some areas it would make sense. Finally, there was also the question of how good Netscape was. From what I could see from the outside, it was a perplexingly mixed picture; they had done some things brilliantly, but in other areas, including tools and architectural strategy generally, I thought they were blowing it badly.

Microsoft presented a different problem. As I analyzed the Microsoft situation, I gradually realized that everything depended on how serious they were. If they got really serious, they could probably kill us. I was also forced to conclude that it was, in fact, in their interest to get serious. Furthermore, while they had some internal political problems, they probably had fewer than Netscape did. Unlike Netscape, Microsoft did not hold high market shares in Internet software and derived essentially none of its revenues from it. Therefore Microsoft would be less concerned about cannibalizing its own revenues, with the exception of a temporary effect on upgrade revenues if they shipped a browser for Windows 3.1. Furthermore, unlike Netscape, Microsoft had a CEO who knew enough to evaluate conflicting arguments and cut through bullshit. I instinctively felt that Gates would not let organizational politics get in the way for too long. Moreover, Microsoft possessed two monopolies, Windows and Office, that constituted powerful weapons. In our case, Office was the more important.

We had already been thinking about how to support Web services that involved Microsoft Office documents for some time. But the conversation with Peters put me on red alert since he specifically mentioned bundling us with Office. There were two critical questions: What could we do to them, and what could they do to us?

I immediately held a series of meetings with Randy, Andy, Peter, and Tom Blumer in order to assess our options and risks. The short-term news was better than I expected. First, by using Microsoft's established public APIs (the published interfaces for outside programmers), we could provide impressive levels of support for integrating Office documents into Web services, and into our tool, without any help from Microsoft. To a lesser extent, we could do the same for other suites such as Lotus SmartSuite. It would be relatively easy for FrontPage to create and manage Web services with links to and from word processor documents, spreadsheets, and presentation graphics, in addition to Web pages. Those would be very attractive features and would put us in the center of the process of making the Web an integral part of the standard office computing environment. The fact that we were building patent positions precisely in some of these areas might give us some further protection against a Microsoft counterattack.

That was the good news. It was also, unfortunately, clear that over the longer term, Microsoft had access to powerful retaliatory weapons. In the first place, they could simply integrate and bundle their tool with Office. Office has a powerful architecture and user interface that is closed to outside applications, and since Office is essentially a ubiquitous product as well as a monopoly, this would be a very hard move to counter. Microsoft developers could therefore build a host of integration features that no outsider could match. (At this writing, the Department of Justice still hasn't noticed that Microsoft's Office monopoly is arguably even more complete and important than their operating systems monopoly.) For example, they could use the common Office menu structure, spell checker, thesaurus, graphics routines, help, and printing, not to mention new features that Microsoft could develop specifically for the Web, such as automatic HTML conversion, importing Web pages into Office documents, and much else. Indeed, with Office 2000, Microsoft has begun to use FrontPage in precisely these ways, and others besides—for example, by enabling Office to use FrontPage server extensions to send Office documents to Web sites.

Hence the only question, really, was whether Microsoft took this area seriously enough. Since Chris Peters had mentioned bundling us with Office in his first telephone call to me, and since he ran Microsoft Office, there was clearly a significant chance that they were pretty serious. It might take them three to five years, especially if our patents were really good, but in the long run, there wasn't anything we could do about it. We would have a fairly clear survival path if we were part of Netscape, since we could offer countervailing integration with a large installed base of browsers and Web servers, but on our own, it looked rough. It was a sobering realization that only strengthened as the weeks passed.

Those reflections, however, led me to conclude that we had several urgent questions to resolve. First, this analysis heightened the importance of our having a strong intellectual property position, either for bargaining leverage or for actual competitive use. I wanted to be sure our positions were as impregnable as we could make them before counterattacks started coming from Microsoft and Netscape. In addition, if we told them anything during negotiations, they might patent around us or try to establish that they were already working on the same ideas, invalidating our patents. So I decided to switch Tom Blumer back to patent work.

I pushed Tom pretty hard, at a time when he was being pulled in a lot of different directions. Tom was a senior guy who'd once run his own company. My sense is that he thought that patent work wasn't very important, and he guessed that something was up. So he pushed me to tell him. At first I told him to shut up and just fucking *do* it. The next day I apologized and told him what was up. Then we acquired another headache. Our lead patent lawyer started to press us for information on our plans because he was worried that, due to conflict of interest issues, we were depriving him of larger revenues from other clients. I pushed back, and he agreed to continue working for us. So Tom started accelerating the patent development cycle.

With both Netscape and Microsoft, of course, the most critical issue was not what they could potentially do, but how serious, intelligent, and ruthless they actually would be. So one major purpose of engaging them in negotiations would be to learn enough to come to some conclusions about that subject. As I'll describe below, it turned out to be very obvious who had the brains.

Finally, there was the John Mandile question. On the one hand, my growing distrust of him substantially increased the attractiveness of an acquisition. On the other hand, acquisition negotiations could provide many opportunities for mischief. I made it very clear to him that he was not to screw around with Microsoft, especially behind my back. He had shown little strategic sense in dealing with AT&T or FTP, so I didn't trust him on that score. But I also didn't want to wake up one day to find that he had wired an acquisition that favored him but screwed the employees and had lined up the board votes behind my back. But while my warnings clearly had some effect, Mandile still tried several tricks and came reasonably close to getting away with murder.

Meanwhile, we had a company to run and a product to launch.

INTERNET WORLD

Trade shows are a huge drain on a start-up, but they're also an unparalleled opportunity to strut your stuff. Internet World was a trade show run by Mecklermedia, which at that time was just emerging from being a husband-wife team working out of a tiny little office in suburban Connecticut. They'd been in business for more than twenty years, but somehow were among the first to notice the Internet. They are now a substantial publishing and trade show conglomerate, focused almost entirely on Internet and Web issues.

Trade shows are exhausting, but in their way extremely impressive. In a few days, you essentially create the infrastructure for a small city and a medium-sized corporation, then you run it for several days at an insane pace, then you tear it down overnight. Even in 1995, Internet World had a couple of thousand people from several hundred companies presenting information to over thirty thousand visitors over three days, often using live high-speed Internet connections. Preparing for this takes weeks—designing the booth and your demos, training everyone, preparing materials, setting up. In the days before the show, the floor is a tangle of cabling, boxes, and screaming people.

We used fully half of our employees in one way or another—staffing the booth, giving demos, answering questions, giving press interviews, checking out the scene. Most of the time, we had at least a hundred visitors lined up at the booth, so it was frantic. The shows run all day; you're on your feet most of the time, and convention centers are noisy, so you're constantly shouting. Adding to this craziness, on the first day of Internet World NYNEX managed to cut our high-speed Internet connection, which disconnected not only our e-mail but also our Web server. If you're a Web development software company, this is kind of a problem. Our Internet service provider, UUNet, identified the problem quickly, but hours were lost arguing with NYNEX before they admitted that it was their fault. More hours were lost before a crew came out, and we didn't get back online until early evening.

Karen Crowley, the communications manager John had hired, did quite a good job. Randy and I were blessedly freed from administration and logistics, which was good for all concerned, since I'm awful at it. All we had to do was show up whenever we wanted. Randy and I went together, and we had the same reaction when we saw the scene for the first time: we were stunned. From several aisles away, we saw a huge Vermeer sign over our booth, overshadowing the Netscape booth nearby. When we got to the booth, there was already an ocean of visitors; one staffer was doing a FrontPage demo on a huge TV monitor to an overflow crowd; at each corner of the booth, smaller crowds surrounded other staffers giving demos on three other PCs. Our crowds were just slightly smaller than Netscape's and far larger than anyone else's.

We got terrific comments throughout the show—even the Microsoft guy running the Blackbird booth came over and said, "You guys did a really nice job"—and we had about twenty formal interviews with the media and analysts. The magazines included *Forbes, PC Week, PC World, Information Week, Communications Week, CIO,* and a long list of Web-zines. Almost all of them followed up with exceptionally good product reviews. The analysts included Meta Group, IDC, and Patty Seybold. We also gave a special demo to technology people from *Newsweek.*

The media interviews, however, sharpened the frictions between me and Mandile. Karen Crowley did a terrific job, but she had worked for John before and took her orders from him. She and our PR firm had set up more than a dozen press interviews. But despite clear prior agreement that the "ambassadorial" function was mine, I was amazed to discover at the last minute that I wasn't scheduled for *any interviews at all,* except for one where the guy had specifically insisted that he would talk only to me. Just as he had done with strategic partnering negotiations, Mandile was trying to take me out of the loop. That was worrisome, and in this case it was also stupid. Interviewing is one thing I do really well and that John did quite poorly. I'm good on my feet and actually perform better when there's an audience, while John was nervous in front of groups and easily became flustered. When I confronted him, he blandly responded that he was only trying to protect my schedule. I was coming to be in awe of his ability not to flinch when caught red-handed. I was therefore included in the interviews I knew about, but he still tried to conceal some, and I ended up inviting myself to several.

As of Internet World, we had no real competitors (NaviSoft was there, but nobody paid any attention to them), but we lived in the constant shadow of the FUD being spread by both Microsoft and Netscape. At the show, we were being asked to compare FrontPage to entirely hypothetical products from both of those companies, and, of course, there are no limits to what a hypothetical product can do. We also heard claims that FrontPage was still only in beta and that the product wouldn't be available for a while. That was an annoying lie that apparently came from several competitors, including Netscape. They certainly knew that we had a product; for one thing, it was for sale at our Internet World booth.

On the final day of the show I was talking with Amy Cortese, a writer for *Business Week* who had been covering the Internet. She asked me if I'd be around over the next several days for an interview. In fact, I would be in Seattle for our first meeting with Chris Peters at Microsoft headquarters. Just as I was about to tell her a bland lie, Rob Glaser, the CEO of RealNetworks (then still called Progressive Networks), came over to talk with me. RealNetworks is headquartered in Seattle. A little alarm went off in my head; its warning light said, Be careful what you say now. I told Amy that I wouldn't be around for a few days because I was flying out to Seattle. "Seattle—or Redmond?" asked Glaser instantly. Seattle, I said; I'm going to a wedding, I'll be back in Boston by Monday or Tuesday. It was a good thing I said that. Two days later, as I walked out of my Seattle hotel, I ran into Glaser on the sidewalk. If I'd told Amy anything different, Glaser would have guessed instantly, and the cat would have been out of the bag.

OPENING MOVES: MICROSOFT

The same day that Internet World ended, Randy headed out to Redmond for the developers' conference, and I followed a day later, so the two of us could meet with Chris Peters. Randy and I agreed that he would handle technical questions and I would deal with business and financial issues. Since I had made it plain to Mandile that I would handle Microsoft contacts, we decided— I decided—that he didn't need to go.

Before I went to the Microsoft campus, I had arranged to have coffee with Adam Bosworth in downtown Seattle. He ran development for Microsoft's PC database product, Access. Adam is quite a character, a very nice guy, smart, feisty, independent, slightly wacky. He came to Microsoft from Borland and has an unusually irreverent view of his current employer. He can also talk literally nonstop for a half hour, as if his brain is on speed. He had sent me an e-mail praising my *Upside* article, so I told him I'd be in the area and would like to meet him, hoping to learn something. Bosworth confirmed that Microsoft had refocused itself toward the Internet and was throwing enormous resources at it—browsers, servers, security software, everything. He said that Peters and the Office people were very interested in authoring tools, and if they didn't buy someone like us, they'd do it themselves. But, he said, for our sake I hope they buy you, because I don't know where they'd get the people. They'd need a couple of dozen good people, and nobody has anyone to spare. I sure as hell don't. Actually, Bosworth was probably wrong about that. Peters's standing at Microsoft was very high, and the Internet had been given top priority. In those circumstances if the vice president in charge of Office, who has known Gates for fifteen years, says he needs two dozen good people for something impor-tant, he's going to get them. But Bosworth's attitude confirmed how tense Microsoft was about the Internet, how far behind they felt they were, and how much they were willing to spend in order to catch up. Very interesting, I thought.

That afternoon, Randy and I met Peters in the lobby of Microsoft Building 12. Peters was in his late thirties and, superficially, he looked like the classic nerd. He was short, pale, skinny and flabby at the same time, wearing jeans and a jeans jacket. But he also radiated a quiet self-confidence in many things that was very un-nerdlike. Chris took us to Building 16, then upstairs to a confer-ence room.

I was determined to avoid the usual fate of small companies engaged in dis-cussions with Microsoft, a fate captured in the industry's expressive phrase, the Microsoft Mindsuck. Inexplicably, many companies answer every question Mi-crosoft asks, while receiving either nothing at all or horse manure in return. In this case they had approached us and, at least temporarily, we held a strong po-sition. Peters was clearly trying to appear helpful, so I exploited the situation. During the week prior to the meeting we exchanged lots of e-mail. I asked him questions about Microsoft's plans and requested meetings with people in charge of them. Every time Peters acceded to one request I followed it with an-other; every time he conceded I pushed further. Now we would see how much he would actually give us.

It turned out we were in the Office "War Room." Peters introduced us to Steve Sinofsky, who was present the entire time, and a couple of other people who came in and out depending on the agenda item. I formed an immediate suspicion of Sinofsky. He agreed enthusiastically with everything everyone said, particularly Peters; he seemed superficial and fawning, yet also calculating. He literally held Chris's presentation for him and turned pages as Peters read from it. This was the first negative sign I'd seen; Peters gave a long, amazingly insipid, obviously canned presentation about Microsoft, how it strove to improve itself, why it was a force for good, what it had learned over the years, etc. Simultaneously a slide version was displayed on a large PC monitor. The effect was somewhat bizarre, and I was surprised that they thought we would swallow this stuff. We tried to be polite, but I think our discomfort and impatience eventually began to show.

Then we got down to something approaching business. As I'd requested, we received briefings on Word and Internet Assistant, their new "Gibraltar" NT Web server, and their general view of the Internet. It was informal, very smart, and with a lot of give and take. The presentations were somewhat informative yet clearly sanitized; nobody said anything nasty about eviscerating Netscape, which clearly had to be uppermost in their minds. But everything confirmed my view that Chris Peters was seriously intelligent. It was also clear that he and Sinofsky knew a lot about the Web and the Internet, certainly more than the Word people did. It was sometime that afternoon that Chris mentioned that he had developed his own Web site. He called it the Bureau of Atomic Tourism; it described tours of monuments and facilities related to nuclear weapons technology. He still runs it. It's at http://www.oz.net/~chrisp/atomic.html and has won a number of awards. So he's got his nerd side.

At Chris's request, Randy gave them the standard demo, which exercised about two-thirds of the product, which is a lot for a demo. There was no question they got it, and from there we moved into a wide-ranging discussion of the Web and its future. It was professional, smart, and a lot of fun. I enjoyed myself, while also taking care not to forget that the subject of our banter was my company's survival. We disagreed sometimes, but registered our differences politely, explored them, and moved on.

There was, however, one area in which they were at least tempted to make a big mistake. They opined that the Office document formats, particularly Word, could effectively replace HTML. This kinky idea posed a risk similar to Netscape's political problems with their own tools. If Microsoft persisted in this folly it would simultaneously reduce the competitive threat they would pose but also, unfortunately, our perceived value to them. When I questioned them about the HTML issue, they were pretty adamant. Randy told me later that Chris Peters already had his doubts about this, but didn't want to get into a public fight with the Word people, who felt threatened.

What do people have on their desks now? Chris said. They have Word and Excel. HTML can't display spreadsheets or good fonts or graphs. True enough, we said, but it was made for electronic hypertext and therefore could naturally do things that Office formats couldn't, and it didn't carry all that paper-document baggage (linear structure, page breaks, et cetera). Further-more, it was already being used by thirty million browsers and half a million Web sites, and by the time Microsoft had anything else on the market, HTML would be entrenched in at least 100 million browsers and a couple of million Web sites. But we didn't press the point too hard. We didn't yet know that the HTML-Office debate had been white-hot inside Microsoft for some time, with HTML continuously gaining. (In his May 1995 memo, Gates had said that Microsoft's Office position offered an opportunity to superset the Web. He may or may not have understood at the time how fundamentally different the two document models in fact are.) By the time Microsoft unveiled its new Internet strategy a month later, the company was solidly in the HTML camp—another demonstration of Gates's and Microsoft's flexibility.

Aside from the HTML issue, they liked almost everything we'd done and every opinion we offered. To make our product easy for Windows PC users to learn, we had deliberately used Windows and Office conventions wherever possible in designing the user interface, so FrontPage looked very much like a Microsoft Office product. They understood the importance of wizards, bots, and the elimination of programming. Some of them, though not everyone, also understood the importance of Andy's client-server architecture; they certainly got the value of remote authoring and the importance of avoiding dependence on any one Web server.

After a couple of hours, we decided to go to dinner. Chris suggested that we follow him to the restaurant and told us to look for a red car, which turned out to be an enormous, brand-new, fire engine red Mercedes. Chris is probably worth several hundred million dollars; I enjoyed the combination of the car, his worn jeans, and the bad steakhouse on the top floor of an ugly skyscraper in Bellevue, where we dined. There were five of us, I think—Randy and I, Chris and Steve Sinofsky, and I believe Peter Pathé, the general manager of the Word group.

Once we ordered dinner we got down to business again, and this time, it was *business*. Chris said there were basically three possibilities. We could give them the right to sell FrontPage, possibly inside the Office box. That was tricky and something Microsoft had almost never done in the past. I suspected im-mediately that this offer was bogus; it would be great for us, but Microsoft isn't crazy, and Chris *certainly* wasn't. Or, second, we could give them a license to our source code, so they could sell FrontPage under their own brand name. This offer was certainly for real, because it was squarely in Microsoft's tradition of eviscerating both suppliers and competitors. Microsoft has a long history of licensing source code and then obliterating its supplier with an identical or im-proved product under their control. They have done this with Sybase (the source of SQL Server, their main database product), Spyglass (the source of their Internet Explorer browser), and even the original DOS operating system (licensed from a Seattle developer for $50,000). I utterly fail to comprehend why people keep licensing their source code to Microsoft, and I can only assume that Chris was offering this option as a test, just to see if we might be stupid after all.

The third possibility, Chris said, was the "full meal deal"—acquisition. But they would acquire us, he said, only if they could buy a functioning engineering organization, so most of the key technical people would have to move to Redmond. Bingo. This was what they were serious about; if they acquired us they'd get the product, but they wouldn't do it unless they could get the people, which meant they'd thought about it carefully. So, what do you think? he asked. Are you interested in working with us? As always, I was impressed with his efficiency. This was our first meeting, yet we were getting to the point. To be sure, Chris would kill us if he could, but not once did Chris torture me with male bonding conversations about sports, stereo equipment, cars, the weather, or stocks. Thank you, Chris, more than you can know. Chris did, however, try to manipulate Randy a bit, by advertising himself as a fellow engineer.

We'd have to be utter morons to license our source code to Microsoft. This was one of the few times Chris behaved as if we could be played for fools; of course, he had to try. I replied, with unusual restraint, that in principle we'd be happy with any of the three options. But as a practical matter, I doubted that source code licensing would work. We would view that as tantamount to an acquisition and would expect to be paid about the same, maybe even more, which would be a lot. Conversely, the idea of Microsoft acting as a FrontPage marketing partner was great, but we recognized that it would be an unusual arrangement for them—i.e., we suspected that hell would freeze over first. Finally, I said we certainly hadn't planned on being acquired. We thought we had a strong product, and we liked our strategic position, so our business plan was to remain independent and do an IPO, which in fact people were already suggesting. But we were businesspeople, and for the right price and on the right terms, we'd consider it. But I warned him that we would be expensive. The dinner adjourned pleasantly; we agreed that we would stay in touch and decide how to proceed further.

The Redmond meeting was on November 3, a Friday. The following Monday and Tuesday, Chris and I exchanged a number of e-mails and phone calls and fairly quickly agreed that acquisition was the only alternative worth discussing. He said he wanted to meet Mandile, which was reasonable, and he also wanted us to meet Greg Maffei, Microsoft's treasurer (he's now CFO), because he handled the financial side of Microsoft's deals. Chris said he was planning to be in the East later in the week anyway, and they would love to come to Vermeer.

I certainly wanted to meet with Chris, but I did not want a Microsoft team showing up at Vermeer. I didn't want rumors spreading, I didn't want them poaching our employees, and I didn't want them wandering around asking questions and picking up competitive information. In fact, I sent an e-mail to the whole company whose message was just short of ordering them to shoot strangers on sight.

I suspected Chris was fibbing a bit and was actually coming east just for us, and I replied in kind. (I later learned that he despises travel and travels only for reasons he regards as very important.) I said we were scheduled to be in New York at the end of the week, so it would be easier to meet him there. I'm sure he saw through it, but he didn't say anything. So we agreed to meet on Thursday morning at the Westbury Hotel, where I often stayed. Maffei was in London at the moment and was also in the middle of negotiating the MSNBC deal, but he would fly to New York to meet with us.

That left only a day or so for Randy, John, and me to discuss our strategy. I had mixed emotions. I was optimistic about our technical position; we probably had a year's head start over everybody else. But I was worried about John, and I was increasingly worried that Netscape was screwing up, so that there would be no countervailing power in Web servers and browsers by the time Microsoft attacked for real. The meeting in Redmond left no doubt that Microsoft would go after the authoring space, and Chris Peters was distressingly smart.

If we were to be acquired, however, I still favored a deal with Netscape as long as the financial outcomes were reasonably close, which came down to price plus an estimation of their prospects. I preferred not to increase Microsoft's dominance, and I knew that several of the engineers felt the same way. But I wasn't dogmatic about it. I thought our minimum acquisition price should be about $100 million, and hoped we could get more. For Mandile's part, because of the way his financial package had been structured, he naturally favored an acquisition. He was careful not to be pushy about it, but did suggest that we "should seriously consider" anything over $75 million. That would net him more than $4 million; remember, this was six weeks after he had started work.

Randy, in contrast, dug in his heels; he was basically opposed to acquisition. He thought we had a terrific product and that we should go public and see it through. In his view, even $100 million wouldn't give him and the engineers sufficient long-term financial security. His share would have been about $3.5 million, or about $2.5 million after taxes, and most of the engineers would make between $300,000 and $500,000. That's a lot of money, but they'd spent ten years in start-ups at low salaries, waiting for the chance to hit it big. Furthermore, getting to do an IPO has an iconic status for many engineers. This was their shot, and Randy didn't want to give it away. Moreover, for personal reasons, Randy initially didn't want to relocate. Microsoft would surely structure the deal to penalize him if he refused. He understood that if the price was high enough, we couldn't say no, but he thought our number should be $150–200 million. But he agreed that we should proceed with the meeting. We flew to New York.

When the issue of price arose in our meeting with Peters and Maffei, I screwed it up by not keeping Mandile on a short leash. Before the meeting, we had agreed on roles. Randy would stay in character as the technical guru, while John and I, also in character, would play good cop and bad cop respectively. We decided we wanted well over $100 million. We would point out that we had already turned down offers in the $60–$70 million range—which was about two-thirds true, if you counted Spyglass and Compuserve as serious companies—and so we would need a *much* higher number now. I should have scripted Mandile carefully, and done so in Randy's presence, but I didn't. This was a big mistake. It left Mandile an opening, which he used brilliantly.

There was another problem, too. Greg Maffei and I took an instant dislike to each other. My first impression, which subsequent interactions only reinforced, was that he was extraordinarily arrogant, obnoxious, vulgar, and amoral, and I didn't hide my contempt very well. In turn, he clearly regarded us as an annoyance that he and Microsoft could simply manipulate at will. When I mentioned my concern that the Justice Department might block an acquisition, for instance, Maffei replied, Forget it, we acquire small companies all the time. There won't be any problem, just leave it to us. I responded by saying No, actually, we're not just some little company, I know at least as much about Justice Department policy as you do, and this could be a serious problem. We didn't pursue the issue further at the time, but the sparks between us had started to fly. This became an issue later, one where Peters's and Mandile's coolness proved useful. Maffei apparently can be charming, but the majority of people I've met, and who know him, share my view.

After the preliminaries, we got right to our asking price. John took over at that point. He said that we had already turned down acquisition offers, and we couldn't consider *anything less than $70 million*. I was stunned. In effect, he had just announced that our asking price was $70 million or perhaps slightly above. I turned to John, trying to keep my voice calm, and said that I thought that in fact we felt that we would need much more than that. I tried to avoid the appearance of pulling rank or appearing angry because I feared that would make us look even worse. But I could already see the glint in Maffei's eye. Our CEO had just told Microsoft that he, at least, would take a very low price. I could hardly have imagined a worse outcome. When the meeting broke up, Maffei and Peters said they would think a bit, and then send us a formal offer contained in a letter of intent. Then they departed, leaving the three of us to confer.

Randy and I were very upset after the meeting. Randy had repeatedly stressed that for him, $70 million was hardly worth it, especially if he had to move to Redmond to vest his remaining options. I was upset about the price too, but I was *utterly furious* at Mandile. Some of the blame was mine for not absolutely scripting what he was to say, but as usual, another of Mandile's supposedly honest efforts greatly favored his self-interest over the company's, since his personal incentives enormously favored a quick acquisition. Mandile then proceeded to make it even worse. He said to us, Don't worry about the price, or about refusing to relocate. I don't think we should sell this company unless all three of us are fully vested.

I completely exploded inside, although I didn't say anything immediately.

If I understand Mandile's conduct correctly, which I am certain I do, this move was at once unbelievably stupid and absolutely brilliant. I should be rigorously honest about this and say that Mandile has never admitted to me that he planned his actions for selfish reasons, and indeed frequently denied it. I am inferring his calculations from his behavior alone. But I am quite confident that I am correct, and the evidence of his subsequent conduct reconfirmed my assessment repeatedly. It goes like this.

Mandile was offering Randy and me a deal, in effect a bribe. It would screw the employees, and to some extent even the VCs, but it would make the three of us, especially Mandile, very happy. On the one hand, he was offering Microsoft a low price. On the other, he was offering Randy and me full vesting if we would support John in getting full vesting too. John never mentioned full vesting for the employees in general, of course. But Randy, John, and I were the three largest employee shareholders, the top management, and two of the four members of the board. If we went to the VCs and told them that we needed to sell, that $70 million was the best price we could get, but that we needed full vesting for ourselves, the VCs might initially object but they would cave. If full vesting for us three was the only thing standing between them and $35 million in Microsoft stock, they would do it. Acquisition alone would increase John's take by half. Full vesting would *further* increase his gain by one-third, Randy's by about the same fraction, and mine by about 20 percent. Furthermore, if Microsoft wanted to keep any or all of us past the acquisition, it would have to give us large additional options, since it couldn't rely on our remaining Vermeer vesting. Thus for us, a $70 million deal with full vesting would be equivalent to a much higher price with continued vesting required. If Randy and I were for sale, it was brilliant. If we weren't, it was stupid.

It was stupid. On the way to the airport, for perhaps the only time in my life I made sure that I arranged everyone's seating carefully, so that John and I were alone in a taxi. Then I told him that I found his suggestion completely unacceptable, especially given the grossly favorable deal he'd already gotten for himself, and that I would oppose any effort on his part to accelerate his vesting. He was silent for a moment, which by now I recognized as a sign that his machinery was processing alternatives. Then he said that he was only looking after Randy's interests, not his own. Bullshit, I replied, I know you by now. If you want to accelerate Randy's vesting, fine, go ahead. But forget about getting full vesting for yourself; I would oppose it. John was silent. Of course, he didn't forget it, and he did try again.

But there were also other issues to worry about in the meantime. It turned out that the antitrust problems I feared in the event of acquisition would be dramatically worsened if we completed our second-round financing.

IMPLICATIONS AND DILEMMAS II: ANTITRUST, AND ANOTHER LITTLE PROBLEM WITH OUR SECOND ROUND

As evidence and logic were forcing me to the conclusion that acquisition might be our best or even only way out, I became increasingly concerned about what the Antitrust Division of the Justice Department might do. If Anne Bingaman really was trying to curb Microsoft, she would be tough on mergers and acquisitions, which for legal reasons are much easier to stop than predatory behavior. They had just blocked Microsoft's acquisition of Intuit. I had just yelled at Anne Bingaman for two hours and might make an attractive political target; furthermore, Vermeer was getting to be a high-profile item. And since Justice had a long-standing record of doing dumb things, including things that helped Microsoft, I thought they might even try to block an acquisition by Netscape. I called a couple of lawyer friends, including Charlie Morris (who is a lawyer as well as a consultant and writer). Charlie told me I probably didn't need to worry as long as we were under the Hart-Scott-Rodino tripwire, to which I replied, What the hell is that? Charlie told me that it was a law that sets guidelines for antitrust clearance of mergers and acquisitions, and that I should check it out. I did.

It turned out that the Hart-Scott-Rodino Act requires all acquisitions above a minimum size (generally, $10 million in net assets or $15 million in revenues) to be disclosed to the Justice Department in advance. Justice can review them before they close and, if it chooses, can temporarily block them pending a full investigation or sue to stop them completely. This is what happened to Intuit; Justice blocked the acquisition and Intuit twisted in the wind until Microsoft unilaterally canceled the deal. However, Hart-Scott-Rodino stipulates that *if and only if a merger or acquisition is below $10 million in net assets and $15 million in revenues, you can close the transaction without notifying Justice.* Their only recourse in that case is to sue afterward to undo the transaction, which is far more difficult.

We weren't over the H-S-R threshold yet, but we were about to close on a second-round financing of $7.2 million, and we still had $1 million from our first round. We also owned half a million dollars' worth of computers. If we drew down the full second round investment, did a couple of partnership deals, and sold a few copies of FrontPage, we could easily exceed the H-S-R tripwire. If we then accepted an acquisition offer from Microsoft, we would have to notify the Justice Department of the pending transaction, *in advance.* That was a nightmare scenario. If Justice blocked our acquisition by Microsoft, we could twist in the wind for months. During this time we wouldn't have a prayer of doing a strategic deal with anyone else, because of the presumption that we'd be part of Microsoft soon. But Microsoft could take advantage of that time, and of everything they'd learned from us, to develop their own competing product. From Microsoft's standpoint, six months of indecision by Justice, or even an eventual ruling prohibiting the acquisition, would be almost as good as doing the deal. Something quite similar could be said of Netscape, particularly since they were already developing their own tools.

On the other hand, if we stayed under the H-S-R threshold, we could close a deal before Justice found out about it. They could still sue, but they would be suing to unwind a deal, which is always much harder. Best of all, they'd be suing Microsoft or Netscape, not us. And while the requested remedy might be to make them divest FrontPage, we'd still keep our money. Thus for us, crossing the H-S-R tripwire at this point would have been insane.

This further reinforced my conclusion that we had a comparatively short window in which to conclude a trouble-free acquisition. Not only were both Netscape and Microsoft getting ready to field competitive products, but the legal complexity and risk of an acquisition would increase sharply as we became a real company, with assets and/or revenues above the H-S-R tripwire. I was certain that antitrust scrutiny of Microsoft, and the Internet generally, would only grow as time passed. Furthermore, at any random point Justice could decide that Web authoring tools themselves constituted a distinct market, that our market share (or Netscape's, or Microsoft's) was excessive, and that mergers in the area should not be permitted.

And finally, if we were going to do an acquisition soon, it would be insane to close the second round even for purely financial reasons. The whole round would dilute us about 18 percent and the effect would be greater upon the employees than upon the investors. So at the last minute we decided to renegotiate the second round, the one and only occasion that time favored us in doing a VC deal. We restructured the round so that the investors committed their money, but we could draw it down in 25 percent tranches, the first tranche right away, and the rest only as we requested it. Mandile took the lead in giving the investors the bad news and negotiating the new arrangement. I must say that he did a good job. It was the kind of task he is genuinely good at, one where his disarming, low-key style serves him well and where tactics, diplomacy, and careful negotiation are everything. I was worried that the investors would balk, but they didn't utter a peep, not one of them—although a couple of them guessed that something (either an acquisition, IPO, or large strategic investment) was in the offing.

As things actually worked out, we only drew the first tranche of $1.8 million. Combining the $32 million valuation we obtained with the fact that we only took part of the round, we got an enormously better deal than if we had accepted Marcuvitz's kind and considerate offer of a quick inside round at $16 million pre-money. It was one of the best deals we ever made. As I mentioned earlier, with subsequent appreciation in Microsoft stock, the difference for the employees was $150 million or more.

But I'm getting ahead of myself. We still had a long way to go, and the journey was becoming more unpleasant by the day.

MANDILE ONCE AGAIN

All this time, tensions between me and Mandile had been steadily mounting. In many ways, this was a tragedy, because our skill sets could have complemented each other very well. Whereas my negotiating style tended to be tough, direct, and abrasive, John was relaxed, smooth, and—as I had learned in his compensation negotiations—supremely patient. He lacked strategic vision, but was superb on details and had a lot of experience with software contracts. He was an experienced general manager. He erred in pricing, marketing, and sales strategy because he was inexperienced in consumer software, but if he had not been so concerned about his power, and if we had had an honest and healthy working relationship, we could have fixed that fairly easily.

But his defects, for me, were fatal. John's interest, always and everywhere, was in somehow improving his own position. In every decision that touched him I became aware of a single overwhelming agenda item: Was this good or bad for John Mandile? And I gradually realized that this could compromise the company seriously, because his hoarding of information and control made it impossible to make optimal decisions.

Our first overt conflict after he started as CEO had been over the conduct of discussions with potential strategic partners. We had agreed that John would take them over, both because he had negotiated a lot more contracts than I had, and because he was less likely to create enemies. The problem was that once he took control he kept the information secret. Even that might have been okay if I trusted his strategic abilities, but I didn't. The FTP and AT&T contract negotiations convinced me that, smart as Mandile was, I couldn't rely on his strategic judgment. It wasn't that I assumed I would always be right, but he clearly wasn't infallible. So at a minimum I wanted to be kept in the loop, at least for major decisions, as indeed he had agreed.

My complete psychological break with Mandile, however, came over something quite different. It occurred in early November, shortly after Mandile made a play for full vesting at the New York meeting and pretended that he was doing it for Randy's benefit.

We had just told the board about the possibility of either an acquisition or an IPO. Wade pointed out that some of the early employees, those who held large options but did not yet own their stock, might have a serious alternative minimum tax (AMT) problem. I didn't have the faintest idea what this meant; this was one of many occasions when the VCs proved that they did, sometimes, add value.

Wade explained that the AMT problem arose if you held unexercised options at a low valuation. After an IPO or an acquisition made with public stock, your options now have large value that the IRS can calculate. If you exercise your options and purchase your stock, you are subject to an *immediate* tax on the difference between the option price and the market price, whether or not you sell the stock. Often this forced people to sell yet more stock in order to pay their tax bill, and if they had to sell it quickly, then they lost capital gains treatment, which increased their taxes even further. This could be an extremely serious matter to an engineer whose stock represented nearly all of his or her wealth. Andy and Peter were in exactly that position, so Wade suggested that they should buy their stock *now,* while the price was still low. You're allowed to buy unvested shares, which become "restricted" stock; it must still vest, but you avoid the AMT problem and your capital gains holding period starts.

I was extremely grateful to Wade for pointing out this problem. I knew that Andy and Peter didn't have much money. In light of the risks they had taken and the work they had done, I suggested we give them a cash bonus sufficient to allow them to buy their stock. It was about $25,000 each. Their contribution to the company was already so large that, in my view, it would have been virtually impossible to overcompensate them. I was pleased that Wade and Andy Marcuvitz agreed without hesitation, and I informed Andy and Peter accordingly.

A couple of weeks later, I asked Andy and Peter if they had received their stock. No, they said, John had told them it would take a while to get the paperwork for the loan. What loan? I said. We're giving you the money. Oh, they said, John said there were problems with that, so it's a loan, but that's cool.

For some reason Mandile and I weren't in the office together, so I called him. Over the telephone, I said, What the hell is this about a loan instead of a bonus for Andy and Peter? Oh, he said, we're working out a bonus plan for the whole company, so I wanted to separate the stock issue from their bonus, which we'll give them later. So I decided to make it a loan.

Then I remembered Mandile's hiring negotiations. He had wanted to own stock when he joined the company, and Marcuvitz had let him buy a lot of it. Then Mandile had wanted a loan to finance that purchase. Andy had given him the loan, but had collateralized it with the stock, so that if Mandile left the company or didn't pay back the loan, he would lose that stock. I thought to myself, I'll bet that John has learned a new trick, and I'll bet he's using it now. John, I said, are these loans by any chance collateralized with their stock? John was quiet for a moment, that deadly reaction I had come to recognize. Well, actually yes, he said, they are, I thought that would be prudent.

I thought to myself, The little shithead. This would provide John with enormous leverage over Andy and Peter. Once they'd borrowed money to buy their stock, he could take it away, or at a minimum cause them considerable hardship, simply by firing them or insisting that they immediately repay the loan. He could potentially strip them of everything they had earned. I went completely ballistic, or postal, if you prefer. John, I said, you promised me, and I promised Andy and Peter, that we would give them the money. The board agreed to it. You then went back on this promise without telling me. You made an arrangement that Andy and Peter almost certainly don't understand, which could cause them to lose all of their stock if some accident or personal financial crisis forced them to leave. You can't possibly understand what they've done for this company, which is ten times more than you will ever do. You will give them the money and ensure that they purchase their stock immediately, or I will cut your balls off. Don't ever lie to me about something like this again. After another long silence, John said, Charles, I understand how you feel. I was just trying to do the right thing for the company. We hung up.

Later I told Randy what had happened. He agreed that Mandile's behavior was wrong and completely shared my feelings about Andy and Peter, but he was also worried about my tendency to react too aggressively and emotionally. He also worried, very reasonably, about the impact on the company if Mandile and I couldn't get along. Randy's instinct was always to avoid conflict and to believe the best about people. But for me, in combination with Mandile's little act in New York, this was a breaking point. I would never again trust him. He'd had years practice playing this kind of game, and he was a lot better at it than I was. That's when I really started to fear that I would have to sell the company or eventually force him out. In retrospect, I may have exaggerated the importance of this particular episode, because (for better or worse) loans collateralized with stock turn out to be a frequently used mechanism, and even have some tax advantages. However, Mandile hadn't been straightforward about it and this followed an increasingly clear and disturbing pattern. My fears grew into a virtual certainty when I saw that Mandile really had serious limits as an executive, and that because of his obsession with self-interest and control, he wouldn't allow himself to rely on me or anyone else for help when he needed it. But I also couldn't leave now, because that would place my employees at his mercy, and for that matter I didn't trust him with my own wealth. At this critical stage, I couldn't risk an explosion with the board, which I might lose in any case. So for the time being, Mandile and I were going to be handcuffed together, as in a bad thriller in which two mortal enemies have to work together against the world—until they are free to fight each other to the death. What fun this was going to be.

Needless to say, I was not in the best of moods as we flew out to California to see whether Netscape wanted to buy us too.

CHAPTER EIGHT

The Making of a Deal

My center is giving way, my right is retreating, situation excellent, I am attacking.
—*Field Marshal Foch, battle of the Marne, 1914*

THE NEXT STEP WITH NETSCAPE: BARKSDALE IN CALIFORNIA

At this point in the proceedings, I still preferred a deal with Netscape and was willing to accept substantially less money from them as opposed to Microsoft, if everything else worked out. But I also wanted the best deal we could get. If we were to be acquired before we exceeded the Hart-Scott-Rodino threshold, Netscape and Microsoft were the only serious candidates, and regardless of which we preferred, it was in our interest to create a bidding war between them. We also wanted to learn as much as possible about them in order to assess their relative prospects and to increase our bargaining leverage by more knowledgeably playing on their fears of each other.

Therefore our next step was to accept Andreessen's offer to talk further. After waiting a decent interval so as not to appear overly eager, we called him and said that we'd like to explore a deal. Andreessen responded quickly and arranged a meeting with Barksdale in California, only a day or two after our New York meeting with Microsoft. By this time I had decided that I couldn't let John out of my sight. Thus all three of us—John, Randy, and I—would go together.

So, in early November, we found ourselves sitting in a conference room in Netscape's headquarters building on East Middlefield Road in Mountain View, half an hour south of Palo Alto. Barksdale and Andreessen walked in, and we all introduced ourselves briefly. Barksdale was strikingly handsome, white-haired, distinguished, superficially informal and deferential yet clearly quite image-conscious. I sensed that he was simultaneously extremely smooth, as Paul Ferri had said, and yet in some ways painfully obvious. He was a salesman in every sense—a suit, as Andy Schulert would have said. He made a point of flattering everyone, particularly Andreessen. He teased Andreessen about the fact that his phone service had recently been disconnected for nonpayment.

Marc had already seen FrontPage, of course, but it turned out that Barksdale hadn't, so we started off with a Randy demo. Once again Andreessen said virtually nothing during the demo, and neither did Barksdale. Afterward, we discussed business options and quickly converged on acquisition as the only sensible one. They made no mention of their own tools, which according to their September 18 announcement were to be released in less than two months. We were by now virtually certain that those products had been mostly imaginary, or were very far from commercial release.

Unwisely, we became enmeshed in a discussion about whether we would move to California if Netscape acquired us. This was partially our fault. Both Randy and John were reluctant to move. I'm sure that Randy could have been persuaded, in the end, if it had been the right thing to do, just as he was later persuaded to move to Redmond, but at this point he was still hesitant to relocate, particularly to California. We blew it by saying that we preferred to remain in Boston, and to his credit Barksdale was more concerned about Randy than John or me, one of only a few times I saw him display any respect for technology. (I never saw him display an *understanding* of technology.) At this point we should simply have said, Don't worry about this now, we'll resolve it if everything else works. I don't think that it changed the eventual outcome. The fundamental problems turned out to be that Barksdale underestimated our value, while I came to have a low opinion of him and of Netscape generally. Over the next two months I saw far too much evidence that these guys were an accident waiting to happen.

During this meeting we didn't actually say we were talking to Microsoft, although we made it clear that they were an alternative. But I made it equally clear that, other things being equal, we much preferred a deal with Netscape. This was quite true, despite my reservations about the company's management and strategy. Along with many of the engineers, I initially preferred to beat Microsoft rather than join it, and I also thought we'd have more fun at a smaller, faster company. This quaint idealism of mine lasted a while, until so many facts hit me in the face that I had to acknowledge them. In particular, when I tried desperately to get through to Barksdale, to impress upon him the danger he faced from Microsoft and our importance as a swing vote, his response was an oblivious arrogance. But in late October and early November, I was actually quite excited by the idea of helping Netscape outwit Microsoft and still naïve enough to think that since I could make a contribution, Barksdale would listen.

Despite the relocation issue, the first meeting with Barksdale ended with fairly positive feelings all around. We agreed that we should get to know each other better, and that Netscape would consider making us an acquisition offer. Barksdale pointed out that the Collabra people were very happy at Netscape, including financially. We left open the possibility of relocating the company over time. Shortly afterward, Netscape's CFO, Peter Currie, called Mandile in Boston to introduce himself. Currie had worked for Barksdale before as CFO of McCaw and was experienced at acquisitions, though not quite this kind. When Mandile reported the Currie conversation to me, I told him that he could handle Currie, but that I would insist on being the primary interface to Barksdale. Mandile agreed, but he clearly wasn't happy about it.

Later, I realized that during our entire two-hour meeting, Barksdale hadn't asked a single question about our product and had said virtually nothing about Netscape's products, much less about competition with Microsoft or the future direction of the Web generally. Warning bell number one.

TIME TO TALK WITH OUR EMPLOYEES

By this time the prospect of acquisition was sufficiently real that, for both ethical and practical reasons, I thought we should begin discussing it with at least some of the employees, beginning with Andy and Peter. John wanted to postpone this, but by this point he had no credibility with me in any question where his personal interests might conflict with those of others, and I simply ignored him. One day during an executive staff meeting, when we were discussing acquisition issues, I got up, went to Andy's and Peter's offices, and asked them to join us. I told them where things stood and asked them what they thought. Later, I also asked them privately. Peter was fine with any of the options—IPO, Netscape, Microsoft. Andy wanted an IPO, would consider Netscape, but preferred to avoid Microsoft. Peter had no problem with relocation; Andy said he'd consider it but would prefer not to. We discussed the merits, our competitive position, and so forth. Then I asked them whether they thought the other engineers would be willing to relocate. They weren't sure; Peter was more optimistic than Andy was.

A few days later I decided to ping Ted Stefanik privately, by asking him simply if he would ever consider relocating at some point in the future. Ted saw through it instantly, as I should have realized he would, and answered with his characteristic reverence for authority. "Sure," he said, "I'll spend a couple of years in Chairman Bill's slopworks if the price is right." I asked him if he thought the other engineers would too. "Charles," he said, "do you think they'd get at least half a million out of it?" Yes, I said, at least the earlier and more senior people; I wouldn't do the deal otherwise. Ted replied, Then I'd bet that most of them would go, at least until they vested. Thus preliminary evidence suggested that enough people would relocate to satisfy Microsoft, and if necessary, Netscape. So we could proceed.

Microsoft's First Offer: We Get What We Asked For

The week before in New York, Maffei had said that he would fax us a written offer in the form of a letter of intent (LOI). Randy's recollection is that it arrived the following Sunday, November 12, a couple of days later than Maffei had promised, and that Randy, John, and I went to Vermeer that morning to wait for it. I do remember that there were other people in the office, obviously curious about why we were guarding the fax machine.

When the LOI arrived, it was an offer to acquire us for $80 million in Microsoft stock. I was disappointed but not surprised. Mandile had opened the door to a low offer, and that's what we got—the $70 million John had said was our minimum, plus a token increase to placate me. Randy and I quickly agreed that we had to turn it down, and John didn't fight us. We called Maffei back and said the offer was much too low. I don't remember the details of the conversation, but it was unpleasant. Maffei said something like, Well you said you wouldn't take less than $70 million, we're giving you significantly more, what the hell are you complaining about. I called Chris Peters separately and told him we were saying no. We discussed it for a while and he agreed to see if he could get us more. But it seemed that he couldn't, or he didn't try that hard.

After we refused the offer, communication declined sharply. We didn't want to appear desperate, and neither did they. In part, we were playing a game of chicken; in part, Peters was truly coming to the conclusion that we couldn't do the deal. But I tried to stay in occasional contact with Peters, for example by forwarding him press coverage of our product, which was still very positive.

There were signs that they hadn't completely given up. Shortly after we declined the $80 million offer, Maffei called Wade Woodson to ask how the board felt about an acquisition—and, I suspect, to probe for a wedge between me, Mandile, and the VCs, hoping the board might go for a low number despite my objections. Wade said all the right things: everybody was fully informed, he'd help wherever possible, but the board was letting the management team drive the decision. And in fact we *were* keeping the VCs informed by then, which we hadn't initially. We had waited until after our first meetings with Andreessen and Peters before telling the board that things were getting serious. At this point Marcuvitz still leaned toward an IPO, probably a vestige of the traditional VC view that acquisition was a second-tier result. He also, of course, didn't yet understand how bad our marketing and sales situation was. John certainly hadn't told him, and I was waiting until our second round was definitively closed, and until I was more confident of my opinions, before raising it myself.

In addition to Maffei's call to Wade, there were two other telephone calls. One came directly to us, from a headhunter who said that he had heard that we were being acquired by Microsoft, asking whether this was true. We said no and asked him where he'd heard it. Oh, people are talking about it, he said, obviously not comfortable saying more. This was disturbing. If our negotiations with Microsoft became general knowledge, it could screw up our partnership negotiations, our hiring, everything.

The other call was *really* weird. Someone involved with Vermeer, whom I will not name, received a telephone call from a prominent VC, whose firm had very close ties to Netscape. My colleague wouldn't tell me who the VC was and to this day regards it as a secret. The VC told my colleague that he was called because he, the VC, had just gotten a call from Microsoft, who was asking about Vermeer—were we real, were we good, what did he know. The Netscape-affiliated VC then called my colleague, who was an acquaintance of his, as a courtesy, and to ask for information about Vermeer to pass back to Microsoft. This was truly bizarre. If this really occurred, and I certainly trust my colleague's report, then by making this request through a Netscape-affiliated VC, Microsoft was in effect notifying Netscape that they were interested in us. This was fine with us, of course, but it struck me as one of the most moronic things Microsoft could possibly do. They might as well have called Barksdale directly and said, Let's have a bidding war. It was thus fairly stupid of them to make calls like this, at least if they really wanted to do the deal. It risked causing antitrust problems, pissing us off when we found out, and also notifying competitors such as Netscape that Microsoft was interested.

Whatever they may have been up to, Chris Peters later told Randy that after a couple of weeks had passed he assumed the deal was dead. So, shortly after we had turned down their $80 million offer, Peters began putting together a development team to build Microsoft's FrontPage killer.

Netscape Again: Barksdale and I Have a Talk, and I Am Unimpressed

At the first meeting in California, Barksdale and I had agreed to have a personal meeting at some point. And, soon after we got the first Microsoft offer, I was in California again. I called Barksdale and we agreed to have breakfast at Il Fornaio in Palo Alto. Il Fornaio is one of the Valley's most popular hangouts, in part because it's below the extremely civilized Garden Court Hotel, whose former manager, Lorilee, kept the place an oasis of calm and saved my sanity (and doubtless many other people's) more than once.

Much to my irritation, Mandile had just told Peter Currie that we had received a $150 million offer from Microsoft. In most cases, Mandile favored anything that would lead to a quick acquisition, even at a low price. In this case, however, he was responding to our shared conclusion that Netscape stock was wildly overpriced, plus the fact that Randy and I had rejected Maffei's $80 million offer. Thus, a financially equivalent stock-based acquisition by Netscape would require a substantial premium over a Microsoft stock offer or a cash offer. Mandile had therefore lied to Currie in order to bluff Netscape into increasing its offer.

I was still shocked at how easily Mandile lied and forced others to back him up. Beyond that, in this case, lying was stupid. We already knew that Microsoft was talking to people about us, including at least one person affiliated with Netscape. If either Microsoft or Netscape caught the lie, which was entirely possible because of the Valley's rumor mill, our position would have become far more difficult. To be sure I wasn't overreacting, I told Wade about it, and he was even more upset than I was. This also placed me in an uncomfortable position with regard to Barksdale; I didn't want to contradict our CEO, but I didn't want to support the lie, either.

But, as it turned out, I had far bigger problems with Barksdale. Our breakfast meeting confirmed my growing suspicion that Barksdale was far out of his depth, that he had a much bigger ego than he pretended, and that he was seriously disconnected from reality. Several incidents remain imprinted on my memory. The first came during a general discussion of the relative positions of Microsoft and Netscape, including the management problems they faced. Barksdale said that Netscape faced the problem of managing rapid growth, while Microsoft's problem was even tougher—maintaining its flexibility and maneuverability as it became very large. That was a perfectly sensible observation. But then Barksdale went on to say, No matter who you take as a benchmark it's just a very hard problem. Take any company you think is the best-managed company in the United States. You might think it's IBM, you might think it's General Motors, they all face the same problem, and now

Microsoft's got that problem too. Barksdale said this, furthermore, with a casual, nonchalant arrogance that suggested he understood these issues and companies intimately.

At this point my main problem was concealing my stunned surprise, indeed my utter wonderment. In Silicon Valley, you do not speak of IBM and General Motors as models of anything except what to avoid, and the idea that Microsoft was in their category was, to put it mildly, insane. Moreover, I actually knew something about these issues; in fact, I probably knew a lot more than Barksdale. I thought to myself, What planet is this man from, and what planet does he think he's on? And why would he think that I would swallow it?

But it got much worse. Barksdale continued talking about Microsoft; they had asked him to be their chief operating officer, but he had turned it down in favor of Netscape. At this point, a lightbulb went on inside my head. Barksdale had spent his entire career being number two, and I think for good reason. With Gates running technology and strategy, Barksdale might actually have been a good guy to make Microsoft's trains run on time. But Barksdale wanted to be number one somewhere, and I increasingly suspected that his behavior at Netscape was a variation on the second-company syndrome. He was going to show the world how to do Something Big. Another red flag. Barksdale proceeded. History, he said, has proven over and over that the way to make serious money isn't to run a company that dominates an industry; it's to create a new industry. Microsoft is basically over with. Maybe they'll get another double out of their stock, but there's no way they'll do as well as we will, no way they'll catch us. This was once again said with a casual assurance that his background, and Netscape's position, did not justify. I thought, even then, that he was underestimating Microsoft. In his two previous companies, Federal Express and McCaw, Barksdale had been competing against slothful incumbents who had grown incompetent in real competition because their core businesses were heavily protected by government regulation. At FedEx, he undercut the U.S. Postal Service and later UPS. At McCaw, he shared local cellular franchise duopolies with the regulated Bell system local telephone companies. Microsoft was a very different beast. Either he didn't get that at all, or he didn't think that I did.

He also insisted that Netscape's stock would keep on going up and that we had no reason to fear a stock-based acquisition. At the time, Netscape stock was at about $55 (this price and all others adjusted for the subsequent stock split: i.e., it was $110 at the time). It actually kept rising for another month, hitting a peak of about $87 in early December, giving the company a market capitalization in excess of $5 billion. Starting just after Pearl Harbor Day, however, it rapidly sank to about $25 and stayed there for months until AOL bought the company for $41 a share in late 1998. So I was right to be nervous.

When i pushed back on the stock price issue, Barksdale conceded that it might be temporarily overvalued, but argued that over the long term it would increase. We're the next Microsoft, he said, that's the kind of value we'll generate. Netscape's competitive and financial decline began only a few weeks later.

We spent some more time on the relocation issue. I defended the idea of a Netscape East, which actually made some sense. There was less start-up activity than in California, but many good engineers, and many key customers for authoring tools were based in the East—the publishing industry, the banks, the advertising agencies, the corporate headquarters of the Fortune 500, and the Internet service providers. But what bothered me even more was that Barksdale focused almost solely on Randy, to the exclusion of the entire engineering staff, not to mention the rest of the company. There was a core team that Barksdale should have been concerned about; Randy was neither a necessary nor sufficient condition for getting the entire team, yet he didn't ask about that. And perhaps most bothersome of all, once again there was not a single question about our product, its functionality, its market, or the competitive environment. He didn't ask how we compared to Netscape's supposedly imminent products, to NaviSoft, Blackbird, nothing. Nor did he discuss Netscape's architectures, technical strategy, or third-party infrastructure at all.

When I brought these issues up, Barksdale's responses were stunningly foolish. First, when I mentioned patents and proprietary control, Barksdale was completely dismissive of our patent effort, and of patents generally. While in my opinion this was an error, it was also admittedly an issue with respect to which people could and did hold varying opinions. But then I asked him about proprietary control and the risk of cloning, particularly from Microsoft. Especially by posting their beta code and specifications on their Web site they were giving Microsoft early information about what to clone. He said, We develop products better and faster than anybody else. We give away all of our specifications to anyone who wants them, including Microsoft. We don't need patents, we don't need to protect our APIs. We win by leading the industry and staying ahead. This was just nuts. By not following well-known principles of architectural strategy—building proprietary but open APIs, developing compatible enhancements over time, covering all possible market segments in descending order of importance, creating a large surrounding infrastructure— they were greatly simplifying Microsoft's task. Not to worry, Barksdale said, we'll stay so far ahead of Microsoft that they can't catch us. To describe this as a dangerously arrogant statement is a kindness to Barksdale. But in fact it was even worse: he showed not the slightest understanding that these issues even existed, never mind how complex, subtle, and important it is to construct architectural strategies and to control proprietary industry standards. I heard no discussion of lock-in, cloning, standard stealing, complex trade-offs, future choices, difficult decisions, or potential Microsoft counterattacks. He was, quite simply, oblivious.

Then there was the issue of Barksdale's outside involvements in government policy and other companies' boards. We talked about several interesting policy issues—export controls on encryption, educational policy, FCC regulation of the Internet industry—and our common acquaintances in Washington. But while doing Vermeer, I wasn't spending very much time on government policy, because I had other things to do. Barksdale, however, was everywhere in the media, testifying in Congress, lobbying on export controls, co-founding the Technology Network with John Doerr, joining the @Home board. So far as I could tell, Netscape had very little management depth, and if I were in Barksdale's position, I'd be feeling *busy*. So while I enjoyed the conversation, it was further evidence that Barksdale didn't understand how urgent his business problems were.

Then we came to the acquisition issue, which was complicated by our differing views of Netscape's stock price. It turned out that John's statement that Microsoft had already offered us $150 million didn't do any real harm. I said that because we expected Netscape's stock price to decline, we'd need at least $200 million to do a deal, even though almost everyone in the company, including me, would prefer Netscape to Microsoft. I argued, quite correctly I still believe, that at this price or even a higher one, the acquisition would be anti-dilutive (i.e., would increase Netscape's earnings and stock performance) due to our revenue potential and the strategic synergy between FrontPage and Netscape's products.

Barksdale replied that if we were worried about Netscape's stock price, it would be easy to arrange a collar to protect us against a price drop, but that we'd have to give up the upside as well. Barksdale said that he could even protect us well past the date on which the acquisition closed, which would have been unusual. (I later learned, in fact, that it would have been *very difficult,* and maybe even impossible, to construct such a hedge, because too many people were already shorting Netscape stock.) But, in any case, he said, he didn't see how they could offer more than $100 million. Then he very pointedly looked me in the eye and said, If Microsoft has really offered you $150 million, then I think you should take it.

Even if Barksdale had correctly guessed that this was a lie and was calling our bluff, his response was yet again foolish. Barksdale told me later that he had decided not to engage in a bidding war with Microsoft. This was dumb. If Netscape really had excellent tools under development, they could perhaps have afforded some arrogance, but they didn't. They *did* have a very strong interest in keeping us out of Microsoft's hands (particularly because there was nobody else on the horizon) and a strong interest in acquiring our product, team, and intellectual property. Barksdale either didn't know how important tools would be or didn't understand the true condition of Netscape's efforts. My subsequent interviews suggest that both were probably true.

Altogether, then, the meeting was a bleak experience. No CEO is perfect, and at that point I was certainly in no position to pretend that I was, or that Vermeer was better managed, particularly given my problems with John and our abysmal sales. But, because he didn't know what he didn't know, Barksdale's conduct profoundly disturbed me. I began to think that Netscape's future success or even survival would depend more on Microsoft's continued inaction than anything else, and that Netscape would make far too easy a target if Microsoft ever got serious. This concern would only deepen in light of what occurred thereafter.

Shortly afterward, Peter Currie called John with a verbal acquisition offer of $80 million in Netscape stock. He indicated some flexibility upward, perhaps to $100 million, but no more. Did Netscape know from Maffei's conversations what the real size of Microsoft's offer was? I've never found out, but it was one hell of a coincidence that they chose exactly Maffei's number. It was also a big problem, because there was no way in hell I was going to sell Vermeer for $80 million in Netscape stock.

However, I was becoming deeply concerned about our situation. For different reasons, neither Microsoft nor Netscape looked promising. The only good news was that neither of them could attack FrontPage in the near term. We had satisfied ourselves that Netscape's September announcements were vaporware, and Chris Peters had effectively admitted that they were starting from scratch. On the other hand, Peters noted that once he assembled a team and started work, our value to Microsoft would begin to decline precipitously, and he was right. My combined assessment of John, our lack of sales, and the long-term strategic issues suggested to me, more than ever, that life as an independent firm would start getting very rough in another year to eighteen months.

Time for a Conversation with Chris Peters

It was amid these reflections, at the end of November, that I decided to revive our discussions with Microsoft. My interactions with Maffei had been quite unpleasant, and it wasn't clear to me that he either understood or cared about our product or its value. So I decided to approach Chris Peters and propose to him, in essence, that we jointly go over Maffei's head. I wasn't sure what the power relationship was between Peters and Maffei, but I knew that if he wanted to, Peters could easily get us a meeting with the people who really ran things, including Gates. So I called him.

Peters took the call right away, and we had a very direct, but very civilized, conversation. I said to him, Chris, if $80 million really is your best offer, then we should just stop, because we won't sell for that price. We really, really, won't. But if you offered us twice that, then we would accept instantly. I'm not bluffing; I'm just telling you the truth. But I have a suggestion, I said. I think that we can convince you that we're worth a lot more than $80 million. I think it would be in everyone's interest for us to give you, and Microsoft's top management, a presentation about our position.

Peters replied, Well, we could probably do that. But I don't know if we could get to $160 million. Is there any point in talking if we come up with a number between $80 million and $160 million? I said, Sure. Obviously though, the closer it is to $160 million the more interested we'll be. And it would also depend on specifics such as vesting provisions. I also thought of Mandile and the full vesting trick he had already tried once. So I said, Chris, you should also understand that you can't rely just on buying me off. I really want the employees to get financial security, so the terms have to be good for them as well as for me, which means a higher total price. I understand, Peters replied.

Then Peters said, I agree that it would be a good idea to set up a meeting. It will be easier to get the right people if you can come to Redmond. Would that be all right? Fine, I said, and the sooner the better. Okay, Chris said, I'll check people's schedules and get back to you. Bill is away on his book tour [this was his first one, *The Road Ahead*] so I don't think we'll get him. But I think I can get most of the office of the president, certainly the technical and product people—probably Pete Higgins, Paul Maritz, and Nathan Myhrvold. Does that sound okay?

Here, I had a big problem. I had never even spoken to Higgins and Maritz; they were the highest-level line managers at Microsoft, and they had good reputations. Nathan Myhrvold, however, was quite another matter. I *had* spoken with him, several years before, and he had struck me as one of the most egotistical, self-important people I'd ever met. A number of my friends shared this opinion. One of them told me that Myhrvold tended to buy hundred-dollar *glasses* of wine, so that he could tell you all about them. He loved to hear himself talk, didn't spend much time listening, and did not enjoy hearing that he might be wrong. This was particularly dangerous, because he *was* often wrong, and in fact had been so in a way directly relevant to us. Myhrvold was the genius behind the original, proprietary MSN and its Blackbird development tool and had ignored the Internet for quite a while. Yet for some reason, he was in favor with Gates. This was exactly what we didn't need: someone whose ego and political position were directly threatened by our message, and who was also powerful.

So I replied to Peters, very guardedly, that while the others were fine, I didn't think that having Myhrvold at the meeting was necessary. Very elegantly, without saying anything explicit or quotably incriminating, Chris let me know that he got the message. Shortly afterward, he got back to me about scheduling. We set the meeting for the afternoon of Friday, December 8.

Then, a few days after we had set up the meeting at Redmond, life started getting interesting again.

How Nice to Feel Wanted, Even If Their Intentions Are Not Honorable

It started with an e-mail from Marc Andreessen to Randy, sometime in the last days of November or the first days of December. Andreessen said that Netscape was about to make a huge announcement involving scripting languages, Java, and Sun, and that they'd like us to be part of it. Would it be okay if someone from Netscape called us to describe the announcement and the kind of support they wanted? Of course, Randy replied, and sure enough, we got a call.

Netscape and Sun were about to announce an alliance based on a Netscape-designed scripting language called LiveScript, which allowed very simple programs to be written into Web pages and executed in browsers. Although the language had very little technical relationship to Java, the programming language and environment that Netscape had licensed from Sun, the language would be renamed JavaScript. Netscape was about to license JavaScript to Sun, which agreed to support it along with Java. They both wanted endorsements for JavaScript from influential Internet software companies, of which we were one. They were clearly in a rush and needed an answer before we could perform any serious analysis, but we agreed anyway, because it was harmless. Randy wrote a brief, generic, nonbinding statement that would be distributed to the media as a quote from John, speaking as Vermeer's CEO.

Randy then sent the following e-mail to everyone in the company:

Dear Vermeeroids—

!!NEWS!!!
This may sound a bit surprising, but we are part of a big announcement that Netscape and Sun are making on Monday. Those companies are announcing a "new" scripting language called JavaScript, which is a cross-platform, multi-vendor, object-oriented scripting language that can be embedded into HTML pages . . .

We are participating in this announcement because: (1) Netscape invited us to; (2) with some study, it appears that JavaScript is actually quite useful;

(3) with all these companies announcing support, it looks like JavaScript has at least a shot of becoming some sort of industry standard; (4) our customers who use Netscape browsers will probably want to type JavaScript scripts into their HTML pages from FrontPage; and (5) we get some free publicity and get some visibility as a company that swims with the big fish and supports multi-vendor cross-platform "standards."

Then, a couple of days later, we began to understand what was going on. I got a call from Chris Peters. He said that Microsoft would be making some announcements soon, and they wanted us to endorse them. Would it be okay if someone called me to describe what they were doing? It had to do with scripting languages . . .

I was highly amused, but tried not to show it. Why certainly, I said, please have them call me. I promptly received a call from a man named Cornelius Willis, who said that he was in charge of Visual Basic. Bingo. We'd been waiting for this. Visual Basic was and is a wildly popular language for writing simple Windows applications. Peter had used it to construct our original product demo in late 1994. It was a natural for use as a scripting language for Web applications, except for two things. First, it ran only on Windows, and second, it had certain technical kinks derived from its Windows heritage. We had examined this issue one year earlier, when we contemplated putting a scripting language into our product, for use by professional programmers and "power users." As a result of these limitations, we had therefore tentatively planned to use a Visual Basic *clone*, of which there existed several that ran on all major operating systems, and which we could tailor to Internet requirements.

Now, Mr. Willis informed me, my worries were over. First, Microsoft was about to announce that it had licensed Java from Sun and would provide a Java interpreter (virtual machine) in its browsers. Even better, though, Microsoft had also developed a special dialect of Visual Basic called VB Script, which was just the thing for scripting Web applications. Oh, I said, and I suppose Netscape can use it too, in Navigator? Why of course, replied Mr. Willis. I could already tell that, like just about everybody else I'd talked to at Microsoft, Willis was obviously very smart, and he didn't waste time.

In fact, Willis continued, Microsoft was developing an open reference specification of this language, which, out of the goodness of its heart, it would donate to the world as a nonproprietary standard. The standard would be controlled by an Internet industry standards committee so that everyone, including Microsoft's competitors, could have equal access to it. Of course, there were already three million people using Microsoft's Visual Basic, so it would be easy for people to learn this new cool thing. And of course Microsoft had developed this new thing, so it might show up in Microsoft's browser first. But wasn't this just wonderful, and as an important Internet software company, wouldn't we like to endorse it?

Yes, we would. Randy dutifully drafted another endorsement letter to go out over John's signature, virtually identical to the previous one for Netscape, and sent another virtually identical e-mail to the employees. It said:

Dear Vermeeroids—

Yet more . . . !!NEWS!!!

Believe it to not . . . we are going to be part of a big Microsoft announcement tomorrow (!). This is VERY similar to the Netscape/Sun announcement that we were part of on Monday. In fact, some of the same companies are in the announcement . . .

Here's the deal in a nutshell: Microsoft has licensed Java (!!) for use in its web browser, Internet Explorer. Furthermore, Microsoft has come up with a web scripting language called VB Script that is based on Visual Basic. VB Script is positioned identically to JavaScript . . . The guy at Microsoft in charge of getting third-party support for this announcement said that of all the companies participating in this announcement, he was most excited to get Vermeer, because we are cool and because of our buzz. He was probably just blowing smoke at me, but I ate it up anyway . . .

We are participating in this announcement because: (1) Microsoft invited us to; (2) it sounds like VB Script will actually be fairly useful; (3) with all these companies announcing support, it looks like VB Script has at least a shot at getting some industry support, along with JavaScript; (4) our customers who use Microsoft's browser may want to type VB Script scripts into their HTML pages from FrontPage; (5) it strengthens our vendor-independent position (we are supporting both JavaScript and VB Script); and (6) we get some free publicity.

There was no way our brilliant, cynical engineers would let us get away with this, of course. Rob Mauceri, one of our best client-side developers, circulated a third company e-mail announcement a few days later. It was based on COBOL, an obsolete mainframe language, and a nightmare avoided by all PC programmers. Rob's e-mail:

Dear Vermeeroids—

Yet again, even more fabulously unbelievable . . . !!NEWS!!!

Believe it or not . . . we are going to be part of a gigantic IBM announcement tomorrow (!). This is VERY similar to the Microsoft or Netscape/Sun announcements that we were part of this week . . .

Here's the deal in a nutshell: IBM has come up with a web scripting language called Visual Cobol Script (VC Script) that is based on VisualCobol which is based on Cobol (. . . you can read about Cobol in a good history of computing text book, or visit the Computer Museum). VC Script is positioned identically to JavaScript and VB Script, except nobody will use it. Further still, IBM is paying $1M to anyone who licenses the VC Script run-time engine . . .

We are participating in this announcement because: (1) IBM invited us to; (2) Charles was away when IBM invited us to; (3) with these companies announcing support, it looks like VC Script has a snowball's chance in hell at getting some industry support; (4) Lou Gerstner paid me personally $5M; (5) it strengthens our open-systems-based-platform/vendor-independent-hyphen-hyphen position; (6) we get some free publicity and there is no such thing as bad publicity.

By the time we were through talking to Microsoft about their upcoming announcements, I realized that we had better take advantage of our moment, because it might not last long. Netscape had been in a rush with the JavaScript announcement because they had found out about Microsoft's impending announcements, including VB Script and the Java license from Sun. Netscape executives, including Andreessen, had been furious when they learned that Sun was planning to license Java to Microsoft. There had been an enormous, very bitter fight about it. Sun argued that since Microsoft was developing a Java clone (which was true: they were), the control associated with a license was better than nothing. Netscape thought that they and Sun could drive the Java standard, and keep Microsoft permanently behind. But Sun disagreed, and Netscape decided to preempt Pearl Harbor Day with the JavaScript announcement. Sun had agreed to license and endorse JavaScript to mollify Netscape.

But I was very impressed, and sobered, by what Mr. Willis had said. Even if he was lying through his teeth, his comments showed that Microsoft understood, extremely clearly, exactly what the world needed to hear. There wasn't any egotistical bullshit of the Barksdale variety, just cold clear thinking. I called Chris Peters and asked whether Microsoft's upcoming announcements would say anything about tools. I was worried about FUD and interested in how Chris would handle the issue. He replied, We would have liked to have gotten a definitive answer from you guys by now, but since we haven't, we will be silent on the issue.

And so they were. But, as they say in the movies, Microsoft did something convincing. While they didn't directly make any statements about tools, about one-third of their announcements were in one way or another directed at the problem of Web site development. And the comparison between Microsoft's actions and Netscape's response was even more telling. Microsoft went to war, but Netscape just continued to party.

Pearl Harbor Day

Any lingering doubts I may have had about Microsoft's conversion to the Internet were eliminated by Bill Gates's December 7 announcements. The specifics of the announcements were extremely impressive, but for me, they were overshadowed by Gates's unequivocal declaration that Microsoft was now "hard core" about the Internet, as Gates put it. He also said, smiling, that he would be monitoring Microsoft's browser market share "on a very regular basis." In short, he would do whatever it took to win.

First of all, Microsoft would provide its browser free, bundled with all its current operating systems—Windows 95 and NT. Microsoft announced that it would even release free browsers for Windows 3.1 and the Macintosh, which it subsequently did. Pointedly mocking Netscape's "free but not free" pricing policy, Gates said: "Not free sometimes, not free for 90 days [like Netscape Navigator], not free except for business, not free for most people; just *completely free, period.*" Microsoft's Web server, IIS (often known by its code name, Gibraltar), would also be bundled free with NT, and Gates promised that all Microsoft's browsers and servers would be compatible with all existing Internet standards, *including all features supported by Netscape Navigator.*

Microsoft made several other announcements designed to cut off Netscape at the knees. In the first place, Gates announced that Microsoft had indeed entered into an agreement with Sun to license Java, the cross-platform programming language that Netscape, and people like George Gilder, had predicted would kill the Windows platform. The agreement between Sun and Microsoft—it would be several more months before a contract was signed—was reached just a few hours before Gates's announcement, after an all-night session, which several months later was codified in a quite sloppy contract. Predictably, Microsoft went its own way, and in 1998 Sun sued Microsoft for allegedly violating the contract by undermining the cross-platform nature of Java.

Microsoft announced VB Script and a mechanism to make it an open, nonproprietary standard just as Willis had said. Microsoft also announced a new architecture called ActiveX that would extend its technology for linking software objects (for example, putting a spreadsheet in a word processing document) to work in Web browsers. Although it posed some potentially serious security problems, ActiveX allowed complex, powerful programs to be placed in Web pages and used by browsers.

The announcements contained a number of subtle and not-so-subtle messages for us. As Chris had promised, Microsoft's announcement said nothing explicit about Web development tools. But JavaScript, VB Script, Java, and ActiveX all targeted our general space, albeit indirectly. Both Microsoft and Netscape clearly recognized that to grow their markets they would have to offer Web development solutions. Both of them, in short, would eventually want either to own us or to kill us. Indeed, Chris Peters had already said so. The days when we could just build a cool product were over.

Furthermore, my already bleak assessment of Netscape became even darker. Netscape had already repeatedly botched its opportunities in the *absence* of significant competition. Now, when the wealthiest, most relentless competitor of them all declared war on them, their only response was a scripting language, and an easily cloned one at that. Netscape took no other visible action: no pricing changes, no technology licensing or acquisitions, no intellectual property, no major new alliances.

Pearl Harbor Day finally softened Randy's opposition to an acquisition in general, and to one by Microsoft in particular. He received a tape of Gates's presentation a few days later and gave it to me. You should watch this, Charles, he said. Bill gets it. He really does. I distinctly remember watching the tape one evening, a few days after our December 8 presentation, sitting in bed with Camille drinking wine. It was an hour and a half long, and I found it riveting. I never, ever, thought that my idea of an interesting evening in bed with my girlfriend would be watching a video of Bill Gates. I doubt that it will ever happen again.

THE DECEMBER 8 MEETING

I had flown out to Seattle the evening prior to our meeting, in order to make sure that at least one of us made it. I took the risk of staying at the Woodmark, the hotel in Kirkland at which many Microsoft visitors stay. Randy and John showed up just after noon the following day, a couple of hours before the meeting.

I had written my presentation in WordPerfect. Randy suggested, humorously but also seriously, that it might be better if I made the presentation using Microsoft's presentation graphics package instead, and he spent an hour typing it in and formatting it. Following a private conversation between John and myself, we had agreed that I would give a presentation, Randy would give a demo, and John would keep his mouth shut. John would not, for example, indicate that we were for sale for $81 million.

When it was time for our meeting, we headed over to the Microsoft campus, where Chris Peters met us and took us up to a conference room full of people. At the table besides Peters were Sinofsky, Maffei, Higgins, and Maritz, and several others I didn't recognize. Then Nathan Myhrvold came in. He came over to me, introduced himself, and said, I just wanted to say hello, I've heard great things about you guys, but unfortunately I have a conflict, so I won't be able to attend. And then he left. I thought to myself, thank you, Chris, very well done. Peters, or someone, had clearly also talked to Maffei, who was completely silent and quite deferential throughout the entire meeting. And on our side, after the introductions were over, I don't believe Mandile said a single word.

Chris thanked everybody for coming and then turned to me and said, This is your meeting, proceed however you see fit. I said I would make a presentation, Randy would give a demo, and then we'd be happy to answer questions. Randy then set up our laptop, which he connected to a huge Barco projector that showed the PC screen across an entire wall of the room. Because Randy knew that I was an incompetent software user in general, and had never used PowerPoint in particular, he had carefully set up the system so I just had to click the mouse to move from slide to slide. But I didn't know that, so I started by turning to Randy and asking, How do I work this thing? I wasn't the least bit embarrassed, but Randy certainly was, and the Microsoft guys broke out in incredulous laughter. Randy told me that all I had to do was click the mouse. I replied that as a Ph.D. from MIT, I couldn't be expected to handle such complexities, which provoked more laughter. Then we got down to business.

I had worked hard to make the presentation very cold-blooded, logical, and direct, without (I hoped) sounding arrogant or boastful. I started out by acknowledging the impressiveness of the previous day's announcements, but then listed the many respects in which Microsoft remained far behind Netscape. Microsoft's browser market share was still under 10 percent, and since its Web server ran only on NT, it wouldn't become an industry standard anytime soon. In authoring tools, of course, they had nothing at all.

Then I described what we had done and why it would take Microsoft a long time to catch up. I made the case for the importance of authoring tools: why they were a critical enabler for the expansion of the Web; how much more complex and harder to clone they were relative to browsers and Web servers; and why good tools would improve Microsoft's other businesses. I described the external APIs we had created to support an infrastructure of custom add-ons to our product, and how they created lock-in once used. I described our intent to create industry standards, and how our server extensions created a server-side standard while commoditizing Web servers by covering over differences between them. I named a dozen or so companies we were negotiating with. I said we had just closed a $7.2 million investment round. I then laid out three scenarios and the strategic logic and consequences of each one.

The first was acquisition by Netscape; the second was continued independence; the third, acquisition by Microsoft. If Netscape bought us, their 80+ percent browser share and substantial server share would give us huge distribution leverage, and we would probably immediately bundle a low-end version of FrontPage with the Netscape browser. The package of server, browser, and authoring tools would also give Netscape an important edge in the corporate Intranet market, as well as with Internet service providers and Web hosting firms that needed our remote development capability. It would therefore be Netscape, not Microsoft, who killed Notes and dominated the Internet services industry, foreclosing huge revenue opportunities for Microsoft. Furthermore, during the year or more it would take Microsoft to catch up there would be no Web development support for Gibraltar, the new NT-based Microsoft Web server, since Netscape would presumably not support server extensions for Microsoft products. This would not only hurt Microsoft in the Web server market, but also slow NT's progress in the server operating systems market. They'd also suffer in Web-based applications such as financial software, MSN, and the like. I guessed we'd add $50 million to Netscape's 1996 revenues and certainly make them a much more formidable competitor, while causing substantial damage to Microsoft's business and Internet position.

The second possibility was that we stay independent. We would then become the Switzerland of the Internet, the neutral country used by, and trading with, all of the warring parties. We'd have the market to ourselves for six to twelve months. We guessed that Netscape would beat Microsoft to market with competitive authoring tools, but we were first by a wide margin and would assert our patents against everybody who followed. At this point, Paul Maritz interrupted to say that we wouldn't get anywhere on patents, because Microsoft had done lots of editors and had patented lots of stuff having to do with editing, so we'd violate as many of theirs as they violated of ours. We clashed for a couple of minutes; I noted that Stac, Wang, and others had cost them hundreds of millions of dollars. But you just have an editor, Maritz replied; we've already done that. Then Peters said, Let's move on. I don't know what effect this had; I'd like to think that later, when Maritz saw Randy's demo, he realized that we might be patenting a lot more than HTML editing.

In any case, I said, we'd have our second-generation product on the market before either Microsoft or Netscape had anything out at all. We planned an IPO in mid-1996, and if things got too hot after that, we could still be acquired by Netscape, Oracle, Adobe, AT&T, or IBM. If Microsoft was interested, however, this was their last chance, because the antitrust authorities would almost certainly block a deal with them once we exceeded the H-S-R threshold. Mandile had wanted me to drop this section, but I think it would have been a mistake; I wanted to make the case that *we* didn't have to do a deal now with anybody at all, but if *they* were interested, they had to move fast. I was concerned, among other things, that they might learn the true state of our negotiations with Netscape. If they thought we were desperate to conclude an acquisition, we'd be in a very weak bargaining position.

The third option, of course, was that they could buy us. The business case there was essentially the flip side of a Netscape purchase. They would immediately gain a big lead over Netscape in a critical Internet-enabling technology; they could bundle it with their own products, like Office and their Web server; and they would be making the decisions on how to tie authoring to servers, scripting, browsers, and everything else. My guess was that it could mean an incremental boost to Microsoft revenues of as much as $500 million a year.

There were very few interruptions and no challenges except for Maritz's comment on patents. At one point, when I mentioned that we had a huge list of enhancements scheduled for the next several releases, both Peters and Higgins jumped in. They said, Please don't tell us anything confidential. We absolutely do not want to know anything confidential or proprietary, or anything you might regret telling us in the event that we end up as competitors. I laughed and replied, Your concern is touching, but I can't *possibly* tell you how unnecessary it is. We aren't going to tell you *anything* about our future plans, technical or otherwise. You can put your minds completely at ease. It was a light moment, which was good, and it also suggested that despite Maffei's comments in New York, they were actually quite concerned about legal exposure, either through Justice Department antitrust actions or private lawsuits, which I found interesting.

I finished in about an hour and turned the floor over to Randy, who proceeded to give the most amazing product demonstration I've ever seen, anywhere, by anybody. He started by running through our standard demo. Unlike me, he was continually interrupted with questions, including a number from Higgins and Maritz. Maritz, in particular, was clearly very technical and seriously smart. Several times they made Randy deviate from his script, both to answer questions and also, probably, to see if they could throw him off balance. He was absolutely flawless: relaxed, articulate, completely self-confident, but in his inimitably helpful, easygoing, gentlemanly way.

After running through the demo, Randy said offhandedly that he hadn't shown them every feature out of concern for time, but he'd be happy to keep going if they wanted. Somebody asked what else there was. Well, Randy said, a number of things—for example, creating forms for data entry over the Web, and storing the information that people entered in the forms. We didn't directly support real-time database applications but had very intelligently taken advantage of the fact that HTML included specifications for forms, buttons, and pick lists. FrontPage could create those objects in HTML pages and also allowed developers to specify the format in which new data entered by users would be stored. It was then easier for programmers to write procedures that would process the data.

They asked Randy to show them how that worked. So with no canned demo or script, and everything showing up on the wall projector, Randy built a very complicated form, with many different fields and data types, amid repeated interruptions to change fields or use data supplied by the audience. When he finished, he said, Gee, I hope this works. He crossed his fingers, smiled, and clicked the mouse. It came out perfectly.

Someone said, Great, thanks. Is that it? Randy said, Well if you're *really* interested, we've done a prototype application for the *Chicago Tribune,* one of our partners. It's for an electronic newspaper, still in the early stages, but it's a good example of what we can do. Would you like to see that? Yes, they replied. In many ways, this was the most powerful part of the presentation. Nobody in that room had thought about the Web for as long or as seriously as we had, and for most of them, it was probably the first demonstration of what the Web really *could* do once everyone had good development tools. The *Tribune* demo opened with an electronic newspaper for a small town. Then Randy clicked on links to the classifieds, which were searchable, and then to the real estate listings, and then to specific real estate agents and houses, and then finally to local banks. He finished by showing the banks' mortgage products, comparison shopping for rates, and directories and maps of their local offices. It blew them away.

When Randy finished, there was silence, a clearly impressed, sobered silence. I said, Well, that's our presentation. How would you like to proceed? Higgins said, "We should confer for a few minutes. If you don't mind staying here, we'll go outside." They were gone for about three quarters of an hour, which seemed an eternity. I knew we had done a very good job, but they were keeping good poker faces, so we couldn't really tell what their reaction would be. We mostly just sat there. We didn't want to say anything substantive in case we could be overheard, and we were too tense for idle conversation. I later found out that they'd been trying to contact Gates, who had just flown to Tokyo, but hadn't been able to reach him.

Eventually they all came back in. Higgins said, Thank you for coming to talk to us. This was impressive. Very impressive. We came in today with one number in mind. But now we have to think of another number. We hope we can have the chance to make you another offer. We need to talk to Bill about this. Could you give us a couple of days, say until next Monday or Tuesday? It won't take any longer than that. Sure, I said. We'll be back in Cambridge and available. Thanks, said Higgins. We'll be in touch soon.

For our part, I think we were as sobered and impressed as they were; I know I was. These people were *smart,* and to an amazing extent, despite all the powerful egos in the room, they didn't let egos get in their way. Keeping Myhrvold out, reining in Maffei, the neutral, utterly matter-of-fact tone of the whole discussion, the sharp questions, the lack of extraneous interruptions, the patience to listen for more than two hours, the readiness with which they conceded that they had undervalued us. It was blindingly obvious to me that Netscape and Barksdale were no match for these guys. It was equally clear to me that we weren't either, at least in our current form, and maybe not ever. If my fortune depended on Mandile leading Vermeer to victory against these guys, I was in serious trouble. And I wasn't at all certain that the VCs would have the nerve, or the good judgment, to replace Mandile fast enough, if ever.

Later, at Microsoft, Randy learned the politics behind the meeting. Higgins trusted Peters's judgment absolutely, and Chris wanted to do a deal, so that was two votes for us. Maffei was neutral to negative, as I had thought. It was also a macho point of pride for him, and his standard operating procedure, to try to beat down acquisition prices by telling companies they weren't worth anything. Sinofsky didn't have a vote, so the key player was Maritz, who was deeply technical, greatly trusted by Gates, and so held a veto. Maritz had been put off by my presentation, because he really believed we just had a page editor that they could easily replicate. But when Randy showed them what a powerful and complete solution we had developed, Maritz suddenly understood the damage Netscape could do to Microsoft with our product. From that point, he was a believer. Thus, it may have been a mistake for me to start; perhaps Randy's demo should have come first. But part of the reason I wanted to go first was that I wanted to preempt the possibility of any cute maneuvers from John by immediately setting the tone and indicating that, CEO or not, I was the guy in charge.

GOOD-BYE TO NETSCAPE

When we got home, I decided to make a final appeal to Barksdale. My principal goal was not, in fact, to create a bidding war; it was to clear my conscience. Despite my now overwhelming skepticism about Netscape, I still didn't feel right about selling out to Microsoft, in both senses of the word, without giving Netscape a final opportunity to acquire us and a warning about what they faced. I felt an ethical obligation to tell Barksdale that I had seen the armada and that it was heading straight for him. Randy felt the same way; while his enthusiasm for Netscape was dimming fast, at the emotional level they remained his preferred partner. John called Peter Currie to arrange a meeting. But it had to happen fast; if Microsoft came back with a superb offer, they would pressure us to commit quickly, including signing a binding letter of intent, and I didn't want to delay for long.

Barksdale was traveling, so we couldn't arrange a face-to-face meeting in the time available. We did the meeting as a conference call, with the three of us in Cambridge, Peter Currie in California, and Barksdale in a New York hotel. I rewrote the presentation I had made in Redmond, keeping its structure and logic but making the case for an acquisition by Netscape, which I in fact believed. We faxed the presentation to both Currie and Barksdale just before the call. Although Barksdale had not seen the product demonstrated in as much detail as the Microsoft people had, I doubt that it would have made any difference. Neither he nor Currie had the technical background or intuition to understand it, and they clearly didn't realize how important this was. Perhaps if the senior technical managers—Rick Schell, Eric Hahn—had seen a complete demo they would have weighed in. But we never spoke to them. And once again it was telling that Barksdale didn't have anyone with a technical background join the conference call.

I went through the presentation, being if anything even blunter and tougher than I had been with Microsoft. Since Pearl Harbor Day had already come and gone, I pointed out that Microsoft was now clearly serious and that Netscape's revenue was certain to suffer as a result of Microsoft's free browser and Web server. I noted that our server extensions, with the remote development they enabled, would probably be the largest proprietary differentiation available to Netscape Web servers, at least for the next year or two, while our tool itself would be Netscape's only product that would be extremely difficult to clone. Then I described the consequences of Microsoft buying us. This part of the presentation read in part:

Microsoft instantly becomes the best authoring solution, supporting personal Web
    servers and Gibraltar.
Netscape now 6–12 months behind in a critical market.
Microsoft now kills Netscape:
    FrontPage bundled with MS Office, free or cheap
    FrontPage supports links to/from MS Office docs
    Patents (you have none, they have ours)
    FP server extension licensed . . . for UNIX, NetWare servers to kill you
    [Etc.]
Large uplift for many Microsoft platforms, applications, architectures . . . an incre-
    mental $250–500 M/year?

You lose browsers, servers, and tools.
We cash out with a highly secure currency.
Microsoft wins.

I warned Barksdale that this was not the same as FedEx competing against the post office, or McCaw competing against the telephone monopolies. Gates is different, I said, Microsoft is different. Look what they just announced. They mean business, your browser and server leadership is fragile, you need to run scared. And I ran through all the reasons why, just as I had explained at Redmond, a Netscape acquisition of Vermeer would greatly strengthen their hand against Microsoft. I argued that even at a very high price, the additional revenue and proprietary control would make the acquisition antidilutive, which was in fact true. When I finished, Randy gave me a thumbs-up indicating that he thought I'd done a good job. I thought so too; I'd given it my best shot.

But Barksdale made almost no comment during the presentation, and at the end his only response was to push us to specify a number. Randy remembers being quite impressed with how controlled and neutral his voice was and how little he gave away. I was *unimpressed,* for the same reason: this guy was the quintessential suit. Randy and I had agreed that we'd need at least $250 million from Netscape to compensate for the fragility of their stock. I gave Barksdale that number, and he made me repeat it to be sure there was no mistake. Then he said, Thank you, we'll discuss this and get back to you, and hung up. Currie later told Mandile that he felt like drinking a triple scotch when I was through. Barksdale apparently did not: ignorance is bliss.

Shortly after the conference call, Mandile and I had separate, very short, telephone conversations—John with Currie, me with Barksdale. The message was the same. They said that we might be able to convince them to go up another $10–$20 million to $100 million or so, but nothing like what we were asking. I said that we couldn't do a deal at that price. I knew then that there was no point in further discussion.

But then I had yet another suspicious thought. By this time it was clear that Netscape was talking regularly to the Justice Department. I feared that if we turned Netscape down definitively, Barksdale would immediately warn Justice that we were about to be acquired by Microsoft, despite our nondisclosure agreement. Although we were under the H-S-R tripwire, Justice could still initiate an investigation, subpoena all of us, and make our lives sufficiently difficult to endanger a Microsoft acquisition.

So I asked myself, What would Mandile do in these circumstances? And so I decided to lie, or at least to mislead, as Mr. Clinton would say. Barksdale had given me his private pager number. I sent him a pager message imploring him to reconsider and saying that it would be another three weeks before we had to do anything irrevocable. While technically true, I actually hoped to have the acquisition closed by then, and it nearly was. And as it turned out, Barksdale *did* get in touch with Justice as soon as the acquisition was announced, gave them our presentation materials, and convinced them to investigate the transaction, perhaps because he didn't realize that the H-S-R tripwire protected us. As I'll describe below, Justice did indeed investigate us, but there wasn't anything they could do.

MICROSOFT'S BETTER OFFER

Pete Higgins called from Microsoft four or five days after the December 8 Redmond meeting to make us a new offer. It was a large conference call with Chris Peters, Higgins, and I believe Maffei also on their end, and the three of us on ours. I did the talking. After very brief preliminaries, Higgins offered us $130 million. I replied that we would need to see the offer in writing, but that it seemed reasonable and we were disposed to accept it. A failure of nerve. I learned later that they would have gone up to $150 million if I'd shown the slightest hesitation.

The formal letter of intent (LOI) came by fax a couple of days later, and we sent it to our board and attorneys. The VCs were delighted: the first-round VCs were getting thirteen times their money after one year. I am struck by how little involvement they had in the entire process, although I suppose they would have gotten much more involved very fast if the terms had not been to their liking. We negotiated the details of the LOI for about a week—triggering several clashes between Maffei and me—but we got it done, and it was signed on December 19.

My next fight with Maffei was over the conditions for Microsoft's due diligence review. We had nothing to hide, but I didn't want them spending a lot of time on site sucking out our brains in the event that the deal fell through. Fortunately, Peters had obviously decided that we were for real, and he was content with a minimum review. I think he also realized that anything more would be hard to get. Throughout the entire process beginning in late October I had been extremely hard-core about preventing them from seeing our people, our technology, our patents, and even our offices. Peters had also read the *Upside* article, in which I made my opinion of Microsoft clear, and although our conversations were never heated, he understood that I never intended to let my guard down. In the end, we agreed that Microsoft could make two visits to our offices. One would be a legal and financial review led by Maffei. The other would be a technical review conducted by Peters and Sinofsky.

We spelled out the ground rules carefully and negotiated what they could see. Peters and Sinofsky were allowed to interview Andy and Peter, but only with Randy present. We would show them a list of our source code modules, let them observe us do a product build, and then let them pick three modules at random and watch them compile correctly. They would not be able to inspect our source code, or the comments within it, except for a few selected modules, which they would inspect in our presence. Nor would they be allowed to talk with anyone unsupervised. We ensured that they were escorted wherever they went and we warned all of the employees to report unauthorized conversations. Altogether, Microsoft conducted as minimal a review as one could imagine for a transaction of this size.

I was, however, quite concerned about one condition in the LOI, with respect to which Microsoft was deadly serious. The LOI (and the final contract) required that Randy plus two-thirds of Vermeer's "key technical personnel" would move to Redmond, and Microsoft alone would determine who was "key." Peters was willing to create jobs for most of the nontechnical people who wanted to move—he viewed that as a cost of the deal—but he made it clear that he had no interest in Vermeer unless it came with a functioning FrontPage engineering team. Nor was there any interest in creating a "Microsoft East," along the lines I had suggested to Barksdale; I don't think I even brought it up. I still wasn't sure how many engineers would move; a number of them were married with families and had strong ties to the Boston area.

As it turned out, getting the engineers to move was easier than I expected—in fact, it was very easy indeed. Randy was quite reluctant, but the economics were overwhelming, and Randy also felt intense loyalty to the team and the product. Although everyone's options accelerated somewhat upon the acquisition, anyone who turned down the move to Redmond would be leaving a lot of money on the table. They would lose their unvested Vermeer options, plus new options that Microsoft planned to grant to everyone who became a Microsoft employee.

I had feared Andy Schulert would be the most difficult to persuade, because of his anti-Microsoft UNIX background. But as he put it, for that much money I'll mop the floors at Redmond. Peter was no problem; he was delighted to get back to the West Coast anyway.

The married engineers, however, were almost all worried about their wives' agreeing to go. I therefore found it quite amusing that the spouse's reaction in almost every case was, Let me get this straight, you're *worried* about whether I would move for a million dollars. Are you crazy? *Of course we'll move.* There were, however, some tough special cases. At least three developers, including Rob Mauceri, one of the most important members of the team, were either engaged or in serious relationships, and the acquisition forced the issue of whether they'd get married. All three couples worked it out, and all three sub-sequently married. Chris Peters got Rob's then-girlfriend a job at Microsoft to help close the deal; she's done very well. Then there was Manda Schossberger, whose boyfriend had a child custody agreement that required him to stay in the Northeast. Manda had moved up from office manager into marketing, but Peters would give her a marketing job only in Redmond, and even that was not given casually. Microsoft is careful about marketing jobs, and Manda was seriously grilled before they made her an offer. In the end, she got the job and moved, still got married, was very successful, and recently transferred back east. In the end, all the engineers went except one. He had the nerve to ask me for a quadrupling of his options as a condition of his going. I said no, pleasantly at first, and less so when he persisted.

But there was one member of the technical team that Microsoft didn't want, and that could have become a *really* serious problem. When the deal was about to close, Chris Peters told me that he'd prefer to terminate Frank Germano. He said there was no point in deluding ourselves; Frank was not the kind of person who would do well at Microsoft. Oh God, I thought. I replied, Chris, look, I agree with you on the merits. Frank was critical to our finishing the product on time, but we were already considering replacing him because of his problems. But one of those problems is that he fights harder, more nastily, and more stubbornly than anyone else I know, including me. You run a Web site devoted to nuclear weapons. How would you like to become, yourself, personally, ground zero of a nuclear explosion? If you want to terminate Frank, you should get ready for the time of your life. Chris took my advice and had Mandile negotiate an arrangement whereby Frank took a job as head of FrontPage documentation and quality assurance, with a Microsoft QA guy under him who really did the work. As soon as Frank vested his Vermeer stock he resigned and moved to New Mexico.

THE REAL DEAL

The deal closed on January 12, 1996. Following negotiations and signature of the letter of intent on December 19, the final acquisition contract negotiations consumed only about three weeks. But it was an extremely tense period, as emotionally draining as any part of the Vermeer experience.

Microsoft sent an army of attorneys to Cambridge, along with Peters, Sinofsky, Maffei, and someone from Maffei's staff. They also had attorneys working full-time on it back in Seattle. All of them were very good, but the lead guy, Rick Dodd, from Bill Gates's father's firm, Preston Gates & Ellis, was fabulous, and razor-sharp. He had a rumpled, frumpy, deferential, soft-spoken effect, but he ran circles around our guys. We had switched law firms after closing the first round, and our new lawyers were very smart, competent people, but they had never done a merger this complicated this fast. They learned a lot during this time, enough that I got worried. I called Wade, who once again showed that beneath his easygoing exterior he was no pushover. He said, Decide now. If you need to change attorneys, find someone new *before* you fire them and do it fast. Let me know if I can help. He asked if I thought we should hire an investment bank, and I said no, which was correct. Hiring bankers would have cost us a ton of money, slowed everything down, increased the risk of leaks, and added virtually nothing. Indeed the experience made it clear that with smart people and good lawyers, investment bankers are quite superfluous in these situations.

Fortunately, our legal interests were highly aligned with those of Microsoft. We all wanted the deal done, quietly and fast. But there was enormous complexity in structuring the transaction to get favorable accounting treatment, melding the different stock option programs, and using a structure that allowed us to avoid delays and news leaks associated with conventional requirements such as the need to hold a shareholders' meeting. I found it interesting to watch, and despite a few disagreements, most of the legal issues were resolved amicably. There were innumerable details: a 5 percent escrow in the event that problems were discovered afterward; representations about legal and financial conditions; the procedures required for us to sell stock. The final structure was complicated and legally arcane—a "reverse triangular merger" by which Vermeer merged with Bumbershoot Limited, an empty shell created for the merger that then changed its name to Vermeer. This structure required a special registration statement by Microsoft and foot-thick consent forms for all shareholders. Microsoft's recommendations were in fact the best way to proceed and cut weeks off the normal closing process.

I had been very concerned that our employees be treated fairly, and Microsoft was really quite generous. They allowed the one-year acceleration of everybody's options to stand. In addition, John found a clever ploy that they also allowed. In order to align Microsoft's 4.5-year option plan with our 5-year option plan, John suggested an additional six-month acceleration of all Vermeer options. Of course, this benefited him too, and he already had an outrageously favorable deal, but I let it pass because this provision benefited all employees equally. Depending on when they had joined, the people moving to Redmond had between two and three more years to go for full vesting. Chris Peters thought this was fine. He said that his experience was that any engineer who stayed two years at Microsoft would remain there for the long term, and he was mostly right. In addition, Microsoft agreed to add $10 million worth of new options (computed using the standard Black-Scholes options pricing formula) for the people who went to Microsoft. Peters and Maffei actually gave them considerably more than that, and those new options are now worth a couple of hundred million dollars.

In part, this generosity reflected Microsoft's interest in keeping the engineers, and in part they were responding to a major concern of ours. Microsoft uses so-called nonqualified options, or NQOs. These options are more tax-efficient for Microsoft but less favorable in their tax implications for employees than the incentive stock options, or ISOs, that our option plan used. The favorable tax status of ISOs, however, is only available to small companies, since ISOs are intended to reward employees who form and join new businesses. We used this issue to push for larger new options for employees. I was still worried, however, and discussed it with John, Randy, and Wade. In a very classy move, Wade agreed to let us use the $3 million in cash we had in the company to give the employees large bonuses. If Microsoft allowed it, this would be enough to let the employees purchase their restricted stock and/or pay their alternative minimum tax obligations. I feared that Microsoft, particularly Maffei, would object, since it would lessen their grip on employees they wanted to relocate. But when I mentioned it to Maffei, he was merely amused. Oh, I see, he said, bonuses on steroids! Andy Marcuvitz, however, was not amused at all. But Wade supported us on the proposal in a board conference call, and Andy M. capitulated, although quite unhappily. Andy said, You better make sure you understand just how unusual and generous this is and make sure everybody knows it.

We tried to distribute the bonuses based on merit, but also to ease any previous inequities and to cushion any vesting losses for the few people who didn't get Microsoft job offers and/or could not go. Randy compiled a complex table of all the employees, their options positions, their relocation status, their salary, and our estimates of their contribution. Andy and Peter got the biggest bonuses, which they completely deserved, and Ted Stefanik got a large one too. So did Ed Cuoco, who had functioned as our entire marketing department under considerable stress. On the first iteration Randy, John, and I received no bonus. In fact, I made a point of this at the board conference call, in order to say that this was not self-interested on our part. This caused me a very painful problem shortly afterward, as I'll describe.

Thus the mechanics of the deal went smoothly. Microsoft didn't haggle over pennies and was generally willing to treat people fairly, while their lawyers were extremely competent and straightforward. Concurrently they were beginning to involve their human resources people to structure relocation packages, facilitate purchases of Seattle-area houses, and so forth. But there were still some serious confrontations. They centered on three related but quite different issues—Mandile's vesting, my termination agreement (which became a casualty of the personal animosity between me and Maffei) and, finally and most embarrassingly, my severance pay.

Mandile Yet Again You can't keep a good man down. I had already told John more than once that he would get full vesting over my dead body. I was amazed that he would ask: he was getting more than three years' vesting for about four months' work, not to mention the huge block of stock he already owned outright. But the issue of John Mandile's vesting just would not die, because John never gave up.

Halfway through the final contract negotiations, just before Christmas, Mandile came to me and raised the issue again. Charles, he said, you started this company. You deserve full vesting. *I* would certainly support *you* in seeking full vesting for your stock. Don't you think it would be fair if you supported me? By this point we were barely on speaking terms, and I'm sure that the Microsoft people sensed tension, although I don't think they knew just how much. I replied, No John, actually I *wouldn't* support you. I might deserve it, Randy might deserve it, but you definitely *don't* deserve it. You're going to make almost $10 million for about three months' work, I kind of think that's enough. In fact I think it's obscene that you're getting more than Randy and twice as much as Andy and Peter *combined*.

John was awesomely, marvelously, breathtakingly unfazed. Well, he said, there's a way we could do this that would benefit Andy and Peter, too. We could just insert a sentence into the acquisition agreement that lifts restrictions on any restricted stock. This was actually quite clever of John. Restricted stock is stock that you have paid for but not yet vested. All of Randy's, John's, and my unvested stock was in the form of restricted stock rather than options, and in late summer, I had gotten a bonus for Andy and Peter to buy their options too, and now Mandile was taking clever advantage of this. Since Andy and Peter now held restricted stock too, the insiders' deal could include them.

John, I said, I'm not going to help you improve your vesting. But your idea is a good one for Randy, Andy, and Peter, so will you support me in trying to get it just for them? Sure, he said, but to comply with pooling, it would have to include me, too, in the contract. So will you agree, I went on, that if you get extra vesting too that you'll give it to the other employees? Of course, he said. Great, I said. Will you sign something to that effect? There was the characteristic silence, then John said, No, I think it would be better to keep it flexible and informal. John, I said, you are one serious piece of work.

I wasn't sure if I could beat him on this. I called Bob Davoli and told him how Mandile was behaving. Bob heard me out and said, Well, he's young and ambitious, he doesn't always have the perspective that comes with experience, but I wouldn't worry about it too much. I didn't exactly see it that way, but Bob said he agreed with me on the vesting issue and would talk to John.

A short time later, I received the new draft acquisition contract. Upon reading it, I found a boldface paragraph (indicating changes since the last version) containing exactly the provision lifting restrictions on unvested stock that Mandile had proposed. I pulled John aside and told him to take it out. He refused. He said, Charles, I think I deserve this. I want the board to decide. I said, I'll never let this pass, surely you understand that. I'll call a special board meeting and we'll take it out. Fine, John said, but I want to let the board decide. I'll confess that this worried me. I wondered whether John had done a deal behind my back.

John would not get to vote because the issue concerned his compensation, and the VCs couldn't allow that blatant a conflict of interest to go on the record in the board minutes. But even so, to win at the board meeting I needed Randy's support, and it was a source of great personal satisfaction to me that he gave it. By this time I felt as if my nerve endings were made of piano wire. I had put Randy in a very painful position, and I blamed myself (correctly) for misjudging Mandile so badly that it had come to this. I knew Randy had trouble believing the worst about anybody. He respected Mandile's diplomatic skills and his negotiating and managerial abilities, and he was properly upset at my propensity to force confrontations. I had been extremely angry and tense over the past several months, which I knew had affected Randy. I also knew that by asking Randy to oppose the lifting of the stock restrictions, I was asking him, Peter, and Andy to give up a lot of money, at least in the near term.

Randy wanted to think about it overnight. But Randy realized that Mandile's request was outrageous, and he agreed to support me. Once I had his support, I convened a special board meeting by conference call. Mandile came into the room at the start, very nervous and upset, then left us to deliberate and vote. I summarized the issue and said I wanted extra vesting precluded, including my own. Andy Marcuvitz stunned me with his response. Well, he said, I'm not sure there's anything underhanded about this. In fact it might partially be my fault, because I told John in his compensation negotiations that he would get equal treatment with you, Charles. And you have favorable vesting arrangements, and this will just bring him up to about where you are in terms of stock ownership.

This was absurd, and I resented it, to put it mildly. For one thing, this was the first I'd ever heard of Mandile deserving or getting equal treatment with me. Long before, in persuading me to accept Mandile's compensation package, Marcuvitz *had* justified Mandile's enormous acceleration of vesting in the event of acquisition by saying that it gave him incentives similar to mine, and that this was desirable for the firm. Even this was false, but I'd been worn down by then and put up only token resistance. But never, then or at any other time, had Marcuvitz or Mandile said that parity between us was either deserved or promised. If Marcuvitz had said this, he had kept it from me despite an explicit promise to keep me fully informed about the negotiations, and he had no right to make private deals with Mandile. Furthermore, knowing Mandile as I now did, and knowing that we had sold a grand total of 289 copies of our product, I found it outrageous for Marcuvitz to equate four months' of Mandile's time with everything I had put into the company, and I let him know it.

Marcuvitz then tried to defuse the situation, suggesting that John and I may have just miscommunicated. I replied, with considerable heat, Look at the most recent draft of the acquisition contract. You'll find a paragraph about lifting vesting requirements on restricted stock. Now, please tell me where the hell that came from, and how it just happened by accident. At that point Wade intervened and said, with obvious weariness in his voice, Yeah, Andy, unfortunately I think we've got to believe something was going on here. Shortly afterward we took a vote and John's request was formally refused.

But Mandile *still* wasn't done, and this time he finally got somewhere. After the deal closed, he negotiated a consulting contract with Microsoft to assist them during the transition. As part of this agreement he got them to agree to continue his vesting during the six months of his consulting contract. He didn't quite get everything, but he came awfully close. Randy, Andy, and Peter, I'm pleased to say, didn't suffer financially as a result of my action. They stayed at Microsoft long enough to vest their stock, and in fact Andy and Peter are still there. However, blocking Mandile's full vesting cost *me* about $2 million at the time, or about $20 million at the current stock price, but I would willingly have given up even more.

Maffei and My Termination Contract By this time Maffei and I detested each other, a condition that unquestionably interfered with the negotiations. Maffei is extremely smart, but I found him oblivious to everything and everyone except himself, and I was in no mood to put up with him. I've already mentioned our clash over due diligence. Then Maffei insisted on a heavy breakup fee if the deal didn't go through. I was seriously opposed to this, because I was afraid that *Microsoft* might leak the deal, particularly since Maffei himself had been calling outside people about it. This might let the Justice Department block it, not to mention the effect it would have upon our continuing business if it were revealed that we had been negotiating with Microsoft for months.

Later I learned that Maffei had the same fear in reverse. I gave in on the breakup fee when Chris Peters sat me down and said, Look, we *really* want to do this deal—we aren't just toying with you. Marcuvitz later said that if it hadn't been for Mandile's diplomacy the deal might never have happened, and Peters apparently also once said that he thought that I might blow the deal. I don't think so. I was extremely tense, angry, and frequently unpleasant, but I'm not stupid. But there is no question that Chris Peters, on their side, and Mandile on ours were both very helpful in maintaining minimum diplomatic relations.

Indeed, it was equally clear that Peters told Maffei to behave himself and meant it seriously. I remember one moment that came the morning after a particularly brutal exchange. It was during a long session at our attorneys' offices, just before Christmas. Maffei pulled out a package and, trying his very best to be civilized, he gave it to me and said, Merry Christmas, Charles, I'm sorry I've been so difficult. It was a huge Starbuck's coffee mug, which became my favorite. I was highly amused and shameless about showing it. Gee thanks, Greg, I said, you're such a sweet guy.

The final clash between Maffei and me came over the restrictions on my future activities. Even if we had had the best of relationships, this would have been a touchy question. I had long been critical of Microsoft, and in fact in the early 1990s I believe that Bill Gates personally banned me from attending analyst meetings, because I once asked him a tough question about antitrust issues in front of a dozen other people. In addition, I was politically well connected and had written and published widely about the industry. Consequently Microsoft wanted to gag me. The Microsoft attorneys told me so quite explicitly and said that my refusal would be a deal breaker. Maffei was gleeful and proposed a five-year noncompete agreement plus a five-year prohibition on my saying anything about Microsoft or the Internet. I thought this was outrageous, but, fortunately, without my prompting, our normally mild-mannered attorneys stood up and told Maffei that both the proposal and his conduct were out of line. I was quite impressed and grateful to them.

In the end we agreed on two years, which expired in January 1998. The agreement didn't just prevent me from making public statements; it prevented me from making any statement about Microsoft that *became* public. I asked one of the Microsoft attorneys, How can I control this? What if I have a dinner conversation that someone overhears? Well, he said, you better be damned careful where you have dinner and what you say, because we mean this *exactly* the way it's written. We intend to buy your silence as a condition of this deal. So I signed it, and for two years I was indeed careful about what I said.

My Severance When I had originally argued for giving the employees $3 million in bonus payments, I had said that I didn't want any of it. That wasn't a trick; I really meant it. But a week or two later, just before the deal closed, I suddenly realized with a jolt that I didn't have any money. *I really didn't.* My salary was about to end, I had a mortgage payment, rent, and other expenses totaling $9,000 a month, and I had virtually no cash left in my checking account. I had about $200,000 in a Keogh plan, but if I withdrew that money before retirement I would immediately pay a 10 percent penalty plus income taxes, and that was literally the only money I had to my name. I was about to become very rich, but I couldn't sell my stock until I established a brokerage account. With the amount involved, I wanted to be careful about that. At the time I knew very little about stock, brokers, and money management. If I'd thought about it calmly for ten minutes, I would have realized that with $14 million in stock, I wouldn't have much trouble raising whatever cash I needed. By this point, however, I was far too exhausted for calm reflection, and the last thing I wanted was another set of financial negotiations. I needed quite badly to stop thinking about money for a little while.

So I called Wade and asked for a $100,000 severance payment. He was very nice about it, but he said no. I explained that I had virtually no money and just needed something to tide me over until I could think about my financial arrangements. Wade said, Charles, I realize you don't understand yet how this works, but, trust me, as soon as the deal closes, money managers will be falling all over themselves to get your business. You will be able to borrow literally millions of dollars almost instantly, so you won't have to worry about paying your mortgage.

I've never properly apologized to Wade for how I behaved next. I snapped. What I really wanted to say was, Wade, please, I'm so completely exhausted, I don't want to bargain with anybody, especially not money managers trying to get my business. I've been fending off Mandile. I've been getting everybody bonuses and watching everybody else's back, and nobody's watching mine. I just want this one simple thing so I can clear out and vegetate for a bit until this all sinks in, and then I can think about money management and financial planning. Can you do this for me, please?

But that's not what I said. Instead, I screamed at him and threatened him, and he yelled back at me and hung up. We eventually worked it out; of course, John had to get his pound of flesh too. John and I each got a $75,000 bonus; Randy got $100,000, but Randy gave $20,000 of it to a developer who had felt mistreated. Then the Microsoft lawyers decided that they needed to pay me for my two-year gag agreement to make it enforceable and paid me $50,000 for my signature. So I suddenly had plenty of cash, but it was a bad way to end things with Wade. We've since gotten over it.

Actually, there was one final moment of dark humor. I proposed to Chris Peters that I might do some consulting for them during the transition. I didn't need to be paid, I said, I just wanted to be helpful. The truth is, I had absolutely no interest whatsoever in assisting Microsoft; I just wanted to be able to roam around inside the beast, to learn about it from inside. Chris saw through this in a nanosecond. He replied, Charles, thanks very much for the offer, we'll think about it, but I'm not sure it would work out.

AFTERMATH

The deal closed at 5:00 P.M. on January 12, 1996, and was announced a few days later. It received considerable press coverage. There were articles in *The New York Times,* a substantial segment on CNN Financial News featuring an interview with Chris Peters, and a long article in *The Wall Street Journal.*

I didn't go to the closing. Instead I had booked a flight to California departing that afternoon—the first time in my life I ever bought a full-fare first-class ticket. I felt a vast sense of relief at leaving the conflicts, the tension, and the vile weather in Boston. I felt quietly happy that I really had done something very clear, something that was good, that had made a difference. I also felt some guilt at having helped Microsoft extend its empire. I felt numb yet free. I felt an enormous sense of gratitude to Randy, Andy, Peter, and the other people at Vermeer, many of whom would still have to work several years more to finish vesting their stock. I was completely drained, light-headed, contentedly alone. A couple of hours into the flight, I realized the deal had just closed and that I had officially become worth $14 million. I drank several glasses of bad airplane champagne.

I spent the next several weeks at my house in the Berkeley hills, decompressing, contemplating how beautiful the house and its surroundings were. But the house was a mess; I started looking for an apartment in San Francisco so I could have a place to live while renovating the house. Then, one Friday evening, I got a voice mail message from a Justice Department attorney, saying that it was extremely urgent that I contact him immediately. I tried calling him throughout the weekend but got only voice mail. This is apparently standard practice at Justice; their goal in forcing you to wait through the weekend is to make you tense and therefore more cooperative or more apt to say something stupid.

When I finally talked to the lawyer on Monday, he told me that I was being subpoenaed in connection with Microsoft's acquisition of Vermeer. His tone was extremely cold and unpleasant. I responded in kind and said I wouldn't have anything to say without a lawyer present. I made some phone calls and found that Mandile and Microsoft had been subpoenaed too. Microsoft told me that their counsel would attend my session, but I decided I wanted my own lawyer as well. I had consulted Dale Collins, a lawyer from Shearman & Sterling, on antitrust issues before the acquisition, and I liked him, so I retained him as my personal attorney. I flew back to Boston a couple of times to meet with Collins and Steve Holley, one of Microsoft's principal antitrust attorneys.

My deposition, when it eventually came, took a day. The Justice Department attorney was a consultant from a San Francisco law firm. I found him absurd—expensive haircut, pinstriped suit, suspenders, Mont Blanc fountain pen, no idea whatsoever what he was doing, hours of pointless questions. I wondered whether he might be just running his clock. There were only two moments of interest. The first was when he asked, Didn't you contact the Justice Department and Ms. Bingaman in order to warn her that Microsoft was a dangerous, predatory company and that Justice should take action against it?—Yes, I said.—Didn't you advocate a series of measures to contain Microsoft and limit its power?—Yes.—Didn't you discuss acquisitions in that context?—Yes.—What did you say about acquisitions?—I recommended that Justice be very tough on them. He seemed confused by that and dropped it. I was exceedingly tempted to tell him that if Justice had been doing its job more effectively, we might not have needed to sell, but I didn't.

Later he asked about my meetings with Netscape and produced a copy of my presentation to Barksdale outlining the consequences of a Microsoft acquisition of us.—Did you write this? he asked.—Yes.—Does it represent your truthful views about competition for the Internet?—Well, yes, I said, although I probably exaggerated a bit, since I was trying to goad Barksdale into action. After all, I gave a very similar presentation to Microsoft just a few days before about the trouble *they'd* be in if they didn't buy us. Once again, he dropped it.

The only point at which I got testy—almost surprising myself at my anger—was when he asked whether Barksdale had correctly represented our discussions. By this time I realized that Barksdale was behind this. I said, I don't know whether he has or not. He certainly lied through his teeth to me about a few things, like Netscape's stock price and prospects and our ability to hedge our stock if we were acquired, so I wouldn't exactly take his word as gospel.

I assume it was just a fishing expedition. They deposed a number of others and subpoenaed a huge mass of files, including a lot of e-mail. The investigation seemed to just wander until it finally stopped. To give them credit, they've certainly done better in the current antitrust suit against Microsoft, and they obviously have reached out for a far more competent team of lawyers.

FrontPage proceeded to take over the field of Web authoring, as I knew it would. I still feel an enormous though slightly ambivalent pride when I encounter rows of books, stacks of boxes, articles, evidence of its growing role in the world.

Almost everyone who went to Redmond seems to have flourished, and most are now quite wealthy. Randy and Ed Cuoco have left Microsoft; Randy wants to start another company. Chris Peters went on a leave of absence but then returned part-time. Andy is now running the FrontPage business unit—quite a change for an erstwhile UNIX snob—while Peter became the development manager for PhotoDraw, Microsoft's new graphics product, which has received superb reviews. John Mandile has become a VC with Sigma Partners, joining Bob Davoli in Sigma's Boston office. Wade Woodson is now managing partner of Sigma. Camille and I separated as a couple but have remained close friends. After taking some time to relax and renovate my house, for the last year and a half I've been writing this book. I've also started investing in start-ups, returning to policy research, and learning filmmaking. Life is returning.

CHAPTER NINE

Speaking Ill of the Dead:
A Strategic Analysis of Netscape's Failure
and the Future of Internet Software

Streets flooded. Please advise.
—*Robert Benchley, upon arriving in Venice*

Either he's dead, or my watch has stopped.
—*Groucho Marx, A Day at the Races*

*T*he final three chapters of this book attempt to reflect on large-scale issues related to the Internet. In this chapter, I analyze the strategic competition between Netscape and Microsoft. I ask whether Netscape could have survived if it had behaved differently, thereby preserving an independent Internet software industry and curbing Microsoft's power. Despite Microsoft's power and ruthlessness I believe that the answer is probably yes. This was a situation in which a few early mistakes, such as the choice of Netscape's top management team and their basic strategic decisions, changed history. However, those mistakes are now unrecoverable, and Netscape can no longer discipline Microsoft's monopoly power, so one must consider Microsoft as a policy problem in that light. Thus in the next chapter I consider the Microsoft problem and argue a somewhat hawkish middle ground. I think that Microsoft's power is a problem and that the company should be split up, but only if this can be done without destroying the enormous benefits Microsoft has bestowed upon the industry. In particular, a divestiture into an operating systems company and an applications company makes sense, whereas other more extreme proposals could easily do enormous damage to the technology sector and even the world economy.

In the final chapter of the book, I consider three other issues: the tension between privacy rights and legitimate information requirements; the beneficial, but also sometimes destabilizing economic effects of the Internet revolution; and finally, the huge impediment to progress represented by monopoly telecommunications industries—particularly the local telephone and cable TV companies.

NETSCAPE BOWS OUT

Netscape was effectively pronounced dead on November 24, 1998, when it agreed to be acquired by AOL for $4.2 billion in AOL stock. At the time, Netscape's browser market share was about 50 percent; it has since declined to under 40 percent and is clearly doomed to decline further. Microsoft's browser share is over 60 percent and growing; in other words, the browser wars are over. To the extent that the Netscape acquisition made sense, AOL bought Netscape primarily for its Netcenter "portal," or Internet directory and news service, which at the time had about nine million users. AOL was buying subscribers, just as other media companies do. It may also have wanted Netscape's browser as a way of disciplining Microsoft's monopoly power, though I doubt that this will provide much leverage. Netscape's motivation in selling itself to AOL was simpler: it was basically dead as an independent company, as one of its senior executives privately admitted to me in mid-1998.

As part of the acquisition, AOL essentially handed control over development and marketing of Netscape's Web server products to Sun Microsystems. AOL said that it would use Netscape software in developing custom Web sites for large customers and that Sun would take over the development and sales of Netscape's software products. In March 1999, AOL and Sun announced a new alliance based on this agreement. But it's awfully hard to take this seriously, and it is highly unlikely that either AOL or Sun will become a major force in Internet software. Sun will do well selling Netscape Web servers on Sun hardware, but cannot and will not become a major force in the Internet software industry, and certainly not an industrywide standard.

The principal beneficiary of the acquisition, therefore, is actually Microsoft, despite Microsoft's claim that the acquisition of Netscape by AOL proves the folly of the Justice Department's antitrust case. With the takeover of Netscape's software business by Sun, the Internet software industry and the Web lose their last significant independent industrywide software vendor. Inevitably, Sun will favor its own hardware and operating systems in supporting Netscape software and will almost certainly *not* support Microsoft's. This will probably accelerate adoption of NT and Microsoft's Web server, because while Microsoft's Web server runs only on NT, NT does at least run on hardware from many different vendors. Thus, Microsoft's Internet software products will probably soon be more cross-platform and hardware-independent than Netscape's Web server products under Sun's control. I would argue that the acquisition actually should strengthen the government's antitrust case and increases the importance of curbing Microsoft's power.

However, I don't think this result was inevitable: Netscape could have lived, if it had behaved differently. While I certainly agree that Microsoft played dirty against Netscape and should be brought under control, Netscape died unnecessarily—primarily because it was unspeakably arrogant and stupid. Here, I will try to explain why. In doing so, I will be breaking a taboo; criticizing Netscape is politically incorrect (not to mention uncool) in Silicon Valley. However, I also think it's important.

The mangling of large companies by polished, politically astute, nontechnical CEOs, which is a major part of what happened at Netscape, is a movie that the Valley—and the technology sector in general—has seen many times before. If Jim Clark, John Doerr, Netscape's executives, and Silicon Valley's most important people had openly and directly confronted the fact that Netscape was blowing it, things might have turned out differently.

But they didn't. Alas, firing highly visible CEOs is all too rare, no matter how bad they are. Ben Rosen has done it twice, when he replaced the CEO of Compaq in 1991 and again in 1999. More often, however, everyone sits around, afraid to be the first to blow the whistle and provoke a fight. But by the time an obvious crisis forces action, it's often too late. In the long run, I would argue, the Valley didn't do itself any favors by keeping quiet about Netscape's problems. Keeping quiet in the face of similar incompetence and strategic disaster at Apple, IBM, Lotus, WordPerfect, and Novell during the 1980s didn't help the Valley, either. If anything, lack of public criticism increased Microsoft's power by reducing pressure on its rivals to put their own houses in order. Consequently, mismanagement was allowed to continue longer than necessary, which reduced the competitive discipline Microsoft faced.

Netscape's story also provides a remarkable case study in how to run a high technology company, and how not to, at both strategic and operational levels. Perhaps never in American history has a new company faced larger opportunities, and such profound choices, as Netscape did. And although Netscape certainly provided enormous financial returns for its early investors and employees, in the larger scheme of things it failed. Netscape thereby joined a short list of companies—certainly Apple, probably also Novell and Sun—that once had a chance to affect technological and industrial history, but failed to grasp their opportunity. It is unpopular in the Valley to point out that Microsoft owes much of its success to the fact that it is simply *smarter* than most of its opponents, but it's true. It's bad to make mistakes large enough to change the path of an industry, but it is worse not to assess them and learn from them.

And while Netscape did some things well, and a few things brilliantly, its overall performance was shockingly bad. From the beginning it blundered strategically, technologically, managerially, and operationally, yet was dismissive both of criticism and of the challenges it faced. In the Internet industry, and when your opponent is Microsoft, that's fatal.

INITIAL DECISIONS: BRILLIANCE, THEN STUPIDITY

Marc Andreessen and the original NCSA group had a remarkable insight when they conceived the original Mosaic browser, and they deserve to go down in history for it. While Andreessen later blundered in attempting to change the software industry, he had already done something that profoundly changed the entire world.

Andreessen's achievement with Mosaic carried over into one important and insightful commercial decision. Clark and Andreessen concluded fairly early—by March or April 1994—that the Web offered a massive business opportunity and that browsers and servers would become high-volume commercial products. Most people took far longer to figure that out. It is nonetheless still a bit surprising that even Clark and Andreessen didn't get it *instantly*, since Andreessen had, after all, conceived Mosaic more than a year earlier and other people were already commercializing it. Yet he and Clark spent several months talking about other ideas before they realized that the Web should be the basis of their future.

Their second key decision was that their company would concentrate first and foremost on a *browser*. This was not something to be taken for granted. Netscape had a clean slate, the Internet was still virgin wilderness, and there were other alternatives (Web servers, development tools, custom services). Furthermore, browsers were in some ways the most problematic choice. NCSA Mosaic was effectively free for most individuals, and Mosaic-derived commercial browsers from Spyglass and other companies were proliferating rapidly in 1994. And in the long run, there was also Microsoft. Thus, in some ways it would have been safer for Netscape to concentrate on, say, high-performance Web servers, as Open Market did, or special-purpose browsers, or development tools, as we did.

The decision by Netscape's founders to focus on browsers was not necessarily wrong. But it was a major strategic decision whose profound implications they clearly did not understand. The decision to dominate the browser market locked them into an extremely demanding strategic and technical trajectory, including an eventual collision with Microsoft. Randy and I had looked at doing a browser in 1994 and decided against it. It was already clear to us, as it was also clear to others, that browsers would become a ubiquitous PC utility, like word processors or electronic mail software, of a kind that would naturally be integrated into either Windows or Office. In other words, if you were going to go into the browser business, you had to assume that your ultimate competitor would be a Microsoft product that was free and/or tightly bundled with one of their core monopolies. That is not just hindsight. Randy and I had *exactly* that conversation in mid-1994, and I also had it with Andy Marcuvitz, Wade Woodson, and others I spoke with around the same time.

But again, even the fact that Microsoft would eventually be the competition does not imply that targeting the browser market was a mistake. It was daring, aggressive, and risky, but it was not crazy. Microsoft was obviously tangled up in MSN and Windows 95. Netscape could count on having a substantial lead and having temporarily uncontested access to the installed base market of pre-Windows 95 PCs. Moreover, the area was new, so there might be large patent opportunities and application markets. If you did everything right, you might just pull off the stunt of the century.

However, if you were going to try this, *you had to assume that Microsoft would eventually come after you in a very serious way, and prepare accordingly.* The same strategy that would provide the only effective protection against them—creating a proprietary industry standard platform with APIs that you controlled, and that couldn't be easily cloned—would also threaten them the most and trigger the most intense counterattack. Thus, choosing the browser as your platform for launching a major company was a huge strategic commitment, and once you did it there would be no going back. You couldn't declare war on Microsoft, change your mind, and then retreat to a safe, profitable corner with 20 percent of the market: it was win or die. While I assume that at some general level Clark and Andreessen knew this (neither agreed to be interviewed for this book), they clearly did *not* understand what it really meant. They were visionary and daring in identifying the Web as a revolutionary opportunity, in targeting browsers and Web servers as their markets, and in choosing to distribute their first products over the Web. But they did almost everything else wrong.

Hence, we come to Netscape's first big mistake. Clark and Andreessen failed to understand that in order to create a sustainable competitive position in browsers (and servers as well, by the way), they had to use their lead time to create *a highly proprietary industrywide standard, a.k.a. an architectural franchise,* strong enough to withstand Microsoft's inevitable assault. This would require coverage of all major market segments with Netscape's products; creating new content standards and APIs that enabled programmers to customize browsers and Web sites; creating a supporting infrastructure of consultants, application developers, etc.; establishing a proprietary position through patents, functional complexity, and continuous improvements that defeated cloning; and creating lock-in with content developers, end-users, and programmers. Netscape would have needed to provide a continuous stream of enhancements in order to obtain upgrade revenues, and also to keep Microsoft permanently off balance, unable to compete against Netscape either through developing a comparably powerful rival architecture or by cloning Netscape's. Furthermore, Netscape should have tried to seem unthreatening for as long as possible, so that by the time Microsoft woke up, it would be too late.

In other words, Netscape had to play exactly the same game that Microsoft has played so brilliantly over the last fifteen years with DOS, Windows, Office, NT, and BackOffice. Settling for anything less would be suicidal. The proper standard for evaluating Netscape's performance, therefore, is how intelligently they set about creating such architectural franchises for their browsers and Web servers. Well, they flunked. I'll begin with Netscape's conduct prior to Microsoft's Pearl Harbor Day counterattack and then consider their subsequent responses. I'll discuss their products and technology first and then proceed to organization, personnel, acquisitions, and strategic management.

Some Successes: Capital Structure, Distribution, and Sales

Unlike Microsoft, of course, Netscape was a start-up. It had to raise money, establish structures of corporate governance and control, and build all of the infrastructure and industry relationships that Microsoft could take for granted. In some areas, Netscape did this quite well. After Clark put $4 million of his own money into the company, he rapidly secured another roughly equal injection of capital from Kleiner Perkins. Less than a year later, Netscape raised $11 million at a valuation of over $150 million—astonishing for a start-up. By mid-1995, the company had a very well-connected set of investors, directors, and advisors.

In addition, Netscape's decision to distribute the first browser over the Web—free for the beta version, and mostly free to individuals for the final product—was simply brilliant. That single decision forever changed the nature of the software industry and pushed the Web into the center of the market's imagination. It allowed Netscape to enter both the retail channel and corporate markets quickly and on far stronger terms than most start-ups can obtain. By early 1995, therefore, for a company that had yet to celebrate its first birthday, Netscape could point to an extraordinary list of accomplishments. Unfortunately, they did almost everything else wrong.

NETSCAPE'S EARLY PRODUCT, TECHNOLOGY, AND STRATEGY DECISIONS

Architecture and Engineering The need to create and control an industry-standard platform had quite specific implications for Netscape's engineering efforts, most of which were ignored. One of the most important was the need for good architecture and design and appropriately experienced development management to ensure excellent implementation. Because software products evolve in unpredictable ways, but predictably become more complex over time, it is critical to establish a rigorous architecture before the product becomes prohibitively complex.

Yet Netscape's browser was a mess from the very beginning. Their first browser was relatively simple, so choosing hacker style and spaghetti code to reach the market fast was tempting. But there is a general rule in software engineering that the cost of fixing an error doubles with every step down the engineering sequence, from initial conception to architecture to commercial release, and that these costs continue to double with subsequent releases. To do its first product correctly would have cost Netscape an extra month, maybe two at most, and as I describe shortly, Netscape made other technical and strategic errors that actually *lengthened* its development time. Thus, if Netscape had approached the problem correctly, it could have developed a vastly superior product, with sustainable long-term technical and strategic characteristics, approximately as fast as it produced Navigator 1.0.

But Navigator 1.0 had almost no architecture, and therefore none of the clean, flexible interfaces that mark the work of someone like Andy Schulert. In Netscape's rush to market, it was *conceivably* justifiable to do this, although I very much doubt it. Even if so, the failure to fix it immediately by developing a real architecture for the *next* product was utterly, totally fatal. Navigator 1.0 was throwaway code that they didn't throw away. It had about one hundred thousand lines of code and was written by about ten people. This overstates its complexity, since there was a known model (Mosaic) and some of the code came from existing freeware.

But Navigator 2.0, which was released fifteen months later, was the real thing. It ventured into new functional territory, had seven hundred thousand lines of code, and required 30 developers. Then, Navigator 3.0 required 50 developers and had one million lines of code. Their corporate browser suite, Communicator 4.0, which was released ten months after Navigator 3.0, had three million lines of code and required 120 developers. Underlying each of these products, however, was the non-architected Faustian bargain of Navigator 1.0. With each release, Netscape's cost structure, technical limitations, and development times worsened relative to Microsoft's, as did its ability to support new features and interfaces, with the result that Netscape's lead, which was at least a year on Pearl Harbor Day 1995, was eliminated within two years. Indeed, in some important respects, Microsoft's browser was superior to Netscape's by mid-1997.

Netscape's failure to architect its browser was just one of many engineering errors. Another, also serious, concerned testing. Software quality assurance (QA) is a complex activity, with a range of best practices and capital-intensive software tools for automating testing, bug tracking, and error correction. For complex products, you even design the testing systems into the original architecture of the product. That's not the way Netscape did it, to put it mildly. According to some reports, Navigator 1.0 testers were hired by placing notices on bulletin boards offering to hire random college students at ten dollars an hour. A dangerously casual attitude toward QA persisted even well after Netscape had focused on mission-critical application and server products for conservative, quality-conscious Fortune 500 clients.

Each release pushed Netscape deeper into the swamp. As the code base got bigger and the product more complex, the pain got worse, but it also became more difficult and expensive to start over. Once Microsoft arrived in force, Netscape's window of opportunity to fix the product effectively vanished; from that point, there just wasn't time. They tried to do it once, far too late, and in a bizarre, foolish way. During the development of Communicator 4.0, which was begun in 1996 and released in mid-1997, Netscape allocated about half its browser development team to an effort to redesign the browser from scratch, *using the Java language.* It would be difficult to exaggerate the idiocy of this choice. At this writing, three years later, nobody yet uses Java to write large Windows applications, because its performance is still mediocre and its tools, environment, and user interfaces are insufficiently mature. When Netscape tried to write the "Javagator," as they called it, Java technology was far less stable and nobody, including Netscape, had any experience using it for major applications. After a few months Netscape canceled the effort.

Netscape's Windows-Aversion Psychosis Unlike Netscape's general neglect of careful architecture and other good software engineering practices, some of its worst technical problems were the result of deliberate choice. I said that Netscape's browsers lacked an architecture. This was not *entirely* true. In one area of browser technology, Netscape went to great lengths to make its own life more difficult, and succeeded. Netscape decided to develop its early browsers so that they could be developed and released for many operating systems simultaneously, not just the multiple versions of Windows but also the Macintosh, OS/2, and a half dozen varieties of UNIX. These operating systems and their user interfaces are fundamentally different from one another. Consequently Netscape developed a major piece of software, the Netscape portable runtime layer, that covered up the specific features of various operating systems—such as Windows. Netscape developers then wrote code targeted to this generic intermediate layer rather than to specific operating systems. Later this generic code was adapted to each operating system.

This decision was an enormous strategic error for reasons I describe shortly. In addition to being strategically foolish, however, it was also a major technological and engineering disaster. It meant that Netscape deprived itself of the best available tools for developing software, particularly for Windows. Microsoft has long understood that the loyalty of the world's programmers is a major source of competitive strength, and over the years it has created superb development tools for the Windows environment. Indeed, this area was Bill Gates's original personal specialty: Microsoft's earliest software products, some of which Gates wrote himself, were development tools for PC programmers. At Vermeer, we used their then-standard (and very state-of-the-art) development environment, VC++/MFC: Visual C++ with Microsoft Foundation Classes. Together with other software tools, from Microsoft and several other vendors, the development tools for the Windows environment, which run almost entirely on Windows and NT, constitute an enormous advantage in developing Windows applications. Furthermore, in most areas they are now substantially more advanced than tools available for other platforms, and the gap is widening.

But Netscape did not use these tools. In part this was because it had decided to use its portable runtime layer, which was not supported by any of the standard development tools. In part the decision came from Netscape's early employees (who came from NCSA and Silicon Graphics, not from Windows software companies), who preferred to use UNIX as their development environment. Furthermore, developing the portable runtime layer itself took time, and it had to be kept current as computer and software companies continuously updated their various operating systems. As a result, Netscape's development efforts were slowed down considerably, at least for Windows products. Indeed, their development efforts even for non-Windows platforms might have gone faster if they had chosen to start with a well-designed Windows product.

Netscape's decisions to avoid Windows tools and Windows-specific development affected both the quality of Netscape's products and the engineering behind them. Different operating systems have their own look, styles, advantages, and disadvantages. Netscape could not easily take advantage of the unique features offered by each operating sytem, and in some cases, particularly Windows and Office, it deliberately chose not to. These decisions also affected the quality of Netscape's people, because extremely good Windows programmers either saw their talents wasted or were dissuaded from joining the company.

Strategic and Business Implications Netscape's technical failures in architecture and engineering, together with related decisions I describe shortly, probably cost the company hundreds of millions of dollars. In addition to increasing Netscape's costs and lengthening its development cycles, which allowed Microsoft to catch up faster, these problems limited Netscape's strategic options. For example, Barksdale admitted to me in 1998 that the lack of properly "componentized" browser code was a major cause of AOL's decision to use Microsoft's browser. Microsoft's browser, unlike Netscape's, was specifically designed so that it could be integrated into other products. Because Netscape's was not properly designed, it was much harder for AOL to embed Navigator in its own software. This would also have been a major problem for other OEM customers, such as Internet service providers and Windows application vendors who wanted to embed a browser in their products. Indeed, this problem was also apparently a factor in Intuit's decision to use Microsoft's browser.

Product Functionality and Programming Support (APIs) Netscape's early products contained both very intelligent decisions and huge mistakes. Navigator 1.0 maintained rigorous compatibility with preexisting Web standards, which was wise, while offering greatly increased performance and several useful enhancements to HTML. Netscape also developed and deployed the SSL security architecture for encrypted communication between browsers and Web servers. Taken together, these features represented a major advance over other browsers, and Navigator deservedly took over the browser market.

However, even in its first products, Netscape made extremely serious technical errors, which worsened over time and interacted with related strategic mistakes to produce a disastrous situation. Navigator 1.0 failed to adhere to the user interface conventions of Microsoft Office, which are used by nearly all PC applications (not just those from Microsoft, or those in Office). Furthermore, it provided no interfaces—so-called APIs—that would enable programmers and software companies to add new or customized functions either to the browser or to Web pages displayed with the browser. And finally, Netscape's browser was not structured in such a way that once installed on a PC it could be used by other applications, which would have been an extremely attractive, novel feature. For similar reasons, and as I mentioned above, Navigator could not be embedded in other software products, ranging from Intuit's tax package to the Macintosh operating system to AOL's viewer software. In addition to generating major strategic problems, these technical limits made Navigator a less desirable product, limited its market penetration, and made it easier for users to switch to Microsoft later.

Navigator 1.1/1.2, released in June 1995, fixed none of these problems. In later releases Navigator began, quite slowly and clumsily, to address some of them. Netscape's priorities were, to say the least, bizarre. Over the following year, Netscape introduced *three* interfaces for programmers (APIs)—the Plug-In API, JavaScript, and Java—that served similar purposes: they allowed programs to be inserted into Web pages and to run while the page was displayed in the browser. The Plug-In API had serious problems, e.g., that it required users to download and install Plug-In programs manually, and Netscape neither patented it nor enhanced it rapidly. As a result, it was easy for Microsoft to clone. Netscape also allowed cloning of JavaScript, its language for writing simple programs within browsers.

However, at least in these areas Netscape provided something, whereas it didn't address some of its browser's other problems at all. It did not, for example, "componentize" its browser so that it could be used by other applications. It did not make use of MS Office standards. And it did not introduce any APIs that permitted programmers to embed the browser in other software products or to add functions to the browser itself (as opposed to Web pages that the browser displayed), which were major functional limitations. For example, if Netscape had provided a reasonable architecture and suitable APIs, Vermeer could have used Navigator within FrontPage. This would have allowed Front-Page users to verify instantly that their pages would look the same in the Navigator browser as they did in our tool. Netscape finally provided an appropriate, componentized browser only in late 1998, long after Microsoft had done so and far too late to have made any competitive difference.

Beginning in 1995, Netscape made a further series of errors in adding functional enhancements to its browsers. It overemphasized multimedia and video technologies, which depended on faster Internet access speeds than were generally available, while neglecting less advanced functions with larger, proven markets (such as playing audio). It also failed to create preferential functional integration between its browsers and its servers, which could have enhanced the attractiveness of both products in a number of ways.

And then, of course, there was Netscape's tools effort. Independent of whether Netscape should have acquired Vermeer, Netscape's tools effort was extremely poor. Of the three products Netscape announced in September 1995, only the low-end HTML editor, Navigator Gold, was successful. None of the products approached the ease of use or functional power of FrontPage. They did not enable true remote development, they did not eliminate programming, they did not include personal Web servers, and they did not have external APIs to allow programmers to add additional functions. More generally Netscape failed to appreciate that, unlike Web browsers and servers, tools were difficult to clone and were a business in which Netscape could charge real money, at least if the products were good. Seemingly, Netscape just didn't understand how important tools were. Indeed, only Navigator Gold survived; Netscape's other products were withdrawn from the market.

Netscape's most serious error, however, probably concerned its bizarre decisions regarding the relative importance of providing cross-platform support in browsers versus server markets and its view of how to create and control industry standards in both markets, the issues to which I now turn.

NETSCAPE'S RECORD IN ARCHITECTURAL STRATEGY

The establishment of industrywide architectural leadership was a critical and demanding requirement for Netscape to survive, but probably an achievable one—if Netscape had heeded the lessons of Microsoft, Intel, and others in establishing such positions. One of the most basic requirements for establishing and controlling a standard is that your products, architectures, and/or programmer interfaces (APIs) must be available to the entire market—i.e., on all of the industry's principal computer platforms. Yet Netscape did the opposite. This failure was an important special case of the broader failure of Netscape's architectural strategy. In addition to covering the whole market, an aspiring architectural leader must also create proprietary advantages and lock-in so that it is difficult for competitors to clone its products, and create switching costs so that it is difficult for programmers and users to switch to a competitor's products. For an ambitious software company these should be basic precepts. Netscape ignored all of them, thereby making Microsoft's job far easier. I will address each of these issues in turn, beginning with market coverage.

Netscape's Platform Strategy in Browsers and Servers In the browser market, Netscape developed an obsession with "cross-platform development," which it described as a major tenet of its strategy. As Andreessen once put it, Netscape products "will run on all the different desktops, NCs [network computers], previous versions of Windows . . . Ours is an approach of cross-platform, cross-version, cross desktops, cross-servers, cross-databases, cross-applications, and cross everything." Even as a general principle, this was not necessarily wise, but more important, what Netscape actually *did* was quite foolish. Essentially Netscape decided to pretend that Windows was not the world's dominant PC operating system and that Microsoft was not a serious competitor. Netscape therefore massively *overinvested* in dysfunctional forms of platform independence and coverage in browsers, where Windows was dominant, while massively *underinvesting* in platform independence and coverage for servers, where support for multiple systems was in fact strategically essential.

Browser Strategy Navigator 1.0 was released simultaneously for Windows 3.1, the Macintosh, and half a dozen varieties of UNIX; the same was true for Navigator 1.1, released in mid-1995. Navigator 2.0, released in early 1996, also supported Windows 95. As I mentioned above, Netscape achieved this by creating a generic intermediate layer and adapting general-purpose code to all these operating systems simultaneously. When questioned about this, Netscape executives told me that this strategy helped them win business in corporations that had a mixture of Windows, Macintosh, and UNIX systems. Andreessen also argued that Netscape's cross-platform browser strategy actually helped it dominate the Windows market. Since Microsoft initially released its browser only for Windows 95, Netscape was able to dominate the installed base of Windows 3.1 systems by virtue of its cross-platform strategy.

Actually, Netscape's behavior was insane. By 1995, Windows 3.1 accounted for about 90 percent of PC shipments; by 1997, Windows 95 accounted for nearly 95 percent of PC shipments. To compromise support for these platforms in order to support over a half-dozen other platforms accounting for less than 10 percent of the market is, to put it mildly, questionable. When this dominant platform also belongs to your largest prospective competitor, it is wildly irrational. In fact, it was even worse than that. In order to produce generic code, Netscape was forced to use least-common-denominator technology. But all Windows operating systems—Windows 3.1, Windows 95, NT, as well as more recent systems such as Windows 98—share many common characteristics in their APIs, development tools, and hardware environments. If you take advantage of these, you can cover the total Windows market, including the installed base initially neglected by Microsoft, much faster. Thus, Netscape's behavior slowed down its coverage even of the Windows 3.1 installed base and on a market-weighted basis was therefore contrary to its own expressed strategy of covering all markets. Netscape's cross-platform browser strategy also reduced the marketability of its browser in substantial segments of the Windows market that expected use of the MS Office standards. Taken together, these actions not only reduced Netscape's market coverage but also made it dangerously easy for Microsoft to recover market share in its home territory, which constituted over 90 percent of the market. Furthermore, adoption of a Windows-centric engineering strategy by Netscape would not have precluded support for other platforms; if a product is well-designed, only three to six months' effort is required to port it to the Macintosh and UNIX systems.

Netscape eventually abandoned its cross-platform browser strategy and started giving priority to Windows, but only after it had caused itself enormous damage over several years. Moreover, at the same time that Netscape was neglecting Windows and overinvesting in minor operating systems, it was also neglecting portions of the Web server market, where a cross-platform strategy was actually very important.

Web Server Strategy Unlike the personal computer industry, the corporate server world is extremely heterogeneous, and the platforms used to run Web servers are even more so. In 1995 no operating system *family* had more than perhaps 25 percent of the server market, and within each family there were several variants. Sun, Hewlett-Packard, IBM, and Silicon Graphics each had dialects of UNIX running on their own server hardware; in addition, Linux freeware—which is essentially a UNIX dialect—ran on server hardware from many vendors, including Compaq and Dell. Microsoft's NT server operating system was already gaining market share, but even now is still not dominant. There was also Novell's NetWare, which dominated the market for small servers used for sharing files and providing printing services among work groups. Finally, and quite important, a large number of Windows PCs, NT workstations, and Macintosh PCs were, and still are, used as Web servers too. Moreover, these PC-based Web servers are often used by programmers, and/or in conjunction with authoring tools, for Web site development. Thus they are an unusually important market segment. This was one reason that we included a PC Web server within the FrontPage authoring tool. Netscape could have provided Web servers for these PC and workstation systems and probably should even have bundled them with its browser. This would have provided many benefits to both Web users and Web site operators, as well as added differentiation for Netscape's browser and server products.

Consequently, and unlike the Windows-dominated PC market into which browsers were distributed, the Web server market actually did require a cross-platform approach. The importance of covering all major platforms was further increased by the fact that, for various technical and historical reasons, most large organizations—even including server vendors themselves—used a wide array of server systems from multiple vendors, in addition to PC-based Web servers.

Thus, information systems (IS, or sometimes MIS) managers within these organizations attempt to purchase software products that run on all the major server platforms they must administer. System management is greatly simplified when a single vendor and product can be used for all systems. In addition, for software vendors such as Netscape there is an important "guerrilla marketing" benefit to having their products running on small, PC-based servers. These systems are usually below the radar of IS managers, allowing technically skilled individuals to introduce new technologies into organizations without formal approval. Often, these technologies spread so fast that IS managers are presented with a fait accompli and later must support them as corporate standards. This was another reason that we included a Web server with FrontPage and adopted our "free PC Web server" strategy (which we should have exploited much more aggressively than we did). And finally, a comprehensive cross-platform strategy would have enabled Netscape to differentiate itself from Microsoft, whose Web servers run only on its own operating systems, as a truly industrywide standard.

Therefore, the correct strategy for Netscape was to deploy its Web servers on as many platforms as possible, including PCs. But it did the opposite: its server products were *less* cross-platform than its browser. Netscape didn't develop a Web server for NetWare for years. None of its Web servers *ever* ran on Windows 3.1 or the Macintosh and of course were never bundled with the Navigator browser. Netscape's FastTrack Web server initially supported Windows 95, but Netscape later withdrew Windows 95 support. A reasonable calculation is that over Netscape's lifespan, its Web server products were, on average, available to only half of the total market. In part for this ridiculously obvious reason, and in part also through overpricing and failure to use the retail channel for selling Web servers, Netscape's Web server market share never exceeded 20 percent, and in early 1999 it was less than 7 percent. There is no way on earth you are going to control the direction of an industry if you hold only 7 percent of the market, especially if you're competing with Microsoft.

How Netscape could permit this to happen remains somewhat mysterious. In part, they were again led astray by their UNIX-centered early technical employees. In part, they may have feared cannibalization of their expensive UNIX Web servers if they provided (necessarily inexpensive) Web servers for PCs, and their disdain for Windows and Microsoft again clouded their thinking. But there really is no good answer: Netscape's platform strategy, in both browsers and Web servers, was just wrong.

CREATING AND CONTROLLING INDUSTRY STANDARDS

In fairness to Netscape, the subject of architectural strategy—the creation and control of standards for competitive advantage—is complicated and subjective, an art rather than a science. Nonetheless, it is susceptible to analysis, and it is extremely important if you're in for the long haul, not just the quick buck. Netscape not only made fundamental errors in this area; in some cases it ignored the existence of the issue.

In the technology sector, control of an industrywide standard is a license to print money, at least if you manage it intelligently. If you control the standard, then you have advance knowledge of how it will evolve and probably the deepest knowledge of how it works. You can therefore develop the earliest and best products that depend upon it, while others are reduced to trying to clone you, follow behind you, or serve minor niche markets. Beyond any doubt, Microsoft is the master practitioner of these strategies. And once again, Netscape proved itself incompetent. As a result, Microsoft was able to do something very rare in high technology competition; it was able to wrest control of an existing industry standard from the leading firm. Microsoft first cloned Netscape's browser successfully, pulled even with its rival in the market, and then created a proprietary standard of its own built on top of the technical foundation created by its rival. This strategy, which I had described in 1993 and termed "standard stealing," is infrequently observed and even less frequently successful. It is normally extremely difficult to dislodge an architectural leader who manages its position effectively. Netscape, however, made it easy for Microsoft to clone Netscape's browser and for users to switch from it to Internet Explorer.

Indeed, my introduction to Netscape's world of illusions came at my breakfast with Jim Barksdale in Palo Alto, when I asked him about precisely this subject. Barksdale said Netscape's strategy was based on some combination of two propositions. First, he said that Netscape didn't need to control industry standards because it could develop new technologies and products faster than anyone else, so Netscape's products would always be better. Second, he said that the best way to establish and control standards was to let others clone them at will, thereby guaranteeing their universality.

This is dubious even as a general matter, and when your opponent controls the operating system upon which you depend, has $10 billion, and is brilliant, it's very dubious indeed. Netscape's implementation decisions made things worse. First, as we have already seen, Netscape failed to use architecture to maximize the value that its products and standards could provide to customers. Second, it also failed to create lock-in to its products and standards— with users, with the community of programmers, and with other software products used in major computer systems. Netscape probably overpriced both its browsers and Web servers (a mistake we at Vermeer made too). This reduced Netscape's Web server market share seriously from the very start, because there exists an excellent freeware product, the Apache Web server, whose source code is available free. As of this writing, the Apache server's market share (in unit terms) is about three times higher than Netscape's.

Furthermore, as already noted, Netscape failed to provide appropriate programming interfaces for its browsers and servers, such that programmers could add custom functions, embed Netscape's products in larger systems, or have Netscape's products cooperate gracefully with other software products. Its first browser had no APIs *at all,* and even in later releases they were inadequate. This not only reduced the market penetration of Netscape's products, but also the cost of switching to Microsoft's, because it was literally impossible to invest in customizing Netscape's browser to your specific needs.

The contrast between Netscape and Microsoft in this regard is telling. There are armies of small developers writing to Microsoft APIs, creating special-purpose applications for Windows, Office, BackOffice, and other Microsoft platforms. Microsoft provides them with development tools, invites them to frequent developers' conferences, and so forth. Of course, this information and control also allows Microsoft to cherry-pick the most attractive markets for itself, once a small application developer has pointed the way. Thus Microsoft has the advantage of a large industry infrastructure dependent on its platforms and also the opportunity to exploit the largest markets itself. Netscape behaved in precisely the opposite way. It neglected and even alienated outside developers and failed to create a large infrastructure of custom solutions based on its platforms. In fact, Netscape antagonized virtually every company in the industry, including its natural allies.

Netscape also failed in managing its APIs and standards themselves, even when it eventually developed them. If Netscape had behaved wisely, it would have been exceedingly difficult for Microsoft to produce such a complete, accurate, and current clone of Netscape's browser. But Microsoft was able to do it. For example, I've mentioned several times Netscape's disdain for patents and other forms of intellectual property. Barksdale shared this view, one that apparently he had absorbed from Andreessen and the other student UNIX hackers, a community in which intellectual property is viewed as evil.

It was foolish for Netscape to publish its APIs and specifications, essentially giving Microsoft and freeware competitors such as Apache a map of what to do. But if you are going to take that path, it is essential to cover the market completely with your own products. Otherwise, you leave large market segments for competitors, which hands them a large gift in the form of free market share. Since control over standards nearly always accrues to the vendor with the highest market share, leaving large market gaps is an invitation to disaster. This helped Microsoft rapidly gain market share in the browser contest (through AOL's and Intuit's need for a componentized browser) and allowed the balkanization of Web server markets when Netscape could have supplied an industrywide standard.

Netscape thus should have been more careful about when, how, and to whom it disclosed its interfaces and standards. Furthermore, standards and APIs should be continuously enhanced over time while retaining compatibility with prior versions. In this way, systems and Web sites using earlier versions of your technology can continue to operate, but you can continuously raise the ante for competitors. Since you control the standard, you know about new features before the competitor does. In this case, it would have meant that Microsoft would have been permanently behind and off balance. Yet Netscape failed to do this. For example, the Plug-In API had technical limits, but Netscape failed to remedy them or continuously enhance its capabilities. This enabled Microsoft to clone it completely and also caused the industry to shift toward other technologies, one of which, called ActiveX, is a technology developed by Microsoft that Netscape's browser didn't support.

Finally, a product or architecture that aspires to become an industry standard should coexist well with the industry's other principal standards and architectures. In this way, your product becomes an integral part of your customers' computing systems and services. Yet Netscape sometimes failed to integrate gracefully with the world's principal software systems, particularly Microsoft's, but others as well. Sometimes Netscape also developed its own standards in areas dominated by others while simultaneously neglecting to support important standards that already existed. Thus for example Netscape developed its own standard for so-called directory services, a major function for server software, despite the fact that Novell already possessed an excellent standard and Novell should have been a natural ally against Microsoft. Yet at the same time, Netscape failed to support Microsoft Office standards used by virtually all PC applications. As a result, Netscape's products were unnecessarily isolated and therefore, once again, more easily replaced.

Netscape's defense might be that they didn't have the luxury of hindsight, the way writers of postmortems do. But I'm afraid this doesn't exonerate them. What I've described is precisely the way Microsoft has behaved for years and the way we designed Vermeer's strategy during precisely the same period. Moreover, if you decide to go to war with someone like Microsoft, you should study your opponent enough to understand how it became so powerful and how it might respond to your assault.

HIRING, PERSONNEL, AND MANAGEMENT

Mistakes like Netscape don't happen by themselves. It takes people to foul up a company, and Netscape's problems derive in large part from flawed personnel decisions from the very start, and at the very top. These early errors propagated until they produced a huge organizational, strategic, and engineering fiasco. The problem seems to have started with Jim Clark, who made Netscape's early hiring and organizational decisions. Clark's mistakes may have been related to the fact that his entire business experience had been in the world of high-end UNIX workstations for engineering and graphics, rather than with Windows software and high-volume business markets.

What I find more puzzling, however, is the selection of Jim Barksdale as CEO, which involved not only Clark but also John Doerr of Kleiner Perkins. Doerr, who is now perhaps the most famous venture capitalist in the United States, became a major Netscape investor and board member within weeks of the company's founding. Doerr is brilliant and has an extraordinary depth of experience with Silicon Valley and the technology sector. Although he has made some very large mistakes (GO and 3DO, for example) he has also been spectacularly successful. Doerr has invested in and/or served on the boards of Netscape, Sun, Amazon, @Home, Intuit, Compaq, and Drugstore.com, among others. And while we unfortunately haven't always gotten along, I greatly respect Doerr's insight and strategic abilities. But I think that hiring a nontechnical, big-company CEO for Netscape was a mistake.

At the working level, a casual, or perhaps just misguided, attitude toward technical hiring was evident from the start. In an ambitious software start-up, you should do technical hiring from the top down, starting with rigorously trained, extremely experienced architects, lead programmers, and managers. If, as with Netscape, your original product idea comes from someone who is brilliant but very young, its later commercial implementation requires the addition of disciplined, experienced architecture and management. As you grow, it gradually becomes easier to use less experienced technical people, as Microsoft does, for working-level programming.

But Netscape's very first product development effort, and its key strategic and technical choices, were controlled by a childrens' crusade, headed by Andreessen and his college friends from the NCSA. Clark and Andreessen hired the entire Mosaic team and apparently gave them enormous freedom. There were a few experienced engineers involved in Navigator 1.0, whom Clark brought in from Silicon Graphics. But even they were from the high-end UNIX world, with little or no experience with Windows technology or with competition in Windows-dominated markets. There seems to have been no countervailing force within the company against the choices to write hacker code, to snub the Windows platform and the Windows development tools, and generally to act like students. It's hard to blame the kids, who were too young to know what they didn't know. But Clark made a mistake there.

The most serious element of this mistake was making Marc Andreessen the chief technology officer of Netscape and giving him unchecked power in choosing Netscape's product directions and technologies. Andreessen is brilliant and precocious, but he was only twenty-three and, except for a few months at EIT, he had never even had a job. Andreessen was completely inexperienced in commercial software, and his previous work had given him no understanding of architectural or strategic questions. It astounded me that Netscape's management not only gave him such power, but allowed him to make public statements such as his now-infamous assertion that Windows would be reduced to the status of a badly debugged set of device drivers.

This hiring pattern and psychological approach seem to have persisted throughout the first six months—a lot of young people without extensive Windows development experience. Hiring of experienced senior people seems to have commenced with Rick Schell, who became VP of engineering in the late summer of 1994. He started bringing in experienced people, and he should have known better himself, but he seems to have deferred to Andreessen, and/or decided not to get into a fight with all the kids. Netscape did not really get a serious infusion of adults until after the Collabra acquisition in September 1995. Collabra technical managers gradually took over many of the senior technical management jobs at the company.

But even after Schell arrived, Netscape continued another mistake: the pace at which they hired people, including developers, was far too aggressive. You simply can't choose and integrate good people that fast; even in the Internet industry, there are natural limits to the rate at which a start-up organization can grow. (Another famous maxim of Fred Brooks from *The Mythical Man-Month*: "Adding manpower to a late software project makes it later.") Surely, Barksdale and Schell had to know that hiring engineers wasn't the same as multiplying FedEx telephone operators. Somehow they apparently decided that raw growth was paramount. As a result, they ended up in a wild tangle and threw away most of the huge lead that they initially possessed.

Ultimately, of course, responsibility for Netscape's performance belongs to its CEO and to the board that selected him and structured Netscape's top management team. Jim Barksdale might have been up to the job if Clark and Doerr had surrounded him with superb, experienced technologists—especially a chief architect, someone like Eric Schmidt (who might also have made an excellent CEO). But Netscape never filled that position.

BARKSDALE AS AN EXAMPLE OF THE NONTECHNICAL PROFESSIONAL CEO PROBLEM

I think Jim Barksdale is a decent, intelligent man who did not understand what he was getting himself into until it was too late. When I walked into his office in mid-1998 to interview him for this book, I was stunned at how much he had aged since I'd last seen him three years before. In that instant, I felt for the man. The effects of severe chronic stress were painfully evident, and since I had felt them myself, I knew what they could do. To his credit he had hung in there when things got rough, rather than retiring to Hawaii. But he was responsible for many of Netscape's problems, and in our meeting he once again showed the odd lack of perspective I'd come to associate with him. He started the meeting by telling me that he had just been to a wedding in Seattle where he had seen all his *friends at Microsoft,* among them Nathan Myhrvold. These friends were executives of the company that had been destroying Netscape by using, according to his personal testimony in the antitrust case, a wide array of illegal and unethical practices. It was an odd way to begin.

When I first met Barksdale in 1995, I had wanted badly to discover that the CEO of Netscape was able to keep up with Gates, so that I could negotiate an alliance with him or sell my company to him in good conscience. Instead I found him to be rather typical of nontechnical professional CEOs. First, he overvalued smoothness and charm relative to doing the right thing. Second, he had been managing traditional companies for too long and I suspect had become habituated to deference and the absence of overt conflict. I wonder about his tolerance for extremely smart, aggressive people who knew more than he did and dared to criticize him. This may partially account for the intellectual vacuum at the top of Netscape, at least in comparison with Microsoft and Intel.

But third, and perhaps most important, Barksdale lacked a deep understanding of technology and how pervasively it affects not only engineering choices per se but also organization, strategy, management, and hiring in high technology firms. He may also have suffered from the common disease of thinking that technology is a commodity—any time you need some, you can simply order it, like stationery. Along with many people in the industry, I have come to believe that to be a good high technology CEO, you must have a deep respect for, and understanding of, technology itself. I wish more venture capitalists and boards of directors understood this. On the other hand, I'm painfully aware that given my behavior at Vermeer, I'm in no position to give anyone lectures about how to choose good CEOs. It is a truly hard problem.

Technology Assessment, Licensing, Alliances, and Acquisitions

As soon as Netscape did its IPO, it could afford almost anything it wanted—people, technology, companies. Stock-based acquisitions have become a common technique for technology acquisition and market coverage; Cisco wrote the book on making adroit acquisitions with high-priced stock, and Microsoft has made its share. A similar strategy made a lot of sense for Netscape. And Netscape indeed made a considerable number of acquisitions beginning shortly after its IPO.

Unfortunately, with a few exceptions (such as Kiva, which developed high-performance Web application servers, acquired in late 1997), Netscape's acquisitions didn't make sense. Furthermore, Netscape failed to acquire several companies that could have enormously strengthened its position. Netscape's first major acquisition was Collabra, a groupware company acquired in September 1995. The Collabra acquisition is sometimes portrayed as successful because most of its engineers remained with Netscape and several executives joined Netscape's top management. But Collabra's product was based on pre-Internet proprietary systems and was incompatible with the Internet, so Netscape had to throw it away and start over from scratch. Indeed, Collabra was willing to sell in part because it feared that the Internet would destroy its business. In effect, Netscape got a few executives and some good engineers for $100 million. Perhaps not highly destructive, but a bit on the expensive side. Other deals ended much the same way. They were either thrown away or people wasted a lot of time trying to glue together products that didn't quite fit. For example, two small acquisitions were apparently the basis of Netscape's abortive tools effort.

Far more damning, however, are the acquisitions Netscape *didn't* make. The two acquisitions they certainly should have made were RealNetworks and Vermeer Technologies. Either one would have given Netscape proprietary technologies that would have greatly complicated Microsoft's cloning efforts and improved Netscape's strategic, technical, and financial position. If Netscape had purchased *both* of them, or even developed close alliances with them, it would probably dominate the Internet software industry today.

RealNetworks developed the first successful commercial software for sending audio over the Internet in 1995, then developed similar systems for video, and until recently it dominated these markets. It distributes both a player that runs within a browser and a server that manages audio and video files, analogously to the way a Web server manages Web pages. Anyone can download a free low-end version of the player over the Web, and the audio player now has a huge installed base—about thirty million users.

RealNetworks also developed proprietary technology that greatly enhanced "streaming" performance—managing the flow of Internet packets to maintain a realistic audio and video flow. If Netscape had purchased RealNetworks and integrated its technology into its own browsers and servers, it would have held a major competitive advantage over Microsoft, and one difficult for Microsoft to clone. However, this opportunity was lost when Microsoft bought an equity stake in RealNetworks, licensed its technology, and then developed its own player, which is now integrated with the IE browser. Rob Glaser perhaps thought that as an ex-Microsoft executive, he'd be treated differently from other Microsoft licensees. Dumb. Microsoft is now in the process of destroying RealNetworks through techniques virtually identical to those used against Netscape. It will take a while, but I would be surprised if Microsoft loses. As a technology executive once said to me, a partnership agreement with Microsoft is like a Nazi nonaggression pact—it just means you're next. But if Netscape had gotten to RealNetworks first, and protected its intellectual property, things would be different.

The logic for Netscape's acquiring Vermeer was roughly the same as that for acquiring RealNetworks. We had a year's head start on both Microsoft and Netscape in the market for end-user authoring tools and had applied for several valuable patents (several of which have now been issued to Microsoft). Netscape could have directly integrated FrontPage technology into Netscape browsers and servers and distributed FrontPage server extensions for competitors' servers, creating a powerful, industrywide Netscape standard—which is precisely what Microsoft is now doing. In addition, we would have given them a PC and Mac Web server, with integrated FrontPage server extensions, that they could have sold, distributed free, and/or integrated with their browser. FrontPage-Netscape Web servers and server extensions could have become the standard Web server API on all Windows PCs.

I don't know why Netscape never did a deal with RealNetworks or whether Glaser ever approached Netscape. Nor do I fully understand why Netscape didn't understand the value of buying us. Barksdale's own explanation was unconvincing. It was clear that he was edgy about the subject. He told me that he hadn't wanted to enter a bidding war with Microsoft, since any price would be "micenuts" to Gates. He also said to me, "You were so hard on me about how dumb we were to not understand the value of this thing . . . I had had a terribly long day doing a bunch of other stuff. And I just felt like I was being beaten up on it. I know that wasn't your intent. But after a while I said, 'Damn! I don't want to mess with this guy.'" Here I am completely unsympathetic. I had had some long days myself, but I still sold Vermeer on the basis of what made sense, not whom I liked talking to (Greg Maffei isn't a frequent dinner guest). Furthermore, as I saw it, and events have borne me out, they were heading into combat without a helmet. I was trying to warn Barksdale that Netscape was about to get shot to pieces, and he wasn't listening.

In the final analysis, however, better acquisition decisions *alone* would not have done Netscape much good. The profile of Netscape's acquisition activity once again suggests that Barksdale, Andreessen, and the company didn't have a clue about architectural strategy. In all likelihood, if they *had* acquired Real-Networks or Vermeer, they would have posted all the RealAudio specifications on their Web site, not bothered to manage their proprietary interfaces, and let Microsoft clone their technologies. Foolish acquisition decisions were just a symptom, albeit a major one, of deeper problems.

Finally, one of Netscape's most mysterious and self-destructive obsessions concerned Java. First, Netscape endorsed Java and licensed it from Sun; fair enough. Then Andreessen and others began proclaiming that browsers with Java spelled the end of Microsoft. Around the same time, in the fall of 1995, Netscape purchased and developed Java technologies in an attempt to compete with Sun, which not only alienated Netscape's principal natural ally but risked fragmenting the Java standard. Thus Netscape's outrage when Sun licensed Java to Microsoft was more than slightly hypocritical.

More important, however, Netscape simply should not have placed such enormous importance, both publicly and internally, on this technology. As I mentioned earlier, Java technology was immature, and trying to use it to rewrite the browser was severely irrational. Netscape also invested heavily in creating Navio, a joint venture that was intended to develop Java technology for so-called thin clients, palm-top systems, and other non-Windows computing devices. All of this constituted a serious diversion of time, energy, and money from Netscape's real problems and opportunities. The source of this appears to have been Andreessen. Barksdale, of course, was incapable of judging the technical issues. It remains a mystery, however, why Netscape's engineering organization, which by 1996 included not only Rick Schell but also several experienced technical managers from Collabra, did not steer the company back to reality.

ATTITUDE AND STYLE

In the press, and in the antitrust suit against Microsoft, Netscape is often portrayed as the victim of a predatory bully. In the large-scale context of the industry, this is true. But it is hard to sympathize. Until recently, Netscape was one of the most arrogant companies in Silicon Valley history, which is saying quite a lot. The consensus of almost every company that tried to deal with Netscape was that it was insufferably unpleasant and unhelpful. Microsoft can be insufferable as well, but its arrogance is grounded in real achievement, and there is surprisingly little of it relative to the company's power. In Netscape's case, the arrogance was baseless and cost them dearly. They alienated many people and companies eager to help them, and their incessant public denigration of Microsoft drew a reaction that was faster and more vicious than otherwise would have been the case. In addition, Netscape's attitude toward Microsoft alienated many potential customers, who correctly viewed Netscape's behavior as immature and potentially indicative that the company would not prove to be a reliable supplier.

Netscape's arrogance also fostered a pervasive intellectual laziness. If you think you're automatically superior, you don't think, period. Consequently, Netscape never ran scared, even after Microsoft's Pearl Harbor Day announcements, didn't think ahead about how to save itself, and reacted slowly to

Microsoft's attack. Microsoft started giving away its browser in late 1995, but Netscape refused to do so until early 1998, even though its market share declined precipitously starting in 1996. Amazingly, when Netscape competed with Microsoft for the contract to become AOL's default browser, Netscape insisted on charging AOL ten dollars per copy, when Microsoft had a componentized browser, which Netscape did not, and Microsoft was in effect paying AOL to use it by giving AOL space on the Windows desktop screen. Netscape also failed to befriend and support third-party suppliers, developers, and resellers, behaving as if they should be grateful and honored that Netscape dealt with them at all.

Barksdale and other senior Netscape officials seemed oblivious to the fate that awaited them and spent too much time on outside involvements. Barksdale was an active director of @Home, a cable-based Internet service; he led the formation of Navio, a "thin-client" company later absorbed by Oracle; Barksdale and Doerr formed the Technology Network lobbying organization; and Barksdale became one of the most visible Silicon Valley spokesmen on policy issues, testifying in Congress and giving press conferences. Given the challenges Netscape faced, this was not the way Barksdale should have been spending his time. IBM executives used to behave like this on the way to their company's collapse in 1992.

Netscape also failed to understand the importance of appearing consistent and stable to the industry and to large customers. It developed a pattern of unnecessarily extreme lurching and backtracking. For example, Netscape made a major commitment to the corporate groupware market and developed the Communicator product suite for this reason. But when Netscape introduced Communicator, which included not only a browser but other functions specific to large organizations, it also decided to discontinue distribution of the Navigator browser as a separate product. Netscape hoped to force all customers to buy its expensive, and initially rather bad, e-mail, groupware, calendar, and browser software as a package. This alienated many customers and strategic partners, and Netscape was forced to reverse itself fairly quickly. Similarly, it announced that it was entering the tools market, but didn't deliver products for six months, and then withdrew them shortly afterward. Such decisions reinforced the impression of a company without a strategic compass, moving aimlessly from one decision to the next.

The kindest words I have heard about Netscape came from Eric Schmidt. He reminded me that "there is nothing harder to do than to set up a positive-returns monopoly in the presence of an existing monopoly. It is the hardest business challenge in the world." His point is that Netscape could win only by achieving a virtual monopoly in Internet platform software comparable to Microsoft's monopoly in operating systems. And it had to do so in the teeth of all the weapons that Microsoft naturally derived from its current monopolies. That's an entirely fair comment, and it reminds us what a difficult challenge Netscape faced. But Netscape failed even to understand that they faced it.

MICROSOFT'S COUNTERATTACK AND NETSCAPE'S DECLINE

Microsoft, of course, didn't do everything perfectly either. Its largest mistake was simply being slow to notice Netscape and the Internet generally. It appears that the company had been getting soft. The Internet challenge came at a time when Bill Gates got married in a wedding that sprawled over half of Hawaii. In August 1995, he spent a month touring China in a rented private train with Warren Buffet, accompanied by an entourage of consultants tutoring him in Chinese history, art, and other subjects. He wrote a book and went on a prolonged book tour, built a home only slightly smaller than the Pentagon, and became a media celebrity. In short, he started acting like someone who'd worked insanely hard for twenty years, had accumulated an astronomical fortune, and was starting to relax and smell the roses. When your company has $5 billion or $10 billion in cash and all of your enemies of the past decade are dead, it gets hard to maintain a healthy state of panic.

But once Microsoft woke up, their performance was almost flawless, a textbook example of architectural strategy both in conception and execution. In the half year between Gates's "Internet Tidal Wave" memo of May 1995 and Pearl Harbor Day, he completely redirected Microsoft's focus and strategy, which is no trivial matter for an enormous company. The day after Pearl Harbor Day, they decided to buy us, and then they licensed RealNetworks's technology in order to kill them faster. By the release of Explorer 3.0 in 1996, and certainly by the release of Explorer 4.0 in 1997, Microsoft's browser was at least equal to Netscape's, and in some ways it was substantially superior. Microsoft took full advantage of its Windows monopoly to lock in the browser's competitive position, integrating it into Windows 98 in ways that make Web access from applications like Word and Quicken convenient and transparent for the user. Microsoft also courted major strategic partners aggressively, paying Internet service providers and major Web sites to use and distribute its browser.

One consequence of the Microsoft-Netscape wars was that the confrontation reenergized Microsoft. On the evidence of Microsoft e-mails and internal memos released during the antitrust trial, Gates made the absolute worst case assumptions about Netscape's capabilities and intentions, including the threat that Java and browser-based thin clients might supplant Windows. A more relaxed executive, with as deep an understanding of technology as Gates, would perhaps not have reacted so viciously or exploited his monopolistic position so unrestrainedly. More relaxed executives, of course, don't build companies like Microsoft.

Characteristically, Netscape was very slow to understand how serious a threat Microsoft's counterattack posed, and to react to it. In some areas, it barely reacted at all. Over the subsequent three years, it took a series of defensive steps, always too little and too late, as its market share in both browsers and servers declined continuously. By late 1998, Netscape was in a desperate situation. Its browser no longer provided any revenue, and its server revenues were stagnant at best. Its Netcenter portal was growing, but this business, too, was in serious trouble. Netcenter derived a high fraction of its users from the fact that its home page was the default page displayed every time someone opened the Navigator browser. But Netscape's browser market share, even with a free browser and free source code, was continuing to decline. This would soon force Netcenter into an equal-terms competition with Yahoo!, MSN, and AOL, in which Netscape probably would not have fared well.

I don't know whether a prompt, strong reaction by Netscape after Pearl Harbor Day could have saved the company, or whether it was already too late. Certainly, a forceful response would have prolonged Netscape's life and increased its value. But the contrast between Microsoft's assault on Netscape and Netscape's casual, meandering, and then eventually desperate defense is once again very stark.

THE FUTURE OF NETSCAPE SOFTWARE: MAYBE GOOD FOR SUN, NOT FOR ANYONE ELSE

AOL bought Netscape primarily for its Netcenter portal customers, which were certainly worth something, but it's not clear to me that the acquisition helps AOL very much. While AOL and its partner, Sun Microsystems, have made all the right noises about continuing the Netscape software business, it is highly unlikely that Netscape can remain a viable software company. It is quite possible that Sun will make money from it, because it can effectively bundle Netscape servers with Sun hardware while gradually discontinuing support for Netscape Web servers on rival hardware platforms. But as a force in the Internet software industry, Netscape's days are over.

In the first place, it is difficult to imagine AOL selling software effectively—Netscape's or anyone else's. AOL is a media company. All of AOL's previous software ventures, such as its early browser, or its NaviSoft authoring tools and Web server, were abject failures. In addition, neither AOL nor Sun can be credible as honest broker vendors of Internet software. Many of Netscape's major customers—Internet service providers, other portals, e-commerce sites, and a variety of commercial Web sites—are direct competitors of AOL and will be justifiably extremely wary of becoming dependent upon it. Sun, of course, will not be credible as a software vendor for rival hardware or operating systems.

Finally, Netscape was already a seriously unsettled company for two years before the acquisition, and its integration into AOL and/or Sun will only worsen matters. AOL is headquartered near Washington, D.C., while Netscape is in the middle of the Valley. With Internet software developers at a premium in the Valley, there is already a major exodus of talent from Netscape, particularly because many Netscape employees received a huge payout from the deal and can leave as soon as they are liquid.

Nor will Sun be a hospitable employer or manager for most of Netscape's engineers. Sun is so anti-Microsoft that it even banned Windows machines from company premises. As a consequence, it has little development or marketing experience with Windows products and is not likely to sustain a product line that runs on Windows clients or NT servers. I therefore expect continued fragmentation of the Web server industry, which favors the long-term trend toward Microsoft and NT. The gradual decline of UNIX and eventually Sun at the hands of NT will therefore continue, so that while Sun will remain profitable for another five years or so, it will gradually cease to be a major force in the industry. And the period during which Netscape software shaped the Internet industry is definitely over.

Thus, my conclusion concerning the competition between Netscape and Microsoft would be the following. First, if Netscape had managed itself effectively from the beginning, it probably could have survived and even flourished as an independent company, albeit one constantly fighting a very tough, smart, ruthless competitor. Second, given Netscape's actual behavior, Microsoft's victory was virtually preordained—at least if Microsoft could make its browser and server free, could integrate them into its operating systems, and could pay users to switch. Given how incompetent Netscape was, I think that only very severe constraints on Microsoft's conduct could have preserved Netscape's long-term viability. However, this does not exonerate Microsoft, nor does it imply that Microsoft's power poses no threat to the technology sector. On the contrary, the failure of Netscape's challenge, whatever its causes, only makes the Microsoft question more pressing. But Netscape's extraordinary record of technical and managerial bumbling suggests that the inquest verdict must be that Netscape died by its own hand.

Netscape's self-immolation had effects far beyond its own organization. If Netscape had been able to establish itself as the Microsoft of Internet software, or even maintained a fragile leadership of Internet software standards, it would have disciplined Microsoft in important ways. Microsoft's abuse of its operating systems position would have been curtailed, because Netscape would have had reciprocal leverage over Microsoft and users would be able to run industry standard (Netscape) Internet software on non-Microsoft operating systems and Web servers. Furthermore, Netscape's strength would have protected and nurtured a wider independent Internet software industry, enabling firms such as Vermeer, RealNetworks, and others to survive in the face of Microsoft attacks. Netscape would have encouraged start-ups to challenge Microsoft and supported the further development of Linux. And, as technologies and applications continued to arise, Netscape would have supported Microsoft's rivals, rather than Microsoft, in their commercialization. (As we shall see, a similar result could probably be obtained if Microsoft were broken up along technological and product lines by an antitrust judgment.) Over time, Netscape would have inevitably loosened Microsoft's grip on the world—perhaps enough to make antitrust action unnecessary, perhaps not. But it is quite clear that with Netscape's death, a whole industry died with it, almost before it was born. Now, the only significant challenges to Microsoft's power in software come from the game and palm-top markets, and even there Microsoft could obtain a dominant position.

Thus, with the death of Netscape, Microsoft must be declared the winner in current Internet software markets. Interestingly, Microsoft is the only major incumbent to hold a strong position; Oracle, Sybase, SAP, and others have not become significant forces in Web servers or Web-based applications. Microsoft seems to have the field to itself, with the possible exception of IBM and Sun's Netscape software business. However, in novel applications, Web-based services, and electronic commerce infrastructure, the situation is less clear. Indeed, in these areas I would invert my conclusion regarding Netscape and say that unless Microsoft is permitted to play very dirty indeed, it is unlikely to dominate the major Web services and electronic commerce markets. However, for reasons I will discuss later, the risk that Microsoft *will* play dirty is very real and deserves more attention than it has received.

Thus, I now turn to the most obvious question raised by the death of Netscape: Microsoft. The Microsoft question is a difficult and nuanced one, with no demonstrably correct answer. On balance, the evidence suggests strongly that Microsoft is too powerful, has abused its power, and needs to be curbed. Legal sanctions on Microsoft, including forced divestiture and a prohibition on entering Web content businesses, are therefore justified—as long as they are designed intelligently, which unfortunately is not to be taken for granted. For one thing, and as with the Netscape question, some of the most important issues related to the Microsoft issue are rarely discussed and have not played any official role in the Justice Department's antitrust case.

CHAPTER TEN

The Microsoft Question

Power tends to corrupt; absolute power corrupts absolutely.
—*Lord Acton*

One more such victory, and we are lost.
—*Pyrrhus*

*A*t this writing in mid-1999, Microsoft has about $30 billion in revenues, $10 billion in profits, more than $20 billion in cash, and the highest market capitalization of any company in the world. Even if its growth rate slows dramatically, Microsoft will be a $75 billion company less than a decade into the twenty-first century. And, as the preceding narrative I hope has made clear, Microsoft now casts a shadow over the entire technology sector. Once the most admired of companies, Microsoft has become widely reviled, in part because of its conduct against Netscape and its behavior in the Justice Department's antitrust case. Here, I will argue that Microsoft's power has become so great, its behavior so unrestrained, and its abuses so dangerous that intelligent and decisive government intervention is now justified to prevent serious damage to users, the industry, and even the entire economy.

The word *intelligent*, however, is a very important qualifier, and in the antitrust arena, not one to be taken for granted. Microsoft should not be dismembered casually. In the current uproar against Microsoft, it is easy to neglect the great contributions it has made, contributions that could be easily destroyed by sufficiently foolish government policy. If Microsoft had never existed, the technology sector would have remained a much worse place, and if we're careless it could become that way again.

In what follows, I first describe the innovative model Microsoft created and some of the enormous benefits it has generated. I analyze its current monopolies, potential future monopolies, and its use and abuse of monopoly power. I then analyze the risks and benefits of alternative policy measures. I recommend that Microsoft be broken up along technological and product lines, while rejecting as extremely dangerous the so-called Baby Bills proposal advocated by Netscape, Sun, and Gary Reback. I also comment on the rather disastrous state of the antitrust system, a problem I explore further in the final chapter of the book.

THE MICROSOFT MODEL

Microsoft is justifiably criticized for its lack of technological vision and innovation, but is given too little credit for its innovations in strategy and organization. The Microsoft model, which is essentially an internalized version of the Silicon Valley industrial model, is a major contribution to management, perhaps on a par with the lean-production manufacturing model created in postwar Japan. The creation of the Microsoft model alone secures Bill Gates a place in the pantheon of American business geniuses.

At the level of broad strategy, Microsoft competes by establishing and controlling industry standards, and relatedly by commoditizing the businesses of others. It develops products by licensing, acquiring, or copying the innovations of others and commercializing them in the form of high-volume industry standard platforms, with proprietary but usually externally accessible APIs. It takes great care to ensure that its products run equally well on many competing hardware platforms. This not only provides for standardization and compatibility, but simultaneously forces the computer systems industry into an unending cycle of fierce commodity competition based on price and performance, rather than any proprietary or architectural advantage. Not surprisingly, Microsoft takes great care never to become dependent upon others' proprietary architectures or intellectual property. Microsoft's licensing of Java from Sun in 1995 was a rare exception, and it should have surprised no one that Microsoft would immediately create its own variant of Java, with Windows-specific features under its proprietary control.

Microsoft was not the first to employ architectural strategies in high technology; IBM did it quite impressively in its mainframe business in the 1960s and 1970s. But no company, not even Intel or IBM in its heyday, has employed architectural strategy with the brilliance, clarity, or ruthlessness of Gates. Microsoft's model follows well-defined steps, which are no less impressive for being predictable: First, create or acquire at least adequate software to attack a market opportunity of interest, and steadily improve it. Cut prices to drive out competition. Turn the product into a platform that covers the entire market space, with APIs to attract third-party developers and supporting products. Leverage relationships with Microsoft's neighboring, preexisting platform monopolies to broaden and deepen penetration and control over the market space. Start with comparatively simple products for low-price, high-volume markets, then enhance them over time in order to reach higher-priced, higher-margin markets, as Microsoft is doing now with server operating systems and database software. Conquer additional markets created by interesting third-party point products, by entering these markets with products preferentially linked to Microsoft's platform. Steadily expand into adjoining spaces, e.g., for applications dependent on the platform. Repeat the process as new markets arise.

This is the strategy that Microsoft has followed almost to perfection starting with DOS and the transition to Windows, Windows and the rise of Office, Windows and NT, and with the linkages between NT, Web servers, and BackOffice. Now, Microsoft is repeating this process with Windows, NT, and Office in conjunction with both BackOffice and its entire Internet software suite (the IE browser, FrontPage, Visual InterDev, the FrontPage/Office server extensions, and Web servers). Microsoft has also initiated strategically similar efforts in palm-top, set-top, and other consumer devices, as well as in Web-based content and electronic commerce services.

Microsoft has already obtained at least three monopolies through this strategy (DOS, Windows, Office) and takes enormous profits from them. One can argue that these stunningly high profits represent a loss to consumers, and there is some truth to this. Far more important and beneficial for consumers, however, Microsoft has also created a compatible PC and server hardware industry. It has attempted to stay clear of hardware dependencies, ranging from the original IBM Personal Computer to current palm-top devices, and striven to ensure that its software works equally well on many vendors' hardware systems.

In fact, Microsoft actively promotes the commoditization of computer hardware. It supports not only Intel but also Intel's competitors and clones; since the early 1980s it has supported not only IBM's PCs but clones and rivals such as Compaq and Dell. Now Microsoft is doing the same thing with server hardware. As new hardware functions arise, Microsoft, often in cooperation with Intel and/or a group of PC vendors, seeks to standardize them in a nonproprietary way. This prevents hardware vendors from exerting countervailing power against Microsoft and also prevents them from insulating themselves from competition against one another. This benefits Microsoft, but it also has huge benefits for consumers: Microsoft ensures that the computer industry will be ruthlessly competitive and at the same time will display a high degree of interoperability. Everyone's floppy disks, CD-ROMs, software applications, memory chips, PCMCIA cards, modems, microprocessors, network connections, and printers work equally well with everybody else's machines. This is not to be taken for granted.

As testimony in the antitrust case has made clear, Microsoft not only controls the PC industry but has even forced Andrew Grove and Intel to dance to Gates's tune for the past decade, far more than the other way around. (Intel wasn't happy about it: at one conference at which I spoke, when Grove and Gates shared the podium, Grove referred to Gates as "His Majesty" in front of two hundred executives.) The problem for public policy, of course, is that Microsoft has sometimes used its leverage with PC vendors as a predatory tool against software rivals—for example, in its war against Netscape.

At the same time, with minor exceptions, Microsoft has avoided entering hardware businesses itself. In a similar fashion, Microsoft does not directly distribute its own software on the mass market, but exercises strong leverage over retail distribution and sales channels, working to keep them fragmented and powerless.

One frequent criticism advanced against Microsoft is that the company is not a technological innovator. This is correct, but innovation is not necessarily central to Microsoft's value (or lack thereof), which lies in its role in organizing the entire industry. Microsoft has been compared to Rockefeller's Standard Oil in the scope of its monopoly power, and there is some justification in this. However, there is another parallel from the same era that is equally accurate and relevant: J. P. Morgan. Morgan was a tough guy, and not without his problems, but he brought badly needed order to a chaotic, unstable financial system and to industries such as railroads. Microsoft has played a similar role in the personal computer and server industries through standard setting, and by exercising this function Microsoft has provided gigantic economic benefits.

Microsoft is also the world's first mass-market software company—there has never really been another one—and its strategies are appropriate to that objective. Procter & Gamble, FedEx, and Wal-Mart don't invent any revolutionary products, either; it's not what they're about. But although Microsoft doesn't compete primarily on technological grounds, Gates has a deep respect for technology and technical expertise. In a technology-intensive industry, he understands the need for a technologically deep top management, not just for product development and purely technical choices, but for strategy, organizational decisions, and marketing as well. This was a crucial insight on his part that many others still fail to grasp.

Microsoft's organization is an internalization of the structure of the Silicon Valley start-up sector—a corporate structure that I have called the "Silicon Valley model." Although elements of the Silicon Valley system developed simultaneously in the semiconductor industry and elsewhere, Gates grasped it early, and he has pushed it the furthest. In earlier chapters, I described the concept of well-architected software. A complex program is disaggregated into many small modules, each operating relatively independently of the others, but with cleanly defined interfaces within a clear overall technical specification. The architecture of FrontPage, as I said, was a good example; that of Netscape's browser, a bad one. Well-architected software is easy to maintain, repair, and enhance as needs arise. Individual modules can be upgraded—say, to accommodate new generations of hardware devices—without affecting any of the others.

Well, it turns out that the same issues arise in companies and industries. The first place to exhibit the Silicon Valley model was Silicon Valley itself, an entire industry composed of companies specializing in an architecturally defined market and related to one another accordingly. In the case of a company producing architected products, the architecture of the company should mirror the architectures of its products.

Microsoft was among the first companies to apply this model systematically to its internal organization and to the strategic management of an entire industry. This allows many product teams to work with great independence but within a shared, clearly defined specification of both technology and high-level strategy. It has enabled Microsoft to maintain an extraordinary level of productivity and flexibility for a company that now employs more than thirty thousand people, with minimum overhead and bureaucracy and extreme geographic concentration in Redmond. To a remarkable degree, Microsoft is still a meritocracy and is perceived as such by its employees. Consequently, there is relatively little of the highly dysfunctional internal politics that for years crippled decision-making companies like Apple and Lotus, and which causes problems even at Sun and Oracle. The relative lack of destructive politics is partly a consequence of the powerful presence of Gates himself at the top of the company. As Chris Peters once remarked, nobody at Microsoft thinks they're smarter than Bill Gates, and nobody thinks they, or anyone else they know, could do a better job of running the company. After a few months at Microsoft, Randy told me the same thing.

The loyalty of Microsoft's employees has been easier to retain, of course, with heavily stock-weighted compensation and a stock that has been rising stratospherically over a prolonged period of time. All those overworked young engineers and marketing managers know that if they hang in there and put up with the pressure, they'll get rich. It's a mixed blessing; many people get rich enough to leave after only five years, and now that Microsoft is a large company, recruiting and retaining people is getting harder. Microsoft hires primarily at the entry level, especially for engineers, and promotes almost entirely from within; its business managers almost always have a strong engineering background. While the commitment to internal promotion is undoubtedly good for morale, Microsoft may have overdone it. For example, its prolonged neglect of the Web and the Internet suggest a company that had become ingrown and insular. More mid-level and high-level management hiring from outside, especially of people with start-up experience and recent advanced degrees in computer science, would probably help.

Microsoft has also evolved a unique software development model, one that is quite consciously adapted to its mass-market, standard-setting competitive strategy. The best-practice software development model for ambitious start-ups, and the one we used at Vermeer, is quite different. We relied heavily on top-flight senior engineers and used an engineering team that was far more experienced, and market-sensitive, than most of Microsoft's engineers. Lacking Microsoft's infrastructure and developing a visionary product for a highly novel market, we needed to move lightning fast while still remaining extremely flexible, without the luxuries of massive infrastructural support. Thus we needed engineers who deeply understood what the product should do and what kind of business and competitive environment it would be selling into. The senior engineers played a major role in specifying the product, and we changed that specification more, and later in the development process, than Microsoft can afford to.

Gates has developed quite a different system. The evolution of Microsoft's engineering system in part reflects Gates's dropout hacker origins; in part, it reflects the need to become a huge organization with literally hundreds of millions of customers. Gates was correct in concluding that neither start-up methods nor conventional methods for managing large software efforts (the "megaproject" techniques pioneered by IBM and U.S. defense contractors) would scale well enough for Microsoft's requirements. There is probably also a lingering distaste for making concessions to the technically inept—i.e., most end-users. At the same time, Gates realized that the company had to jettison its earlier "testosterone-based development" style in which young, smart, arrogant, but inexperienced developers made virtually all important decisions themselves, often with disastrous results. (Like in the early Netscape . . .) The tangled code that still haunts DOS and Windows dates from that era.

The new Microsoft development model continues the heavy reliance on extremely bright but young and inexperienced engineers. It then surrounds them with an elaborate infrastructure to fix, prevent, or at least mitigate their mistakes. The model is becoming quite disciplined and formalized. For each product, a small number of program managers develop specifications, and a rigorous but time-consuming planning process integrates specifications, engineering schedules, and product launch, including such matters as manuals, books, packaging, and national language translations. Code is written by development teams composed mostly of young engineers with little say in specifications, but who are supervised by experienced managers who are former software engineers. In fact, Microsoft development managers generally still spend half their time writing code, to keep in touch.

Direct engineering is supported by two testing groups—usabililty testing, and a huge traditional testing organization for quality assurance. Most Microsoft system software efforts use at least one tester per developer (in contrast, Vermeer's ratio was about one to four). Microsoft also tries to compensate for the inexperience and technical bias of its young engineers by having them observe and participate in elaborate usability analyses, including extensive consumer testing, as well as other exercises such as forcing engineers to answer customer support lines. (Speaking as a user, I would say that these techniques have produced only mixed results . . . but the effort is clearly serious.) There is also a very impressive product release infrastructure to manage documentation, production of books, manuals, training programs, and national language adaptations. When that infrastructure works well, as it has with Microsoft Front-Page, its efficiency and comprehensiveness are simply awesome. Relative to start-ups, it delays development by about six months, but then greatly accelerates product launch and global market availability (it takes start-ups six to eighteen months longer than Microsoft to internationalize their products, acquire high-volume distribution channels, and cover the world market).

Developing and marketing software on the Microsoft scale was a wholly new problem. Nobody had ever really done it before—the only other company that came close was Lotus, which peaked at about 25 million spreadsheet users in the late 1980s, and whose internal organization was a mess, to put it gently. So Gates and Microsoft deserve enormous credit for creating an obviously workable model for the industry. It's far from perfect, however, and unless development efforts are led by unusually good people, the system tends to produce mediocre products. This ought to be fixed, because it isn't necessary. By all reports, for example, Peter Amstein did a spectacular job on Microsoft's new consumer graphics product.

There are signs that Gates and Microsoft have realized that there is a problem here and are trying to fix it through increased reliance on corporate acquisitions, hiring experienced development managers, and trying to hire people who have good taste as well as technical skills. But Microsoft has never been big on good taste, and people without it cannot easily choose people who have it. The Vermeer acquisition was in some ways unusual, the result of choices made by a few farsighted people, especially Chris Peters. It was also one of the few times that Microsoft has bought both a visionary product and a mature engineering team. In this case, however, Microsoft did keep the team intact and did not force Vermeer into the Microsoft development mode. On the other hand, I doubt that Microsoft will soon, or perhaps ever, be widely known for developing innovative, truly superlative products. If your corporate goal is to produce the white bread that 90 percent of the population uses in their sandwiches, reliability and consistency may be more important than vision.

The more serious problem for Microsoft may be in the size and complexity of its systems. Windows is getting awfully big and still crashes more than I would like; even Word displays some rather curious and sometimes dangerous behavior. Yet Microsoft is trying to scale upward to extremely complex, mission-critical server systems, which must also be highly reliable. For example, Microsoft's delays in delivering NT 5.0 (now called Windows 2000, perhaps optimistically) have stretched into years. Software is still, at bottom, a craft that depends upon people, and with increasing size and complexity, software products and companies are permanently at risk of falling into a hopeless snarl. Microsoft has not managed this problem as carefully as I think it should have, in part because of its financial incentives favoring upgrade cycling, an issue I discuss below.

There are early signs of Microsoft drifting into the behavior that seems eventually to infect all dominant firms, as it claimed IBM, the old AT&T, and still seems to grip the likes of General Motors. Quite unlike IBM's founding dynasty, the Watsons, Gates really is a technologist and has a great appreciation of the implications of technology for organizational structure and strategic decision making. But the harbingers of excessive complexity and bureaucracy are certainly there. Gates's heir apparent, Steve Ballmer, is an MBA and a salesman rather than an engineer. Few people think that any of Microsoft's senior managers have Gates's stature, and he won't be able to keep everything in his head forever. I have begun to hear of good people screwed by political middle managers and human resources bureaucrats.

The inevitable onset of sclerosis might be the strongest argument for a breakup of Microsoft. History indicates that the monopoly power of dominant firms lasts far longer than their technical and managerial efficiency—as my economist friend Joe Farrell has put it, monopolists who control industry standards have a great deal of excess momentum. Before considering the arguments for curbing Microsoft, however, I will discuss the benefits Microsoft has brought to the industry, and why they should be preserved.

IN PARTIAL PRAISE OF MICROSOFT

Praising Microsoft is now politically incorrect. Microsoft has always been the company that antiauthoritarian technologists love to hate, although as with

IBM thirty years ago, these attitudes have so far had no effect on the company's growth. For a number of reasons I too believe that on balance the costs of an unconstrained Microsoft are beginning to outweigh the benefits, and that the trade-off will continue to worsen.

At the same time, we should be clear on what an enormously positive force Microsoft has been throughout its existence and in many respects continues to be—for the computer industry, for the advance of technology, and for the consumers. Many of the benefits Microsoft has provided are a side effect of its greed or are unglamorous, so they are not widely discussed. But they are enormous, probably totaling hundreds of billions of dollars over Microsoft's history. Microsoft should be constrained or disassembled only in such a way that these benefits are left largely intact. The major proposed antitrust remedies vary widely in the degree to which they meet this requirement. Thus, it is worth understanding precisely what's going on here.

First and foremost, Microsoft has reshaped the personal computer industry, and more recently the server industry as well. The world's personal computer users tend to take for granted the open, neatly layered, highly compatible structure of the PC industry—many hardware and software companies competing ferociously within the open "Wintel" (Windows plus Intel) standard. In fact, however, the personal computer industry was the first generation of computing that had this structure. Like the proprietary online services industry, all previous computer markets—mainframes, minicomputers, UNIX servers—were dominated by an oligopoly of closed architectures, with proprietary hardware and software combinations supplied by vertically integrated firms. This could have occurred in the personal computer industry as well; in fact, a conservative forecaster might have predicted this until the mid-1980s or even later. Prior to the rise of pure clones and the Windows standard, it appeared that the industry could easily be an oligopoly dominated by the tightly closed Macintosh standard on the one hand and a technically retrograde IBM-controlled industry on the other. In fact, that's what the PC industry was like until the late 1980s in the United States, and such a structure persisted in Japan until the mid-1990s, when proprietary Japanese systems gave way to Windows. The server industry initially took the same path, as hardware vendors such as Sun, Hewlett-Packard, and Silicon Graphics developed their own proprietary variants of UNIX.

In every case, this vertically integrated and oligopolistic structure reduced the intensity of competition, facilitated tacit collusion in pricing, and substantially reduced both scale economies and the rate of technological progress. This regime also drastically reduced compatibility, interoperability, and therefore everyone's ability to communicate with everyone else. Yet IBM and Apple both sought to impose this structure upon the personal computer industry—Apple through Macintosh, and IBM through a series of fiascos such as the OS/2 operating system and the MicroChannel Architecture, happily now forgotten.

Microsoft was a major force in preventing this outcome and creating a level playing field in which IBM had to fight it out along with everyone else, because PC software ran identically and equally well on everyone's machines. To be sure, Microsoft was not alone in promoting this result; Intel and Compaq helped greatly. So did IBM's stunning incompetence, which prevented it from achieving the dangerous level of architectural control it could have obtained if it had behaved intelligently. But Microsoft was a major force in defeating both IBM and Apple, and the primary driver from the software side of the equation.

More recently, the same firms—Microsoft, Intel, Compaq, and to some extent others such as Dell—have been playing a similar role in the restructuring of the server industry, with Intel-based NT servers taking market share from the proprietary UNIX systems. In this effort, however, there is a split between Microsoft and the hardware vendors. Microsoft promotes NT, of course, while Intel and the hardware systems vendors seek not only to displace UNIX but to contain Microsoft's increasing power by promoting Linux, the freeware variant of UNIX that runs on nearly all Intel-based hardware. Even counting Microsoft's desire to destroy Linux, however, Microsoft's role in the server industry is at this point still, on a net basis, highly positive, because it disciplines both the incumbent UNIX server sector and the insurgent vendors of Intel-based hardware. As a result, the entire server industry must fight a brutal commodity battle based upon price and performance, which maximizes technological progress in hardware.

Furthermore, by standardizing operating systems and hardware architectures, but permitting wide variations in the details both of hardware underneath and applications software above, Microsoft has vastly improved compatibility and simplified hardware and software development. The vendors of applications for UNIX servers must port their software to each proprietary UNIX variant, whereas all versions of NT-based systems are essentially identical. Similar statements hold for vendors of PC applications software and peripheral hardware systems such as modems, printers, and so forth. This is not to say that either the Wintel PC standard or NT server standards are perfect, or complete. They're not; for many reasons, sometimes including mistakes by Intel and Microsoft, things are still, in some ways, quite messy. But what many PC users (and even people working in the industry, not to mention certain antitrust authorities) may not realize is that things could easily be much worse, and that in fact it is in the interest of the hardware systems vendors to *make* them worse.

Moreover, even within the software industry, Microsoft's effects are far from universally bad. Despite their frequent tendency toward mediocrity and bugginess, Microsoft's PC software products are generally serviceable, not consistently worse than those of vanquished competitors such as Lotus 1-2-3 or WordPerfect, and sometimes better. And at the corporate level, Lotus and WordPerfect largely deserved their fate; they had mismanaged both their technology and strategy to an appalling degree. In fact, Lotus probably got more than it deserved as a result of its high-priced acquisition by IBM.

Finally, there is no question that Microsoft has dramatically lowered the price of software in a way that none of the other major application software companies would have done on their own. The Microsoft Office suite preloaded on a PC today sells for less than the price of a single word processing or spreadsheet application in the early 1990s, and it was Microsoft that took the lead both in creating suites and lowering prices.

Microsoft is now having a similar effect on server software. Just as in PCs, Microsoft's assault on corporate servers is exerting strong downward pressure on software prices and margins. NT and its BackOffice application suite, which includes substantial Internet server software and the SQL Server relational database management system, together sell for a few thousand dollars per processor, roughly a tenth the price of a commercial UNIX operating system plus the Oracle database system. Microsoft's products are still functionally behind Oracle's and do not yet scale to very large processors and transaction loads, but the gap is closing and Oracle and others are already feeling pressure.

Furthermore, Microsoft disciplines Intel. Microsoft and Intel also collude in important ways, for example in setting standards that keep the PC hardware industry in line. But out of purest self-interest, Microsoft also seeks to strip Intel of its market power and margins, so it can increase its own prices and margins without affecting total demand. Microsoft's new Windows CE operating system for palm-tops, for example, runs on non-Intel processors, and Microsoft openly works with Intel clone vendors such as AMD and Cyrix. Intel reciprocally tries to discipline Microsoft—for example, via its recent investment in Red Hat Software, the leading Linux vendor—but so far with less success.

Finally, Microsoft is unquestionably quite a good, and fair, employer by technology sector standards, and remarkably so by the standards of large corporations generally. Microsoft is also refreshingly honest with its employees in granting and administering stock options, in sharp contrast to the frequent duplicity found in Silicon Valley start-ups. And, as I mentioned earlier, the company has managed to sustain a visibly less politicized, more meritocratic management and promotion system than any of its major competitors. Developers, in particular, enjoy working at Microsoft, and many of them stay long after they are multimillionaires.

Taken together, the benefits of Microsoft's success over its history have thus been enormous. I suspect that their cumulative effect up to the present has been highly positive, with the benefits of standardization and hardware industry competition far outweighing the negative consequences of Microsoft's pronounced tendency to engage in predatory behavior. In the corporate server market, moreover, the benefits of Microsoft's pressuring the industry toward less expensive, commoditized hardware and software are just beginning to show themselves.

That is quite a creditable record. So why is it time to rein in the company? In the rest of this chapter, I will examine this question. I consider the nature of Microsoft's current monopoly power and where it may exercise monopolies in the future. I examine Microsoft's use of monopoly power, the damage it already causes, and the damage likely to flow from the predictable growth of Microsoft's market power. Finally, I discuss the "excess momentum" problem that, in the absence of divestiture, would inevitably afflict the company and the industry in the future as Microsoft's power continued beyond the era of its effectiveness.

MICROSOFT'S CURRENT MONOPOLIES

At the moment, Microsoft possesses two clear monopolies: personal computer operating systems, and office applications—word processors, spreadsheets, databases, and the like—for those same machines. The Justice Department's antitrust case has oddly ignored Microsoft's Office monopoly, which is in some respects more powerful and dangerous than its operating systems position. Ironically, as we shall see, the fact that Microsoft possesses two layered monopolies actually improves the benefits of a divestiture that splits the company technologically. Unfortunately, as we shall also see, this point seems to have been lost on many participants in the case.

First, let's be clear: Microsoft's claims notwithstanding, Windows and Office *are* monopolies. The unit and revenue market share of Windows and DOS-based PC operating systems is now about 95 percent, and their share of the installed base is more than 90 percent. IBM has stopped development of OS/2, the Macintosh is down to about 5-percent market share, and Apple has terminated efforts to sell the Mac OS on non-Apple hardware. Microsoft even owns an equity stake in Apple, has rights to all of Apple's intellectual property, has contractual guarantees that Apple will use Microsoft's IE Web browser, and holds at least 50 percent market share in application software for the Mac. In other words, not only does Apple have a tiny market share, but Microsoft also has Apple by the balls. Other rivals are literally trivial; sales of DR-DOS, various UNIX dialects, and Linux for desktop PC systems are small, and there is little application software available for them.

Microsoft's unit market share in Web browsers is probably at least 60 percent and growing, as Windows 98 rolls over the PC installed base. Microsoft's browser, furthermore, now includes an Internet e-mail client and Microsoft's streaming audio and video player (the Media Player). While RealNetworks still has a larger installed base in streaming audio—the RealAudio player has been downloaded to thirty million users—Microsoft's share of new shipments may be as high as 80 percent, and I think the result of this contest is a foregone conclusion.

In traditional PC applications software, Microsoft Office's share of the installed base is now probably more than 75 percent, and its share of current shipments is more than 90 percent. This will increase to nearly complete domination of the market, in part through the advantages afforded by the Front-Page/Office server extensions in allowing business users to post Office documents to Web servers. The competing office suites offered by Corel (based on WordPerfect) and by IBM/Lotus have only tiny, and declining, market shares and no significant competitive advantage. Adobe still leads in PC graphics and publishing software, but its revenues are essentially flat and its market share is declining, while Microsoft's share is increasing.

Thus we are long past the point at which Microsoft's only source of power is the Windows operating system. I remain surprised that analysts still overlook the very powerful platform position of Office, which is largely closed to outsiders. Intuit, Adobe, and others—including Netscape and Vermeer—would have greatly benefited from access to the facilities and APIs of Office, which include menu systems, scripting functions, and user interfaces. Users could then use any application as an Office application, and applications developers could use standard Office functionalities and develop graceful relations with other Office applications like Excel. But in these respects, Office is closed.

This is not an academic point, and it's also a very personal one. Before Vermeer's acquisition, we explored the issue of integration between FrontPage and Office and found that, while we could have achieved some integration on our own, the most important interfaces were closed to us. When it became clear that Microsoft would build a competitive product if I didn't sell Vermeer, a major factor in my decision was the clear possibility that Microsoft would integrate its product with Office in ways we couldn't match. In the same way, Microsoft now uses the FrontPage server extensions for its own high-end authoring tool, Visual InterDev, and for Office as well. As I argue shortly, a similar process is being repeated in server software with NT and BackOffice. One must expect Microsoft to manage those APIs similarly, closing portions of the platform to other operating systems and applications while using its own privileged access to confer advantages on Microsoft products.

Microsoft's two existing monopolies, PC operating systems and office applications, account for about three quarters of its revenues and an even higher proportion of its profits (perhaps more than 100 percent, since Microsoft is losing money in some areas). Since Microsoft's overall profit margins are extremely high, the margins and profitability of these two businesses must be truly extraordinary. There is no practical possibility of either of these monopolies being overturned in the foreseeable future, at least by the workings of the free market. It would cost billions, probably tens of billions, for a new entrant to develop competitive products and to build the marketing, sales, and support infrastructure to challenge Microsoft in world markets. Even then it would face the certainty of years of losses as it amortized huge fixed costs over an initially tiny market share.

No sensible company would even try this; certainly no start-up would. In word processors and spreadsheets, one can argue that this is no loss to the world. But more important, anyone will think twice before trying it even in *new* applications, if those applications can be logically integrated with either Windows or Office. This is not contradicted by my earlier argument that Netscape could have survived if it had been smarter. While Netscape made enormous mistakes, it also possessed huge advantages that most innovative start-ups do not have: an eighteen-month lead, a dominant market share, and enormous financial resources by start-up standards.

Realistically, therefore, the markets in which Microsoft has established its monopoly are closed to competition, as are new product markets in the same or adjacent competitive and architectural domains. They will remain so at least as long as desktop computers are the primary platform for office applications and Microsoft retains its current corporate structure.

THE COST OF MICROSOFT'S MONOPOLY POWER

Microsoft's assault on PC applications software markets in the early 1990s exerted heavy downward pressure on prices, much to the consumer's benefit. But wherever it has already succeeded in establishing a monopoly, its behavior has been quite different. First, there is strong evidence that Microsoft has more than once manipulated its operating systems, and access to information about them, to damage competitors—e.g., with its alleged use of error messages to discourage use of a DOS clone, DR-DOS, in the early 1990s. Second, it is completely clear that Microsoft has repeatedly used its monopolies as leverage to enter and dominate other areas—online services and Web browsers, for example. Microsoft is also, now, beginning to use its Office monopoly in order to strengthen its position in server software, by linking various Office applications, including Excel and FrontPage, to server applications such as Web servers and the SQL Server database system. Third, the average price of Microsoft's PC operating systems has been increasing continuously and substantially for the last five years, since Windows clearly vanquished the Macintosh and OS/2. Office is just beginning to exhibit the same pattern, with recent high-end versions beginning to move upward in price even as volumes increase and unit costs decline.

Microsoft has defended its pattern of increasing prices for operating systems by pointing to the many new functions that are bundled with the basic OS. There is some truth in this. For example, Internet Explorer replaces a product that in Netscape's hands was originally a $39 retail product and a $10 OEM product. But in the end, Microsoft's defense is nonsense. It made Internet Explorer free primarily in order to destroy Netscape. And personal computers are dozens of times more powerful than a decade ago, but are also much less expensive. While there *are* new functions in Windows, the unit cost of the software has been falling rapidly. Development costs are spread over unit volumes that have increased dramatically, and that continue to increase perhaps 25 percent per year. Microsoft's average costs in marketing, distribution, and sales have also declined sharply. The steady increase in its unit volumes, the conversion from floppy disks to inexpensive CD-ROMs, and the shift toward PC preloading, Internet-based distribution, and high-volume corporate licensing agreements have all been driving down unit costs and driving up margins, for both Windows and Office. In fact, Microsoft's profits have consistently increased much faster than its revenues over the last decade.

But this is not all. Microsoft also uses another technique, the forced upgrade cycling of its installed base, which increases its revenues but imposes huge costs on consumers by forcing them to replace their hardware more frequently than necessary. Clearly, the rapid progress of computer hardware technology helps ease the pain of the high rate of obsolescence Microsoft creates, but there is considerable pain nonetheless. The pace of updates and sheer number of new features results in the often bug-ridden bloatware that consumers and businesses are forced into accepting.

With each new round of operating systems or applications updates, Microsoft also generally discontinues or at least deemphasizes sales and support for older versions. In effect, therefore, all new sales automatically result in some new documents that can't be read by the installed base. The introduction of backward-incompatible new features, even if each feature is used by only a small percentage of users, will quickly result in a high fraction of new documents being unreadable by older versions of the application. The whole user base is therefore forced into a kind of perpetual motion machine of rapid version updating. Some large-volume contracts actually *require* that customers update their software. Only a monopolist could get away with that.

This forced version cycling imposes enormous costs on users that are probably beginning to approach, or even exceed, the size of the benefits discussed earlier. First, users must buy new hardware more frequently. Even larger, however, are the increased installation, service, and maintenance costs imposed by this regime. The generally accepted rule of thumb is that corporations spend three to five times their hardware costs in service. New hardware and software products must be installed, debugged, and then serviced; employees must be taught how to use them. These costs increase greatly with the novelty and heterogeneity of systems in use; hence, the more upgrade cycling, the higher these costs.

Microsoft's behavior in this regard takes place with at least the implicit collusion of Intel and the PC hardware industry, which benefit from the rapid cycling of processors and hardware systems. To be fair, this is a subtle issue. Theoretically, one might expect Microsoft *not* to collude with Intel. In principle, if all of Microsoft's software, including its newest upgrades, ran on old processors, then hardware costs would shrink, allowing more room for Microsoft to increase software prices. As a practical matter, however, it would be much more difficult and expensive to push the same cycle of frequent feature upgrades using only the old processor base. First, Microsoft has much more direct leverage over new PC sales, where it can effectively force PC vendors to preload the newest versions of its software. And second, developing upgrades that older machines could use would require well-designed, compact, efficient software, which is harder to write. Furthermore, users might sit on their hands. There would be the risk that new features would not be adopted by a critical mass of users, with the result that the installed base would remain happily stable for too long. But if PC manufacturers preload only the newest releases of Microsoft's products, users *can't* go on strike, at least not for as long, because the new machines will inevitably start producing documents they can't read. Microsoft, with the implicit cooperation of the PC industry, thus guarantees that the whole user base will eventually be forced to upgrade.

Since there is rapid technological progress in semiconductors, plus genuine competition in the hardware sector, PC costs have been flat to falling. Recently, direct and Internet retailing have further reduced manufacturing and distribution costs to extraordinarily low levels. As a result Microsoft has been able to pursue its strategy without causing unacceptable increases in hardware prices. Nonetheless, even $599 PCs are probably $100 more expensive than they would be if Microsoft wrote products more carefully and without artificial feature increases. More important, people would not need to replace their computers as frequently or spend as much money servicing them. These costs affect everyone, but they probably affect poor people and the developing world more than the average business user. While it's not clear that antitrust action would change this—it might, but it might not—it's still worth pointing out that this behavior does impose significant social costs.

Furthermore, too much Microsoft software is just *bad*. With some justice, Microsoft can argue that it faces unique challenges—a huge number of users, running a very large number of slightly different hardware platforms, in an industry with an unusually high rate of technical change. But Cisco routers have most of those characteristics, and they work much better. If routers crashed as frequently as PCs, we'd never get our e-mail. It is also noteworthy how often freeware outperforms Microsoft's commercial products. By all reports, for example, Linux is a much more reliable operating system than NT. And despite more than a decade of development and enormous levels of investment, Windows still comes out poorly in ease-of-use comparisons with the Mac.

Microsoft's position as the monopolist purveyor of mediocre software is another source of large, and unnecessary, social costs. Training and recovery from software errors and crashes are, along with rapid version cycling, major contributors to service costs. Every large corporation devotes a substantial fraction of its technical and consulting resources to cleaning up after Microsoft's mess. Although Apple made huge mistakes, it did produce software that is elegant and easy to learn, and the available evidence suggests that this reduces maintenance and service costs. Conservative estimates are that the cost of maintaining a desktop is several times higher than the cost of purchasing it. Cleaner, simpler, better-designed software could reduce these overhead costs, thereby freeing large numbers of technologists to do useful work.

Once again, to be fair to Microsoft, this is a complex issue. Some of Microsoft's quality problems derive from earlier design errors, which must be carried forward to preserve compatibility, rather than recent or deliberate actions. My impression is that the average quality of Microsoft software is slowly improving, perhaps because the development system has stabilized and Microsoft is hiring more experienced developers from the outside. Furthermore, Microsoft's quality problems don't derive entirely from its monopoly position: the hacker tradition, which is where Gates comes from, has always been accepting of complex software that only technical users like. But Microsoft's rate of improvement seems to have been faster in markets in which there is, or has been, real competition; if there were more real competition, people might start to switch if rivals produced higher-quality products.

Finally, there is Microsoft's effect upon potential and actual innovation. It is abundantly clear that any new entrant who creates a large market or a threat to Microsoft's monopoly platform position will be the object of brutally effective, often predatory retaliation in which Microsoft will use every unfair advantage it possesses. While Netscape brought much of its fate upon itself, Microsoft certainly helped and the results were impressive and sobering. Venture capitalists now generally avoid funding companies that will compete inside Microsoft's monopoly-controlled spaces, because they assume it's hopeless to try; for example, it's now virtually impossible to get funding for high-volume PC application software ideas, even though VCs are overflowing with money. And once again, while Netscape made many errors, the world is a better place because it dared to exist. We should recall that in 1995 Microsoft had ignored the Internet for nearly two years and was seeking to use its PC operating systems monopoly as leverage to enter and dominate the online services industry via a technically retrograde, proprietary service—MSN—bundled with Windows 95. Microsoft's excellent free browser came only in response to Netscape's entry. Without any question, Netscape hastened the advent of the Internet age and, at least for a year or two, increased the rate of improvement of browser technology. It would be a very bad idea to permit an industry structure that precluded or dissuaded such efforts, either in PC software or elsewhere.

To summarize: Microsoft now enjoys two software monopolies, is using its market power to extract excessive profits from consumers and businesses, to destroy competition, and to force software purchases that impose significant economic costs. While I believe that the cumulative net effect of Microsoft on computer markets has been greatly beneficial, its current and prospective actions, at least in PC markets, are causing increasingly serious damage. Of major concern is the fact that monopolistic profits from the two core monopolies can be, and have been, used to fund scorched-earth attacks on innovative new entrants. That's a pretty good textbook definition of a monopolist taking advantage of market power. Furthermore, Microsoft isn't done yet.

MORE MONOPOLIES? PROBABLY. MORE USE OF MONOPOLY POWER? ALMOST CERTAINLY.

The penetration of the Windows NT client operating system into the workstation market has been very impressive and within a few years will approach monopoly control. Windows NT client is Microsoft's version of NT for workstations, with excellent compatibility features with both Windows and NT server, which is particularly useful for developing software. Until recently, the workstation market was completely dominated by various flavors of UNIX, but Windows NT now has a 50 percent share and is gaining fast.

This is a small market, but a disproportionately profitable and influential one, because its customers are primarily leading-edge, price-insensitive designers and developers of technology, including software engineers. Like so many of Microsoft's victories, this is one where it's hard to feel sorry for the competition, since it is the failure of UNIX vendors to unite behind a single, hardware-independent UNIX standard that created Microsoft's opportunity. Microsoft offers excellent development environments and tools for NT client, NT server, and Windows, so for most client-side or even midrange server applications, Windows NT is rapidly becoming the development platform of choice. We used it at Vermeer, and the reasons to choose it have become only more compelling since that time. Within a few years, NT will totally dominate the workstation market, except for high-end 3-D graphics workstations.

The *server* operating system and applications markets are more complex. Although Microsoft is still a long way from achieving dominance, it has been making extremely rapid progress, and I would argue that within two or three years, Microsoft will begin to possess real market power in these areas. In the high-end server market, NT is not yet competitive with UNIX-based operating systems from Sun, Hewlett-Packard, and IBM that support very large multi-processor systems. The Windows 2000 (formerly NT 5.0) system, which should ship in late 1999, will close the gap but not eliminate it.

In addition, there is significant competition in two other market segments: the low end of the server market, and systems used for technical applications by technically proficient users. In the former, the competition is Novell's NetWare; in the latter, Linux. NetWare still has a large installed base and is becoming the preferred system to support fast, efficient servers for filing and printing, as well as embedded control of dedicated hardware such as routers. Under Eric Schmidt, Novell is also trying to obtain control over industry standards for directory services, an area in which NT remains behind (but is catching up).

Linux's market share remains small, but seems to be gaining steadily, particularly among highly technical users, such as software firms. A number of major technology vendors including Intel, Dell, Oracle, and IBM have announced support for Linux and/or equity investments in Red Hat Software, the leading Linux distributor. In a fair world, Linux would do well. It is vendor independent, it runs on both workstations and servers, it is virtually free, and it is far more stable than NT, a major concern for many server applications.

However, as we shall now see, life isn't necessarily fair. NT has been gaining market share rapidly for the past several years, with unit shipments and revenues both growing about 100 percent per year, versus perhaps 40 percent per year for UNIX, 10 to 20 percent per year for NT, and perhaps 50 percent per year for Linux. BackOffice has similarly been gaining share, with its shipments and revenues growing approximately at the same rate as NT, versus roughly 30 to 50 percent per year for competitors such as Oracle in database systems and Netscape in Web servers. Increasingly, Microsoft's market-share gains—particularly against NetWare and Linux, both of which are hardware independent and compliant with major industry standards—will reflect not only the proper benefits of Microsoft's hardware-independent position and the quality of its products, but also the use of leverage from its existing monopolies.

Microsoft has already announced that Office PC applications will be increasingly integrated with BackOffice server applications, and in some ways they already are. With the use of FrontPage server extensions as the Office server extensions, and the insertion of Microsoft-specific features into Front-Page itself, Microsoft will begin to leverage its Office position into competitive advantage for BackOffice, which runs only on NT. In addition, Microsoft has announced that Excel will be increasingly integrated with SQL Server, allowing data to be exchanged between them in ways that are potentially very attractive and powerful. Microsoft has *not* announced equivalent arrangements with other database systems sold by competitors such as Oracle and IBM.

Combining simple extrapolation of NT and BackOffice shipments with their increasing integration with Office, we can expect that within a few years Microsoft will effectively dominate the mid-range server market and will be steadily chipping away at NetWare.

Linux may have a permanent niche, perhaps 10 to 15 percent of the market, but it is unlikely to discipline Microsoft seriously. BackOffice will never run on it. Office will never preferentially integrate with the applications that do run on Linux, and Office will not directly run on workstation versions of Linux at all (while Office does, of course, run on the Windows NT workstation operating system). Furthermore, while Linux is technically quite strong, the current Linux freeware open source license is a problem. All Linux code enhancements must be distributed free to everyone, including competitors, which makes it difficult to see how Linux can attract the levels of investment and infrastructure required to mount a serious challenge to NT. Furthermore, this situation permits the balkanization of Linux dialects, which makes it harder to establish a standard. One could conceive of modifications to the Linux freeware license that could solve these problems, but the Linux freeware community would probably resist them, and the existing license is highly entrenched. And while major applications software vendors threatened by Microsoft—Oracle is an obvious one—can begin to distribute and maintain Linux themselves, they face very real problems. Oracle would alienate its existing distribution channels, including resellers of UNIX servers, by supporting a free operating system. Thus the degree of software support that Linux can attract remains highly questionable, and it will certainly not include most Microsoft server applications.

Thus, while it may take a while before products like SQL Server and Back-Office can challenge high-end Oracle and IBM DB2 installations running on large multiprocessors, NT and BackOffice will steadily take over the mid-range and chew their way up into the high end. The rapid evolution of FrontPage as the world's Web development tool of choice will accelerate this process, as

FrontPage is preferentially linked not only to Office and Visual InterDev, but also to the NT Web server and the Microsoft Internet Explorer browser. Inevitably, FrontPage and its users will start producing more and more Web pages that can be viewed only with Explorer. I also expect the FrontPage server extensions available on the NT Web server to gradually become richer and more capable than those available on other Web servers and operating systems.

Ironically, these strategic decisions, which are enabled by Microsoft's existing monopolies, are having the effect of gradually reducing the vendor and platform independence of software that Microsoft originally created in the industry, and which remains its greatest contribution. Since Microsoft possesses monopolies in more than one layer of the industry, it can use each layer to reinforce its control of the others. It can use Windows to defeat Netscape by integrating the browser, while using Office to restrict the growth of Linux simply by not porting Office to Linux.

This kind of behavior is, I think, further compelling evidence that Microsoft needs to be reined in. It is also evidence that Microsoft's current behavior causes economic damage; while integration between Office and SQL Server is a good thing, equivalent integration with all database systems would be a better thing and is technically quite achievable. Only Microsoft's monopoly positions and aspirations prevent it. In the absence of divestiture, I think it is quite predictable, actually, that five years from now we will be looking at serious antitrust complaints related to these issues, derived from Microsoft dominance of the broad mid-range of server software.

MARKET POWER ON THE WEB?

Despite the billions Microsoft has spent pursuing content and services businesses, most recently on the Web, the company's performance in this area has been poor. A Microsoft takeover of major Web-based content and services businesses does not look imminent. Microsoft's share of the "portal" market is growing, but Yahoo! and AOL certainly show no signs of imminent collapse, to put it mildly.

For several reasons, Microsoft has more difficulty dominating Web content and services than traditional software businesses. In the first place, the market is so huge, growing so fast, and so application-specific that no one company can dominate it. Microsoft may not fare well at all in markets that it cannot dominate; its entire strategy is predicated upon control over industry standards, which requires domination. Second, Internet commerce in physical goods requires complex inventory and logistics infrastructures with which Microsoft has little experience. Netscape, by comparison, was competing in a business that Microsoft understood completely, so that although Microsoft was late to awaken, it obliterated Netscape quite easily, exploiting every error and opportunity, once it focused. Microsoft clearly does *not* understand electronic commerce as well as Amazon.com, financial services as well as Charles Schwab or E*Trade, or portal and media services as well as Yahoo! and AOL. Amazon's revenues already place it in the Fortune 500, while Schwab has hundreds of billions of dollars in Web-based assets under management.

Nonetheless, I would argue that there is still reason for concern in these and related areas that Microsoft could soon possess enough market power to affect them, and that antitrust sanctions (once again, *if intelligently applied*) might well be indicated. Microsoft does not *yet* dominate the browser market or related software such as Web-based audio and video players, but it probably will quite soon. It will also dominate the market for Web development tools and will become increasingly powerful in Web servers as Netscape fades from the scene. Microsoft already has monopoly positions in applications that have potentially attractive synergies with many Web services—downloading financial data into spreadsheets, for example. Taken together, these positions represent potentially very powerful leverage of precisely the kind Microsoft has repeatedly used to convert each of its monopolies into the next.

And Microsoft is clearly not quitting. There is every reason to expect that Microsoft, if left unconstrained, will ruthlessly use its operating systems and applications monopolies to leverage its way into Web services and electronic commerce. Furthermore, Microsoft's performance in the Web arena is now starting to improve, particularly that of its MSN portal. It has also spent more than a billion dollars acquiring Web-related companies, including WebTV; Hotmail, a Web-based free e-mail provider; Firefly, a Web privacy software vendor; and Link Exchange, a Web advertising exchange service. Further acquisitions and equity investments will undoubtedly occur; Microsoft now has more than $20 billion in cash and a market capitalization of about $500 billion, so money will not be a problem. And I would argue that the ability to affect freedom of speech, even slightly, merits even stronger intervention than actions that merely cost us a lot of money.

SUMMARIZING THE CASE

Microsoft now possesses great power, causes significant economic damage, and has demonstrated an almost complete lack of restraint in exploiting any advantage at its disposal, fair or unfair, ethical or unethical. It has not hesitated to force the bundling of Microsoft products, or the unbundling of others. The notorious per-processor licensing fee that was ended by the 1995 consent decree was worthy of John D. Rockefeller. Railroads paid rebates to Standard Oil even on competitors' shipments, and PC makers had to pay for Windows even if they loaded a competing operating system.

In the case of Netscape, Microsoft freely used its monopoly position and profits to obliterate the only major hardware-independent Web software vendor in the industry. When Compaq dared to try to preload Netscape's browser instead of Microsoft's, Microsoft canceled Compaq's Windows license, and Compaq capitulated the next day. Netscape, to be sure, played its cards stupidly, but the sheer ruthlessness and efficiency of the Microsoft assault has sent a chill through the entire technology sector. When you see a company as well funded as Netscape, with such a huge installed base, 80 percent market share, and experienced founders, brought to its knees so quickly and viciously, you will be extremely wary of doing, or investing in, anything that could elicit a similar reaction.

Microsoft's style also, I think, further lowers ethical standards throughout an already brutally competitive, ruthless industry. Microsoft is alleged to have engaged in such a wide array of unethical conduct that one cannot dismiss it. These actions have included disconnecting rival software, as RealNetworks alleged; inserting error messages, as alleged by DR-DOS; causing application errors, a technique allegedly used against Lotus in the early 1980s; spreading FUD by false product announcements and claims, as with Blackbird; blackmailing Apple by threatening to withdraw applications support for the Macintosh; and a well-established pattern of Japanese-style intellectual property violations that have resulted in major patent disputes with Stac, DEC, and Wang.

Not all of these acts have been proven, and while some may not be true, some clearly are. More important, the collective weight of the evidence is overwhelming. In sharp contrast to the generally high standard of ethics that marks its treatment of employees and investors, Microsoft's competitive behavior often skirts the edge of the law and routinely oversteps ethical boundaries. I think there is a strong argument that Microsoft's actions, and the fact that the government has done nothing to stop them, have had a deleterious effect on business ethics throughout the industry. If there was any doubt on this score, Bill Gates himself put it to rest in his videotaped antitrust deposition, in which he made the most absurd, obvious, and sometimes quite funny statements about his strategies, his knowledge of them, and his dealings with competitors.

In short, despite all of its contributions, the case for restraining Microsoft is now very strong, particularly if such restraint can be achieved while preserving the benefits it provides. Microsoft already possesses two powerful monopolies and is almost certainly on its way to having several more. It exploits its monopoly positions ruthlessly, and there is no sufficiently effective countervailing power within the industry. Microsoft's intellectual property violations, preda-tory behavior, FUD, false dealings, and strategic use of monopoly power are integral to its ability to create further monopolies and to deter or destroy inno-vative competitors. Its exploitation of its monopoly power is also critical to its ability to impose dead-weight costs on the industry and users via excessive up-grade cycling, forcing users to bear concomitant quality problems, hardware costs, service and maintenance costs, and compatibility problems.

There is, finally, another serious problem associated with Microsoft's monopoly power, one that over the long run could prove more important than Microsoft as an efficient and brutal monopolist. This is the prospect of Micro-soft as an *inefficient, declining, politicized* monopolist in the manner of General Motors, pre-divestiture AT&T, or pre-1993 IBM. In this regard, the record of in-dustrial history, including the technology sector, is extremely clear. Monopolists with captive customers inevitably succumb to the temptations of laziness and decline, and when they do, they impose enormous costs upon the economy derived from this decline, and from the political maneuvering of their incom-petent or self-interested employees.

In every case in which a long-standing monopoly has been dismem-bered—certainly in the cases of Standard Oil and AT&T—the successor firms have outperformed their monopolist parent. Conversely, where such firms have *not* been divested into multiple competitors, their performance has usually re-mained abysmal for long periods of time, until competition either forces change or wipes them out. In the meantime, their employees and customers pay dearly. Consider General Motors, the U.S. integrated steel industry, or—even more pointedly—IBM under Akers or Apple under Sculley. During the 1980s, IBM probably forced the world to buy *several hundred billion dollars* worth of obsolete, overly expensive, proprietary mainframes and minicomputers, while retarding the technological progress both of its own systems and of the open-architecture personal computer and server industries. In the end IBM could not sustain this behavior, lost $30 billion, replaced its CEO, laid off two hun-dred thousand employees, lost half its market value, and then reformed itself. But before that happened, IBM's market power had lasted a decade longer than it deserved, and it had cost the U.S. economy—indeed the world economy—a great deal of money.

Already, Microsoft is beginning to show the first hints of this syndrome. I think that it is completely inevitable at some point; the only question is when. At the latest, it will become a serious issue whenever Gates effectively loses the ability to understand and manage the enormous span of activities in which Microsoft will be engaged. It will certainly become a problem whenever he be-gins to retire. At a guess, this deterioration might begin about five years from now and last a decade or more, as it did with IBM. Once again, it would be enormously beneficial to forestall this result, if this could be done without eliminating the benefits Microsoft has provided.

It therefore makes sense to examine what is now being done about this and then conclude by considering what *should* be done, and how.

THE ANTITRUST RECORD: MOSTLY DISASTERS, GETTING SOMEWHAT BETTER

As I write this, the Justice Department has presented its case, and Microsoft its defense, in the department's antitrust suit; only final arguments remain before a verdict. It Microsoft is found liable, another phase of the trial will begin, devoted to the question of remedies. The government's performance in this case, while frequently poor, represents an enormous improvement over Justice's prior record with Microsoft and high technology antitrust issues generally, which has been awesomely bad. But the night is still young. In recommending and monitoring remedies, Justice will have ample opportunity to revert to its traditional performance level. There is already disturbing evidence in this regard, as I will describe shortly. Economic and industry analysis has been the weakest part of the government's case, and the prosecution has erred needlessly in several ways—e.g., by failing to make an effective argument that Microsoft's conduct has harmed users. Worse, press reports indicate that at least some members and advisors of the prosecution team favor the so-called Baby Bills policy, which would be disastrous.

This is particularly worrisome because, as I said, the federal government's record in high technology antitrust issues has been abysmal. Its first nightmare was the IBM case, which was filed in 1969 and abandoned in 1982, after thirteen years and literally hundreds of millions of dollars. The case went to trial; the trial had lasted for six years, heard by a judge who had flunked the bar exam three times, when the government simply gave up. The AT&T case, filed in 1976 and settled in 1982, led to AT&T's divestiture in 1984 and was a model of efficiency and wisdom by comparison. That settlement at least led to the introduction of competition in telecommunications equipment and in long-distance services, though it preserved local monopolies in both voice and data services, which are becoming particularly dangerous in the Internet era. I will return to that issue in the final chapter of this book.

The government's scrutiny of Microsoft began in 1990 with a level of stupidity difficult to surpass. Antitrust responsibilities are informally divided on industry lines between the Federal Trade Commission (FTC) and the Justice Department's Antitrust Division. This causes problems, since software is the FTC's responsibility, while hardware and telecommunications are controlled by Justice; in reality, they are often related. Antitrust action against Microsoft began with an investigation initiated by the FTC, apparently on the basis of newspaper articles read by FTC lawyers who seem to have lacked the faintest understanding of the computer industry, even at the level obtainable by reading *The New York Times*. The hypothesis of the investigation was that IBM and Microsoft, which had just evolved into brutal competitors over control of operating systems, were *colluding* to divide the market between them.

Eventually the FTC realized that this was not a problem, since Microsoft and IBM were quite obviously at war, and the investigation shifted toward Microsoft's control of DOS and Windows. After three years of investigation, in 1993 the FTC commissioners deadlocked in a vote on whether to proceed. In a highly unusual move, and to her credit, Anne Bingaman, who had just become head of the Antitrust Division in the first Clinton administration, took the case over from the FTC. However, she blinked. She won a narrow, virtually meaningless settlement related to pre-processor licensing and walked away.

Unfortunately, however, in another case around the same time, the Justice Department assisted Microsoft in controlling the PC-application software industry. Borland, a then-significant competitor of Microsoft's, acquired Ashton-Tate, the vendor of the popular dBase II PC database program. In its infinite wisdom, Justice decided that *Borland* was a potential monopolist in the market for PC database software. As a condition of approving the acquisition, and apparently with the concurrence of its economists, Justice required that Borland license dBase technology to a competitor, FoxPro. One month later, Microsoft acquired FoxPro. Of course, Justice approved *this* transaction with no restrictions, once again with the concurrence of its economists. Microsoft then proceeded to eviscerate Borland by performing its first "cashectomy," in the industry's nice phrase, while Justice stood by and watched. Microsoft, of course, now holds an effective monopoly in PC database software, which Justice has never challenged. The department's actions in the Borland and FoxPro cases were yet further evidence of the appalling condition of high technology antitrust policy. Strengthening Borland's hand in database software was actually a rare opportunity to create a countervailing independent Windows application vendor, with a suite of products potentially capable of challenging Office, whereas Justice forced precisely the opposite result.

The department's first productive action came in 1995, when the Antitrust Division, still under Anne Bingaman, blocked Microsoft's acquisition of Intuit. It was a few months after this action that I warned—well, *berated*, actually— Ms. Bingaman about Microsoft's prospective dominance of Internet software. In that same year, Justice decided not to oppose Microsoft's bundling of MSN into Windows 95, which in my opinion was a serious mistake. While it is quite true that MSN posed no great threat, Justice set a precedent that suggested to Microsoft that leveraging an operating systems monopoly was okay. Shortly afterward, Microsoft used exactly this technique in its deal with AOL, in which AOL agreed to abandon Netscape in favor of Microsoft's browser. Microsoft has also used similar techniques in other portions of its attack on Netscape.

Under pressure from Barksdale and other Silicon Valley companies, Justice began to investigate Microsoft's Internet behavior, especially with regard to browsers, in 1995. A case was filed in 1997, based on the 1995 consent decree. The consent decree prohibited forced bundling, but permitted integrating additional functions into Windows. Justice won the case, and Judge Thomas Penfield Jackson ordered Microsoft to unbundle the browser. With extraordinary insolence, Microsoft responded by distributing a broken operating system, suggesting how arrogant and insular Microsoft had become. This prompted an enormous and immediate uproar; Microsoft retreated and began offering a working unbundled operating system and browser. But Judge Jackson's decision was reversed on appeal, and Microsoft immediately resumed bundling of its browser. Microsoft has since slightly loosened its contracts with PC manufacturers, so it is now possible to preload non-Microsoft browsers, although almost nobody does so.

Justice's Current Case Evaluated

The Justice Department lawsuit against Microsoft was originally based almost entirely on Microsoft's use of Windows to destroy Netscape. Since David Boies was hired to try the case, it has expanded somewhat to include Microsoft's behavior toward the PC industry, America Online, Intel, and Apple. However, the case is still largely confined to Microsoft's predatory use of Windows; the Office monopoly isn't part of the case.

The government's principal success has been in eliciting a wide-ranging and unflattering portrait of Microsoft's predatory behavior and an equally unflattering pattern of evasion and dishonesty by some of Microsoft's witnesses and employees. Microsoft's courtroom performance has been poor, and Bill Gates's deposition was almost laughably implausible. Gates's performance alone seems to have affected public perception of the company. I'm not a lawyer and will not attempt to analyze the legal issues in the case. But the shift in mood on the part of the public, the industry, and the government seems to have increased the likelihood that some action will be taken against Microsoft.

However, the government has also made some unnecessary, and possibly quite dangerous, errors. First, as I mentioned, it has restricted the case to Microsoft's Windows monopoly. This means that there has been virtually no discussion of Office or of Microsoft's increasing use of Office as leverage to dominate other markets. This is important not only because it would strengthen the case, but also because of its implications for how Microsoft can be curbed. If Office is powerful, then splitting Microsoft into an operating systems company that included Windows and an applications company that included Office would yield two powerful firms capable of disciplining each other. This has barely been mentioned because the Office monopoly hasn't been mentioned by the government.

Second, the government has fared poorly in the competition to analyze the economics of Microsoft's position and conduct. Microsoft's primary economics witness was Richard Schmalensee, who is dean of the MIT Sloan School of Management. His performance wasn't perfect, but it was superb. His major errors were that he was caught contradicting himself a couple of times, and portions of his deposition are just silly—for example, he claims, apparently with a straight face, that Microsoft possesses no monopolies or monopoly power. However, his deposition was extremely well argued. Of course, Schmalensee does not spend much time estimating costs of deterring or destroying innovative entry, the costs of unnecessary upgrade cycling, the costs of Office not being available in Linux, the costs of Office being linked only to SQL Server, the costs of FrontPage server extensions being available preferentially to Microsoft applications, and so forth. But Schmalensee made something approaching the best case that can be made in Microsoft's favor.

But in cross-examining Schmalensee, the government didn't challenge him on any of those issues, and Boies didn't fare well in the cross-examination. Worse, the Justice Department's own principal expert economic witnesses failed to make these points in their own direct testimony. One of them, Frank Fisher, a professor at MIT who has practically made a career of corporate antitrust consulting, made the astonishing statement that Microsoft's conduct had probably not done any damage to consumers. At this writing, it is not yet clear how much the government's poor performance in the economics battle will affect the outcome of the case. Fisher's rebuttal testimony repaired some of the damage, but not all of it.

The real risk, however, is that after a finding of antitrust liability against Microsoft, the government will try to do the wrong thing and the courts will agree. Given Justice's record, this risk must be taken extremely seriously. And it does appear, unfortunately, that serious attention is being paid to proposals that could make the industry worse, not better, than it is with Microsoft's current structure and power.

Before turning to the question of what should be done, therefore, it is worth saying something about the quality of antitrust policy, procedures, and enforcement. In the first place, the antitrust system is archaic; it is not structured to deal with high technology questions. There are no special provisions for technically trained judges or juries. Nor are independent experts usually available; expert testimony is dominated by highly paid witnesses working for the opposing parties. Legal procedures are lengthy and cumbersome, with the result that even the fastest trials last longer than most technology generations. Perhaps worse, the Antitrust Division is not staffed or structured for effective analysis of high technology industries, and it never has been. This might seem odd, given that the three most notable and important antitrust cases in recent history—against AT&T, IBM, and Microsoft—have all been in high technology. I would further argue, and do so in the next chapter, that the most important cases that Justice *ought* to bring are in local telecommunications and data services, another area with serious technological content.

There are two problems: the lawyers and the economists. The Antitrust Division has roughly 900 employees, about 350 lawyers, and 40 economists. How many technologists? I hear you ask. Zero is the answer. Even the Federal Communications Commission, which is not a model of *anything,* has a chief engineer, but not the Justice Department. It would not seem such a dramatic or difficult reform to hire some technically trained attorneys and a cadre of computer science Ph.D.s. It is possible to get such people into the government—DARPA and NSF, for instance, have people like that by the carload, and they're smart. But both the lawyers and economists at Justice guard their turf fiercely, and they certainly don't want to create a new organization defined precisely by knowledge of important things that they don't understand at all. Furthermore, there is virtually nobody in the Justice Department with significant industrial experience *of any kind,* never mind experience in a serious high technology company. The Antitrust Division's professionals fall into one of two categories: career civil servants and people on two-year rotations who are getting their ticket stamped to make themselves more marketable to consulting firms, law firms, and corporate antitrust defendants. I'll say more about *that* later, too.

It is perhaps not surprising, therefore, that the department's antitrust activities in high technology tend to be sporadic, reactive, inconsistent, and ineffective. The general pattern is to wait until something comes along and someone is making too much noise to ignore. Each situation is then narrowly, often erroneously, analyzed, and a narrow, often erroneous response is then crafted. In static, low technology industries, Justice might do a much better job; I don't know. But with Microsoft, the local telecommunications monopolies, and even IBM, its record is far from encouraging. The very fact that Justice would appoint people like Rich Gilbert and Daniel Rubinfeld (both of whom derive the majority of their wealth from corporate antitrust consulting) to be its chief economist speaks volumes about antitrust policy in telecommunications. The entire computer industry has known about the Microsoft problem for at least a decade, since the Windows 3.0 launch. Indeed, Microsoft's style, power, and toughness—the dirty tricks, the FUD, the pattern of coercion against computer manufacturers, the version cycling, the leverage of operating systems information and control—all date from the company's earliest days.

Thus, by the early 1990s at the *latest,* it was clear that there was a problem here. And, even within the constraints of the current system, the Justice Department could have done something about it. They should have permitted Borland's acquisition of Ashton-Tate and blocked Microsoft's acquisition of FoxPro, not the other way around, and filed cases on DOS, Windows, and Office much earlier. In fact, a number of the most potent arguments against Justice intervention against Microsoft, and in high technology generally, derive from the inefficiency, unpredictability, conflicts of interest, and randomness that have characterized the antitrust process, including Justice's own behavior. I certainly would agree that major reforms are necessary.

In the meantime, however, there is the question of what should be done to Microsoft now.

OPTIONS AND RECOMMENDATIONS

While I am an antitrust hawk on Microsoft, I very much fear that the wrong remedy could do more harm than good. If Microsoft were to be regulated à la Judge Greene's oversight of the telecommunications industry—or even worse, the FCC's regulatory processes—I would prefer continued monopoly power. Similarly, I think a continuation of the current situation would be preferable to the so-called Baby Bills proposal, whereby all Microsoft products and code would be owned and sold by multiple, competing successor firms.

There are, however, strong arguments for some combination of three proposed remedies. None is perfect, but I think that any of them would be an improvement. The first remedy would be the forced disclosure by Microsoft of its major APIs, including the internal APIs of Office. The second would be prohibition of Microsoft's entry into certain industries adjacent to its existing monopolies, particularly Web services. The third, and I believe the best, would be the divestiture of Microsoft along technological and product lines, into one company that sold operating systems and another that sold applications.

After analyzing the defects of regulation and Baby Bill divestiture, I will discuss the merits of these three possible solutions, singly and in various combinations. Parenthetically, I should note that the majority of my personal wealth is still in the form of Microsoft stock. If you wish, you may regard the following analysis as either self-interested or masochistic. For what it may be worth, I would say myself that neither extreme is required. First, I consider myself absurdly wealthy; I cannot imagine spending more than a minority of my money over my lifetime even if I never make another penny. Even a sharp drop in Microsoft's stock price would have little meaningful effect on my personal security and comfort.

Just as important, however, the history of antitrust divestitures suggest that when they are intelligently done, shareholders usually do *better* after the breakup of a monopoly—even Standard Oil's did. While Microsoft is certainly not a bloated bureaucracy like pre-1993 IBM or pre-divestiture AT&T, it is beginning to exhibit early symptoms of incumbent's disease and would inevitably suffer from it over time. Over a twenty-year horizon, I suspect that investors would be well served if Microsoft is broken up now, rather than permitted to acquire enormous power and then gradually deteriorate into the Bell Atlantic or General Motors of software. Bill Gates and a few senior Microsoft executives might not like it, because they'd have to compete again, but that is another matter.

I can't think of any substantive reason why the country would continue to be better off with an intact Microsoft as opposed to a divestiture into two successors, one each for operating systems and applications. There are two arguments for leaving Microsoft alone, both of them serious, but they are primarily reflections of the poor quality of the antitrust system, as opposed to the merits of this case. The first is that the process could easily be interminably ghastly and resource consuming, with never-ending appeals, retrials, reversals, etc. The second is that the Justice Department could recommend, and the courts could agree, to do the wrong thing. Hence the following analysis. I think that the country would be better off with a *properly* split-up Microsoft; the question is whether it's realistically possible to get there, and to do so without destroying the city in order to save it. What follows is my attempt to point at the right target.

First, I think it is hardly necessary even to mention the argument against permanent regulation of a high technology company. The mere thought of the FCC, the FTC, the Justice Department, or some similar organization holding continuous hearings about whether and how to develop new operating system interfaces is simply too horrible to contemplate. Enough said.

The Baby Bill proposals, however, have apparently attracted significant support, even within the prosecution team. This tells me that we should be very careful about how we press the case for action against Microsoft, because this option would be disastrous.

Gary Reback, of the Silicon Valley law firm of Wilson, Sonsini, has been leading the Silicon Valley guerrilla war against Microsoft for a long time. He has recently represented Netscape, but also has several clients whose names have never been revealed. They are widely assumed to be Sun, Novell, and/or Oracle. Because of Reback's prominence in the Valley, his proposals are widely quoted and, I'm afraid, taken more seriously than they deserve. Reback and several others propose various mechanisms to partition Microsoft into several competing successor firms, each with a full set of Microsoft's products and intellectual property. This is a profoundly bad idea.

Consider what could occur after such a divestiture. One possibility, the most benign by far, is that after a few years of chaos and major compatibility problems throughout the world, one of the successor companies would pull ahead and become the new industry standard, in which case we would be right back where we started. This wouldn't be great, but the outcome could easily be far worse.

The next best result would be a *permanently* balkanized software industry, with a serious decline in software standardization and compatibility, but with no other ill effects. Each competitor would develop its own enhancements, almost certainly incompatible with one another, and develop its own proprietary installed base. This would be a major economic drag, with enormous maintenance costs as well as the myriad costs of pervasive incompatibility. These costs would be very large even if the rivals actually tried to maintain compatibility, because accidental incompatibilities and desynchronization would inevitably occur. Such problems sometimes occur even within Microsoft itself. And there is of course no guarantee whatsoever that all of the successor firms would even try. The record of the industry—in the UNIX market, in pre-Internet proprietary online services, in mainframe computers, with the Macintosh—does not suggest that the lure of a proprietary, captive installed base can often be resisted. And, dear reader, you have absolutely no idea how much you take the current situation for granted. You go to any PC, you send an e-mail, you insert a floppy disk, you print a document, you look at a Web page, you write a memo, you know what to do, things work. It doesn't have to be that way, and believe me, it wouldn't.

However, even this would still be a quite benign result. How could it be worse? you ask. Think about the *hardware* industry is the answer.

The personal computer and server companies do not love Microsoft for commoditizing them and forcing them into permanent, brutal competition stripped of all proprietary advantage. Most of them would love to revert to the structure of the mainframe industry, the minicomputer industry, and the UNIX server industry led by Sun Microsystems. Then they could have a proprietary installed base, insulated from immediate competition, and much higher margins—like IBM used to have. This would also facilitate tacit collusion of the kind that occurred during the mainframe era, when IBM used to set "price umbrellas." Well, with a Baby Bill divestiture of Microsoft, the PC industry could get there. Compaq could acquire one of the Baby Bills, Dell another, IBM a third, Sony a fourth. They wouldn't even need outright acquisitions; an exclusive licensing agreement would be enough, perhaps accompanied by an equity investment. In fact, they wouldn't even need to do *that*. PC and hardware peripheral manufacturers could simply start introducing proprietary, incompatible hardware features that Microsoft would not currently support. But the Baby Bills, unlike Microsoft, would not have the market power to prevent such behavior. Sometimes, monopolies aren't all bad.

The Justice Department, moreover, would sit by and do nothing. Your average Justice economist would look at this industry, see multiple competing vendors, conclude that it was competitive, and recommend no action. The Baby Bills would love it, the personal computer industry would love it, and Sun Microsystems would *really* love it, because this would place Sun on an even footing with an industry that otherwise will surely kill it. Users, however, would get screwed.

These risks, and the Baby Bill proposal, are sometimes defended as being necessary in order to discipline Microsoft. On this argument, a structural or technological divestiture would be ineffective, since the result would simply be two monopolists instead of one. As we shall see shortly, this is false; the successor firms would have strong incentives to discipline one another and perhaps even compete with one another, while also cooperating to maintain compatibility. Their relationship would be similar to that which currently exists between Microsoft and Intel. Thus, the Baby Bill proposal has essentially no redeeming features except that it might serve the proprietary interests of firms currently forced to compete harder than they would like.

We now come to the several proposals that might make sense. Forcing Microsoft to open its APIs is intellectually attractive, but poses difficult problems of definition and enforcement. Would Microsoft have to publish every component interface, or just those used by separately sold products? What about the internal APIs inside Office? It would also be difficult to monitor Microsoft's compliance and to enforce sanctions against violations. There might be some argument for one-time disclosure of a set of APIs currently identifiable as important, if industry agreement could be reached—itself not guaranteed. I tend to think, however, that tempting as the idea is, it would prove less effective, less efficient, and less durable than structural solutions. But I do think that there are two attractive structural solutions, which can be used either individually or together. Each would have major benefits, and if both were used, I think we could obtain nearly all of the benefits Microsoft has provided, but with far fewer problems.

The first structural remedy is to preclude Microsoft from entering certain new business areas, most critically Web services, and to divest those it has already created. Even a prohibition that expired after, say, five or ten years would have real merit and would allow the Web to grow without coercion from

Microsoft. If a more radical dismemberment of Microsoft was judged infeasible, then constraints on Microsoft's *future* predation, particularly in the realm of Web services, should be a minimum fallback. There is ample precedent, and such prohibitions can be easily defined and enforced. In addition, businesses like Web content and financial services are already teeming with competitors, so there is no conceivable economic loss from keeping Microsoft out.

Finally, the cleanest alternative, and the one I prefer, would be a structural (or technological, or architectural) divestiture along architectural boundaries, taking advantage of Gates's own organizational innovations. One could separate operating systems and applications into two companies, probably divesting Web services into a third. This would yield two monopolies, each desirous of reducing the other's power.

The resulting companies would still be the largest, most profitable software companies in the world, well able to compete and innovate. If anything, the American software industry would become stronger and more competitive. In contrast to the Baby Bill proposal, the benefits of standardization and interoperability would be mostly preserved. There would be increased opportunities for competition in new spaces, yet also a continuation of discipline on entrenched incumbents, such as NT's attacks on UNIX and BackOffice's attack on Oracle. There would be much less chance of a single incumbent becoming a dead weight on the entire market and much less opportunity to use the leverage of one monopoly to create others.

Moreover, each of these firms would be given an incentive to discipline the other in ways that would benefit consumers. The applications company would want to make Office available to Linux and BackOffice available on both commercial UNIX and Linux. The operating systems company, conversely, would want to support competing applications vendors and/or to develop applications of its own. The increase in competitive pressure that each would generate on the other might also motivate them to open their APIs in their own interest. Thus, for example, the applications company would have an incentive to open the Office API lest the operating systems company begin to sponsor rivals. Yet both firms, as controllers of major industrywide standards, would remain interested in maintaining standardization, compatibility, and commoditized competition *throughout the hardware industry,* and they would be powerful enough to do it. Thus, while we cannot predict exactly how this process would go, it would almost certainly increase competitive discipline without destroying incentives for standardization, compatibility, and competition in both hardware and software.

That having been said, even this solution is complicated. In addition to product development, Microsoft includes marketing, distribution, sales, and other internal service organizations, international operations, intellectual property, key management personnel, and many other people and assets that do not cleanly belong in any one product group. Nonetheless, it could be done; Microsoft just reorganized itself in a fairly major way, along lines not entirely different from this proposed divestiture. Another complication concerns Bill Gates's personal holdings. If Microsoft was dismembered but Gates was allowed to keep his stock in all successor firms, he would be a 20 percent shareholder in them, and he, Paul Allen, and Steve Ballmer together would own nearly a third. To avoid a Rockefeller-style interlocking trust, they should be required to divest their stock in all but one successor firm. Thus, even with a "clean" structural divestiture, at least part of God is indeed in the details. Given the Justice Department's record, this makes many people, including me, quite nervous.

However, something should be done. There are powerful reasons why structural divestiture would be best for the economy and for consumers. Failing this, a prohibition on entering Web services and improved (not merely increased: *improved*) Justice Department vigilance should be the bare minimum that the country should settle for. Microsoft is too important and valuable to destroy, but also too important and valuable to leave in one piece.

CHAPTER ELEVEN

The Future, and Some

Large Questions

The empires of the future are the empires of the mind.
—*Winston Churchill, 1943*

Heaven sends us good meat, but the Devil sends cooks.
—*David Garrick, 1777*

A lawyer with his briefcase can steal more than a hundred men with guns.
—*Mario Puzo,* The Godfather

At the dawn of the Industrial Revolution in the latter half of the eighteenth century in England, it would have been impossible to predict most of its consequences. It led to the rise of England as the world's dominant power, but also to the emergence of America. Industrialization generated a great increase in wealth and life expectancy, yet also the misery of nineteenth-century working-class slums. There was a wave of economic globalization as a result of transportation and communications technologies such as steamships, railroads, and telegraphy; there was also an enormous increase in the deadliness of war as a result of new weapons such as the machine gun and high explosives.

Thus, while the rise of the Internet represents a major development in world history, it is impossible to predict what it will eventually yield. I should say that, on balance, I am very optimistic about the Internet revolution, including its cultural, political, social, and artistic consequences as well as its economic effects. Like movable type and the printing press, the Internet is astonishingly liberating. But it will also produce some stress. The conventional wisdom, which for the most part I believe is correct, is that the Internet will have three large-scale effects on economic behavior. First, it will absorb and largely supplant other information distribution and communication industries such as telephone service, traditional data communications, music distribution, and eventually video distribution. Second, it will improve distribution generally, by rationalizing distribution and retailing, and also through the competition provided by direct Internet-based electronic commerce. And third, the Internet will accelerate economic and financial globalization, by integrating many industries and markets currently separated by geography or information costs.

But these are extremely general statements, and they leave out a great deal—effects on culture and individual rights; the risk of Internet accidents, terrorism, or warfare; effects on education; effects on government and international relations; economic dislocations as the winds of change blow through unprepared industries. I will therefore end this book with a few highly personal comments about three large-scale issues associated with the Internet revolution, selected from among the almost infinitely many one could choose to discuss.

First, I will consider the inherent conflict between privacy and legitimate control, an old question that is sharpened by the rise of the Internet. Second, I will consider some of the economic effects of the Internet, including its destabilization of traditional industries and its possible effects on the distribution of wealth both within and between societies. And finally, I will discuss a specific industry, one that is deeply threatened by the Internet but also essential to its further progress. This industry is local telecommunications, curently dominated by monopoly telephone and cable television companies. The telecommunications case is much more important than is generally understood and shows that progress in the Internet isn't automatic; it must be fought for.

FREEDOM VERSUS CONTROL: PRIVACY, FREE SPEECH, CENSORSHIP, ENCRYPTION, METERING, AND PIRACY PREVENTION

On a net basis, the Internet unquestionably represents a profound leap forward for political freedom and the free flow of information, *especially* in controlled societies. The Internet is becoming so important to so many economic, social, and governmental processes that effective political censorship will soon be prohibitively costly. Only regimes such as Iraq and North Korea, whose leaders are willing to slaughter and starve their citizens, will be able to do it, and they will fall ever further behind the rest of the world as a result. The only other nations where such censorship will be effective are those too poor to have large numbers of personal computers. China and others make various attempts at Internet censorship, but in the long run, and even to a large extent now, they're hopelessly doomed. In some cases U.S. policy goals might benefit from creating a "Radio Free Internet" to send information into closed societies, but for the most part it just isn't necessary.

On the other hand, the Internet does pose some problems related to individual rights, even—perhaps especially—in highly industrialized, generally free societies. The primary risk is the disappearance of privacy. I take this risk quite seriously and tend to be a privacy hawk, though for different reasons than some others. My principal concern is not misuse of personal information by the United States government, but rather the use and abuse of such information by other private individuals, the mass media, corporations, criminals, and foreign governments.

The Internet is a powerful means of information distribution and consumption, but it is also a powerful means of information collection. The pervasiveness of the Internet, and of electronic control systems generally, is generating increasing tension between individual freedom and privacy rights, on the one hand, and the requirements of law enforcement and the economics of information industries, on the other. On one side are privacy rights and freedom of speech; on the other, the need to regulate financial systems, prevent Internet sabotage, and enforce restrictions against illegal activities.

I am concerned even about the degree to which the Internet facilitates discovery and disclosure of accurate information. But I am even more concerned that as a pragmatic matter, widespread availability of personal information makes major abuses both more likely and more difficult to police. Wide availability of individual information makes it easier to spread errors, lies, half-truths, and rumors. It also increases the likelihood of accidental or deliberate privacy intrusions into the lives of friends, family members, colleagues, and other third parties, and it increases the likelihood that private information can be obtained by people who really should not have it.

Broadly speaking, there are two classes of policy tools for dealing with these tensions, which can be used singly or in combination. They are: technological solutions (either voluntary or required by law) and legal restrictions on behavior. Technical solutions include mechanisms such as technological escrow of sensitive personal information. Escrowed information is kept in some secure, trusted system and remains anonymous and/or private unless there is a demonstrated need to unlock it, e.g., through a law enforcement search warrant or because of a medical emergency. In some cases, such as the tension between privacy rights and controlling piracy, it does appear that technical solutions can at least reduce the trade-off between privacy and legal control. In other cases, a major trade-off may be inevitable.

In principle, these problems are not new. But the Internet marks a huge, qualitative change in their potential scope. I have several friends who have been caused considerable pain as the result of media coverage of personal matters whose disclosure served no legitimate purpose. I have other friends whose families could be at quite serious risk if their lives were open to random investigation. If you're an American working in Russia, for example, or in the Middle East, it's not a terribly bright idea to let anyone publish a complete diagram of your life, or your family's. That's especially true if you work for, say, the Defense Department, or if you're an investigative reporter.

But we're going in that direction. Recently, an extreme anti-abortion group in the United States posted on its Web site detailed information about the doctors in an abortion clinic—home addresses, descriptions and license plate numbers of their cars, names and occupations of family members, personal habits—in order to harass and threaten them. In that case, a court order put a stop to posting such personal information, but one can easily imagine many similar abuses, and their legal status is disturbingly unclear in the United States. Many commercial Web sites in the United States have adopted a voluntary policy of not providing individual Web usage information commercially, but the financial incentives to sell this information are increasing, and there will clearly be abuses.

Thus, consider the following cool business idea. I'll purchase data from anyone—not just the tame financial data that credit bureaus get, but *everything*. Your Web page usage, the times you use electronic card keys (hotels, offices, garages), and dull easy things like public property and tax records, voter registration records, legal and court records, telephone and Internet directory listings, marriage and divorce records, any financial disclosure forms you've filed, anything your employer, your bank, and even your government is willing to sell.

Then, for a mere $29.95, I will allow anyone to search this database and to purchase information about anyone else over the Web. For serious money, I'll do customized searches—how often have John and Jane been in the same hotel? This is not, unfortunately, entirely a fantasy. Electronics is now pervasive, and ever more actions are metered and recorded: when you open your office door or hotel room with your electronic key, when you turn your office computer on, exactly where you make every phone call. The rise of electronic money may worsen this situation, since electronic money is an architected information object like any other. There have been proposals for deliberately anonymous electronic cash, and other proposals for complete traceability. Both are technically feasible.

At the moment, privacy is losing ground. Intel wants to put identification numbers on every microprocessor in every personal computer. In early 1999 it was discovered that Windows 98 automatically stamps an identification number on every document it handles, enabling tracing of every electronic document created on a personal computer, including tracing the path back to where a document was created even after it has been e-mailed repeatedly. When this was discovered, Microsoft removed the feature, but many other systems already perform similar identification stamping.

Ironically, however, one of the people who discovered and complained about this Windows 98 feature used this same feature to track down the source of the Melissa e-mail virus, which corrupted more than one hundred thousand PCs before being stopped. Thus, once again, the inevitable trade-off between privacy and legitimate controls. Sun's new Java technology for consumer electronics, Jini, does the same thing as Windows 98, issuing unique identification numbers for every message transmitted between devices. When asked about this, Scott McNealy, Sun's CEO, replied in his inimitable fashion, "You have zero privacy now. Get over it."

This would not be my answer. Furthermore, the Europeans have taken a different view of these matters, and the European Union issued a stringent privacy directive that clashes with U.S. policy and law. The EU directive is stereotypically bureaucratic—rigid, possibly too stringent, imposing large administrative costs, and in danger of becoming technically outdated even before being implemented. I do not nominate it as a model for U.S. policy. But I think that some intermediate course would be desirable, and an eventual collision with European policy now seems inevitable.

Encryption and Export Controls Currently, U.S. policy prohibits the export of advanced encryption technology, so that the National Security Agency can continue to read other people's mail and so that international wiretaps can still be effective. The U.S. technology sector is overwhelmingly in favor of relaxing or eliminating these controls, for obvious and selfish reasons. In addition, libertarians (who are numerous in the technology sector) want encryption to be widely available so that governments cannot read their mail.

For the moment, I'm not terribly worried about the U.S. government reading my mail. The strongest arguments for relaxing controls are that American companies will lose business to foreign vendors who don't have such restrictions; that, without strong encryption, international customers won't commit business to the public Internet; and that encryption actually *increases* security by reducing the risk of information terrorism and sabotage. A related argument is that the bad guys can get access to strong encryption software anyway. There is some truth to these arguments, but there are counterarguments as well.

Outlaw regimes cannot steal encryption technology as easily as they could if it were freely available on world markets. We derive at least some benefit from reading other people's mail, particularly people like the Iranians, North Koreans, Iraqis, Syrians, Libyans, Serbs, terrorist groups, drug cartels, and others. The intelligence establishment has many problems, but there are also some pretty scary people out there, and we're better off knowing more about them rather than less. On balance I tend to think that the current de facto policy, which is gradual but not complete relaxation of controls, is the right way to go.

Piracy One of the strongest arguments for enabling the identification of Internet users and the metering of their usage is that without such capabilities, fear of piracy will prevent the use of the Web for distribution of creative works. These include software, music, literature, photography, journalism, radio, academic research, videos, and film. The Web is often cited as a potentially huge benefit to artists and information creators who are currently hostage to expensive, restrictive distribution systems such as the music industry or the large movie studios. There is much truth to this; the Web offers a potentially remarkable opportunity for direct distribution of creative works. However, there is just one little problem. One thing that recording companies, publishers, and movie studios do well is make sure that they get *paid*. The creators or authors may not get much, but they do get something. On the Web, they might get nothing at all, which is not fair. Piracy using the Web is spreading fast, as is subsequent copying of downloaded materials via corporate networks.

The music industry and other major distributors of information and creative products are getting worried about this, for obvious reasons. So are creative artists and authors, although their lobby isn't as strong. Various technologies are being developed to monitor and control the distribution, redistribution, and use of information and creative works. All such technologies require some form of usage metering, identification, payment, restrictions on redistribution, and/or authentication of property rights. These technologies would enable the collection and sale of personal and in some cases extremely sensitive information. Many people, including me, find this prospect quite disturbing. Once again, therefore, there is a tension between privacy and legitimate rights of ownership and control.

Although the industry has thus far not agreed, I would argue that in this situation, stringent legal protection of privacy and personal information is actually in the industry's interest. Such legal protections would accelerate the development and consumer acceptance of technologies that would stimulate demand for computers, Internet services, and Web-distributed information products. But even if this effect is small, I would argue for such protections on ethical grounds. Freedom of speech, and freedom to consume information, isn't quite the same if everyone knows exactly what you're reading.

In all of these cases—protection of personal information for privacy rights, design of electronic money, encryption, piracy control, anonymity—both technological and legal systems have been proposed to mitigate the tension between the goals of privacy and individual freedom, on the one hand, and legitimate controls, on the other. None of these systems are perfect, and it is difficult to predict in advance how well they would actually function. I regret to say that I have no magic answers. My guess is that the best way to proceed is incrementally, with substantially increased legal protections for privacy while experiments are conducted on technological protections.

ECONOMIC ISSUES AND INTERNATIONAL ECONOMIC POLICY

Technology, Growth, and Income Distribution Although a far more general problem deserving of separate treatment, it is worth noting here that the Internet, and the rise of information technology generally, is worsening an already severe problem, namely, the gulf between the economics discipline and reality. Although academic economists seem to be eminently pragmatic when highly paid to testify on behalf of monopolies, they (and consequently economic theory) have become remarkably divorced from actual economic behavior. This problem shows up in attempts to understand economic growth (or the lack thereof), the effects of globalization and trade upon economic welfare, determinants of the distribution of income and wealth, the sources and implications of financial crises, and the role played by technology in these processes.

Modern information technology and particularly the Internet will clearly have profound effects on economic behavior. I am quite optimistic that on balance, and over the long run, these changes will be tremendously beneficial, yielding economic growth, improved education, and more efficient use of limited natural resources. As with the first Industrial Revolution, however, I suspect that the Internet will also cause some major stresses and temporary, but severe, pain to some nations, industries, and people.

The underlying source of these problems is the differing rates of change exhibited, and that can be tolerated, by different institutions, cultures, and social groups. Internet technology, and the institutions that are developing and deploying it, are moving much faster than many of the nations, institutions, and people that will be affected by it. This is true both within the United States and, more markedly, across social and economic groups throughout the world. Not everyone is habituated to, or ready for, 100 percent per year technical change in his or her industry, profession, or society. But the Internet industry will be delivering the technology, and start-ups will be using it, whether the world is ready or not. Small, independent U.S. bookstores and the highly price-controlled

European book retailing industry weren't ready for Amazon.com. But Amazon .com is here anyway—as indeed it should be.

This process of "creative destruction," as Joseph Schumpeter termed it, will be repeated a thousand times throughout the world economy over the next several decades. For the most part, it will be tremendously healthy. But not everyone will be able to get out of the way in time. This is a problem that deserves some attention. In part, the Internet is qualitatively new in this regard, as a result of its ferocious speed. In part, it represents a continuation of processes that appear to have been under way for at least a decade, and maybe longer. The rise of information technology is driving a globalization of industrial behavior, an acceleration of rates of change and competitive intensity, and an increase in productivity. It also seems to be creating an increasing premium on people with high levels of education and widening the gap between winners and losers at every level of the world economy. One consequence of this is increasing inequality of income and wealth, both within and between nations.

Many of these developments are good. I would argue that personal computing, the Internet, and the start-up-driven U.S. technology sector deserve at least partial credit for the current prosperity of the United States, which reversed a previous period of stagnation. For a quarter century, starting in the early 1970s, the entire industrialized world experienced a slowdown in productivity growth that neither the economics profession nor anyone else has satisfactorily explained. Recently, U.S. productivity growth has begun to improve again, or at least so the conventional numbers indicate, and I think if anything they understate the change. This is an enormous subject, which I will not discuss in detail here. I will, however, advance a personal view that is supported by the available evidence (which is rather spotty).

The Productivity Conundrum Following the end of World War II, the U.S. economy developed a particular structure heavily based on stable, large firms— the likes of GM, Exxon, AT&T, and IBM. These firms easily dominated not only U.S. but also world markets for the first quarter century after the war. During this time—until the early 1970s—U.S. productivity growth was very high, more than 3 percent per year.

Over time, however, the Fortune 500 got lazy. The management and governance of these firms became inbred, inefficient, and increasingly disconnected from many changes occurring in the world, ranging from the rise of Japanese lean manufacturing to the revolution being spawned in Silicon Valley. This led to a period of stagnation and decline, which, I would argue, is now being partially reversed by the rise of start-ups and the Internet.

This phenomenon shows, for example, in the contrasting performance of mature industries such as automobiles, textiles, steel, and mainframe computers (the old IBM) as opposed to newer companies and industries. In general, the U.S. economy is extremely good at generating entry where there is a continuous stream of new technology and new market opportunities with initially low capital requirements. Happily, U.S. research in information technology is well provided for, as is biomedical research. However, the U.S. economy is generally poor—less good than Japan or Korea, for example—at generating new entry in mature industries where start-up-based entry is unlikely (cars, for example). I am not sure how to solve this problem, although I think that improved corporate governance would help, as would federal policy that promoted it. You don't see many Fortune 500 CEOs get fired, no matter how dismal they are. Other helpful measures might include more vigorous and intelligent antitrust enforcement and continuation of aggressive science policy, which will keep the start-up sector supplied with raw material. In Europe, which came to have a similar stagnation of productivity associated with declining large firms, the required policy measures are probably different: privatization, lower taxation of employment, and measures to create venture capital and start-up systems that for the most part do not exist there.

But now we come to the 1990s, the rise of personal computers, and the Internet revolution. As Internet technology becomes an increasing fraction of all economic activity, previously stable and separate industries will experience greatly increased competition. The Internet will also accelerate the global integration of many markets previously divided by national, social, or other boundaries. I can now buy British and French books previously available only by special order and only through a half-dozen foreign language bookstores in the United States. Europeans can now buy books from Amazon at U.S. prices, which often saves them 30 to 50 percent. Anyone, anywhere, can buy London theater tickets and check the schedules for museum exhibitions and symphony performances anywhere in the world. I think this is *great*. But at the same instant, global provision of information and transactions will also cause enormous economic and political stresses.

For example, many European and Asian nations, including Germany and France, have highly restrictive regulations that limit the behavior and competitiveness of the retailing sector. Such regulations will become decreasingly enforceable and will quickly become completely untenable in the absence of artificial regulatory controls on Internet-based commerce. Such controls are, in principle, possible; one could apply extremely high taxes to Internet transactions, or even to use of bandwidth. Such controls would cause major economic distortions and reduce consumer welfare. They would also be extremely difficult to enforce, and indeed would be effectively *impossible* to enforce in the absence of international agreements. Substantial difficulties may also emerge in other large policy questions including regulation of financial services industries, contract law, taxation, and consumer information requirements. In many nations, the competitive pressure generated by the Internet will also cause major domestic tensions, not least in foreign (especially third world) telephone monopolies that make the United States look like a model of competitive perfection by comparison.

The Inequality Issue The first Industrial Revolution that began with steam engines and textiles in the latter half of the eighteenth century in England clearly generated enormous improvements in living standards. Equally obviously, it led to miserable conditions for some who were left behind, or rendered powerless, by its demands. Although there is not yet any clear evidence on the matter, my personal suspicion is that the speed and voraciousness of the Internet revolution will cause a similar, temporary, but sharp increase in global economic inequality, lasting perhaps a generation. For those who can effectively use the Internet—who have the required skills, money, computers, intellectual flexibility, institutional support, information, and social approval—the Internet provides such enormous advantages that it will often make the difference between competitive success and failure.

This is not all bad. In many cases, this will enable the previously powerless to improve their situation relative to the previously privileged, in highly desirable ways. In situations ranging from political dissidence in controlled societies to the ability of E*Trade to challenge Merrill Lynch, the Internet will make the established and wealthy work harder for their privileges. Equally, however, the skilled, wealthy, computer-literate, flexible, and simply lucky will pull rapidly ahead of the uneducated, illiterate, innumerate, and those trapped in inflexible situations or societies that cannot adapt to the pace of Internet-driven change. Many organizations, people, and nations are *not* particularly well prepared to flourish in such an environment and will pay for it, both within nations and between them. The available statistical evidence, while not as reliable as one would like, suggests that this is already happening, both in the United States and elsewhere. My own impression is that neither the U.S. government nor most foreign governments are reacting fast enough to mitigate the damage, which will primarily affect the poorest 25 percent of the population. Twenty-five percent of the U.S. population is a lot of people, and 25 percent of the world population is even more.

This problem, I think, is not receiving the amount of attention it should. Even more important, it's not receiving the *kind* of attention it should. The economics discipline has contributed remarkably little to understanding the sources of economic growth and stagnation, either in the United States or in the developing world. Economics does not spend much time investigating the policies, institutions, and norms that clearly have much to do with economic performance. The U.S. start-up system, for example, exists nowhere else in the world. Smaller versions of it exist only in Israel, Poland, and Taiwan—but not in Europe. The Silicon Valley system depends on a rich set of government policies, habits, and private institutions that have evolved over the last half century. Economics has had remarkably little to say about why this is so, or how the system could be replicated elsewhere. Nor has it been effective in coming to grips with the implications of information technology for globalization, or the determinants of growth in a technology-based era.

These problems even show up inside economic methodology. Economic theory remains dominated by highly stylized, quite rigid mathematical models. This leaves out both primary research about facts and also newer theoretical methods. In a wide array of disciplines, ranging from evolutionary biology to epidemiology to political science, computer simulations are revolutionizing theoretical research. This new field, complexity theory, uses evolutionary or so-called agent-based simulations to develop and explore models that often have highly original implications. These new models, which are heavily dependent upon computer power, have already generated interesting results that potentially undermine much of conventional economics. These models offer the eventual prospect of far richer, and more realistic explorations of social, political, and economic phenomena and their interactions than the traditional models of these disciplines, which have become quite isolated from one another.

Yet the social sciences in general have been slow to employ these new computer-based models (relative to biology, for example). Economics is not alone among academic social sciences in this regard, but has been the slowest, most rigid, and most resistant discipline. For example, two of the most important books in the new field, Axelrod's *The Evolution of Cooperation* and Epstein and Axtell's *Growing Artificial Societies,* were written by political scientists. It has been apparent to many people in the technology sector, and even outside of it, that information technology is profoundly remaking economic life. Yet the economics discipline has remained a lagging indicator. In fact, the best empirical investigations of how technology and its management affect economic behavior have been conducted by noneconomists such as Kim Clark at Harvard Business School.

Since the economics discipline still has considerable influence in economic policy analysis and policy making, this rigidity in the face of rapid change could become dangerous. In fact, perhaps it already has. Slowly, grant-making foundations and agencies such as the NSF are increasing their support of newer, interdisciplinary, computer-based research that uses complexity theory. But we have a long way to go.

It also turns out, however, that there is one regard in which economics has become eminently practical. It has sold out to the lobbying interests of the one industry that really is in a position to slow down the Internet revolution. I will close this book with a discussion of this question.

THE TELECOMMUNICATIONS BOTTLENECK AND THE CORRUPTION OF ECONOMICS

The rise of the Internet is profoundly destabilizing to existing structures of economic and political power, which of course generates resistance. And the telecommunications sector does resistance very well. Local telecommunications is the last bastion of retrograde monopoly behavior in American high technology. Relative to its potential, it is therefore one of the worst-performing industries in the world. This condition is just on the verge of becoming dangerous, because the progress of the Internet now requires major advances in communications services. But the enormous bureaucratic incumbents who dominate telecommunications—particularly the regulated monopoly local exchange telephone carriers and cable television providers—do not want to provide these advances, and/or seek to slow them down, limit and control them. Even the long-distance companies have mixed incentives in this domain.

The reason for their stonewalling is quite simple: they will be among the first to go. Future systems for carrying telephone calls, videoconferences, images such as fax or photographs, and even television will (or at least should) be provided by a system that looks much more like the Internet than like current telephone or cable TV systems. Furthermore, Internet telephony systems based in the United States are already affecting domestic telephone monopolies throughout the world. But for historical reasons, most telephone and television systems are regulated monopolies, often owned or tightly controlled by governments, and the telecommunications sector also has the special characteristic that the current Internet depends upon it technologically for local access. This makes things very tricky.

The stakes are huge. Traditional telecommunications is a $150 billion industry in the United States and a $700 billion industry globally. It is critical to the Internet yet deeply threatened by it. If local telecommunications markets were truly competitive, traditional telephone and data services would decline sharply in price and would be rapidly absorbed and/or destroyed by the Internet once high-speed Internet service was widely available. Since most of the telecommunications companies are monopolies, and since they are currently necessary to the provision of Internet services, they have chosen to be part of the problem rather than part of the solution. Even long-distance companies such as AT&T are deeply threatened by advanced Internet service, which will eventually absorb long-distance and international services too. Furthermore,

AT&T has purchased TCI, the largest operator of local cable television monopolies in the United States, and is acquiring more cable companies as well. Consequently, the long-distance industry cannot be counted on to discipline the monopoly local providers.

In the dangers it presents to U.S. and global economic progress, and possibly even to freedom of speech, the telecommunications situation dwarfs Microsoft, probably by a factor of ten. Unlike Microsoft, the local telecommunications industry already causes a huge drag on U.S. economic growth and the Internet's technical progress. Yet while the Justice Department has taken action against Microsoft, however incompletely and ineptly, it has done virtually nothing about the telecommunications monopolies. In part this is because telecommunications has until recently been dull and unsexy. There is another reason, however: the industry wields enormous power, in part by paying lots of money to academic economists, former telecommunications regulators, and politicians. In some cases this results in appalling conflicts of interest, some of which I will describe shortly.

The Problem As the Internet grows, Internet speeds increase, and new technologies permit increased Internet service quality, the Internet will absorb more and more information industries. The economic and social effect of this development will be enormous and will eventually include voice telephone service, traditional data communications services, and virtually all information distribution industries, as I mentioned above. Already, personal computers can download music well enough (using the MP3 data format) to make the music industry nervous. Faster and more advanced Internet services would allow even cooler things: musicians jamming over the Net, long distance, in real time; Web-based direct distribution of high-definition independent films; live distribution of concerts, press conferences, university lectures; good videoconferencing; essentially free self-distribution of many creative works.

But the music industry can't do much, really, to stop the overall progress of the Internet. Neither can magazine publishers, Kodak, the movie industry, FedEx, software retailers, or the U.S. Postal Service. Unfortunately, however, the monopoly telecommunications companies *can* do something to slow down the Internet, *because the Internet depends upon them*. The ability of the Internet to absorb new functions and industries, including telephone and data communications services, depends upon continued progress in three commercial technologies. One is personal computers; the second, networking equipment and fiber optics that provide high-volume Internet transport; and the third, the local communications channel that carries Internet service to and from your home or office. The first two—computers and Internet "backbone" services—are highly competitive, and the price and performance of their technologies are progressing extremely fast—50 to 100 percent per year. The third, local telecommunications, is dominated by regulated monopolies (the local telephone and cable TV industries), and—surprise!—the price and performance of *their* services are lagging badly. And when these companies do supply advanced services, they do so in artificially controlled ways designed to prevent exactly the competition against their traditional services that the Internet ought to provide.

In addition, many of these companies are quite simply incompetent. AT&T and the Bell system local monopolies are, in many ways, a bad joke in the way they do everything except basic voice telephone service (the one thing that, in fairness to them, they seem to do well). They have been regulated monopolies for the entire careers of their executives and have neither the incentive nor the ability to compete in rapidly changing, advanced networking markets. Until recently most local telephone companies would not even let you send them e-mail, pay your bill with a credit card, or use the Web to order services or equipment. Some of them *still* don't let you do these things. Their service is appalling; compare what happens when you call your telephone company to what happens when you call FedEx. In fact, *the federal government* has used the Web faster and in more innovative ways than the telephone companies.

Much of the problem comes from the management culture of the telephone industry. The top management ranks of local communications carriers are still dominated by Bell system career bureaucrats from legal affairs, public relations, government relations, and finance; out of the top thousand telecommunications executives in the United States, there are probably fewer than a dozen who have advanced technical degrees. Their executive pay and corporate governance arrangements are awful. Their boards of directors include very few high technology executives and many ornamental nonentities such as retired executives and college presidents. Director compensation is strongly linked to longevity rather than corporate performance, hardly a recipe for vigilance.

These companies also have many interlocking business and political relationships, giving them an incentive to avoid competing with one another. And in fact they *don't* compete with one another, despite laws and federal policies that encourage them to do so. For example, the local telephone companies complain that through its interpretation of the 1996 Telecommunications Act, the FCC is forcing them to sell facilities to competitors at artificially low prices. Yet none of the regional Bell monopolies has attempted to use this alleged condition to invade the territories of any others and offer competitive services.

The rise of the Internet, together with the Telecommunications Act of 1996, began to place pressure on the telephone industry's cozy arrangements. The 1996 act mandated "unbundling" of the telephone monopolies' systems so that Internet providers and others could lease their local wiring in order to provide advanced local services, such as high-speed Internet access. The monopolies' primary response was to stonewall—litigating against the government, refusing to provide adequate technical information and support to aspiring local services competitors, and merging with one another to form even larger and more powerful monopolies. Bell Atlantic has already acquired NYNEX, and Southwestern Bell (SBC) has already acquired Pacific Telesis. Now Bell Atlantic has also agreed to acquire GTE, SBC has agreed to acquire Ameritech, and AT&T has purchased TCI. Soon, there will be only four or five local communications providers in the United States. Worse, all of them will have strong incentives to retard, or warp, the provision of advanced Internet services.

The industry, and its defenders—we will come to them shortly—generally advance two arguments in response to these criticisms. The first is that the regulators made them do it: they are so constrained by the complex and archaic regulatory regime that if only they were let free, all would be well. There is little truth to this. The regulatory regime is indeed awful—the FCC and the state regulators are astonishingly inefficient and often as devoid of high technology expertise as the industry itself—but the regulatory system is as much the creation of the industry as the other way around. Furthermore, the direction of regulation over the last decade has been to give the industry far more leeway, not less. The industry has used this leeway to increase profits, dividends, mergers, and diversifications into cable television and foreign telephone monopolies. Investment in new technology has remained very low and in some cases has even declined. Through most of the 1990s, the telecommunications industry spent less than 1 percent of revenues on R&D (versus 5 to 10 percent for competitive high technology companies). Their capital investment levels have generally remained flat for most of the decade, and their capital investment is dominated by traditional, low technology systems rather than Internet-ready technology.

The industry's second defense is that competition between the telephone companies and cable television providers is now, finally, yielding progress. There is indeed some progress, but it is very slow, very limited, and its structure is quite worrisome. For example @Home, which is affiliated with AT&T/TCI, is providing high-speed Internet access to about half a million people. But @Home gives technical advantages to certain preferred Web sites and prohibits video clips longer than ten minutes from being stored on its servers—because good video over the Web could compete with TCI's cable TV programming. TCI also prohibits other Internet service providers from connecting to its network, which has generated protests from AOL and other Internet service providers. Similarly, although Pacific Bell and other telephone monopolies are starting to provide advanced Internet services, the technology and pricing of these services are carefully structured to make them unsuitable for voice telephone service and to require use of the telephone companies' own Internet services subsidiaries.

The overall situation, therefore, remains bad. As of late 1999, more than half of U.S. households have personal computers. Yet only 1 million U.S. homes and businesses *combined* have high-speed Internet access based on modern technology, despite the fact that this technology is readily available and inexpensive. The rate of technical progress and price-performance improvement exhibited by local telecommunications monopolies ranges from zero to a maximum of perhaps 20 percent per year, versus 50 to 100 percent per year for every other information technology industry (computers, software, networking equipment, business networking systems). One major reason for this, of course, is that the telephone companies are still near-monopolies in providing traditional, extremely expensive data services. Conventional data services such as T1 and T3 (1.5 megabits per second and 45 megabits per second, both services widely used for Internet access by commercial Web sites) are now probably five to ten times more expensive than they would be in a competitive market using modern systems.

And these are not trivial matters. T1 service is a $10 billion per year business in the United States and growing rapidly owing to the Internet. The price data are less clear than one would like, because telephone companies generally refuse to provide rate information, and state utility commissions usually keep only *paper* files, and often throw away old price schedules. But T1 service clearly remains very expensive and has not declined in price at the rate technical progress implies it should have. T1 installation costs range from $300 to $2,500, with monthly charges varying from $300 to $1,000 per month. Yet the underlying cost of this service is probably about $50 per month, and declining rapidly due to improvements in electronics.

This situation is reminiscent of the way IBM retarded progress in the computer industry until the late 1980s. It is already causing a major drag on the growth of the technology sector and the U.S. economy. For a $150 billion industry, there is a big difference between 0 to 25 percent per year technical progress and the 50 to 100 percent per year progress exhibited by all competitive technology sectors. Furthermore, this problem cascades into the technology sector and indeed to all users of information technology. The total effect is to reduce U.S. productivity and GNP growth by 1 percent per year, possibly even more. And things are still getting worse, as telecommunications becomes a major bottleneck to computing and Internet services and the mismatch between computer speeds and local telecommunications performance continues to grow. As one Intel manager said to me, "We make Ferraris, but unfortunately they have to use dirt roads."

The Problems of Lobbying and Economics Given the importance of Internet services, why does this situation persist, and why is it so little discussed in academic and policy circles? At this writing the Justice Department has not blocked a single merger, has not filed a single lawsuit, and has not initiated any major investigations of anticompetitive or collusive behavior by the telephone companies. The FCC has been similarly passive, with the exception of prohibiting the local carriers from entering long-distance markets until they open themselves to more competition. But given the size of the problem, there has been remarkably little policy response. Why? Here, we come to the telecommunications industry's true core competencies: litigation, lobbying, and buying people, especially former government officials and prominent economists. The local carriers have been lobbying, among other things, to merge with one another, to have the FCC regulate the Internet industry, and to force Internet service providers to pay fees (so-called access charges) for the right to use the telephone network. And when the telephone industry lobbies, it doesn't fool around. Let me first give you a general idea, and then provide a few examples.

The local telephone companies alone have about five hundred full-time employees lobbying in Washington, *not* counting the innumerable law firms, lobbying firms, and public relations firms they also employ. They also have large lobbying efforts at the state level. Local, long-distance, and cable companies are also among the largest contributors to political campaigns and political action committees at both state and federal levels. In total, the telecommunications industry probably spends half a billion dollars a year on lobbying in all forms; that's serious money.

And the people they choose aren't file clerks. The use of former government officials is well known; somewhat less well known, but equally pervasive, is the corruption of the academic economics discipline. Let us consider, for example, a few federal officials and prominent economists and what they are doing these days.

The chief economists of the FCC and the Justice Department's Antitrust Division are usually senior economists who serve at Justice during a two-year academic leave. In the 1990s, three of Justice's chief economists were Rich Gilbert, Carl Shapiro, and Daniel Rubinfeld (the most current officeholder and still a consultant to DOJ). All three are professors at UC Berkeley. Until they entered Justice, all three had also been employees of a most extraordinary firm: the Law and Economics Consulting Group, or LECG. (If you don't believe what I'm about to say, look them up at www.lecg.com.)

LECG is the largest corporate antitrust consulting firm in the United States, with revenues of more than $50 million. It gets over a quarter of its revenues from the telecommunications industry and most of the rest from other current or potential antitrust defendants. Rich Gilbert was a founder of LECG. When he entered the government, he sold his LECG stock back to LECG, thus avoiding conflict of interest restrictions. Then, when he left Justice two years later, he repurchased it; his LECG stock is now worth more than $30 million. After his government service, Carl Shapiro formed his own antitrust consulting firm with Michael Katz, another Berkeley professor who had just been the chief economist of the FCC. Their firm, the Tilden Group, was recently acquired by the *other* large corporate antitrust consulting firm, Charles River Associates. Katz and another Berkeley professor, Glenn Woroch, run a research project, the Consortium for Research on Telecommunications Policy, which is funded almost entirely by the Ameritech Foundation. Woroch also consults for Bell-South. Daniel Rubinfeld, the Justice chief economist until late 1998, owned more than $6 million in LECG stock while working for Justice, representing the overwhelming majority of his personal wealth. LECG's newest senior partner is Laura Tyson, the dean of UC Berkeley's business school, who is also a director of Ameritech and was the chairwoman of the National Economic Council in the first Clinton administration.

Berkeley is in no way unique. MIT's Jerry Hausman recently published a highly polemic paper in a Brookings volume, attacking the FCC for not giving the telephone monopolies more freedom in the Internet industry. What Hausman did not mention in the paper is that he has received millions of dollars from the telecommunications industry for regulatory consulting and expert testimony. A similar story is found in most major economics departments, including the most prominent industrial economists in the United States. NYU's William Baumol, another famous economist and a past president of the American Economic Association, has a confidential consulting version of his curriculum vitae containing a fifty-page supplement listing his expert witness engagements, for which he is paid more than one thousand dollars per hour. Professor Baumol does not seem to have encountered many things he won't testify about. Peter Temin, former chair of the MIT Economics Department, has consulted for AT&T on antitrust and regulatory matters since the 1970s (I spent the summer of 1980 working for him). Robert Crandall at Brookings consults for Bell Atlantic.

I could go on in this vein for quite some time. I should say, to be rigorous about this, that I do not possess any smoking guns, and I don't know some of these people well enough to have a personal assessment of their individual ethical standards. But to put it bluntly, the entire situation smells very, very bad. Enormous conflicts of interest among former government officials and/or economists, particularly those who specialize in regulation or antitrust policy, are now the rule rather than the exception. In addition, many of these economists violate their own university regulations by spending more time consulting than doing academic work, by not fully disclosing their consulting relationships, and by publishing research favorable to their clients without stating that they consult for the industries discussed in their publications.

Now, given this situation, suppose you're a graduate student in economics or management, writing a Ph.D. thesis on telecommunications policy. Choice A: attack the clients and publications of all the senior professors supervising your work, and who are critical to your career. Choice B: make lots of money working for them, and then continue in their footsteps. Perhaps unsurprisingly, very few seem to opt for choice A. A number of prominent economists are privately very disturbed by this situation, but they are outnumbered and few dare to comment publicly about it. University administrators seem to be remarkably timid about reining in this problem. Neither Congress nor the administration seem to be much better. Former high-level government officials and managers of political campaigns lobby for the telecommunications industry with the same regularity. Indeed, the prostitution of the political system is even greater than that of academia and economics, and is by no means confined to the Clinton administration or to Democrats. Republicans in Congress, such as Senator John McCain, have been by far the worst offenders in pressuring the FCC on behalf of the telecommunications monopolies—especially the local telephone companies, but the cable TV industry and broadcast networks as well. Despite the huge deficits of Clinton administration antitrust policy and personnel, congressional Republicans have worsened that situation as well. They receive the overwhelming majority of political contributions from telecommunications monopolies, Microsoft, and other antitrust defendants, and regularly call for "freeing" the incumbent telecommunications industry from antitrust scrutiny.

The condition of the antitrust system in regard to high technology issues of course makes things worse. In any potentially major case brought against the telecommunications industry, the Justice Department would be outspent by at least ten to one, probably more, by the defendants and would be intellectually outgunned just as badly. Furthermore, the condition of the economics discipline has become so extreme that it is difficult to find prominent economists who do not have massive conflicts of interest and who would be willing to testify for the government. (The federal government's maximum consulting rate is about one tenth the rate generally paid to corporate expert witnesses.) Only a highly competent and self-confident organization, and one quite free from political pressure, would dare to go to war under such circumstances. Neither the Justice Department, the FTC, nor the FCC appears to be such an organization. Indeed, the FCC is even worse than the Justice Department's Antitrust Division in some ways; to my knowledge, no FCC commissioner has ever come from a high technology industry.

Some Potential Reforms Substantively, the major policy goal related to advanced telecommunications services is that the Internet services industry have an open, competitive structure, with incentives to generate technical progress for all users. Thus, both the cable television industry and the local telephone companies should be required to open their networks to independent Internet service providers. Moreover, *all* advanced communications and Internet service providers should be prohibited from providing or restricting Internet content, except at the specific request of customers (e.g., to filter out sites unsuitable for children at the request of a parent). In the current situation, immediate anti-trust investigations and FCC regulatory proceedings directed against both the cable industry and the local telephone companies are more than justified. However, there are also major problems with the underlying structural conditions, which cripple the antitrust system and economic policy analysis.

One can envision a number of policy reforms in these areas. In the antitrust system, special courts with technically trained judges have been proposed and might be an excellent idea. It is also necessary to improve the high technology expertise of the Justice Department and the FCC and to control the conflict of interest problem, both within the government and in university economics departments. In addition, something should be done about the expert witness situation. Recently, in a highly unusual but encouraging development, a federal judge in a major product liability case appointed a panel of independent medical expert witnesses who were paid by and reported to the judge, rather than the contending parties. In the case of high technology antitrust cases, this would be extremely helpful, perhaps even necessary.

This would not, however, be sufficient in itself. Tighter conflict of interest guidelines for relationships between government service, academic research, and consulting are also required to avoid the LECG phenomenon. Such policies could be implemented directly by universities, but if the universities fail to act, they could and should be implemented by the grant-making agencies (NSF, DARPA, NIH) or by new legislation. Measures to increase the political independence of the FCC and Justice Department would also be useful, as, obviously, would campaign finance reform. The political feasibility of such measures is, alas, quite another issue.

Finally, the telecommunications industry is an issue that U.S. foreign policy and international institutions such as the World Bank should take much more seriously. For historical reasons, most of the world's telecommunications systems, particularly in the developing world, are even more monopolistic and retrograde than the U.S. system. Yet U.S. trade policy has sometimes been driven by the telecommunications monopolies, who wish to acquire or partner with foreign monopolies. Foreign governments also prevent progress because privatization of national telephone companies yields more money if they are monopolies. But for these countries, increased competition and technical progress in telecommunications is vital to economic development, particularly in an Internet-based world economy.

In Conclusion

Despite the many acerbic comments I've made in this book, I would like to make it clear that I don't regret being a dilettante, getting a Ph.D. in political science, or starting Vermeer. The world is of course an imperfect place, and will remain so. But for all its problems, the system has worked awfully well in my case, and it's very hard for me to complain. Vermeer was an amazing experience, often a lot of fun, and FrontPage was and remains a remarkable product. I worked with some of the best people in the world, and I learned an enormous amount. Vermeer has given me the freedom to pursue political, charitable, and artistic interests and to speak my mind in this book. And the Internet still contains many cool opportunities, some of which I'm investing in. I can't talk about those, of course. If you have a good idea, let me know . . . But I think it will be a while before I run another company myself.

ACKNOWLEDGMENTS

*D*ue to the nature of this book, two statements frequently made by authors are unusually important and serious in this case. First, I owe many debts, large ones, related to this book, both in regard to writing it and to the emotional sustenance I received while doing so. It would have been impossible to finish it without the help and companionship of those I thank below, and others I do not mention, either from concern or neglect. Second, none of these people bears any responsibility whatsoever for my opinions, nor for any remaining errors of fact or judgment. Indeed, several people registered serious, intelligent objections to some of my interpretations and arguments, and thereby greatly improved them. If I didn't take enough of their advice, you must fault me alone.

Without any question my greatest debt is to Charles Morris, who is in many ways the chief architect of this book as well as a careful reader, editor, writer, dear friend, generous human being, relentless but always well-meaning critic, and dangerously witty, perceptive observer of all things. Charlie is in no way responsible for whatever may still be bad; but to whatever extent this book has a coherent structure and logic, he deserves much of the credit.

A number of people did quite a lot of hard work on this book. Marc Gorenstein, Kim Malone, Diana Propper, and Camille LeBlanc, close friends who I drafted to become readers and critics, read the manuscript carefully, providing extremely valuable comments even (perhaps especially) when they disagreed with what I said or how I said it. I would also like to thank three other important readers who must remain anonymous, all of them intimately familiar with the events I describe. In addition, I owe much to my long-suffering editor, John Mahaney, and his good-natured assistant, Luke Mitchell; Carie Freimuth, the wonderfully kind and efficient publisher of Times Books; Will Weisser, for publicity; Nancy Inglis and Dennis Ambrose for production; John Castro, for being the most amazingly efficient and good-natured fact-checker in the world; and Adam Goldberg of Tigerfish, for interview transcriptions. Thanks to everyone I interviewed, including those I should not name. To my friends, who provided moral support, alcohol, sanity, and laughter, my debts are huge: Rocky, for dinners outdoors and piano soirees indoors; Camille, for her kindness and house and dogs; Maria Kukuruzinska and Susanna Kaysen, who gave me trio dinners before, during, and after Vermeer. Jonathan Miller and Diane Fassino gave me music and dinners and their home. Heather Shively not only was witty and inspiring, but put up with more eccentricity than anyone should. Good friends, old and new (a few from whom I have regrettably become estranged), gave me what friends give, for which there is no substitute. I owe deep thanks to Marc Gorenstein, Alex Schuessler and his wonderful circle of friends, Suzanne Delbanco (now, Dr. D) and her wonderful circle of friends, Kim Malone, Chris and Lisa Suits, Patrick Nee and Deborah Dyer, Elizabeth Burney-Jones, Joe Farrell and Suzanne Schotchmer, Kathleen Morris, Jeff and Laura Critchfield, Dale Murphy, David Hale, Elizabeth Charles and Daniel Cox, my astounding thesis advisor Carl Kaysen and his wife, Ruth Butler, Sybil Francis, Karen Kornbluh, Louisa Koch, Bill Docken, Dorothy Robyn, John Seely Brown and Susan Haviland, Paul Ricci, Diana Propper, Michael Scriven, Lili Matsuda, Patricia Barbizet, Antonella Vergati, Janicke Jensen, Vibeke Jensen, George Smoot, Lea Sewell, Maryann McGrail, Bob Metcalfe, Ellen Pope, Henryka Manes, Jocelyn Byrne, Leslie Koch, John Caldwell and Zane Blaney, Vered Sharon, Philippe Maniere, Koranyi Noemi, Laura Stanford; the wonderful people I met through the French American Foundation Young Leaders program and the German Marshall Fund; Bo Cutter, Wilf Corrigan, Stephanie Flanders, Jasmine Dellal, Ralph Gomory, Lucy McCauley, Laurie Dill, June Komisar, Shelley Harrison; the many remarkable people I met in Eastern Europe, Russia, Israel, and the former Soviet Union; and everyone at the The After School Corporation, a good cause if ever there was one.

I also owe much to my family: my mother, my aunt Nancy and uncle Leslie, cousins Doug, Cynthia, Wallace, Judy, and Jon; and cousin Cori and her husband, Fred, and their children, who provided a wonderful Thanksgiving during Vermeer's most tension-drenched period.

There are also professional and/or academic acquaintances from whose help and kindness I have benefited, some of whom I cannot or should not name. Some of them have become friends too. First and foremost are Randy Forgaard and the people who joined us at Vermeer Technologies. Randy is a very special human being, and I will always owe him more than I can possibly say. Without him, this would have turned out very differently, and not nearly as well. To Andy Schulert and Peter Amstein, the first two people who joined us, and who were critical to our success, all I can say is: how the hell did we con you into doing it? Once Randy and you two joined, at least there were some rational people around, which made it a lot easier to persuade everyone else . . . but it was still an insane plunge. Thank you for taking it—Rob, Ted, Ed, Tad, Tom, Stu, Manda, Scott, Kelley, all forty of you, including Frank and others I sometimes criticized, and the early consultants who took stock instead of the cash we didn't have. And, Wade, thanks for that term sheet. Outside of Vermeer, I also want to thank Larry Summers, Les Gelb, Larry Korb, Tom Kalil, Eric Schmidt, Kim Polese, Eric Hahn, Bob Litan, John Guttag, George Downs, Josh Epstein, Robert Axtell, Josh Cohen, Robert Lieber, Michael Iovenko, Paul Klingenstein, Josh Lerner, Marty Manley, Anno Saxenian, Dominick Orr, Esther Dyson, Bob Palmer, Bruce Holbein, Ken Flamm, Kevin Werbach, Lael Brainard, Peter Anastos and everyone at the Alliance Technology Fund; several executives at Motorola and Texas Instruments; and a number of journalists. Then there are the really important institutions: Berkeley's cafés, particularly Strada, Milano, and Brewed Awakening, where I wrote most of the book; Chez Panisse and Oliveto, Berkeley's essential restaurants; and the two most civilized hotels in America, the Lowell Hotel in Manhattan, and the Garden Court Hotel in Palo Alto.

And finally, I must try to thank Shoshana Haulley adequately. I can't, but I have to try. She's so smart, so organized, so trustworthy, so patient and appropriately impatient, so relaxed and utterly effective, so humorous and good-natured in every circumstance, so understanding of my very eccentric personality, so omnicompetent, so fearless, so unflustered by crisis and disaster, so completely well-intentioned and yet wily, so willing and able to do the strangest things at my request, so kind, and so generally wonderful in every way, that without her, my life would simply collapse. She was as essential to my finishing this book as she is to everything else I do, or attempt. How she puts up with me I have no idea.

Once again, I must emphasize that none of these people or institutions can be blamed at all for how I, or this book, turned out. It's all my fault.

NOTES

Introduction

3. "A billion here . . .": Judith Evans and Frank Swoboda, "Going on the Road Takes a Bigger Toll," *The Washington Post*, 8 February 1999.
4. Jeff Bezos: Doug Levy, "Flying High on the Future Net Elite: 'It's Not About Money,'" *USA Today*, 22 February 1999.
6. Apple under John Sculley: For a full discussion of John Sculley's tenure at Apple, see Jim Carlton, *Apple*. New York: Times Business/Random House, 1997.
6. who'd never had: Robert H. Reid, *Architects of the Web*. New York: John Wiley & Sons, 1997, pp. 3, 20.
7. When Jobs took: Author interview, confidential source.
7. Then he sold his own: Carlton, *Apple*, p. 412.
7. and he flushed NeXT: Stewart Alsop, "Alsop on Infotech," *Fortune*, 22 June 1998.
7. The industry is: Author interview, confidential source.
8. John Moussouris: "Karmic balance?" *PC Week*, 26 August 1996.
8. zero to $1 billion: Andrew Kupfer, "America's Fastest-Growing Company," *Fortune*, 13 August 1990.
9. plus a couple: R. Colin Johnson, "WYSIWYG for the Web," *Electronic Engineering Times*, 27 November 1995. NetObjects company Web site: www.netobjects.com/aboutnetobjects/html/profile.html.

10. Lou Gerstner: Saul Hansell, "Now, Big Blue Is at Your Service," *The New York Times,* 18 January 1998.

11. East Coast companies: For a detailed discussion of the origins of these companies, see Annalee Saxenian, *Regional Advantage: Culture and Competition in Silicon Valley and Route 128.* Cambridge, Mass.: Harvard University Press, 1994; and Ernest Braun and Stuart Macdonald, *Revolution in Miniature: The History and Impact of Semiconductor Electronics.* Cambridge: Cambridge University Press, 1978.

11. Those companies alone: www. morningstar.net/home.html.

13. Virtually all: Reid, *Architects of the Web,* pp. xx–xxiii.

13. $10 billion commercial: Lorraine Sileo, *Online Services: 1994 Review, Trends, and Forecast.* Wilton, Conn.: Simba Information Inc., 1994, p. 2.

14. CEOs should not: Adam Cohen, "A Tale of Two Bills," *Time,* 25 January 1999; Joseph Nocera, "Witnesses in Wonderland," *Fortune,* 1 March 1999; and James Wallace, *Overdrive: Bill Gates and the Race to Control Cyberspace.* New York: John Wiley & Sons, 1997, p. 45.

15. good at lobbying: "Clinton Defends Ethics Policy on Lobbying," Reuters North American Wire, 8 December 1993; and Douglas Turner, "The Political Influence Industry Enters the White House Door," *The Buffalo News,* 13 December 1993.

15. UC Berkeley economist: "Antitrust Division Names Two Additions to Leadership Team," Department of Justice Press Release, 18 September 1997.

15. owns over $6 million: LECG, Inc, form S-1, 16 October 1997. Available at www.sec.gov.

15. This firm: see LECG, Inc., Web site at www.lecg.com/html/pri_frm.htm.

ONE

16. "The best electric train": "A Recluse Flirts with the Spotlight," *Sunday Times* (London), 14 February 1999.

16. take his Porsches: James Wallace and Jim Erickson, *Hard Drive: Bill Gates and the Making of the Microsoft Empire.* New York: HarperBusiness, 1993, p. 241.

19. notorious womanizer: Cliff Joseph, "Network: Meet Larry Ellison," *The Independent* (London), 29 April 1997.

20. for buying supersonic: James W. Michaels, "Keeping Score," *Forbes,* 14 October 1996.

20. securing the felony conviction: Benjamin Pimentel, "Woman Who Accused Oracle Chief Guilty of Perjury," *The San Francisco Chronicle,* 29 January 1997.

20. winning an Australian: Kevin Fagan, "Race Tragedy Tale: Oracle CEO Tells All to St. Francis Yacht Club," *The San Francisco Chronicle,* 20 January 1999.

20. Larry perceived the: Richard Shaffer, "Oracle and the Database Warriors," *Personal Computing,* 20 March 1990.

20. Oracle grew up: "Market Timing," *The New York Times,* 19 March 1995; For a detailed discussion of Oracle, see Mike Wilson, *The Difference Between God and Larry Ellison: Inside Oracle Corporation: God Doesn't Think He's Larry Ellison.* New York: Quill Trade Paperbacks, 1998.

20. semiconductor industry: For a general discussion of the semiconductor industry, see Kenneth Flamm, *Mismanaged Trade: Strategic Policy and the Semiconductor Industry,* Washington, D.C.: Brookings Institution, 1996.

21. by the late 1980s: Richard Shaffer, "Oracle and the Database Warriors," *Personal Computing,* 20 March 1990.

22. superior designs and flexibility: John Markoff, "Yankee Ingenuity Wins Out in PC's," *The New York Times,* 23 November 1992.

22. There is a risk: Robert Heller, "Whodunit to IBM?" *The Independent* (London), 20 March 1994.

23. *Computer Wars:* Charles H. Ferguson and Charles R. Morris, *Computer Wars: The Fall of IBM and the Future of Global Technology,* New York: Times Books, 1994.

23. Their conduct: Saul Hansell, "Now, Big Blue Is at Your Service," *The New York Times,* 18 January 1998.

23. declined by 60 percent: Clint Willis, "Money Rates the 30 Dow Stocks," *Money,* May 1993.

24. Gerstner's previous job: Marc Levinson, "Can He Make an Elephant Dance?," *Newsweek,* 5 April 1993.

24. More than half: Michael Cooney, "IBM Makes Further Cuts in Networking Systems Unit," *Network World,* 5 December 1994.

24. "The last thing": Dan Blake, "Maybe It's Vision; Maybe It's Lose Some, Win Some," The Associated Press, 17 October 1993.

24. those systems *are:* Robert Lee Hotz, "Fragile Virtual Libraries," *Los Angeles Times,* 8 October 1995.

25. worried about Sculley: For a full discussion of John Sculley's tenure at Apple, see Jim Carlton, *Apple.* New York: Times Business, Random House, 1997.

25. obviously fraudulent company: Stefan Fatsis, "Spectrum Stock Drops; Details on Company Emerge," The Associated Press, 19 October 1993.

25. four months later: David Einstein, "Sculley Quits After Four Months with New Firm," *The San Francisco Chronicle,* 8 February 1994.

26. disaster followed disaster: For a detailed discussion of Apple's history, see Carlton, *Apple.*

26. for $400 million: Ibid., p. 412.

26. chief technology officer: Colleen Benson, "People in Business," *The San Francisco Chronicle,* 16 August 1997; "Executive Suite: Larry Rabiner Named Vice President of Research, AT&T Labs," *EDGE, on & about AT&T,* 5 October 1998.

26. mutually incompatible systems: Robert H. Reid, *Architects of the Web,* New York: John Wiley & Sons, 1997, p. 14.

28. about a thousand: Ibid., p. xxiv.

29. Notes wasn't the answer: Colleen Frye, "Lotus' Changes to Notes and the Company's Internet Strategy," *Software Magazine,* February 1997.

29. clearly in decline: Steve Lohr, "Lotus Counts on Its New Notes Software to Rekindle Growth," *The New York Times,* 12 April 1993.

29. killed by Microsoft: Steve Boxer, "Connected: Big Bill's Excellent Adventure," *The Daily Telegraph,* 25 June 1996.

29. Lotus product anymore: Colleen Frye, "Groupware Strikes Collaborative Chord," *Software Magazine,* October 1995.

29. astonishing price of: William J. Cook, "IBM's Lotus Position," *U.S. News & World Report,* 17 June 1996.

29. Manzi resigned: Glenn Rifkin, "Chief of I.B.M.'s Lotus Resigns Ninety-nine Days After Takeover Deal," *The New York Times,* 12 October 1995; Glenn Rifkin, "Former Lotus Chief to Lead Business Service on the Internet," *The New York Times,* 24 January 1996; and Wallys Conhaim, "E-Commerce; Business Enterprises on the Internet," *Link-Up,* 13 March 1998.

30. just left 3DO: "Communications Personals," *Communications Daily,* 31 August 1994.

30. Don Emery: "WordPerfect Corp. Expands Marketing and Sales Division; Company Hires New Vice Presidents," Business Wire, 24 May 1993.

36. pay taxes at half the . . . rate: "Tax Planning for Small Business: A Dozen Helpful Strategies," *The National Public Accountant,* 11 January 1998.

36. Stac-like software: Carey Ramos and David Berlin, "Three Ways to Protect Computer Software," *The Computer Lawyer,* January 1999.

37. designed by Dave Cutler: "The Odd Couple," *Computer Business Review,* 1 January 1996.

37. whole team with him: Joseph C. Panettieri, "Can't Beat 'Em? Sue 'Em!" *WINDOWS Magazine,* 1 August 1997.

37. patents as leverage: Ibid.

38. *The Internet Unleashed:* Philip Baczewski et al., *The Internet Unleashed.* Indianapolis, Ind., Sams Pub., 1994.

39. EIT was funded: "Smart Valley Commercenet Consortium Wins Federal TRP Grant," Business Wire, 24 November 1993.

39. sixty thousand copies a month: Michael A. Cusumano, "Judo Strategy: The Competitive Dynamics of Internet Time," *Harvard Business Review,* February 1999; and Reid, *Architects of the Web,* p. 9.

Two

42. as the ARPANET: Wallace, *Overdrive,* p. 16.
42. Bolt, Baranek, and Newman: Brett Glass, "Internet Makes Standard Creation Quick and Consensual," *InfoWorld,* 12 June 1989.
42. DARPA gave research and development: Ibid.
42. telephone company—GTE: Jonathan Marshall, "GTE Buying Internet Service Firm," *The San Francisco Chronicle,* 14 November 1997.
43. National Science Foundation: Robert H. Reid, *Architects of the Web,* New York: John Wiley & Sons, 1997, p. xxi.
43. commercial online services: Kara Swisher, *aol.com: How Steve Case Beat Bill Gates, Nailed the Netheads, and Made Millions in the War for the Web.* New York: Times Books, 1998, p. 15.
43. big industry: Lorraine Sileo, *Online Services: 1994 Review, Trends, and Forecast.* Wilton: Simba Information Inc., 1994, p. 2.
43. destroyed it so fast: Peter H. Lewis, "More Users Now Taking Direct Route to the Internet, a Survey Finds," *The New York Times,* 23 September 1996.
44. not Internet compatible: "Code Dump," *Trading Systems Technology,* 7 March 1994.
45. primary architect of: "Joy in Unixville," *Computerworld Focus,* 16 January 1985.
46. NT is now picking off: "Windows NT Beat Unix in Unit Sales in 1997, Data Show," *The Wall Street Journal,* 30 January 1998.
46. he joined a well-intentioned: "Tim Berners-Lee," *Newsmakers 1997,* 6 January 1998.
46. Web standards group: W3C consortium; Web site at www.w3.org/.
47. In 1990: "Lifetime Achievement Winner: Dr. Tim Berners-Lee. World Wide Web Inventor," *PC Magazine,* 15 December 1998.
47. NSF national backbone: Mark Gibbs, "Open for Business," *Network World,* 4 July 1994.
47. Electronic Frontier Foundation: Web site at www.eff.org.
47. Commercial Internet Exchange: Web site at www.cix.org.
48. Kapor made his case: Stephen Barlas, "Kapor Tries to Rally Industry in Washington; Mitchell Kapor of Lotus Development Corp.," *Marketing Computers,* April 1992.

48. *The Whole Internet User's Guide and Catalog:* Ed Krol, *The Whole Internet User's Guide and Catalog.* Cambridge, Mass.: O'Reilly & Associates, 1994.

48. entitled "NSF Implementation Plan . . .": "NSF Implementation Plan for Interim NREN," *Journal on High Speed Networking,* May 1992.

50. fought him off: Swisher, *aol.com,* pp. 66–74.

50. Nathan Myhrvold: John Markoff, "Top Woman at Microsoft to Leave Soon," *The New York Times,* 30 October 1996.

51. January 23, 1993: Joshua Quittner and Michelle Slatalla, *Speeding the Net: The Inside Story of Netscape and How It Challenged Microsoft.* New York: Atlantic Monthly Press, 1998, p. 51.

51. NCSA Web site: Web site at http://www.ncsa.uiuc.edu/ncsa.html.

51. Ironically Berners-Lee: Quittner and Slatalla, *Speeding the Net,* p. 70.

52. Markoff wrote a long article: John Markoff, "A Free and Simple Computer Link," *The New York Times,* 8 December 1993.

52. IBM announced a pilot: Scott Hettrick, "Blockbuster-IBM Deal Hits Sour Notes with Record Execs," *Video Business,* 11 June 1993.

53. rejected Prodigy and CompuServe: Swisher, *aol.com,* p. 76.

53. "I can buy twenty percent . . .": Ibid., p. 77.

53. consultant to advise: Wallace, *Overdrive,* p. 116.

53. recommendation was rejected: Ibid, p. 115.

55. GO absorbed $75 million: "Penning a Tale on Pen PC," *Los Angeles Times,* 9 May 1995.

55. "You may not . . .": Reid, *Architects of the Web,* p. 20.

58. *The Internet Unleashed:* Philip Baczewski et al., *The Internet Unleashed.* Indianapolis, Ind., Sams Pub., 1994.

62. basically nontechnical manager: Quittner and Slatalla, *Speeding the Net,* p. 147.

63. AOL swooped in: Swisher, *aol.com,* pp. 112–13.

65. on its Web site: See home.netscape.com/

65. academic and commercial protests: Reid, *Architects of the Web,* pp. 35–36.

66. brand name "Mosaic": Wallace, *Overdrive,* p. 201.

THREE

69. "You can get . . ." See www.stampede.org/people/php3.

70. hard times: Lawrence M. Fisher, "Apollo Computer Sale to Hewlett-Packard," *The New York Times,* 13 April 1989.

70. invested in PSI: Matrix Partner's Web site at www.matrixpartners.com/portcos.htm.

72. Eugene Kleiner: Lloyd Watson, "Record 77 Percent Gain in Holiday Sales," *The San Francisco Chronicle,* 25 January 1993.

72. an early investor: "NextCard raises $38 Million from Kleiner Perkins, Sequoia Capital, Highland Capital and Other Leading Investment Firms," Business Wire, 16 November 1998.

72. he funded Intel: "Robert N. Noyce," *Contemporary Newsmakers 1985,* January, 1986.

72. Don Valentine? Oracle: "Sequoia-Capital/Cisco; Sequoia Capital Stakes Cisco Systems for $2.5 Million; Don Valentine, Bill O'Meara Appointed to Board," Business Wire, 25 January 1988.

72. Dave Marquardt? Microsoft: Stephen Manes and Paul Andrews, *Gates: How Microsoft's Mogul Reinvented an Industry—and Made Himself the Richest Man in America.* New York: Touchstone, 1994, p. 176.

73. last ten years: Bob Zider, "How Venture Capital Works," *Harvard Business Review,* November 1998.

79. Ed Anderson: "Two Noted Industry Veterans Join Redstone Communications' Board of Directors," PR Newswire, 2 November 1998.

80. Greylock, we discovered: "Spyglass Unveils Commercial Internet Search Software," *Electronic Information Report,* 10 June 1994.

80. Sprout, the venture arm: See Donaldson, Lufkin & Jenrette Web site at www.dlj.com/busgrp_index.htm.

81. $100 million by Paul Allen: John Markoff, "Interval Research Is Planning to Spin Off Three Software Units," *The New York Times,* 13 November 1996.

88. Gettys is a real star: Bob Metcalfe, "Internet Plumber of the Year—Jim Gettys," *InfoWorld,* 2 February 1998.

88. one of the two architects: "Linux Expo '99 Names Technical Keynote Speaker," PR Newswire, 4 February 1999.

98. Jobs made himself CEO: Jon Swartz, "Next OS Won't Run Old Mac Software," *The San Francisco Chronicle,* 24 December 1996.

99. focus on software: "Steve Jobs' Pixar to Sell Computer Hardware Unit," *The San Francisco Chronicle,* 27 April 1990.

99. voted the deal through: confidential interview and "Notice to All Shareholders of Pixar," letter from Dr. Edwin E. Catmull, 29 March 1991.

FOUR

103. *The Mythical Man-Month:* Frederick P. Brooks, Jr., *The Mythical Man-Month.* Reading, Mass.: Addison Wesley, 1995.

104. best professional programmers: Ibid., p. 30.

104. "Good cooking takes . . .": Ibid, p. 13.
104. Microsoft is doing: For a detailed discussion of this issue, see the Bruce Jacobsen and Jim Barksdale depositions in the Microsoft antitrust trial. Transcripts available at Department of Justice Web site, www.usdoj.gov /atr/cases/exhibits/1455.pdf.
105. commercial Web services: For a detailed discussion of the opening of the Internet to commercial use, see Herb Brody, "Internet Crossroads: Transition of the Internet from Low-Cost Government Service to Private Enterprise," *Technology Review,* 15 May 1995; Michelle Quinn, "Internet Going on Its Own: Business Replaces Government as Cyberspace Supervisor," *The San Francisco Chronicle,* 29 April 1995; and http://www.merit.edu /nsfnet/nsfnet.retired for the official press release on the turnover from Merit Network, Inc.
108. three to nine times: Brooks, *The Mythical Man-Month,* pp. 4–6.
108. kids at NCSA: George Gilder, "The Coming Software Shift," *Forbes,* 28 August 1995.
108. one hundred thousand lines of code: Michael A. Cusumano and David B. Yoffie, *Competing on Internet Time: Lessons from Netscape and Its Battle with Microsoft.* New York: Free Press, 1998, p. 162.
109. *three million* lines: Ibid.
121. one on Borland: see Bruce Jacobsen deposition from the Microsoft antitrust trial, p. 162, lines 9–18. Transcripts available at Department of Justice Web site, http://www.usdoj.gov/atr/cases/ms_excerpt.htm.
121. and on Netscape: Kim S. Nash, "Explorer Beta Gains Ground on Navigator," *Computerworld,* 22 July 1996.
129. new database product, Illustra: "America Online's Internet Services Company and Illustra (TM) Form Strategic Alliance," Business Wire, 11 April 1995.
129. investor in Illustra: "Silicon Valley's New Sugar Daddies," *The Economist,* 12 July 1997.
129. Illustra's largest customers: Martin Marshall, "Buying into Objects," *InternetWeek,* 1 January 1996.

FIVE

135. "It is a . . .": Frederick P. Brooks, *The Mythical Man-Month.* Reading, Mass.: Addison Wesley, 1995, p. 47.
135. allowed Microsoft's bundling: James Wallace, *Overdrive: Bill Gates and the Race to Control Cyberspace.* New York: John Wiley & Sons, 1997, p. 270.
136. acquisition of Collabra: Michael A. Cusumano and David B. Yoffie, *Competing on Internet Time.* New York: Free Press, 1998, p. 31.

137. Apple under Sculley: Carlton, *Apple,* p. 33.

137. become an executive: "James Barksdale Joins Netscape Communications as President and CEO," PR Newswire, 11 January 1995.

137. few seasoned technologists: Cusumano and Yoffie, *Competing on Internet Time.* New York: Free Press, 1998, pp. 42–43.

137. *no chief architect:* For a detailed discussion of Netscape's corporate structure, see Cusumano and Yoffie, *Competing on Internet Time.*

137. something like 80 percent: Ibid., p. 11.

138. bought a 12 percent: Ibid., p. 75.

138. started getting serious: For a detailed discussion of Microsoft's early Internet efforts, see Wallace, *Overdrive;* and Bill Gates, "The Internet Tidal Wave," e-mail to the Microsoft Executive Committee, 26 May 1995, available from the Department of Justice Web site: www.usdoj.gov/atr/cases /exhibits/20.pdf.

139. E-mail messages made public: For copies of admitted government exhibits in the antitrust file, see the Department of Justice Web site: www /usdoj.gov/atr/cases/ms_exhibits.htm.

139. repeatedly attempted to dissuade: See Jim Barksdale's testimony from the Microsoft antitrust trial, 19 October 1998, paragraphs 92–114. Transcript available from the Department of Justice Web site: www.usdoj.gov /atr/cases/f1900/1999.htm.

139. including Barksdale: See cross-examination of Dan Rosen from the Microsoft antitrust trial, 22 February 1999. Transcript available from the Microsoft Web site: www.microsoft.com/presspass/trial/transcripts/feb99 /02-22-am.htm.

139. Clark: See Jim Clark, "Please forward," e-mail to Dan Rosen, 29 December 1994. Available from the Microsoft Web site: www.microsoft.com /presspass/trial/oct98/10-21email.htm

139. John Doerr: See the direct testimony of Daniel Rosen from the Microsoft antitrust trial, January 1999. Available at the Microsoft Web site: www .microsoft.com/presspass/trial/mswitness/rosen/rosen_full.htm.

139. Netscape had already said: Bob Metcalfe, "From the Ether; Without Case of Vapors, Netscape's Tools Will Give Blackbird Reason to Squawk," *InfoWorld,* 18 September 1995.

139. Barksdale also alleges: See Jim Barksdale's testimony from the Microsoft antitrust trial, 19 October 1998, paragraphs 111–14. Transcript available from the Department of Justice Web site: www.usdoj.gov/atr/cases /f1900/1999.htm.

139. almost identical deal: Stephen Manes and Paul Andrews, *Gates: How Microsoft's Mogul Reinvented an Industry and Made Himself the Richest Man in America.* New York: Touchstone, 1994, p. 438.

139. strangling RealNetworks: see Bruce Jacobsen deposition from the Microsoft antitrust trial, 13 January 1999. Transcript available from the Department of Justice Web site: www.usdoj.gov/atr/cases/exhibits/1455.pdf.

140. create browser APIs: Cusumano and Yoffie, *Competing on Internet Time,* p. 77.

140. eviscerate Microsoft: Mary Kathleen Flynn, "The Battle for the Net," *U.S. News & World Report,* 18 December 1995; "Summary of Written Testimony of Microsoft Witness Paul Maritz," PR Newswire, 22 January 1999; Philip Elmer-Dewitt, "Why Java Is Hot," *Time,* 22 January 1996; and Michael A. Cusumano, "Judo Strategy: The Competitive Dynamics of Internet Time," *Harvard Business Review,* January–February 1999.

141. September 18, 1995: Michael Moeller and John Dodge, "Netscape Set to Revamp Web Browsers and Servers," *PC Week,* 18 September 1995.

143. "to implement on-line . . .": "Microsoft Announces Tools to Enable a New Generation of Interactive Multimedia Applications for the Microsoft Network," PR Newswire, 28 March 1995.

143. Spyglass *prohibited* Microsoft: Wallace, *Overdrive,* p. 281.

143. authored a memo: Gates, "The Internet Tidal Wave."

144. apparently deliberately leaked: Wallace, *Overdrive,* p. 265.

144. technology and strategy: Quotes on pages 180–82 from Gates, "The Internet Tidal Wave."

144. sites, like Yahoo!: www.yahoo.com.

146. wholesaling FUD: David Bicknell, "Microsoft Net Plans Leave Users Guessing," *Computer Weekly,* 14 December 1995; "Microsoft Makes Friends with Internet," *The Times-Picayune,* 8 December 1995; "Microsoft Makes Friends with Internet," *The Houston Chronicle,* 8 December 1995; and "Gates Grasps at Internet Strategy for Microsoft," *New Media Age,* 14 December 1995.

147. successfully coerced Intel: Jay Greene, "Microsoft Trial—Bloom Is off Wintel Marriage," *The Seattle Times,* 8 November 1998. See also the *San Jose Mercury News,* 30 August 1998.

147. "livid" about Intel's: Andrew Zajac, "Gates' Stand a 'Threat': Intel Exec," *Chicago Tribune,* 10 November 1998.

147. "caved": "U.S. Investigating Microsoft's Role in Intel's Decisions," *The New York Times,* 26 August 1996.

148. "undeniably, absolutely new . . .": David Bank, "Why Sun Thinks Hot Java Will Give You a Lift," *San Jose Mercury News,* 23 March 1995.

149. August article in *Forbes ASAP:* George Gilder, "The Coming Software Shift," *Forbes ASAP,* 28 August 1995.

149. George Gilder, *Sexual Suicide.* New York: Quadrangle, 1973.

150. "poorly debugged set . . .": "Summary of Written Testimony of Microsoft Witness Paul Maritz," PR Newswire, 22 January 1999.

150. *Only the Paranoid Survive:* Andy Grove, *Only the Paranoid Survive: How to Exploit the Crisis Points That Challenge Every Company and Career.* New York: Currency/Doubleday, 1996.

151. a huge margin: "Novell's NetWare 4.1 Momentum Continues," M2 Presswire, 22 March 1996.

151. no longer functioning: Kathy Rebello, Robert D. Hof, and Russell Mitchell, "Novell: End of an Era?" *Business Week,* 22 November 1993.

152. resisted the acquisition: Jim Seymour, "IBM's bid for Lotus," *PC Week,* 12 June 1995.

152. start-up that sank: Peter Carbonara, "Freewheeling Expansion Ends in Free Fall," *Inc.,* March 1998.

154. NCN was quietly disbanded: "Industry Saddened, Chastened by Demise of NCN," *NewsInc,* 16 March 1998.

154. Oracle announced: Kim Nash, "Groupware Gangbusters," *Computerworld,* 21 August 1995.

154. identical counterannouncement: "Informix and Netscape Bring Production-Strength Relational Data Management to World Wide Web," Business Wire, 18 July 1995.

155. Microsoft finally announced: For a detailed discussion of the Windows 95 launch, see Wallace, *Overdrive,* p. 265.

155. AOL had been complaining: Kara Swisher, *aol.com: How Steve Case Beat Bill Gates, Nailed the Netheads, and Made Millions in the War for the Web.* New York: Times Books, 1998, pp. 123–24.

156. company was profitable: Cusumano and Yoffie, *Competing on Internet Time,* p. 8.

Six

158. "Whatsoever therefore is . . .": Thomas Hobbes, *Leviathan; or the Matter, Forme and Power of a Commonwealth Ecclesiasticall and Civil.* Reprint. New York: Collier, 1962, p. 100.

159. three products: "Netscape Details New Internet Browser, Tools," *Media Daily,* 18 September 1995.

162. Mandile had spent: "Vermeer Technologies Inc. Appoints New Chief Executive Officer: John Mandile, Former Sybase Executive," Business Wire, 18 September 1995.

177. Internet IPO wave: "Internet Goes Public," *Computer Business Review,* 1 July 1995.

179. publish my article: Charles Ferguson, "Fertile Ground," *Upside,* November 1995.

182. enormous Internet conference: "Internet Technology Industry to Reach $13-Billion in Five Years," PR Newswire, 2 October 1995.

184. on September 18: "Netscape Details New Internet Browser, Tools," *Media Daily,* 18 September 1995.

184. LiveWire Pro: "Netscape Introduces Netscape LiveWire and LiveWire Pro Visual Online Development Environment," PR Newswire, 18 September 1995; and "Netscape Navigator 2.0 Intro'd 09/18/95," Newsbytes News Network, 18 September 1995.

185. Oracle had recently: Erica Schroeder, "Oracle Upgrade Taps 'Rich' Data; Version 7.3 to Support Multimedia; Oracle7 Version 7.3 DBMS," *PC Week,* 4 September 1995.

185. probably doing FUD: "Netscape Tests Internet Publishing Software," Reuters Financial Service, 29 January 1996.

185. publicly announced schedule: Ibid.

186. In 1992 for example: For a discussion of the Borland episode, see Michael L. Katz and Carl Shapiro, *Antitrust in Software Markets,* Berkeley: University of California Press, 1998.

192. *The Wall Street Journal:* Michael Siconolfi, "Controversial IPO Allocation Solidified Gap Between Firms," *The Wall Street Journal,* 13 February 1998.

SEVEN

194. "Why, I remember . . .": recollection of author.

197. Fall Internet World: Joe Michaels, "In Focus at Fall '95 Internet World: Growth, Competition, and Opportunity." *Information Today,* December 1995.

201. six months after: "Ventana Launches Netscape Into Retail Channel," Business Wire, 7 June 1995; and Evan Ramstad, "Netscape to Sell Its Internet Software Through Stores," The Associated Press, 2 June 1995.

202. they listed it: Karen Bannan and Kathleen Richards, "Publishers Web-Related Titles," *Computer Retail Week,* 15 April 1996.

204. its Web site: www.microsoft.com.

204. four hundred thousand people downloaded it: "Microsoft Previews New Web Technology in Microsoft Office 97 to Help Organizations Realize the Full Potential of Intranets," PR Newswire, 13 June 1996.

205. new $149 price: "Microsoft Announces FrontPage 1.1," PR Newswire, 8 April 1996.

205. six languages simultaneously: "Microsoft Unveils New FrontPage 97 with Bonus Pack," M2 Presswire, 28 October 1996.

205. sold 150,000 copies: Elizabeth Corcoran, "Inside Microsoft: An Edgy, Driven World," *The Washington Post,* 18 October 1998.
208. irresponsible piece of hype: George Gilder, "The Coming Software Shift," *Forbes,* 28 August 1995.
213. Internet World: Michaels, "In Focus at Fall '95 Internet World."
213. notice the Internet: "Mecklermedia Crests on New-Media Wave; Publishing Company; Magazine Strategies," *Folio: The Magazine for Magazine Management,* 15 June 1994.
219. he's now CFO: "Microsoft Announces Appointment of Two New Vice Presidents," PR Newswire, 10 July 1996.
223. Hart-Scott-Rodino Act: Isaac B. Lustgarten, "Acquisition of an Investment Adviser by a Banking Organization," *S&P's The Review of Banking and Financial Service,* 21 May 1997.
226. After an IPO: "Mergers and Acquisitions: A Strategy for High Technology Companies," *The Computer Lawyer,* November 1998.

EIGHT

231. Currie had worked: "Peter Currie Joins Netscape as Chief Financial Officer," PR Newswire, 5 April 1995.
239. *The Road Ahead:* Bill Gates, Nathan Myhrvold, and Peter M. Rinearson, *The Road Ahead.* New York: Penguin USA, 1996.
240. announce an alliance: Richard Karpinski, "OLE vs. Java; Battle for the 'Net Begins—Netscape, Sun to Woo Users with JavaScript," *InternetWeek,* 4 December 1995.
241. man named Cornelius Willis: Steve Higgins, "Sun's Jazzy Java Attracting Followers and Competitors," *Investor's Business Daily,* 28 December 1995.
241. it only ran on Windows: Jon Udell, "Novell's Campaign," *Byte,* February 1995.
241. open reference specification: Martin LaMonica, "Hot Seat; Riding the wave; Microsoft's Roger Heinen Explains Why OCXes Will Rule the Internet," *InfoWorld,* 15 January 1996.
241. Internet industry standards committee: "Microsoft's Answer to Java—Product Manager Cornelius Willis Says the VB Script Language Could Be the 'Nice Abstraction' That Programmers Are Looking For," *InformationWeek,* 26 February 1996.
241. three million people: Stuart J. Johnston and Kim S. Nash, "Capitulation!; Microsoft to License Java; Internet Standards War Avoided," *Computerworld,* 11 December 1995.

244. bundled with all: David Hewson, "Microsoft Will Make Internet Software Free," *Sunday Times* (London), 10 December 1995; Steve Boxer, "Innovations: Gates Swings Open the Office Door Internet," *The Daily Telegraph,* 19 December 1995; and James Staten, "Microsoft Shoots for Net: Cross-Platform Browser, VRML; Internet Explorer for Mac, Visual Basic Script, Active VRML; Product Development; Brief Article," *MacWEEK,* 11 December 1995.

244. Windows 3.1 and the Macintosh: Ibid.

244. all existing Internet standards: Marcia A. Jacobs, Richard Karpinski, and Karen Rodriguez, "Industry Lines up for JAVA—Microsoft's Net Offensive Embraces Java Technology," *InternetWeek,* 11 December 1995.

244. *features supported by Netscape:* "Internet Access: Microsoft Chooses Diversity over Dominance of the Internet: IDC Evaluates Microsoft's Internet Strategy Announcements," *Edge: Work-Group Computing Report,* 18 December 1995.

NINE

267. acquired by AOL: Jon Swartz and Jamie Beckett, "Future of Netscape Uncertain After Merger," *The San Francisco Chronicle,* 25 November 1998.

267. Netscape's browser market share: AdKnowledge online advertising report. See http://www.focalink.com/corporate/press/pr_990427_oar-1stqtr99.html.

267. Netcenter "portal": "AOL to Acquire Netscape Communications in Stock Transaction Valued at $4.2 Billion," M2 Presswire, 25 November 1998.

267. use Netscape software: Stephen Buel, "'AOL Anywhere' Is Aim," *The Arkansas Democrat-Gazette,* 26 November 1998.

267. development and sales: Leslie Walker and Elizabeth Corcoran, "AOL's New Stage; Firm Faces Challenge Selling Software, Services to Business," *The Washington Post,* 29 November 1998.

269. concluded fairly early: Joshua Quittner and Michelle Slatalla, *Speeding the Net: The Inside Story of Netscape and How It Challenged Microsoft.* New York: Atlantic Monthly Press, 1998, p. 95.

269. conceived Mosaic: Ibid., pp. 36–39.

269. spent several months: Robert H. Reid, *Architects of the Web.* New York: John Wiley & Sons, 1997, pp. 19–20.

272. one hundred thousand lines of code: Michael A. Cusumano and David B. Yoffie, *Competing on Internet Time.* New York: Free Press, 1998, p. 162.

272. seven hundred thousand lines of code: Ibid.

272. 50 developers and: Ibid.

272. three million lines of code: Ibid.

273. random college students: Quittner and Slatalla, *Speeding the Net,* p. 156.

274. Netscape's early employees: Reid, *Architects of the Web,* p. 24.

274. preferred to use UNIX: Cusumano and Yoffie, *Competing on Internet Time,* p. 165.

275. Barksdale admitted to me: Author interview with Jim Barksdale.

276. componentized browser: Lauren Thierry and Steve Young, "Update on Microsoft Trial," CNNFN, 29 October 1998.

277. "will run on all . . .": "The *InternetWeek* Interview—Marc Andreessen, Co-Founder, Netscape Communications," *InternetWeek,* 6 October 1997.

285. "Adding manpower to . . .": Frederick P. Brooks, *The Mythical Man-Month.* Reading, Mass.: Addison Wesley, 1995, p. 25.

287. But Collabra's product: Cusumano and Yoffie, *Competing on Internet Time,* p. 76.

287. Indeed, Collabra was willing: Author interview with Eric Hahn.

287. It distributes both: For a summary of RealNetworks and its products, see the RealNetworks company Web site at www.real.com/company/index.html.

288. He told me: Quotes from author interview with Jim Barksdale.

289. purchased and developed: Richard Karpinski, "OLE vs. Java."

290. Netscape refused: Cusumano and Yoffie, *Competing on Internet Time,* p. 333.

290. "there is nothing . . .": Author interview with Eric Schmidt.

291. might supplant Windows: Gates, "The Internet Tidal Wave."

292. Netcenter portal customers: Elizabeth Corcoran and Leslie Walker, "A Realignment of the Internet's Stars Is Shaping Its Future: AOL-Sun Talks Complicate Deal with Netscape," *The Washington Post,* 24 November 1998.

TEN

295. "Power tends to . . .": Lord Acton, quoted by Harry Summers, Jr., "Next Bombing Run over Ottawa?" *The Washington Times,* 8 March 1999.

296. Baby Bills proposal advocated: Ted Bridis, "Industry Group Endorses Microsoft Breakup," *The Legal Intelligencer,* 5 March 1999; and Steve Young and Bruce Francis (hosts), "Digital Jam," CNNFN, 10 March 1999.

300. testosterone-based . . .": Conversation with author.

308. three quarters of its revenues: Eric Nee, "Microsoft Gets Ready to Play a New Game," *Fortune,* 26 April 1999.

308. manipulated its operating systems: James Wallace, *Overdrive.* New York: John Wiley & Sons, 1997, pp. 45–46.

308. linking various Office applications: See Microsoft company Web site at www.microsoft.com/office/ork/2000/one/10ct_4.htm#dex78.

309. increasing continuously and substantially: See direct testimony of Frederick R. Warren-Boulton from the Microsoft antitrust trial, undated, paragraph 61. Transcript available from the Department of Justice Web site: www.usdoj.gov/atr/cases/f2000/2079.htm.

313. close the gap: Michael A. Cusumano and David B. Yoffie, *Competing on Internet Time.* New York: Free Press, 1998, pp. 125–26.

314. integrated with SQL Server: See Microsoft company Web site at www .microsoft.com/office/ork/2000/one/10ct_4.htm#dex78.

315. share of the "portal" market: Jay Greene, "Microsoft Backs Portals as Door to Profits," *Chicago Tribune,* 7 September 1998.

316. $20 billion in cash: "Software. Data Mining," *The Economist,* 20 March 1999.

316. about $500 billion: See Morningstar, Inc., company Web site at www .morningstar.net/StockQT/VL_Current/_MSFT.msshtml.

317. Microsoft canceled Compaq's Windows license: Carolyn Lochhead, "Microsoft Disparages U.S. Case," *The San Francisco Chronicle,* 21 October 1998.

317. RealNetworks alleged: Connie Guglielmo, "RealNetworks Steaming over Microsoft Streaming," *Inter@ctive Week Online,* 24 July 1998.

317. alleged with DR-DOS: Wallace, *Overdrive,* pp. 45–46.

317. used against Lotus: James Wallace and Jim Erickson, *Hard Drive: Bill Gates and the Making of the Microsoft Empire.* New York: HaperBusiness, 1993, p. 233.

317. blackmailing Apple: see direct testimony of Avadis Tevanian, Jr., from the Microsoft antitrust trial. Transcript available from the Department of Justice Web site: www.usdoj.gov/atr/cases/f2000/2010.htm.

318. the successor firms: William S. Comanor, "Break 'Em Up for Their Own Good," *Los Angeles Times,* 30 December 1992.

319. prosecution team favor: Madeleine Acey, "Microsoft Could Be Split into 'Baby'" *TechWeb News,* 16 February 1999; and Robert A. Levy, "If the Government Wins, Windows Will End Up with a Dozen Variations," *The Connecticut Law Tribune,* 12 April 1999.

320. were *colluding* to divide: Mark Lewyn and Richard Brandt, "Goodbye, Mr. Chips?," *Washingtonian,* December 1993.

320. performing its first "cashectomy": For a detailed discussion of the Borland "cashectomy," see Bruce Jacobsen deposition in Microsoft case.

321. Jackson ordered Microsoft: Russ Mitchell, "From Two Different Planets," *U.S. News & World Report,* 12 January 1998.

326. Reback and several others: Paul Davidson, "Microsoft Settlement Unlikely, *Newsbytes,* 10 March 1999.

329. 20 percent shareholder in them: Jonathan Davis, "Investment: Poor Old Bill Gates Just Can't Stop Getting Richer," *The Independent* (London), 10 March 1999; and Matt Hines, "Founders to Sell Millions of Microsoft Shares," *The Fort Worth Star-Telegram,* 13 August 1998.

Eleven

332. China and others: "China Uses Jail Threat to Keep Control of Internet," *The Independent* (London), 13 December 1998; and Kirk Albrecht, "Cybersurfers of Arabia," *Business Week,* 20 May 1996.

334. identification numbers: Jon Halpin, "Intel Embeds Unique Ids," *Computer Shopper,* 1 April 1999.

334. Windows 98 automatically: Tom Foremski, "Windows in Privacy Wrangle," *Electronics Weekly,* 24 March 1999.

334. one of the people: "Seven Days; Presswatch," *Computing,* 15 April 1999.

334. more than one hundred thousand PCs: "Lawyer Likens the Melissa Virus to Graffiti," *The New York Times,* 9 April 1999.

334. issuing unique identification numbers: Richard Morochove, "Sun Microsystems Lets Jini out of Bottle," *The Toronto Star,* 4 February 1999.

334. "You have zero . . .": Ibid.

340. *The Evolution of Cooperation:* Robert Axelrod, *The Evolution of Cooperation.* New York, Basic Books, 1984.

340. *Growing Artificial Societies:* Epstein & Axtell, *Growing Artificial Societies.* Washington, D.C., Brookings Institute Press, 1996.

341. $150 billion industry: For 1997 revenues for U.S. local exchange carriers, see Jim Lande and Katie Rangos, *Telecommunications Industry Revenue: 1997.* Washington, D.C.: Federal Communications Commission, 1998. Copies available at the FCC Web site: www.fcc.gov/Bureaus/Common _Carrier/Reports/FCC-State_Link/IAD/trsrv-97.pdf. For 1997 revenues for cable TV companies, see Paul Kagan Associates figures, quoted on the National Cable Television Association Web site at www.ncta.com /glance.html.

341. $700 billion industry: http://www.ba.com/speeches/1998/May/1998 0507002.html.

344. Now Bell Atlantic: Deborah Solomon, "Instead of Fighting, They Got Married," *The San Francisco Chronicle,* 8 February 1999.

346. UC Berkeley: "U.C.-Berkeley Professor Michael Katz Named Chief Economist for the Federal Communications Commission," Business Wire, 20 January 1994; and UC Berkeley Web site at www.haas.berkeley.edu:80 /~shapiro and www.law.berkeley.edu:80/faculty/rubinfeld.shtml.

347. formed his own antitrust: "Charles River Associates Completes Acquisition of The Tilden Group, LLC, Adds World-Renowned Economists,"
Business Wire, 16 December 1998.

347. Katz and another: See Consortium for Research on Telecommunications
Policy Web site at haas.berkeley.edu/~imio/crtp/affiliates.html.

347. $6 million in LECG stock: LECG, Inc. form S-1, 16 October 1997. Avail-
able at www.sec.gov.

347. the American Economic Association: Web site at www.vanderbilt.edu
/AEA/.

INDEX